Regional Modernities

Regional Modernities

The Cultural Politics of Development in India

Edited by

K. SIVARAMAKRISHNAN

ARUN AGRAWAL

STANFORD UNIVERSITY PRESS

STANFORD, CALIFORNIA

2003

Stanford University Press
Stanford, California

©2003 Oxford University Press

Originating publisher: Oxford University Press
First published in the United States by Stanford University Press
in 2003.

Printed in the United States of America on acid-free paper.

This title will be distributed exclusively by Stanford University
Press in North and Central America, including Canada, U.S.
dependencies, and the Philippines.

Library of Congress Cataloging-in-Publication Data

Regional modernities : the cultural politics of development in
     India / edited by K. Sivaramakrishnan, Arun Agrawal.
          p. cm.
     Includes bibliographical references and index.
          ISBN 0-8047-4414-9 (alk. paper)—ISBN 0-8047-4415-7
(pbk. : alk. paper)
          1. Economic development—Social aspects—India. 2.
Regionalism—India. I. Sivaramakrishnan, K., date-II. Agrawal,
Arun
HC435.2 .R433 2003
338.954—dc21   2003009922

Last figure below indicates year of this printing:
12   11   10   09   08   07   06   05   04   03

Foreword

Modernity is alive and kicking in most of the world. Some think this is only because of its relative infancy in non-Western societies—modernity having been invented in the West and subsequently transplanted at different dates in other parts of the globe. 'Wait a while,' these lag theorists tell us. 'Soon you will see dark-skinned postmoderns, wizened and jaded, fed up with the boastful certainties of the modern age, yearning to join the party in the garden of contingent identities and playful self-fashioning.' Others continue to warn us, as they have for almost a century and a half, of the vicious snare called modernity. 'Get rid of this craze for progress and development,' they shout into our ears. 'Get out of the trap of historicism, or else the non-Western world is doomed to eternal inferiority.' The world, in the meantime, seems only to have nodded politely and gone on with what it thinks is the unfinished business of modernity.

So have the anti-modernists and postmodernists been proved wrong? Or at least irrelevant? A close look at the trajectories of modernity around the world in the second half of the twentieth century would not support either of those conclusions. It is now apparent that while the project of modernity has been neither abandoned nor superseded in the non-Western world, it has taken on forms that are distinctly different from the familiar institutions and practices of Western modernity. Questions pertaining to the identification and significance of these differences, the extent to which they can be considered generic, whether the genres are autonomously produced or hybrid, have animated debates over modernity in the last two decades. Many terms such as 'multiple modernities,' 'alternative modernities,' 'hybrid modernities,' 're-flexive modernities,' have been in circulation. The editors of the present volume are proposing a new term—'regional modernities'—but this, I feel, is not a mere addition to the list: it has a new and specific theoretical import that is worth serious attention.

If there are different versions of modernity, what is the best way to identify them? Clearly, a great deal depends on the level at which we consider a difference to be significant. If we are discussing genres of modern painting, for instance, the difference between French and Spanish art may not be very significant, while that between Western and Indian art may well be. If we are discussing modern science, on the other hand, there may be no significant differences between Western and Indian physics but quite significant differences between Western medicine and modern ayurveda. The choice of the level of significance must depend on the specific set of theoretical questions that can be suitably addressed within a given context of comparative empirical knowledge. The choice, in other words, is a strategic one. It is as a strategic, middle-level concept that Sivaramakrishnan and Agrawal suggest the notion of the *region*. There is no pre-given or determinate demarcation of regions. Their delineation depends on a strategic choice in a specific regional context. Regional modernity, then, is very much a working concept, something to use as a tool of comparative research until more stable conceptual definitions emerge. Many researchers in the field will find this a useful and sensible approach.

There is a second dimension that Sivaramakrishnan and Agrawal have introduced in order to track variations in the trajectories of modernity in the non-Western world. This is the narrative dimension. Stories are the means by which individuals, groups, and communities represent and remember their changing lives. It is in stories that one can trace agency. By weaving stories around regions, the essays in this volume present a rich, complex, but analytically manageable set of studies about the career of modernity in India.

The contributors to this volume are from different disciplinary backgrounds. They also cover between them a very wide range of locations and case studies of the complicated and diverse process of development. Spanning all of these variations, however, they emphasize the overarching power of the concept of *development* as the very idea of modernity. There have been and will be many critics of the concept of development. But no matter how gigantic the costs or how unsettling the consequences of development, its proponents do not seem to have any difficulty in persuading people that they must not be left behind in its pursuit, for, who wants to be denied the chance to partake of the fruits of modernity? The point is not inconsequential in understanding the course of popular politics and culture in the contemporary world. The contributors to this volume have preferred not to adopt a critical position that is located on an ethical ground external to the phenomena they are studying: they are not *a priori* either in favour or against develop-ment. Rather, they have chosen to stay with their subjects and their stories and to draw out of them regional patterns that might clarify for us the significantly different trajectories of modernity within the nation-state called India. The effort represents a new and eminently worthwhile contribution to the emerging field of the comparative study of modernities.

Professor of Political Science and Director   PARTHA CHATTERJEE
Centre for Studies in Social Sciences
Calcutta

Acknowledgments

This volume is the result of sustained collaboration among a group of young south Asianist scholars and their Africanist interlocutors. The project took shape as part of a collective effort to rethink the place of area studies in international scholarship. The study of development and globalization was an obvious focus for such an exercise, given the historical centrality of development to area studies in the Cold War era. Along the way we, as a group, became convinced of the need to evaluate some long-standing dogmas, and other more recent orthodoxies, in the field of development studies. Among the objects of our critical reflection was the debate around globalization. We approached questions related to modernity, development, and globalization with a skeptical view of dichotomies used to understand these social and conceptual formations. As we have worked on the chapters that make up this book, we have become even more appreciative of the limited utility of terms such as local and global. At the same time, our belief that concepts such as discourses and narratives are in dire need of supplementary revisions led us to explore the concept of stories as a means to generate a more agent-based, nuanced, contingent approach to understanding development as a process. Development, we believe, is inescapably regional in its origins and manifestations, and can best be understood by referring to detailed ethnographic and historical work that is carefully located in a broader context. The essays in this book substantiate these beliefs.

The idea for this book came into being in the summer of 1997, when we were beginning our first year of teaching at Yale University. Many of the essays in this volume were first presented at a double panel we co-organized at the South Asian Studies Meetings at Madison, Wisconsin, in October 1997. Some of the original participants could not continue, others have joined us along the way.

In February–March 1998, we organized a small conference called 'Regional Modernities' at Yale University with the support of the Yale Center for International and Area Studies, and the help of a number of graduate students and friends in the Departments of Political Science and Anthropology, and the School of Forestry and Environmental Studies. We are grateful to all these early 'investors' at Yale for the immense logistical and intellectual support they provided. Pamela McElwee, Eva Garen, and Nina Bhatt deserve special mention for their unstinting contributions to the success of the conference. Robert Harms helped us think through the intellectual objectives of the conference and contributed vitally to its actual conduct.

Discussions during the conference forced us to clarify, and state more explicitly, some of the conceptual arguments related to the terms 'regions' and 'stories.' In this sense, the chief theoretical statements of the book are without doubt part of a collective enterprise. We remain grateful to all the participants in the conference who took time in a special session at the end of the meeting to openly voice their suggestions and push forward the themes with which the conference had started.

We would like to express our special gratitude for the consistent encouragement that Arjun Appadurai, Partha Chatterjee, Robert Harms, William Kelly, Gustav Ranis, and James Scott have provided us from the very beginning of this project.

For their sustained engagements with the arguments in this volume, we would like to thank Itty Abraham, Chris Bayly, Sugata Bose, Fred Cooper, James Ferguson, Richard Fox, Clark Gibson, Vinay Gidwani, Akhil Gupta, Robert Harms, Angelique Haugerud, Amitava Kumar, Melissa Leach, Jens Lerche, Tania Li, Donald Moore, David Mosse, Benjamin Orlove, Donna Perry, Pauline Peters, Vijay Prashad, James C. Scott, David Slater, Jonathan Spencer, Peter Vandergeest, Kamala Visweswaran, David Washbrook, and Eric Worby. Recent iterations of the introductory chapter have further benefited from comments by participants at the South Asian History Conference at Tufts University in June 1999, and at the South Asian Anthropologist Group Meeting at the School of Oriental and African Studies, University of London in September 1999. Others who have read and commented on the introduction include David Apter, Mamadou Diawara, Michael Dove, Robert Evenson, Anil Gupta, Ronald Herring, Michael Lipton, James McCann, Enrique Meyer, Ebrima Sall, Ashutosh Varshney, and Leonard Wantchekon.

We would also like to thank the anonymous reviewers of the manuscript at Stanford and Oxford University Presses. They went through the arguments in the volume and in each of the essays and carefully noted ways to explicate and clarify points that needed further development. Their comments have made this a far more integrated and connected collection of essays. We are grateful to Shara Svendsen for all her help in getting the manuscript finally ready for production. Pamela McElwee undertook and completed an exemplary job of copyediting the manuscript.

Finally, we would like to thank the Crossing Borders initiative of the Ford Foundation for financial support to the conference that helped us bring the authors involved in the project together. Additional support from the Program in Agrarian Studies, Center for International and Area Studies, and the Kempf Fund, all at Yale University, and from the Aspen Institute through their grant number 94-1-NSRF-01, is also gratefully acknowledged.

Contents

Contributors

Itty Abraham is Program Director at the Social Science Research Council. He is the author of *The Making of the Indian Atomic Bomb: Science, Secrecy and the Postcolonial State* (Zed Books, 1998).

Arun Agrawal is Associate Professor and William Dawson Scholar in the Department of Political Science and the School of Environment at McGill University, Montreal. He is the author of *Greener Pastures: Politics, Markets, and Community among a Migrant Pastoral People* (Duke University Press and Oxford University Press, 1999). His research on the politics of environment and development has appeared in such journals as *Comparative Political Studies, Cultural Critique, Development and Change, Journal of Asian Studies, Journal of Theoretical Politics, Politics and Society,* and *World Development.*

Kim Berry is Assistant Professor and Program Leader of Women's Studies at Humboldt State University in Arcata, CA. Her research and teaching interests concern transformations in gendered relations through colonial rule, nationalist movements, 'development,' and globalization, as well as the formation of regional womenís movements and transnational feminist solidarities.

Sonja Brodt is Program Evaluation Specialist with the University of California Statewide Integrated Pest Management Project based at UC Davis. Her research interests range from local knowledge systems and resource management in Asia to environmental and social sustainability of agriculture in the USA.

Partha Chatterjee is Director, Centre for Studies in Social Sciences, Calcutta, and Professor of Anthropology, Columbia University, New York. He is the author of, among other books, *Nationalist Thought and the Colonial World* (1986); *The Nation and its Fragments* (1993); and *A Princely Impostor?* (2002).

Akhil Gupta is Associate Professor of Cultural and Social Anthropology at Stanford University. He is the author of *Postcolonial Developments: Agriculture in the Making of Modern India* (Duke University Press, 1998) and co-editor (with James Ferguson) of *Anthropological Locations: Boundaries and Grounds of a Field Science* (University of California Press, 1997) and *Culture, Power, Place: Explorations in Critical Anthropology* (Duke University Press, 1997). His current projects include an ethnography of state bureaucracies and a book on reincarnation and social theory.

Angelique Haugerud is Associate Professor of Anthropology at Rutgers University. She is author of *The Culture of Politics in Modern Kenya* (Cambridge University Press, 1995), and co-editor of *Commodities and Globalization: Anthropological Perspectives* (Rowman and Littlefield, 2000).

Rebecca M. Klenk teaches women's studies and anthropology at the University of Tennessee, Knoxville. She is working on a book manuscript focused on how gendered subjects are produced through contradictory narratives, discourses, and experiences of 'modernity' and 'development' in rural North India.

Daniel Klingensmith is Assistant Professor of History at Maryville College in Maryville, Tennessee. He is currently working on a book about US and Indian development ideologies and the creation of India's large dams since 1945.

Amitava Kumar is the author of *Bombay–London–New York* (2002) and *Passport Photos* (2000). He is the editor, most recently, of *World Bank Literature* (2002). He has also published recently in *The Nation, Transition, Harper's Magazine,* and *The New Statesman.*

Sangeeta Luthra was a Marion L. Brittain Fellow at the Georgia Institute of Technology (1999–2000). Her research interests include grassroots NGOs and development in India. More recently she has been researching the impact of broader regional NGO movements like the Narmada Bachao Andolan on Indian and international development policy.

Donald S. Moore works on the cultural politics of space, power, and identity in southern Africa. He teaches in the Department of Anthropology at the University of California, Berkeley. As a vegetarian, he has long reflected on the transcultural legacies of Gandhian body politics.

David Mosse is Lecturer in Social Anthropology at the School of Oriental and African Studies, University of London. He is author of *The Rule of Water: Statecraft, Ecology and Collective Action in South India* (Oxford University Press, 2003).

Vijay Prashad is Associate Professor and Director of International Studies, Trinity College. His most recent book is *Everybody Was Kung Fu Fighting: Afro-Asian Connections and the Myth of Cultural Purity* (Beacon Press, 2001).

Paul Robbins is Associate Professor of Geography at the Ohio State University. He is a cultural and political ecologist with research interests on land cover change, remote sensing, agropastoral production, and the social history of geographic technology.

Subir Sinha is Lecturer in the Department of Development Studies at the School of Oriental and African Studies, University of London. He is currently involved in research on new property regimes and the history of community-based development strategies in rural India.

K. Sivaramakrishnan is Associate Professor of Anthropology and Director, South Asia Center, Jackson School of International Studies at the University of Washington, Seattle. He is the author of *Modern Forests: Statemaking and Environmental Change in Colonial Eastern India* (Stanford University Press and Oxford University Press, 1999).

Ajay Skaria is Associate Professor of History and Global Studies at the University of Minnesota—Twin Cities Campus. He is the author of *Hybrid Histories: Forests, Frontiers, and Wildness in Western India* (Oxford University Press, 1999).

Ajantha Subramanian is Assistant Professor of Anthropology at Harvard University. Her research interests include: the cultural politics of development; technological modernity and diaspora cultures; and state formation and differentiated citizenship.

1

Regional Modernities in Stories and Practices of Development

K. SIVARAMAKRISHNAN AND
ARUN AGRAWAL

I promise you the labyrinth made of the single straight line which is invisible and everlasting.

—*Jorge Luis Borges, A Personal Anthology, 1967*

Tarry awhile. You are so beautiful.[1]

—*Goethe, Faust, [1832] 1976*

One would be quibbling with de Certeau (1984) only a little in claiming that discussions of modernity are becoming universal.[2] Habermas tells us that modernity is characterized by a rationalization of life worlds that became most distinctly visible in eighteenth century Europe with the universalization of norms of action,

1. The original in German reads as 'Verweile doch, du bist so schoen.'
2. Habermas [1985] 1996: 2. Berman (1982) remains a confident text on this score. A number of essay collections have appeared recently, including Appadurai's *Modernity at Large*. Others include Jameson and Miyoshi (1998) and Ross (1988). Works specifically dealing with India include Breckenridge (1995) and Niranjana *et al.* (1993). Comaroff and Comaroff (1993) provide a collection of essays engaging developments in postcolonial Africa.

generalization of values, and patterns of socialization centered on individuation.[3] This commonly accepted portrayal of modernity can serve as a blunt but useful point of departure. Modernity as a condition or a concept, however, needs more careful contextual and historical specification. Attention to history and context is necessary whether one deploys the concept of modernity for analytical purchase, or attempts to understand its construction. This volume of essays proposes the concept of regional modernities in moving toward such an objective.

Harvey reminds us that the core aspiration of modernity 'was to use the accumulation of knowledge...for the pursuit of human imagination and the enrichment of daily life.'[4] He could have been talking about development. If modernity is the figure to which social theory unavoidably refers itself, development is the prime index we use to assess efforts toward modernization. Development, in its various guises, has surely been the most powerful influence structuring social and economic transformations in the non-Western world in this century.[5] The rhetoric around it helped legitimate colonial consolidation in the 1930s and the 1940s. Visions of

3. See also Lefebvre's (1995: 1–2) discussion of modernism (modernization) and modernity. He sees the two as antithetical: 'By modernism, we mean the consciousness which successive ages, periods and generations had of themselves; thus modernism consists of phenomena of consciousness, of triumphalist images and projections of self.... By modernity, however, we understand the beginnings of a reflective process, a more-or-less advanced attempt at critique and auto-critique, a bid for knowledge.... Modernity differs from modernism just as a concept which is being formulated in society differs from social phenomena themselves, just as a thought differs from actual events'. Despite their differences, Lefebvre's explicit references to the rise of skepticism as a feature of modernity is shared by Habermas ([1985] 1996: 2) when he argues that modernity is a reflective treatment of traditions that have lost their quasi-natural status. On the other hand, Taylor (1999: 153) articulates a somewhat different conception of modernity when he argues for a cultural theory of modernity in which it is characterized less by the development of a universal transformation, and more by the emergence of a new culture that is comparable to its predecessor as well as to other contemporary cultures. This view runs into the obvious difficulties of treating cultures as independent separate entities (see Gupta and Ferguson 1997).

4. Harvey 1989: 12.

5. See discussions by Escobar (1995), Ferguson ([1990] 1994), Hirschman (1971), and, of course, Rostow (1960).

development formed a rallying cry for independence movements that led to decolonization in the 1950s and the 1960s. And in the post-Second World War period, development became the *raison d'etat* of newly independent states.[6] It continues today to colonize our imaginations about how modern men and women can assert their dignity and control their lives. For example, in his critical essay on development, Esteva suggests, 'Development occupies the center of an incredibly powerful semantic constellation. There is nothing in modern mentality comparable to it as a force guiding thought and behavior.'[7]

One reason the concept of development seems so powerful is the apparent irreplaceability of a congeries of claims made by development theorists that address, and promise to redress, the misery that continues to be the home of billions: 'the power to transform old worlds, the power to imagine new ones.'[8] Another might be the

6. There is some controversy about the period to which thinking about development can be traced. To be sure, the 1930s are no more the magic decade than the 1940s or 1950s when development suddenly became the concern of state policy. Berman (1982) draws an evocative portrait of Goethe's Faust (written in the late eighteenth and the early nineteenth centuries) to elaborate the inescapable, transformative power of development. Cowen and Shenton (1995), in their historical essay on the intellectual roots of development, trace it back to the writings of European political economists in the early nineteenth century. Standard histories of development at least refer to writings from the late eighteenth and the nineteenth centuries as founding more recent theories of development (Arendt 1987; Rostow 1990).

7. Esteva (1992: 8) goes on to indicate the difficult nature of the term when he says, 'At the same time, very few words are as feeble, as fragile and as incapable of giving substance and meaning to thought and behavior as this one'.

8. Crush 1995: 2. More generally, Crush (1995: xi–xiii) provides one account of the power of development when he describes how between 1990 and 1994 legions of development agencies and experts set up shop in South Africa. The new missions, reports, institutions, and planning documents were only the latest in a series of local reinventions of development that had occurred between the 1930s and the 1980s. One can call such missions and reports a public appropriation of societal transformations in the name of development. Similar discursive appropriations of the 'public face' of political and economic transformations have taken place in nearly all developing countries in this century. These appropriations of social processes lead to empirical and analytical 'data, debate, research, and policy' (Ludden 1992: 251).

very elusiveness of this slippery word whose meanings proliferate in blatant disregard of all attempts to fix and stabilize its referents.[9] A measure of the seductive appeal of development is how it is visualized as a naturalized process and common sense objective, its connections with power hidden, veiled, unknown: what else can one strive for if not to develop?[10] In the tensions between the particular performances of development at cascading levels of social aggregation, and the universalist, 'anti-political'[11] claims of its advocates lie clues to its nature. The ensuing essays recognize the complex nature of development and provide some conceptual tools to assist a fuller, more plural, comprehension of these complexities. Two tools we discuss in this introduction—regions and stories— signal flexibility and dynamism in their very description, especially in comparison to 'global/local' and 'discourses of development' that have animated much anthropological study of development and environment in the recent past.

Instead of underwriting a globalized, homogeneous vision of modernity that development is supposed to inscribe, we direct attention toward 'regional modernities.' We highlight the regional nature of development performances and bodies of writings. We assert, with Bourdieu, that 'regionalist discourse is a performative discourse which aims to impose as legitimate a new definition of frontiers'[12] but do not restrict our definition of region to subnational

9. See the contributions in Sachs (1992). In general, writings on development proceed through a brush-clearing exercise where they first define development, and then embark on their particular elaboration about what is wrong with development and how it can be brought about. Some other instances are Arndt (1987), Black (1991), Hobart (1993), and Norgaard (1994).

10. As an instrument of state policy, the objective of development not only allows its framers a sense of control in a time of disorder but also possesses and confers the capacity to pacify. Development possesses a global appeal that underwrites the paths of economic reconstruction and cultural homogenization pursued by many postcolonial states with a more or less single-minded devotion. Thus theories of development have been globally shared even when territorially circumscribed in practice by national or regional boundaries.

11. We are referring here to Ferguson's ([1990] 1994: xv) view of development as an 'anti-politics machine, depoliticizing everything it touches, everywhere whisking political realities out of sight, all the while performing, almost unnoticed, its own pre-eminently political operation of expanding bureaucratic state power'.

12. Bourdieu 1991: 223.

formations as he seems to do. Further, instead of viewing regional forms of development simply as variations on a global theme we see them as layered acts that contribute to an effect of development glossed as universal.[13]

We also believe it is important to explore the multi-faceted relationships of development to modernity. James Ferguson has recently provided some valuable guidance on this subject.[14] He notes, first, that modernity continues to provide perceptual categories shaping peoples' lives well after specific processes of modernization—often named development—collapsed or were exposed for their role in other nefarious purposes. But experiences of disillusionment have not turned Third World subjects into anti-development crusaders as many new social movements and their scholarly sympathizers[15] often expected. In fact, when social movements have resulted in political power for their leaders, the leaders have usually embarked on new development projects or moved unfinished programs to completion.

Second, Ferguson recognizes that development did not 'invent' Third World poverty and other such manifestations of social inequality on an international scale. He reminds us that development became—for a period historically coincident with the Cold War, decolonization, and modern nation-state building in many Third World locations—the hegemonic way of looking at inequality and managing it. This historical turn in the study of development is welcome and it is something that several scholars have advocated in the last decade.[16] This turn recognizes that colonialism shaped, both explicitly and implicitly, the ideal-material frames from which development could emerge as it did at a certain historical moment following the end of Second World War.

We argue that the historical turn also entails two other acknowledgments that become crucial to continuing scholarly

13. In this regard, see also Applegate (1999: 1172) who argues that 'the most promising (direction) is moving toward an understanding of regional politics that sees them everywhere…as constitutive…in effect the infrastructure of the politicial process altogether.'

14. Ferguson 1999: 14.

15. Cf. Sachs 1992; Escobar 1995; Alvarez, Dagnino, and Escobar 1998; Roy 1999.

16. Ludden 1992; Cooper and Packard 1997.

engagements with development. One links the unfinished projects of development to the unfinished projects of modernity. As scholars grapple with how, to paraphrase Dilip Gaonkar, non-Western people everywhere are beginning to engage critically their hybrid modernities, they are revising the distinction between societal modernization and cultural modernity.[17] The other acknowledgement we wish to highlight draws attention to the political struggles in which categories of development are critical—citizenship, agency, privacy, and subjecthood. These political processes around development retread the ground covered by the politicization of the categories of colonialism in struggles over identity, resources, and freedom in the postcolony.

The following essays enact arguments and tell stories situated in India. In part, of course, their geographical focus reflects the expertise and limitations of the authors. But at least in equal part, this location is also an argument about the continued necessity of attending to the nation-state in a time presumably described by globalization. A greater emphasis on the nation-state is critical to understanding the emergence of regional modernities as development policies and projects are enacted.[18] This claim contrasts with recent writings on development that emphasize either its local performances, or its global/international discourses and agents. The modern state, however, serves both as an agent, and as an arena in which other social agents pursue specific visions of growth, democracy, and nationhood. In this pursuit of modernity, development has been the link that provides a common theme and unites programs around economic, political, and cultural reconstructions. Projects of state formation, their links outward to an international political economy, and strategies of localization in relation to internal actors need insistent attention if we are to understand development—both as performed practice and also as a formation to be interpreted.

17. Gaonkar 1999: 1–2.

18. Recently, supranational economic networks and various subnational formations like autonomous districts, export promotion zones or conservation areas have emerged and can also be taken as examples of how we consider regions. In this paper, however, we focus on the nation-state as an example of the region for two reasons. The nation-state remains perhaps the most important actor in the context of development. Additionally, it is likely the most counter intuitive example of the concept of a region.

A second move we make is to highlight the construction of stories of development and underline the contingent nature of such construction. A number of recent analyses of development have argued that those who are supposedly subjected to development are also the subjects of development.[19] We focus upon storytelling as a critical element in the construction of agency that subjectivity always entails. The justification for such an emphasis on agency stems from some obvious antinomies in the account of development provided by its new radical critics. These antinomies set up oppositions between a dominating global vision of development purveyed by international agencies, and conquered localities characterized as anti-developmental.[20] Such a view is oriented to presenting 'development' as an accomplished fact instead of attending to its constantly shifting nature and contested programs. Our emphasis on stories indicates the importance of variable power held by different actors in the creation of the discourse of development and thus complements an existing emphasis on narratives and discourse.

We begin by drawing from recent writings on globalization and the production of locality. Using the implicit division between the local and the global in these writings as a foil, we develop our arguments about regional modernities. We follow our elaboration of the idea of regional modernities by examining some of the debilities in recent writings on development. This includes the instantiation of the concept of region in the form of the nation-state. It is easy to see that region can refer both to subnational and supranational social and political formations. In focusing on the national variant of the regional, we aim to show its suppleness. We finally show why stories are important to understand the construction of development discourses and narratives.

GLOBALIZATION/LOCALIZATION

Early scholarly writings on globalization saw in it a logic of homogenization that resulted from cultural and material forces with a cross-national, even planetary, sway. These pressures were

19. Pigg 1992.

20. The infirmity of such reasoning is captured succinctly by Comaroff and Comaroff (1993: xii) when they say, '[s]uch binary contrast, we would argue, are a widespread trope of ideology-in-the-making; they reduce complex continuities and contradictions to the aesthetics of nice oppositions.'

seen to emerge from Western metropoles and were disseminated by an intrusive media and political–economic domination. Every McDonald's and every Mickey Mouse was evidence of westernization at work.[21] Such totalizing theories of globalization inevitably saw local cultures as existing independently of contact with a putative outside culture and viewed globalization as a process of contact and integration that made the world more unified and homogeneous.[22] Some scholars saw pressures toward globalization emerging from the movements of a truly global capital.[23] Others have seen a greater disjuncture between economic and cultural processes, mapping the cultural to differentiation, and the economic to homogenization.[24] But for many, cultural globalization remains a process of diffusion and homogenization outward from a core located in the West.[25]

21. This continues to be an influential approach that assumes barriers for international economic integration are progressively being broken down. Thus, recently globalization has been redefined as 'that set of processes by which the world is rapidly being integrated into one economic space via increased international trade, the internationalization of production and financial markets, and the internationalization of a commodity culture promoted by an increasingly networked global telecommunication system' (Gibson-Graham 1996–7: 1).

22. For a critique see Appadurai and Breckenridge (1995), Featherstone (1996), Gupta and Ferguson (1992), and Massey (1994). For disagreement and restatement of globalization as cultural imperialism, see Szeman (1997).

23. Such postulations of the relationship between the economic and the cultural, where material forces, in the famous Althusserian last analysis, dominate and underpin cultural production, have not ceased. See Dirlik (1996), who, despite expressing reservations about assigning a fixed meaning to 'local,' suggests finally that the local plays not only a role of resistance to global capitalism, but is also a site where building blocks for a future politics of difference might emerge. Mitchell's (1996) questions about the celebration of hybridity, mobility, and multiculturalism also stem from a postulated close link between the economic and the cultural.

24. In a recent essay, for example, Jameson (1998: 56–7) suggests that cultural analyses of globalization are more likely to discover difference and differentiation but a focus on economic issues brings to the fore identity, assimilation, and integration, making globalization appear as a 'picture of standardization on an unparalleled new scale.'

25. Some of the more interesting recent work on globalization is contained in the collection of brilliant essays by Appadurai (1996), and in the insightful volumes edited by Breckenridge (1995), Featherstone (1990), King (1997), and Wilson and Dissanayake (1996). See also Meyer and Geschiere (1998).

The agonistic poles in the continuing debate on globalization—the local and the global—are not constructed accidentally. For all the difficulties in interpreting the meanings of global and local, these powerful terms facilitate particular narratives of cosmopolitanism vs. parochialism, of oppression vs. emancipation, of conforming homogeneity vs. agency, of placeless power vs. powerless places. The global stands for a certain free-wheeling movement of capital, ideas, and people. The local in contrast is often believed to be locked into timeless tyrannies of tradition. As Gupta and Ferguson remark, there is a surprisingly frequent tendency to use local and global in ways that replicate 'dualisms opposing tradition to modernity, cold society to hot ones, or *Gemeinschaft* to *Gesellschaft*.'[26]

More recently, of course, these meanings of the local and the global have registered a shift. As one comes to accept the connections of local spaces and social formations with other localities,[27] it also becomes more difficult to view globalization simply as a process of integration and homogenization.[28] As Featherstone argues, believing that 'globalization is basically modernity writ large' is to 'miss the cultural variability of non-Western nation-states and civilizations.' It is insufficient to assume that other cultures will just give way to modernity or regard their formulations of national particularity as mere reactions to Western modernity.[29] In different ways the articulation of global flows with the local context has to be made visible.[30] Such an articulation can take

26. Gupta and Ferguson 1997: 28.

27. Appadurai (1996: 178–99) presents an insightful discussion about the production of locality. Hall (1997) presents a view of the relationship between the local and the global that still relies on analogies with the logic of capital. He suggests that globalization proceeds unevenly primarily owing to varying localities that it encounters and the ways in which localities reconfigure global forces.

28. See Giddens (1990: 64) who defines globalization as 'the intensification of worldwide social relations which link distant localities in such a way that local happenings are shaped by events occurring many miles away and vice versa'.

29. Featherstone 1996: 46–7. See also Appadurai and Breckenridge (1995) on a heterogeneous modernity as the hallmark of the current globalization we are experiencing.

30. See for example, the recent collection of essays brought together in Meyer and Geschiere (1998: 602), who argue, 'it is important to develop an

the form of violent identity politics as manifested in ethnic conflict or more localized violence among neighbors and others having some prior social familiarity.[31] It can also lead to the marginalization of national economies rather than their integration.[32]

Take two specific contexts in which these points become evident. A number of recent studies of gender and women in Asia have focused on encounters related to globalization and industrialization. These studies each highlight dynamic and conflictual interactions in processes prompted by inflows of capital into communities and households.[33] Wolf shows, for example, that for some women, involvement in capitalist exploitation has empowered them in struggles to redefine traditional gender roles.[34] The cases of migration and international mobilization are similarly instructive in highlighting disjunctures between economic, political, and cultural flows in the era of 'globalization.' In some situations workers have created dense international circuits that mimic those of capital.[35] In others they have mobilized across national boundaries to federate into associations that can counter the strategies of regional and international consolidation evinced by capitalism.[36] Significant place attachments and new identities often seem to be the outcomes of the uneven impact of globalization as it is mediated by regional forces and creatively appropriated by the subjects of development and modernization.[37]

---

understanding of globalization that not only takes into account the rapid increase in the mobility of people, goods, and images, but also the fact that in many places, flow goes hand-in-hand with a closure of identities which often used to be more fuzzy and permeable'.

31. Appadurai 1998.

32. Discussing the fate of copper export-dependent Zambian economic participation in global economies, Ferguson (1999: 373–4) argues that when fibre-optics replaced copper cable in telecommunications industry it signaled Zambia's disconnection from the modern world. The example highlights the more general point: processes of globalization may differentiate the world even as they link parts of it.

33. Ong 1987; Safa 1990; Kondo 1990; Rofel 1998.

34. Wolf 1992.

35. Rouse 1991.

36. Edelman 1996.

37. Holmes (1989: 9) makes this point elegantly. His work shows how worker peasantries evolve from the basic demands and constraints of rural

It is evident that scholars of cultural globalization now generally accept globalization as a variable process, producing effects that cannot be predicted as a simple gloss on or reflection of the cultural productions of the metropolis. The disjunctions between different types of globalization—economic, financial, cultural, demographic—may be such as to preclude any simple understanding of the metropolis or the margin as stable or fixed sites of cultural (re)production. In recent statements about globalization, the world is seemingly becoming one without borders owing to the facility with which people, images, and objects travel. Communications and the media are contributing to the erosion of national borders, simultaneously making all of us translocal consumers of cultural products and de-territorialized producers of meanings.[38]

But the one world that is emerging is of a rather special type. It may be one, but its oneness derives from the increasing contact among its parts, rather than from some mythical unity or similarity among them. For Giddens, thus, globalization is the intensification of worldwide social relations that link distant localities.[39] For some cartographers of globalization, the intensification of social relations produces labyrinthine complexity, and leads to effects such as illegibility,[40] hyper mobility,[41] and time–space compression.[42] But as Thrift (1995) argues, these 'barometers of modernity'[43] cannot simply be taken at their face value. They need to be seen as 'a multiplicity of often minor processes, of different origin and scattered location, which overlap, repeat, or imitate one another...converge and gradually produce the blueprint of a general method.'[44]

Modernity may be a global experience, but it is an experience that is multi-locally produced. This recognition should move us toward an effort to understand the patterns in the multi-local productions of modernity. Once we make a distinction between the global and the universal, it becomes obvious that the 'oneness' of modernity

---

livelihood, favoring the integration of diverse productive involvements rather than the creation of narrow occupational identities.

38. Hannerz 1992; Robertson 1992.
39. Giddens 1990: 64.
40. Jameson 1991: 51–2.
41. Castells 1996, 1993: 6, 20.
42. Harvey 1989: 306.
43. Descombes 1993.
44. Foucault 1977: 138 cited in Thrift 1995: 33.

scarcely refers to homogeneity of experiences. We come face-to-face with the reality that agents produce many different meanings even out of the same experiences, and that the production of meanings is made sensible only in an appreciation of common elements.[45]

A similar story can be told about current conceptualizations of the local. Whereas earlier discussion of the local saw it as the refuge of the particular, the specific, or the different, we no longer view the local as a site of purity, where difference emerges to haunt tales of global uniformity and homogenization. Localities exist not because of something innate within a particular site in space or inherent to a specific geographical point. Rather, discrete points in an abstract spatial grid have little meaning in themselves, and spaces become localities because of how they are situated in particular networks with other people, places, and social entities. Localities are produced as nodes in the flows of people and ideas, and are thoroughly socially constructed.

In their current uses, therefore, global and local have moved rather far from their traditional connotations of universality and particularity, or of a generalized spatial context versus a specific place. Nor can these terms easily be mapped on to referents that signify homogenization and overwhelming dominance on the one hand, and difference and resistance on the other. Those who have theorized carefully the nature of the global and the local have made it evident that in a very real sense there is no global—since there is always rupture, disjuncture, and variation in what is imagined as the global. In the same manner, not only is it necessary always to be aware of the politics behind the use of the term local, but there is no specific location or site that can be considered as a locality. The local is produced in systematic articulations of social, economic, and cultural processes that may have a far more regional character than a resolutely independent local one or a thoroughly overdetermined global one.

The old meanings of global (universalism) and local (particularism), however, constantly overwhelm the sense in which the terms

45. A related point is that such a view of modernity as multiply and continuously produced allows us to steer away from ethnocentric claims about the end of modernity. Here we fully endorse Gaonkar's (1999: 13) observation that 'modernity today...no longer has a governing center and master-narratives to accompany it...we have to continue to think through the dilemmas of modernity...from a transnational and transcultural perspective.'

are currently used. The contradictory excess that characterizes the meanings conveyed in each deployment of local and global threatens to render them meaningless. The traditional spatial referents of these terms—large, homogeneous, universally applicable vs. small, heterogeneous, and particular—jostle with the new significance they have acquired, making them internally contradictory. If the concreteness of the local is only an illusion made real to the extent and in the ways a locality is connected to other localities, and in the meanings people give to such connections, it makes little sense to insist upon the independence or the autonomy of the local. Both global and local are to be understood in terms of the relations they signify. It is in the context of this particular incoherence of terms such as local and global that we propose the concept of regional modernities. Even if the new experience of modernity is about a particular kind of complex relationality and connectedness, it is difficult to support the notion that this connectedness is unfolding at a global scale. The variations in the nature of connections make it necessary to adopt a regional approach to understanding modernity. At the same time, our understanding of regionality needs to be attentive to differences of scale in social and political processes rather than insist on the primacy of a particular subnational or supranational scale.

REGIONAL MODERNITIES

We use the term regional to qualify the multiple modernities that were and are being produced. Our deployment of the term is a self-conscious effort to move away from the tyranny of the global or the local, as also from their not-so-interesting juxtapositions such as 'global/local' or, even worse, 'glocal.' 'Regional modernity,' like modernities that are qualified by the terms global or local, has a spatial connotation, but it seeks to map the space between these binary polar extremes, refuses attempts at identifying it with a specific scale or geographical size, and focuses instead on the need to attend to the social networks and flows that give it particular form and content.[46] Although a spatial locution may be important

46. Our use of the term 'regional,' thus, is in stark contrast to its use in earlier writings on regional analysis and by regional scientists. For a review of some of these earlier uses, where region connotes a fixed space, see Bookman (1991).

to define regional in particular contexts and agendas, the attempt to yoke the term to a definite size or scale is as misplaced as attempts that try to pin down the local or the global through purely spatial metaphors. Indeed, it would be appropriate to suggest that there are no places that can be located as the necessarily appropriate referent for the terms 'local,' 'global,' or 'regional': these terms emerge only in a relational form.

Although regional, local, and global all have seemingly spatial reference, none has a *necessary* spatial location. We suggest, however, that the semantic and theoretical move we propose regarding regional permits analysis to proceed without being captured by the endless proliferation of difference that 'local' necessarily produces and in some sense enforces. Regional also breaks up the monopolistic, hegemonic, and monolithic connotations of modernity that global invariably introduces and stabilizes. Instead it denotes the possibility of investigating variable patterns in the production of different modernities. It is precisely because the production of modernities occurs in sites with variable spatial and relational features that our proposal of regional becomes meaningful. Unlike local or global, the term regional denotes levels that span subnational to multinational formations.

We propose regional as a descriptor for modernity not just because of its semantic attractions, as a sort of halfway house for a traveler between the global and the local. Instead, we propose regions also because we consider them the social and discursive sites where the production of modernity occurs. Our proposition draws from and builds on the work of a large number of social scientists who have sought to consider the constitutive effects of political, institutional, and cultural processes upon a region's formation and development. They have argued that the regional is neither reducible to an empirical given, nor merely a 'container' for social processes. It should be seen in terms of the practices of individuals and institutions at a variety of spatial levels.[47]

Our arguments about region emphasize the need to take seriously the variations among the many processes that are often loosely and quickly conjoined together to denote a putative globality. Simply because it is possible to witness and highlight multiple kinds of connections across many different parts of the

47. MacLeod 1998; Murphy 1991; Paasi 1991; Pred 1985; Warf 1990.

globe does not imply that all the connections together constitute an emerging global marketplace or community. In much recent work on globalization, however, it is precisely the inattention to how differences characterize processes cited as part of a new globalization that allows analysts to club them together and classify them as markers of globalization. The interconnections among participants in a chat site on the internet, among viewers of TV programs transmitted to more than a billion people at a time, between individuals and corporations asymmetrically located in economic exchange networks, or tourists who bridge vast distances in a search for the exotic may all denote time–space compression. But because these processes have quite different sources, effects, and trajectories it is important to examine them in their specific regional manifestations rather than view them as the basis of something called globalization.[48] Only by focusing on the 'strategic concentrations' among the 'multiple linkages' that characterize seemingly global processes might it become possible to decode globalization. It is toward this that Ong points when she argues for an 'approach that embeds global processes in a regional formation.'[49]

Chatterjee's argument about modernity fits well with this conceptualization of region: 'There cannot be just one modernity irrespective of geography, time, environment, and social conditions. The forms of modernity will have to vary among different countries depending upon specific circumstances and social practices.'[50] Pred and Watts make a similar point when they approvingly cite Octavio Paz, 'There are as many types of modernities as there are societies.'[51] We agree with their recognition that modernities are multiple, but use the term regional to provide a positive content so as to discuss how modernities assume particular forms in regions.[52]

48. See the recent special issue of *Third World Quarterly* in which several contributors highlight the need to pay attention to the variable processes of articulation that connect regions (Boas and Shaw 1999; Boas, Marchand, and Shaw 1999).

49. Ong 1999: 240.

50. Chatterjee 1997a: 198.

51. Paz cited in Pred and Watts 1992: 1.

52. It may be useful to point out, however, that the phrases 'multiple modernities', and 'alternative modernities' are somewhat empty of meaning. Modernities, by definition, are multiple, and there is little need to talk of multiple modernities if they were not being produced as alternatives.

Chatterjee goes on to specify a universe of distinctive non-Western modernities that map onto postcolonial nations and in this vein says, 'it is precisely the cultural project of nationalism to produce a distinctly national modernity.'[53] We would suggest, in response and amplification, that any particular national modernity is but a species of the genus regional modernity. National modernity describes the contingent dominance of political and cultural forces that come together to produce nations in a particular historical period. Regional modernity, thus, is a mid-level concept that allows for geographic divergence, varying temporal rhythms, and institutional differences. It recognizes the influence of historically sedimented social, economic, and spatial structures that shape development.

Regional modernity also describes the different levels of social aggregations at which the cultural unification necessary for the production of modernity takes place. The different terms our authors use in the following essays to qualify modernity—whether it is Skaria elaborating his concept of a colonial or bureaucratic modernity, Subramanian drawing together the elements of a Mukkuvar modernity, or Kumar speaking suggestively of immigrant modernities—the effort is always to specify further the cultural and material politics that is the concomitant of particular regional modernities. Their discussions recognize and emphasize the influence of historically sedimented social, economic, and spatial structures that shape the regional influences within which development occurs.

The recent and powerful discussion of nationalism and patriotism in India by Bayly provides an excellent illustration of our argument. Bayly refutes the idea that Indian nationalism was entirely constructed in dialogue with Western liberal nationalism of the nineteenth century. He suggests instead that 'the particularities of Indian nationalism have to be understood in the context of Indian forms of social organization and ideologies of good governance that pre-date the full Western impact even if they had, in turn, been modified by colonial rule.'[54] In a series of chapters (especially 1–4), that develop a valuable distinction between patriotism and

53. Chatterjee 1997a: 207. For a similar point with regard to Nepal, see Pigg (1992: 512).
54. Bayly 1998: vii.

nationalism, Bayly argues that late nineteenth-century Indian nationalism drew upon and recast some patterns of social relations, sentiments, doctrines, and embodied memories that had come into existence before British rule was established in the subcontinent. He refers to the precursors of Indian nationalism as old patriotisms and political ethics of Indian homelands that assumed a more defined form after the seventeenth century decline of the Mughal Empire and emergence of regional Indian kingdoms.

Bayly's critique of liberal theories of nationalism and its discontents historically anticipates our argument because it points to problems with bifurcating Indian state–society relationship into a local/global dyad where colonial modernity is the global force and local resistance is provided by fuzzy decentralized communities. He is arguing for the recognition of regional formations, of patriotism in his case, that create the social networks and political structures on which both colonial government and nationalist mobilization came to depend after the 1870s. These networks and structures were regional in the double sense of being supralocal and distinctly Indian. They were also seriously transformed by colonialism and nationalism but it would be wrong to argue they were erased or fully replaced by arrangements fashioned entirely in the faithful image of global or even continental models.[55] Bayly's emphasis on the regional and, therefore, on the construction of modernity in non-European locations also stems from a desire to analyse historical change as a dialectic between ideological and material processes.[56]

Given the need to discuss cultural and political–economic aspects of modernity together, our focus on regional modernities is also an attempt to move away from the kind of disciplinary divisions in discussions of the global and the local to which Michael Watts points when he writes about reworking modernity.[57] Watts argues that anthropological work rooted in ethnographic and cultural

55. A similar argument, in respect of China, can be found in Wigen (1999).
56. Bayly 1998: 316.
57. Arjun Appadurai's recent contribution to the debate on globalization, *Modernity at Large*, and the rising tide of interest among economists in the same topic remind us that these analytical and discipline-based separations continue to be pervasive. Reporting on the recent intensive conversation on development and the social sciences, Cooper and Packard (1997: 16) point to a tension between contextualizing and universalizing disciplinary tendencies.

relations tends to be weak in situating local knowledges and meanings on a map of capitalism.[58] Correspondingly, geographers and political scientists often do not incorporate struggles over meaning into the study of late twentieth-century capitalism or globalization. Thus, for Watts the local/global dyad also represents the working out of disciplinary histories. Regional modernities is our conceptual effort to overcome the stultifying influence of disciplinary boundaries identified by Watts.

We would add, however, that reworking modernity by attending to regions is not only a matter of attending to the embeddedness of local forms of capitalism. Recent scholarship has already pointed to the need to deal with 'worldwide facts of colonial and postcolonial coercion...yet not slight the role of parochial signs and values, local meanings, and historical sensibilities.'[59] In counterpoint, Taussig points to the constructed nature of the 'parochial' when he refers to the 'mimesis of the mimesis,' and illustrates it by the example of Cuna women weaving the RCA Victor-dog motif into clothing sold in the United States.[60] In this instance, there is no self-contained or autonomous local, nor a global that is untouched by local processes. We take such observations as pointing toward the need for attempts such as ours: to deploy 'region' to understand how political, economic, and cultural forces articulate to facilitate the production both of local and global processes. Localities, themselves always in a state of production,[61] transform the nature of what is counted as the global only by being aggregated into regional forms. To move the terms of the debate, we need to consider the mechanisms and conditions that are critical to the construction of regions and regional modernities.

The ensuing essays indicate that regions become important when we recognize the enduring importance of the power wielded through state systems and other political institutions in the reworking of modernity. States, for our purposes, need not only be imagined as a locus of national authority but can also be seen as governance structures in which power is increasingly crystallizing

58. Watts 1992a: 15.

59. Comaroff and Comaroff 1993: xiii.

60. Cited in Fox 1997: 66. He provides a useful story about the meanings of Gandhian nonviolence that traces the relationships between the global and the parochial beyond diffusionist models of change and transformation.

61. Appadurai 1996: 178–9.

around subnational and supranational political formations. The imperatives of trade have facilitated continental alliances like the European Union, the North American Free Trade Agreement, or the South Asian Association for Regional Cooperation. An important mode of analysis for these phenomena has been to treat the regional political economy as a series of networks.[62]

On the other hand, the new Balkanization of Eastern Europe and the emergence of regional political parties in India are but two examples of subnational politics that represent the uneasy coexistence of multiple identities and interests that cohere around the concept of region.[63] As Appadurai says in the context of ethnic strife, in an argument that implicitly endorses our concept of regional modernities

ethnic names and terms become highly susceptible to transnational perturbation...modern state-level forces tend to generate large-scale identities (such as Latino, Scheduled Caste, and Serb) which become significant imagined affiliations for large numbers of persons, many of whom reside across large social, spatial, and political divides.[64]

In all these cases localism or globalization poorly describe the processes at work because they do not adequately illuminate the coalition-building and differentiation that on a graduated scale characterizes regional modernities.

In addition to suggesting that a flexible notion of regions is important to understand the variable spatial loci where modernity is produced, we also claim that regional modernities are constantly in a state of production. In this sense we wish to push further Chatterjee's intuition[65] that non-Western modernity is an incomplete project and that elites in non-Western societies are always engaged in a pedagogical mission that seeks to modernize the rest of the society. We should note that the predicament of incompleteness is not peculiar to non-Western modernities because the signifiers

62. As Bernard (1996: 653) points out, in this approach 'regionalization is...seen as an integral part of the broader process of the globalization of production structures.'

63. A nice illustration of this process of conflict and collaboration is provided in Diawara (1998: 114–19), where he discusses the creation of regional pathways of trade and exchange by West African merchants in the context of globalized structural adjustment programs.

64. Appadurai 1998: 906.

65. Chatterjee 1997b: 31.

of modernity are always under debate, in all places and at all times.[66]

The concept of regional modernities also allows us to rethink discussions of power that are so important to the study of globalization and locality. In much extant writing globalization is an expression of the working of 'placeless power'—discourse formations, footloose capital, unaccountable international institutions. Against this formulation the local is identified as the place that makes visible the other face of power: resistance. Alternatively, more nuanced scholarship argues that local cultures, social structures, and environments mediate placeless power and significantly shape the actual consequences of globalization—a line of reasoning that strongly informs the notion of 'reworking modernity.'[67]

Power is surely never placeless. We suggest, however, amending some appropriations of Foucault, that power relations among various social actors are always capillary *and* nodal, social *and* institutional.[68] In contrast to Foucault, we would argue that it is impossible to know *a priori* whether it is through institutions that power is constituted or power that constitutes institutions. Indeed, if we think of institutions as social mechanisms that structure future expectations of actors,[69] it may not even be possible to know where institutions begin and their social context shades off. Channels of

66. It is for this reason, perhaps, that Latour (1993) notes that we will never be modern.

67. A similar point about the role of different historically and spatially situated actors in shaping development outcomes is made by Cooper and Packard (1997: 18) when they say, 'development initiatives came about as much through the initiatives of impoverished workers in Jamaica as those of visionaries in London.'

68. Foucault (1983: 222) in his essay on 'The subject and power' suggests that 'one must analyse institutions from the standpoint of power relations, rather than vice versa...[because] the fundamental point of anchorage of the relationships, even if they are embodied and crystallized in an institution, is to be found outside the institution...[p]ower relations are rooted deep in the social nexus, not reconstituted 'above' society as a supplementary structure whose radical effacement one could perhaps dream of.'

69. See Bates (1989), Calvert (1995), North (1990), and Ostrom (1990) for discussions of institutions and their role in structuring relations among actors. These accounts of institutions have been important in the creation of the new-institutionalism, especially as it has come to be known in political science and development studies.

power are always constricted, diverted, or overflowing depending on the micro-topography of conduits in a region. Continuities and disjunctures of power, we suggest, are a product of the regional geography of landscapes, institutions, and culture complexes,[70] and it is by attending to these variations that the spread and effects of power may be mapped.[71]

To insist on the regional production of the experience of globalization is precisely to argue for the description of networks, struggles, and differentiated place-making that people recreate in everyday contexts. The National Alliances of Peoples' Movements in India, and the movement for the province of Uttarakhand in northern India are different manifestations of the regional imaginary. The first is tied primarily to a belief in the common ground shared by those engaged in a struggle against the high modernist projects of the Indian state. The second is more tied to place, but the place-related ties themselves are produced by a belief in the political and economic discrimination faced by those living in Uttarakhand.[72] To varying degrees the issues these movements raise about development and modernity are circumscribed by regions that are interlocked physical, discursive, or socio-spatial expressions of struggles about place-making.[73] In other cases we

70. Watts (1992b: 31) also recognizes the salience of the region when he talks of three Nigerian regions as 'products of quite different colonial and precolonial histories.' Sivaramakrishnan (1997) provides an example of this from the case of modern colonial forestry in India. His argument about different Bengal regions and their diverse experience of forest conservancy is built on both ecological–geographic and social–political conceptions of the region.

71. Similar points are made in different contexts by Sangren (1995) and Cooper (1994).

72. For a current European example where a similar argument may be found see Lem (1995). A fuller discussion of the different strands of European regionalization can be found in Applegate (1999).

73. This point is in consonance with the recent questioning of teleological and dichotomizing accounts of development in India. In an essay dealing with the first part of the twentieth century, Bose (1997) judiciously shows development emerging from particular combinations of rival nationalist visions that overtake colonial government initiatives. In a companion essay dealing with more recent times Gupta (1997) reminds us that struggles around development in India do not neatly oppose modernity to community, but reveal complex coalitions between cosmopolitan members of international organizations and local social movements.

may have to trace the circuits iterated by seasonal migrants whose numbers shrink or swell with agricultural slumps or commodity-led industrial booms. In this sense, we agree with Kelly who argues that regions are produced by 'a reconfiguration of employment patterns, social relationships, cultural identity, and political allegiance.'[74]

Regional modernities, thus, encompass multiple terrains of localization and point toward the search for patterns generated by socio-political and cultural forces as they act to produce localities. It implies that localities are always produced such that they remain nested in larger networks of relationships best understood as regions. The idea that an imagined locality does not map onto a single place has led many to the concept of de-territorialization. This concept[75] has become a powerful tool in the hands of those creating images of the global ecumene.[76] But there is a concurrent re-territorialization that we have to note and examine, especially in relation to the place-referents of the re-territorializing imaginary.

Imaginations about the homeland of people who see themselves living in a diaspora are a valuable case in point. Constructions of home frequently conflate several nested localities: Indians in the US are able to think themselves South Asians, Indians, Maharashtrians, Bombayites, or natives of Thane with greater ease, perhaps, than

74. In an elegant and perceptive article Kelly (1990: 224) uses region as a new way of conceptualizing the urban–rural (read 'global–local' for the purpose of this discussion) relationship where material and cultural flows jointly constitute many regions in Japan as peripheries of a national state and metropolitan culture. Kelly discusses the emergence of part-time and part-family rice farming in Japan. The regional modernity of this phenomenon can be observed at several levels, where the region would be defined by social, physical, or cultural parameters. Thus, inside individual rural families demarcations of authority and responsibility emerge as the modern reorganization of living spaces and domestic work creates new intra-family groups and divisions. Operating on a larger scale, regions can also be geographically deciphered within rural areas in the gendered and generational distribution of farm work across agro-climatic zones. Lastly, we have new referents for intra-national regional modernity when the countryside relates to the city as the place of rice production, where the economic irrationality of surplus rice production can be offset by the cultural–political rationality of producing worthy national citizens (pp. 213–20).

75. *Pace* Deleuze and Guattarri 1988.

76. See Soja 1989; Gupta and Ferguson 1992; Appadurai 1996.

their counterparts whose lives remain tied to the tenements and suburban trains of Greater Bombay. Kumar's essay (Part III) on immigrant Indian identities in the diaspora provides a portrait of the workings of the textual imagination in ways that cannot be contained. As he shows how the presumed homogeneity of globalization is shattered precisely in the imagination, he argues that this makes regional modernities always already contested projects. Exploring the expanding discursive terrain of Indian writing in the diaspora with brilliant virtuousity, drawing and contrasting themes always under the surface in the works of Rushdie and Kureishi, Spivak and Chakrabarty, Hall and Appadurai, Kumar is most at ease in drawing unexpected parallels and striking contrasts. His text, invoking themes of dispossession, interstitiality, hybridity, desire, imagination and memory, refuses to cleave to a particular narrative or develop the fiction of living subjects whose lives and experiences can wholly be captured through texts. It constitutes self-conscious evidence about simplifications that become necessary in the construction of representations in the diaspora, representations that can have oppressive, disruptive, or oppositional consequences.

What Kumar is attempting to portray about the production of modernity is insufficiently described by talking about how locality comes into being in a global or transnational public sphere. Instead, we are presented with an interlocking hierarchy of localities that the local/global dyad obscures. The concept of the region enables an explicit discussion of this hierarchy and a simultaneous recognition of how every level in the hierarchy is a product both of contingent construction and historical sedimentation of meanings and institutions. In deploying the term 'regional modernities,' we are attempting to write a history of development encounters without being chained to a modernization discourse, or feeling compelled to produce postmodernist narrative fragments. Our effort is to turn instead to dialogic stories about regional modernities.

Three features of 'regional modernities,' in the sense we deploy the phrase, may, therefore, be emphasized. One, it is more a product of cultural, economic, and socio-political forces than a reflection of points or areas on a spatial grid; as much a result of ongoing processes within the non-Western world as a distinctive socio-cultural formation that emerged with high capitalism in the

West. Two, in contrast to scholars like Appadurai[77] who insist on the newness of recent globalization processes, we insist, in agreement with Bayly,[78] on the historic continuities that mark the emergence of regional modernities. The term also interrogates the easy dichotomization of modernity and tradition and points to the incomplete and diverse ways in which modernity remains at the center of a social imaginary in different parts of the Third World. Three, modernity is alive and well in distinctive forms and with distinctive concerns in non-Western societies across the world. This makes postmodernity a peculiar concern of postcapitalist societies like the US.[79]

We use 'regional modernities' as an organizing concept to explore the contested histories of development and the shifting links between ideas about development in different locations. The experience of development across nation-states indicates that far from entering a postdevelopment era,[80] we seem to be in a period when development has become an object of distributed and decentralized production.[81] Urban intellectuals, power elites, forest-dwelling tribes, 'first nations,' poor dryland farmers, and their various interlocutors like NGOs, international consultants, petty

77. Appadurai 1996.
78. Bayly 1998.
79. See the introduction to Kaplan (1996), who remarks on the political freight and stakes associated with discussions of modernity, postmodernism, and postmodernity.
80. See Escobar (1995) for an elaboration of the notion.
81. Consider the construction of super-highways. Such roads have always been emblematic of the implementation of large-scale development in hitherto remote parts of the world. To index the effects of such development projects by the number of miles of super-highways constructed would be to miss the highly variant political coalitions, economic transformations, and social disruptions that are the concomitant of all development projects. To describe the wider consequences of a generalized discursive formation called development that the construction of a super-highway might index we have to document the unstable micro-politics of its performance. It is important, therefore, to scrutinize more closely the details of the transformations experienced in the places where development occurs. This may be the reason for the insistence by some scholars on the need to look at how local cultures process the flows of global capital and modernity (see Pred and Watts 1992). The difference between the local and the global is, of course, just one level of differentiation in examining international development activities and their consequences.

officialdom, and local politicians have joined in the enterprise of castigating, celebrating, and rethinking development. Ironically, with the growth in the numbers of purveyors, consumers, and publicists, the scope and activities of the development industry have also increased rapidly.

THE RADICAL CRITIQUE OF DEVELOPMENT

Our discussion of region establishes the ground for investigating some of the recent literature on development. We focus especially on analyses of development discourses that see development as a project that took birth in the North and has then been used to victimize populations in the South. This literature flows from the attempt to use Foucauldian and other poststructuralist insights to critique the development project. In its focus on the global and the local, in its identification of these terms with particular idioms of domination and resistance, and in its relative neglect of the nation-state it is emblematic of precisely those weaknesses that we wish to highlight and address through the concept of regional modernities.

Scholars in development studies have long documented how social–structural features like class and spatial features like regional asymmetries have distorted the distributional effects of development. It is now clear that development objectives are also redefined as they travel from the rarefied drafting rooms of international agencies to the realpolitik of national and subnational delivery systems, or as they are imagined by analysts hired by international agencies on the basis of experiences in the 'field.' Thus, its power to frame thought notwithstanding, the discourse of development has always been riven by debate. The tremendous energies engaged in producing development, unleashed through the tension between its desirability and challenges to its operations and implementation, are evident in the rapidity with which goals of development have shifted, especially in recent years. Planning, growth, growth with equity, basic needs, participation, appropriate technology, alternative development, sustainability, liberalization, good governance, social capital, and indigenous knowledge are only some of the shibboleths that for varying periods have colonized the lexicons of development practitioners and theorists alike. Each marks a phase shift. The curious characteristic of such shifts—evidence of the remarkable absorptive powers of development—is that instead of dying out, earlier views become part of an increasing unwieldy conceptual formation.[82]

In contrast to these internalist critiques of development which accept the need for development even as they seek ways to improve achievements in its name, the new radical critiques have focused on discourses of development.[83] They suggest that the very processes that were supposed to deliver humanity from oppression and injustice may be at the core of continuing dependency and exploitation. They highlight the tremendous homogeneity of development encounters, evident in such iconic expressions of development as large dams, super-highways, project-based implementation, green revolutions, industrial complexes, and planned cities. The objective of such criticisms is nothing less than exposing the complicity of development with the power of national ruling elites and the hegemony of international reformist ideologies.

New critics of development[84] have important differences among them to which we attend later, but they all denounce the presumed homogeneity of the developmentalist imagination, suggesting that it leads development practice into predictable channels and uniform solutions to diverse problems in manifold contexts. They trace this homogeneity to epicenters in such US-dominated institutions as the World Bank, the International Monetary Fund (IMF), and the United States Agency for International Development (USAID). These institutions have formulated and empowered a particular view of what development stands for and requires. For Sachs, development is not just an oppressive frame of reference guiding the policies of developed countries toward the South. It also embodies a set of assumptions that 'reinforce the occidental worldview' to such an extent that 'people everywhere have been caught up in a Western perception of reality.'[85] Esteva echoes this sentiment

---

82. For discussions pertinent to our argument, see Cooper and Packard (1997) and Bardhan (1993).

83. This critique is present in its most developed form yet in the works of Escobar (1995) who selectively borrows from Foucault to frame his criticisms of the development discourse. See Agrawal (1996) for a critical review of some development writings animated by a poststructuralist idiom and tone.

84. Escobar 1984, 1988, 1991, 1995; Ferguson [1990] 1994; Apffel-Marglin and Marglin 1990; Parajuli 1991; Sachs 1992; Slater 1992.

85. Sachs 1992: 5.

when he proclaims, 'The metaphor of development gave global hegemony to a purely Western genealogy of history, robbing people of different cultures of the opportunity to define the forms of their social life.'[86]

This focus on a global discourse of development in what has come to be glossed as the 'poststructuralist critique of development' contains debilitating elements of the structuralist logic it grows out of and wishes to transcend. James Ferguson, one of the pioneering authors in this genre, writes, 'structures can take on life of their own that soon enough overtake intentional practices...the most important political effect of a planned intervention may occur unconsciously behind the backs or against the wills of 'planners' who may seem to be running the show.'[87] Escobar, similarly, tells us that development must be understood as a discourse by looking not at the elements of the discourse but by looking at the systematic relations that are established among them.[88]

It is no surprise, then, that such a structural and relational description of development starts at a historical juncture when the structure and the relationship within its parts can be shown to have crystallized and become clear. Escobar seems to be arguing that development emerges as a cultural formation from the structure of the conjuncture between various prior formations.[89] Even these prior formations are of recent origin and mostly traced to the middle of the twentieth century. He identifies them as the consolidation of US military supremacy after the Second World War, the division of the world into Cold War camps, the emergence of science and technology as a transformative ideology for agriculture-based societies, and theories of welfare economics that demarcated a set of economic institutions as modifiable by public policy.[90]

86. Esteva 1992: 9.

87. Ferguson [1990] 1994: 17, 20.

88. Escobar 1995: 40. To mention scholars such as Escobar, Ferguson, Esteva, or Sachs as representatives of the 'poststructuralist' moment in studies of development is not to deny the substantial differences across their writings. One significant difference lies in the yearning for a postdevelopment era that characterizes the work of Escobar, and by which Ferguson is scarcely affected.

89. Marshall Sahlins (1981) introduces and exemplifies the notion of the 'structure of the conjuncture.'

90. Escobar 1995: 35–40.

Identifying development post-1950s as vitally different from colonial policies that were somehow an expression of the will of imperialist states is crucial to the argument that development in the postcolonial Third World is an imposed discourse without agents.[91] Both Ferguson and Escobar build their powerful arguments very self-consciously along these lines.[92] Their critique cites dismally regular failures of development projects to meet stated goals. They show how such projects produce other effects: unintended extension of state capacity and its legitimation, instantiation of asymmetric relations of power, and the undermining of challenges to the status quo.

Earlier critics of development, in the face of its failures, attempted to identify alternative strategies. The new radical critics follow a lock, stock, and barrel approach. Some of them advise that the very concept of development be abandoned, together with the institutions, experts, projects, and ideologies that give it shape and substance. They wish to inaugurate a new global postdevelopment era.[93] Others prefer instead, an elaboration of the effects development produces and refuse on principle to explore alternatives.

Among the new critics of development, the works of Sachs, Esteva, and Escobar[94] share some common problems. Their discussion of the origins of development as a beast springing fully formed from the forehead of Truman in 1949 is implausibly abrupt and ignores the complex genealogies that have contributed to its makeup.[95] As Ferguson notes it was not Truman's speech in 1949

91. Critical to this point is our view of agency that we elaborate later in this essay.

92. Ferguson [1990] 1994: xiv–xv; Escobar 1995: 68–73.

93. Ferguson, we should say in qualification of this assertion, participates in this argument more selectively than others, and is willing to acknowledge the colonial antecedents of some aspects of the development discourse. More recently, he (1999) has also expressed dissatisfaction with the poststructuralist critique of development in a way that comes close to our position. We appreciate his efforts to point out the similarities between his position and the one outlined in this paper.

94. Sachs 1992; Esteva 1992; and Escobar 1995.

95. See Cooper 1997; Ludden 1992; Cowen and Shenton 1995; Washbrook 1997; and Sivaramakrishnan 1999: ch. 8. Development is more appropriately and fruitfully considered as a continuous intellectual project, an ongoing

that sent Africa and other colonial territories to the '"back of the queue,"...conquest, colonial rule, and centuries of predatory violence and economic exploitation saw to it that they were already there. "Development" was laid on top of already existing geopolitical hierarchies.[96] Additionally, for reasons to do with the complexities of colonial encounters where development was created in distinct regional discourses, views that regard development as an imposition of the West are likely to be empirically unsustainable.[97] Such views are also hard to connect theoretically to Foucault.[98] It is worth pointing out that for Foucault power always possesses multiple faces, is never simply domination, and is seldom exercised only institutionally.[99] The idea that development is a Northern imposition can only be sustained by holding at bay the immense evidence on the polyvocal, polylocal nature of development performances and appropriations. Almost all the papers in this volume emphatically demonstrate the multiple sources of developmental ideas.

---

material process that bears a complex genealogical link to late colonialism. These historical links have been explored by a number of different scholars (Arendt 1987; Cowen and Shenton 1995; and Watts 1995). A historical approach that traces the origins of development to the colonizing process would need to shade and nuance the story of development to take into account the shifts and modulations in the project that occurred in the 1945–95 period. But the production of the discourse of development, it can be argued, was well under way by the turn of the century, certainly in places like India and the Indies.

96. Ferguson 1999: 379. For similar assertions in the context of South Asian writings on development, see Ludden (1992), Bose (1997), and Gupta (1998).

97. This point is effectively made and illustrated by Rofel (1997: 155–9) who says, 'we must...remain wary of creating unified readings out of local Euro-American practices and allowing them to overpower interpretations elsewhere...polysemous histories are located in several sites: in the specific interpretations of scientific management by local factory managers: in architectural histories rooted in the early years after liberation, as well as the pre-revolutionary era, and finally in workers' memories of past spatial relations...as a result modernity in China does not neatly replicate the hypothetical transnational—that is, European—model.'

98. We make this observation in light of the efforts of several new critics of development, especially Escobar (1995) to find the theoretical wellspring of their arguments in Foucault's writings.

99. Foucault 1978: 95–6; 1977: 122.

The radical critique of development also troubles because it conjures up a particular and singular image of the relationship between the global and the local. It is a picture in which the global is the homogenizing juggernaut of domination, and the local the crucible in which variable forms of resistance are given birth. In this vision, the World Bank, the IMF, and the producers of theoretical writings on development construct and impose particular visions of development on the world, and residents of indigenous, marginal, local spaces resist such impositions with variable results. It is worth mentioning that in this form the new radical critique of development recalls an earlier model of core-periphery relations postulated by scholars belonging to the 'dependency school.' They saw the movement of western capital, an interlocking state system, and unequal terms of trade to be the source of exploitation.[100] The focus in the new critique is on discourses rather than on economic relations, but the direction and nature of the flow of influence remain substantially similar.

Thus, there are troublesome zones that new radical critiques of development share.[101] But it is proper to differentiate between at least two subgroups within this radical critique, each vulnerable to a different criticism.

If the arguments of these critics are taken seriously one might seek from them alternative forms of engagement that could lead to social change that is more in favor of the dispossessed. But one subgroup of the new radical critics of development refuses to outline general programs of political action. The lack of a political program rushes these radical critics of development headlong into

100. For a recent discussion of these writings in the context of globalization, see Hoogvelt (1997).

101. Consider, for example, another tension. Ferguson ([1990] 1994) suggests that the real consequences of development projects such as roads, entrenchment of coercive state capacities, and establishment of new infrastructure can be considered as unintended. Yet, he also believes that international donors and aid agencies, when designing projects with the help of state officials, mistakenly view them as apolitical. But if state agencies and officials are political creatures and entities, one must be careful before seeing entrenchment of state power and extension of the capacity of state agencies as unintended effects of development. Indeed, state actors interested in development, because they are political animals, may view development quite self-consciously as an instrument to extend state capacities.

a paralyzing wall of inaction.[102] Ferguson, for example, prefers to talk about the effects and the mode of operation of the apparatus of development without 'providing any sort of prescriptions.' He asserts that his book 'never intended or presumed to prescribe.'[103] Such a principled refusal to advocate for others must be respected. At the same time the unwillingness to visualize a program of action, especially on a subject as implicated in livelihoods as development, ultimately stems from an inertia-inducing stance that implicitly assumes 'centers of calculation' to be the sources of agency,[104] and a strict separation between those localities where development is experienced, and other locations from which it is criticized. The consequence, then, is the concession of political responsibility to those situated in 'centers of calculation.' Ultimately, this concern about political inaction forces even Ferguson to outline a sketchy and limited statement about supporting 'typically non-state forces and organizations that challenge the existing dominant order,' and 'counter-hegemonic alternative points of engagement.'[105]

The other subgroup develops alternative politics in greater detail. A yearning for a postdevelopment era marks their arguments. But this yearning is unrealistic about the limits of pragmatic politics, ignores the historical consequences of similar aspirations for utopias, and remains unfair in assessing the multiple forms of development. Escobar, for example, turns to grassroots movements, local knowledge, indigenous peoples, and the power of popular protests in his search for a postdevelopment era.[106] He focuses on hybridity as the metaphor to denote the political responses that are necessary to replace development. Esteva talks about a 'new commons' where the laws of economics and scarcity do not operate and suggests that common men on the margins are likely to lead the way out of development.[107] Rahnema finds the

102. Agrawal 1996.

103. Ferguson [1990] 1994: 279.

104. 'Centers of calculation' is a term we borrow from Latour (1987) who uses it to discuss the institutions in which imperial science was produced. In the context of development it conveys the same sense of an imbalance in favor of powerful First World institutions and passive Third World regions.

105. Ferguson [1990] 1994: 286, 287.

106. Escobar 1995.

107. Esteva 1992: 22.

reason for hope in 'traditional and vernacular ways of interaction and leadership.'[108]

These solutions from the new critics of development are founded on the recognition that the problems to which development has been portrayed as an answer are 'real.' They are intended to alter the conditions that existing development solutions have failed to change. But whether the proposed new strategies can be more effective in changing the lives of those who have borne the lash of modernity on their bare backs[109] is not particularly obvious. Apart from the dubious distinctions to which one must resort in drawing lines that favor indigeneity, locality, non-party politics, and NGOs, it is not even clear that these concepts and social formations possess the kind of transformative capacities their advocates believe them to have. A more careful assessment of development strategies would not only consider the multitude of manners in which it is produced, but also recognize the emancipatory politics it can encourage.

One of the most important development ideas to emerge in recent years is that of indigenous knowledge. Brodt's paper (Part III) focuses on how indigenous knowledges come into being. Her discussion explodes the belief that development discourses are imposed from above. She shows the role played by actors in the locality, in the region, and within state structures in the generation of what is later conceptualized and reified as indigenous knowledge. Brodt notes the uneven distribution of knowledge across differently situated actors, and in so doing emphasizes the power/knowledge relationship. But since her engagement is with 'indigenous knowledge,' often glossed as the knowledge of the impoverished or the marginal, she exposes the differences within the field of even such knowledges. Her emphasis on knowledge as the product of local experimentation with ideas derived from all manner of sources is a useful corrective to views that see it as an imposition.

This recent critique of development also neglects the different modernities that have emerged in various parts of the world, except as a reflection of discourses popularized by international funding agencies and Western scholars of development. Regional modernities emerging out of the varied histories of colonialism,

108. Rahnema 1992: 127.
109. We are indebted to Amitava Kumar for this metaphor.

decolonization, and nation-building have powerfully shaped experiences of development.[110] Consider the example of rural development projects in the different political contexts of single-party socialist, multi-party democratic, and authoritarian regimes. The design of these projects, the experiences of their implementation, and the distributive outcomes that attended them have traced different paths. Such variations in the culture and politics of development at the local level can be understood only by attending to the differences in regional modernities that are often embodied in state policies.

Some aspects of these differences are visible when we contemplate the regionally variant development policies of the nation-state implicit in the experience recounted by Prashad (Part I), Skaria (Part II), and Robbins (Part III).[111] Prashad's concern is the politics around urban land and housing in India, especially in the formative years of the 1950s and the 1960s. He locates the regional modern as well as 'the housing question' in the politics of class cultures. Drawing on this idea, and surveying the politics in the early years of the nation, he identifies particular kinds of rights with the interest of different classes: the right to shelter with the interests of the homeless, and the right to property with those of the bourgeoisie. Given the alliances upon which the modern Indian state was and is founded, he suggests it was a foregone conclusion that the housing question would be resolved in favor of those who claimed the right to property. Nonetheless, the process whereby this particular resolution came into force was intensely political.

110. For example, a recent study of urban development in Bogota (Colombia) has effectively shown how the construction of a modern national capital took shape through complex coalitions between international donors and regional elites with the latter leaving their distinctive stamp on the whole process. The precise projects undertaken in the modernization of Bogota reflected more the self-fashioning of an urban elite, and their vision of urban modernity, than any plan thrust upon them by US agencies (see Everett 1995: 45–50). Somewhat earlier, and in another context, Bates (1983) points to the distinctive politics of redistribution in many African countries that left the impress of the state on peasantries in the name of modernization and development.

111. Again, the regional variations within India are evident in the descriptions of development politics that many of the papers in this volume attempt. See especially the portraits by Klingensmith (Part I) and Sinha and Subramanian (Part II).

We see a very different face of the nation-state and politics of development in the Dangs, the region from where Skaria draws his story of development. In a brilliant set of suggestive reflections, he explores the regional politics of the Dangs through the medium of the Dangs Darbar, a royal gathering of Dangi chiefs institutionalized by the British and continued by the Indian state despite Mrs Gandhi's abolition of the Privy Purses in the late 1960s.[112] Thoroughly historicizing development, Skaria draws connections and highlights contrasts between the nature of the colonial and bureaucratic national modernities within which the Darbar is to be located over time. Neither, he suggests, escapes the primitivism of development. His paper, as Moore points out in his commentary, produces a fusion of cultural politics and political economy that is shared by several other papers in this volume, and must be a hallmark of all attempts to articulate regional modernities.

Where Prashad and Skaria look mainly at how development-related policies of the nation-state intersected with particular regional politics of development, Robbins focuses his attention on the constitution, permeability, and self-image of the state itself, in part by focusing on a particular forestry official. Like Brodt's paper about the multiple locations where indigenous knowledge is produced, Robbins also provides an effective lens into environmental narratives of access and control, degradation and rescue. In contrast to Prashad and Skaria, Robbins's paper introduces how regional modernity and politics unfold in the form of discursive tropes within the institutional bureaucratic space of the nation-state.

These three essays, among others in this volume, provide examples of how the literatures on globalization and development falter when it comes to treating the nation-state or other intermediate structures between what they see as the global and the local. Scholars of globalization have yet to move beyond the local/global poles in a meaningful way. Even when they have recognized that the local does not emerge autonomously but always in connection with other localities or in articulation with forces that have a long spatial reach, they do not theorize the particular and systematic ways in which such articulations occur.

112. Privy Purses were stipends to royal houses in India, annual payments from the Indian government until 1969, as compensation for the kingdoms held before Independence.

In a similar fashion, radical critics of development see it as a global discourse that originates in Western institutions and is, then, exported through multiple channels of transmission to sites of application in the Third World. The sites where development is applied and the people that such sites contain are seen as victims of development. A strong version of development discourse that sees such discourse as being produced in international institutions and as producing social subjection also undermines attempts to attend to mediating structures such as the nation-state or other social locations that form sites for the production of development. Almost all the essays in this volume show that an understanding of development as originating in the West not only produces an impoverished sense of how development and modernity are linked, but it also refuses to recognize the actions of literally countless millions of those outside the West who constantly shape and produce development.

The key mid-level structures that exemplify the region in the context of development are the different forms taken by the nation-state. In directing our engagement with writings on globalization and on development along a somewhat circumscribed path—their vision of the connections between the local and the global—has allowed us to pick other themes as well, but a discussion of the nation-state in relation to the emergence of regional modernities permits the clearest articulation of these two provocative literatures, usually thought distinct.

NATION-STATE AS REGION

Those pursuing a poststructuralist analysis of development discourses find sometimes that the state is strengthened in the implementation of development, in the very failures of development projects. This strengthening of the state takes place, Ferguson would argue, not because of the intent behind the actions of subjects, but in the systematic nature of the social reality that results from the actions of these subjects: an unintended consequence.[113] This simple cause and effect relationship between development discourse and unintended state building is untenable. It may be more fruitful to see certain historically emerging state formations

113. Ferguson [1990] 1994: 18.

as accompanied by scientific and developmental worldviews that serve such formations.[114] Further, the strengthening of states may also be accompanied by processes that strengthen those upon whom states seek to impose their will.

Arguments about the relationship between the nation-state, international development agencies, and development discourses need to recognize the changing character of this relationship. There have been, in broad terms, two main phases of development practices and discourse in the post-Second World War era that coincide with a major shift in the global political economy. The first phase was that of international Keynesianism and state-mediated capitalism, Fordist production, American international dominance, and the decolonization and emergence of the Third World. Institutions such as the World Bank and the IMF worked in this period with postcolonial states to create and further development-related policies. The second period is the deregulated neo-liberal capitalism that emerged during the late 1970s, gained force with Thatcher-Reaganomics and the decline of the Soviet Union, and is still with us.[115] This period is often characterized as having flexible production and footloose capital.[116] In the 1990s, the Second World was dismantled, the Third World differentiated into newly industrialized countries, and a Fourth World is constantly poised at the edge of disaster. In this latter period, international institutions have used the idioms of decentralization and participation to argue for a dismantling of the state.[117]

Once we realize the shift in the global political economy that has taken place since the 1980s, we can appreciate that the nation state was always a lynchpin of development in the first phase. The proliferation of government departments and their field offices, ministries, and related public sector undertakings was central to

114. Scott (1998) provides a comparative treatment of this topic that is also instructive on the issue of state autonomy and discursive formations.

115. Moore 1995: 2; Peet and Watts 1996: 20–3.

116. The consequence for patterns of foreign aid in this period has been that overseas development assistance has grown, but has declined rapidly after the 1970s as a proportion of total resource transfers. This means that the second period also marks a massive switch from official to private sources of development funds. See Corbridge (1993: 25–8) for details.

117. For a discussion of the emergence of decentralization as a shaping rhetoric in development politics, see Agrawal (1999a).

development planning that often took the form of state-led industrialization and large-scale area development projects. The strengthening of the state in this phase took place with the support of international agencies, and the United States and the Soviet Union alike. It is in the second phase of development practices and discourse that there is a dramatic shift in the role assigned to the national state, especially when we witness the concurrent emphasis on alternative development[118] and the need to give free rein to market forces. Arguments about state expansion being an unintended instrument effect of development can plausibly be made only for the second phase. In the first phase, expansion of state capacities in the service of development was necessarily an intended effect.

Much work on globalization is also rather inattentive to the nation-state. On the one hand, theorists of globalization see tremendous variation that they attribute to differences in the many sites where modernity is being produced. At the same time, they see the nation-state as a less than significant actor in the production of these multiple forms of modernity, besieged as it is by transnational flows of people, ideas, and capital, and subnational challenges to its authority. But it seems scarcely credible that the nation-state, its agencies and personnel, and other national level actors have ceased to be significant players in the production of localities, or the production of variable modernities in local sites.[119] Empirical investigation of what are called globalization processes more often reveals that 'globalized supervision and control of economic processes become localized not by bypassing the state but rather through the agency of the state and of locally-based powerful social forces.'[120]

118. Veltmeyer 1997.

119. Garrett (1995), for example, questions those writings on globalization that postulate consistent domestic effects because of increasing exposure to trade and capital mobility. He suggests that the political power of the left and the strength of organized labor within the nation-state continue to have a marked bearing on macroeconomic policy. For OECD countries, Fligstein (1997) suggests there is no convincing proof that increasing international exchanges have been responsible for such domestic effects as de-industrialization, a growing gap in income distribution, or the contraction of social policies, or for variations in these effects.

120. Bernard 1996: 657.

To address some of these weaknesses in the literatures on globalization and development, we suggest that it is necessary to attend both to the nation-state, and to the regional production of modernities. We propose that the ideational and material aspects of development come together in the construction and the legitimation of the modern state. By serving as the arena for the pursuit of growth, democracy, and a single nation, development has linked the progressive state with the economic, political, and cultural programs implied in this three-part goal. Efforts of those who led liberation movements during specific moments of colonial rule were aimed at an independence that would secure growth, stable political organization, and cultural unity. Development, as the index of a desired modernity, was throughout implicated in a political discourse of national statism. In all locations, development came to be marked by the specific combinations of state projects aimed at growth, achievement of coherent political form, and/or cultural unity.

In India, for example, the development ideologies and priorities of the late colonial state were shaped significantly by its place in the geopolitical interests of British colonialism,[121] shifts in the regional economy, and the relationship between nationalist and colonialist politics.[122] The transformative potential of the commitment to universal democracy and planned development after independence was muted nonetheless, by the shape of the legal structures and bureaucratic apparatus of control that India's new rulers inherited from the British.[123] The nationalist program of development that was initiated considered the nation-state as the most significant actor in creating a new India, and development planning to be the instrument that would allow Indians to harvest the fruits of a benign development process. The consolidation of state-centric development in India, the changes that took place in the contours of development orientations beginning from the 1980s, and the variations within the territorial confines of the Indian nation-state cannot be understood by seeing development simply as the reflection of a global process writ regionally, or the

121. Washbrook 1997:49.
122. Bose and Jalal 1998.
123. For the massive reliance of the Indian constitution on the Government of India Act of 1935, see Washbrook (1997: 37). A more specific sectoral instance of forest law and colonial legacies is discussed in Sivaramakrishnan (1995).

state simply in charge of promoting development and extending authority.

At least two papers in the following pages show the intimate, explicit, and intended links between the state as the main producer of development, and programs of development initiated in its first phase. Klingensmith's paper in Part I about the Damodar Valley Corporation (DVC), India's Tennessee Valley Authority (TVA), and Abraham's paper (Part II) about the Asian-African Conference of 1955 are written with different objectives. But they both agree on the crucial and self-important place that the nation-state arrogated to itself in developing visions of modernity. The inception and implementation of these programs was aimed precisely to legitimize the postcolonial state as the prime agent of development.

Klingensmith's paper establishes that even in the context of such likely projects as large dams, the kind of borrowing of development ideology that took place was ineluctably shaped by the evolving interests and desires of politicians and technocrats in India. The relationship between the Indians involved in the DVC and their TVA counterparts was less of tutelage; instead it was one that was used to support a variety of different claims on authority and resources. The range of claims that were made is truly astonishing: from the cultivators, supported by local politicians, who refused to pay irrigation levies, to the DVC officials who saw in it means to garner prestige, to national level politicians who viewed the DVC as the key to state-led development. The intended effects were related to state strengthening; the unintended effects more to the appropriations, corruptions, and manipulations of state objectives.

Abraham's paper elaborates a somewhat different genealogy of power in relation to development. In the context of space research, national development was inextricably bound with national security, and both with the postcolonial state. Elaborating this relationship through a fascinating story of espionage and discovery, Abraham clearly brings home the valence that national planners and scientists attached to the state leading the multifarious enterprise that is development. The leadership of the state can be seen in its organization of time and space, instantiation of boundaries, and orderliness of architecture. But juxtaposed to these intended modernizing effects of state-led modernity stand the signs of the recalcitrant 'immodern' that can be transformed only through recourse to violence.

The second phase of development, manifest in structural adjustment programs in various countries, shows again the usefulness of regional modernities in thinking about the process. Consider two instances. An interesting shift seems to be occurring in the relationship between political reform and economic reforms when one looks at some countries in Latin America and in South Asia comparatively. In Bolivia, Mark Robinson[124] shows us, structural adjustment programs went along with the rapid rise of a technocratic neo-liberal elite government supported by World Bank ideas in favor of a strong central government working for swift and substantial economic reforms. The 1994 Law of Popular Participation in that country is working to dilute the centralized culture of governance that has really emerged in the second phase of development. India's comparable 73rd Constitutional Amendment mandating Panchayati Raj in all states, passed in 1993, works not only to strengthen earlier attempts at devolution but also to provide new powers to the central government for direct political communication with regions by circumventing provincial governments. Here, structural adjustment has a very different relationship to political reform that cannot be understood outside a regional Indian modernity and the political negotiations in a putatively federal form of government.

We would also argue that structural adjustment policies constrain the political agenda of nation-states engaged in sweeping macro-economic reforms. They reduce the scope of intra-national discussion on national planning. A political sphere, thus, partially emptied of economic issues is filled by an expanding realm of identity politics. As identity becomes a major factor in formal politics it becomes more relevant to study regionally distinct modernities as they are manifested in middle-class culture—with its combination of corporate assurance and expanding civic participation, new kinds of production and trade, and distinct social movements caught up in regional struggles. To understand development processes that unfold within nation-states, therefore, we need to understand them as a consequence of how efforts of multiple actors came together in diverse arenas within the region.

124. Robinson 1998.

The essays by Sinha and Subramanian (Part II) both provide hints of the multiplicity of actors that come together in diverse arenas within a region, and how actors involved in distinct social movements can get caught up in regional struggles. Sinha takes us to a landscape familiar for its long history of social movements— the forests in the Uttar Pradesh Himalaya in India. He focuses on the Chipko movement. Locating his project contrastingly to those who claim that development is dead and that it should be replaced by an alternative politics based on social movements, Sinha argues that in fact social movements often find their energies in pursuing the goals that have always been espoused by believers in development. Providing a window into the strategies and objectives of many of the actors related to the Chipko movement, Sinha argues that modernity is alive and well in many parts of the Third World, and that it is constructed in the context of the desires of specific regional actors rather than by the theoretical abstractions presented in development narratives. The radical development critique, Sinha would argue, is one such abstract development narrative.

Where Sinha situates his study in the northern geography of the subcontinent, Subramanian moves us to the southern tip of the country in the district of Kanyakumari. She provides a rich portrait of the cultural politics of modernization that brought together the Hindu nationalist Bhartiya Janata Party and the local low-caste Catholic fishers as uneasy electoral allies. In the process she forces an examination of the strange intersections of narratives of Dravidianism, Hindu nationalism, developmentalism, and environmentalism. The outcomes in this case can only be understood by attending carefully to the politics of the region and the locality. As in the papers by Berry and Klingensmith, we see the actors in this story making claims to multiple identities and sources of power. The two essays by Sinha and Subramanian are concrete illustrations and elaborations of what we earlier called interconnected and networked hierarchies of localities. Their discussions uncover the regional politics that the local/global dyad obscures, and shows that is not reducible directly to any national or statist visions of development or modernity.

It is useful to remember here that globalization processes may accentuate certain kinds of cultural heterogeneity and aggregate them.[125] A complementary point follows from the growing

125. Kelly 1998.

scepticism about market triumphalism accompanied by Western models of democracy, as being the panacea for societies where the heavy-handed developmental state is perceived to be in retreat. As White suggests, 'autonomous state capacity depends heavily on the presence of institutional coherence in the constitutional arrangements for the distribution and use of political power, in the relations between different sections of the bureaucratic apparatus, and in the nature of party systems in political society.'[126] The resulting discussion of 'embedded autonomy' or 'inclusive embeddedness'[127] also underscores the importance of regional modernities by showing how state capacity and its constellation of political institutions are shaped by regionally specific patterns in the construction of state–society relations. [128]

STORIES OF DEVELOPMENT

The multiplication of relevant actors in development (state officials, NGOs, grassroots development agencies, villagers, politicians), the differences even within these cursorily identified groups, and the divergences in the processes of development that their goals and strategies introduce forcefully remind us of the impossibility of looking at development through a singularizing lens. For our purposes this means that even where development has become linked to international discourses of conservation, human rights, public health, and economic stabilization, projects and attempts to develop remain a temporally and spatially bounded theater in which whole episodes of development may be played out as a revelatory crisis. We use the idiom of performance wittingly, to serve as reminder that development is most fruitfully studied at the several loci of its practice, and in the multiple genres of its enactment. An advocacy of the histories of doing rather than an

126. White 1998: 30.

127. Evans 1996; Leftwich 1996; White 1998.

128. A good example of this point is provided by the study of welfare administration as a major feature of the Indian state by Jayal (1999) who shows, using the example of calamity relief, that the regional state is a crucial arena for shaping development action as it is forced to negotiate and translate between strident local assertion and diffuse national benevolence. Here the region acts as an intermediate level between local and global perceptions of calamity and concrete development strategies for tackling it.

attention to discourse formations separates the thrust of our argument from that in the works of the radical critics of development. We are distinguishing here between analysis based on the agency of historically grounded actors—individuals and institutions—and the presumption that the discourse of development, as a field of power relations, generates the subjectivities informing the micropolitics that concern us. Foucault provides a salutary note of caution that we take seriously: 'One should not assume a massive and primal condition of domination, a binary structure with "dominators" on one side and "dominated" on the other, but rather a multiform production of relations of domination which are *partially* susceptible of integration into overall *strategies.*'[129]

Both the terms partially and the term strategies are crucial here. Arguably the Foucauldian formulation of power and resistance can be extended, in ethnographic contexts, along the lines suggested by Gupta and Ferguson who point out that 'practices that are resistant to a particular strategy of power are thus never innocent of or outside power, for they are always capable of being tactically appropriated and redeployed within another strategy of power, always at risk of slipping from resistance against one strategy of power into complicity with another.'[130] But to grant that power works through strategies that are multi-form, and partially realized in relations of domination, is to create the possibility for a theory of resistance that is not entirely encapsulated by particular fields of power.[131] This brings us to the question of agency in an effort to grapple with the post-Foucauldian subject.[132]

We suggest that the expression 'strategies of power' requires attention to a particular concept of agency, one that can come to terms with the notion of strategies. The idea of strategies without authors is particularly dissatisfying in the context of development.

129. Foucault 1980: 142, emphasis added.

130. Gupta and Ferguson 1997: 18–19.

131. One such theory has been worked out compellingly by Scott (1990). At least one contributor to Gupta and Ferguson (1997) presents a reading of Foucault in debt to Scott and close to our position. Rofel (1997: 174) says that the project of Foucault is to 'excavate—and hold in tension—the discursive production of subjectivities and equally the ways in which ordinary people embrace, appropriate, and transform these as they recast their embodiment of past practices'.

132. We are grateful to Angelique Haugerud for the phrase.

Without a relationship with authors, it becomes particularly difficult to connect strategies with effects. These considerations turn us towards a theory of agency that is grounded in discussions of lived experience. Livelihoods and identities are constructed in historically formed regions of understanding and action. The micropolitics of these processes have to be viewed from multiple locations.

Considerations of de-territorialization, political immediacy, and collective value do not answer the question of agency which requires, as Homi Bhabha suggests, an articulation of effect and action. We must ask with Bhabha, 'where indeed is agency in a circuit of action and communication that so radically resists a "return" to the subject?'[133] To ask this question is not to advocate a return to an autonomous, fully formed subject. Nor is it to believe that to anchor strategies to agents, it is necessary to appeal to knowing subjects who are capable of comprehending all the unfolding implications of their actions in relation to the social contexts they inhabit. Rather, we advocate a subject who is always in the process of formation, but who, nonetheless, is also an actor. The agents we have in mind define interests and relate interests to actions, always in specific contexts, admittedly in an imperfect fashion. Their stories may define subjective interests at a point in time but over time their stories are also always struggling to control changes in the definitions of interest.

It is only through such a redefinition of the concept of the subject that we can more satisfactorily begin to harness ideas of strategy, agency, and subjecthood to the analysis of development activities. The paper by Rebecca Klenk (Part I) examines the socialization of young women along Gandhian principles at Lakshmi Ashram in the Kumaon region of Uttarakhand in north India. Her examination opens the space for precisely such a linking of subjecthood and development. The Gandhian Lakshmi Ashram educators wish for inner strength for their graduates, wish for them the ability 'to stand on their own feet.' For such an objective the existing, conventional government syllabi are not very useful. Among modern nation builders, Gandhi perhaps had the most articulated vision of the relationship between the fashioning of the self, and the possibilities of development understood as self-reliance. But

133. Bhabha 1998: 126.

this production of modern selves in Kumaon, a self-formation process that may be recognized as roughly parallel to that in other Gandhian ashrams in India, is in stark contrast to official visions of development inscribed by the nation-state: visions that require graduates with formal college degrees, diplomas, and certificates. Klenk's paper points insightfully to the regional processes of the construction of the self where different elements in the regional imaginary cohere around Gandhi's thought. It also brings home the disjunctions between such regional self-transformation processes and those promoted by official development efforts.

If Klenk's paper points to how regional processes of self-development may run counter to official needs, Berry's paper in Part I on the development of women, and Luthra's paper (Part II) on the education of entrepreneurs highlight two very different strategies and relationships in the production of modern selves.[134] At the same time, both these papers also articulate several of the features of regional modernities that we emphasize. Both the papers take NGOs, actors that have become increasingly prominent on the stage of development, as one of the institutional sites where modern women and modern entrepreneurs are produced. Berry's paper focuses on women. She shows the transnational links between US Department of Agriculture Programs for rural American women in the early 1900s, reinterpreted implementation of similar programs by the Nehru government, and the appropriation of such programs in conjunction with a feminist reading of Sanskrit texts about *shakti* by the NGO Sutra in Himachal Pradesh. Showing these links alone make hers a remarkable paper. But she goes further and also examines how women in Changar, Himachal Pradesh, transform the programs sponsored by Sutra because their views of their health needs are born in a very different social and discursive space in comparison to the ones that government officials had in mind when creating women's programs for the entire country. In the process of elaborating these links, Berry also emphasizes how the concept of 'woman' is itself a product of particular conditions, interpreted in multiple ways by particular publics of development.

---

134. These, again, are not the only two papers that invoke the relationship between the transformation of the self and of the nation. See also the essays by Skaria, Robbins, and Abraham in this volume.

Luthra (Part II) also focuses on NGOs and the relationships between seemingly grassroots strategies/stories and global visions of development. But she has a different focus and objective. She looks at how the well known Self-Employed Women's Association (SEWA) creates women entrepreneurs and the tensions between efforts to craft women's subjectivity into a mold resembling that of an entrepreneur, discourses of feminism, and the emphasis on social development. Each of these objectives can be linked rather easily to larger discourses of development. But the actual practices of development that SEWA undertakes and to which its women members relate underline the difficulties in constructing the seamless discourse of development and in classifying its clients into subjects or victims. In no small measure are these difficulties the result of the obstacles that are born as a part of the processes of active self-transformations that projects of development generate (see also Gupta's commentary in Part I). Both Berry and Luthra's papers provocatively indicate that development projects are transformed by those who are supposed to be the victims/beneficiaries of such projects, often because of the multiple positions they occupy. Indeed, the very fact that people occupy multiple subject positions reveals the possibilities of and for agency. Not all subject positions are determined in the power–resistance dialectic.[135]

New options arise for even the most disempowered actors because power works through multiple social and institutional locations—where institutions are broadly defined to include structures, rules, and norms. In this conception, structures, rules, or norms are not static entities, fixed in time and space. They are 'constituted by mutually sustaining cultural schemas and sets of

135. Berry (1993) makes an analogous point when she shows how the spread of cocoa cultivation in west Africa led to the multiplication rather than consolidation of claims to rural land both through the spread of tenancy and because the definition of tenant hinged on issues of descent and/or citizenship as well as land use. This points to the increasing bases for claims and power in the modernization process as community and tradition become rallying cries for traditional elites who feel undermined by the modern state. Berry concludes: 'by simultaneously courting supporters in the name of customary social solidarities and disparaging ethnic loyalties as backward and politically disruptive, African governments have both intensified ethnic tension and political competition and rendered them more uncertain—thereby reinforcing peoples' propensity to invest in multiple social networks (p. 132).'

resources that empower and constrain social action and tend to be reproduced by that action.'[136] Structures do not just constrain. They also empower particular actions of agents who possess knowledge of the cultural schemas that enables mobilization of resources and by their access to resources enact schemas. Again, to insist on the ability of agents to shift the structural context within which they are located is not to adopt a starry-eyed vision about the lack of limits on human possibilities. Rather, it is to focus on the impossibility of structures to constrain actions to a unique singular point. To deny that strategies have authors or agents logically leads to an insistence on the tyranny of the social.

These are some of the reasons that lead us to make two final points. One, there is an urgent need for the ethnographic, micro-historical, micropolitical turn in the study of development and regional modernities. Two, this turn cannot leave the empirically oriented researcher stationed in the locality while the global is left to analysis by modelers and hermeneutically inclined scholars. We are signaling the various ways in which development is a powerful center that is constantly being redefined and reimagined. Stories and practices of actors situated in the flexible realm of regional modernities have to become central foci of inquiry. This requires institutional histories, ethnographies, and accounts of micropolitics in relation to development.

Our critique of poststructuralist anti-development discourse makes clear that its infirmities are produced by the debilitating disease Sherry Ortner recently called 'ethnographic thinness.'[137] Our focus on practice, in turn, leads to a focus on mediation— between local and global, between development agent and development object, between the realm designated modern and the one characterized traditional—or the ways in which nation-states, regional politics, villages, NGOs, MNCs, and multi-layered government bureaucracies create an imagined regional as the variable interface between a mythical local and an equally mythical global.

Rather than a single systematic discourse of development, understood as an overarching cultural logic of globalization, we propose the exploration of stories of development. These stories may seem to resonate in global quarters, but their authors are located in sites within the institutions of regional modernities and local contexts.

136. Sewell 1992: 27.
137. Ortner 1995.

This point can be made clearer by briefly returning to our claims about modernity. We have argued earlier that the origins of modernity cannot be easily traced to western Europe in a particular historical period. If we grant that modernity grows out of the exigencies and exchanges of European empire building, then we have to concede its history is longer and more ambiguous than something neatly emergent from eighteenth century debates on reason and rationality in western Europe.

Outside a highly abstract philosophical realm of consideration it is not even clear that modernity has only a few stable referents like progress, teleological beliefs, the privileging of reason and skepticism, and the reorganization of collective identities around the territorial nation-state.[138] In the everyday world of livelihood and identity, social struggles and statemaking, signifiers of modernity are drawn very quickly into contentious debates and contested practices. It is in these debates and practices that the stability of such signifiers as progress and reason is called into question as they become imbued with more specific meanings.

We find the idea of stories, therefore, useful in that it can consciously be used to move beyond the limitations imposed by the notion of discourse that has come to inform writings on development. The use of the terms stories draws attention to multiple vocalities, multiple points of production, and the more intimate and unpredictable processes through which development as practice has outcomes we too easily attribute to development as rhetoric or discourse. Through an interest in stories, it also becomes possible to attend to issues of human agency at many levels—even if some forms of it are thwarted or only partially realized.

The focus on stories also allows attention to the contingent production of development in many sites. Stories are less closely tied to a schema than discourses or narratives, even if persuasive stories appeal to specific elements of well accepted development narratives. In contrast to a discourse, stories are far less committed to elaborating a hidden structure that underlies and presumes to explain how development works out in practice. They are a more conscious montage of patchy and sometimes disjunctive experiences. Unlike narratives, stories have a limited commitment to

---

138. A working definition of modernity that Gupta (1997: 321) feels is widely accepted within anthropological debates on modernity.

linear development. They are more suited to reporting the unpredictability that is part of the process of any attempt to alter a social status quo.

Our focus on stories recognizes that a growing body of scholarship has come to distinguish a variety of narrative forms. If Jameson's account[139] provides one of the earliest discussions of 'meta-narratives' that exemplify the most monologic and authoritarian forms of narratives, Bakhtin's work has allowed the discovery of polyphony, intertextuality, and dialogism in the analysis of narratives.[140] However, the structure, linearity, and cohesion implied by the use of the term narrative means that multiple narratives only refer to the existence of several competing coherent and meaningful accounts. Stories, in contrast, refer to the more contingent process of narrative construction—a micropolitics of narrative production, if you will. They foreground, thus, all the messiness involved in the power-plays of assembling narratives.[141] We suggest that a 'narrative' comes into focus only when the tensions and indeterminacies of its construction have been relegated to the background if not completely erased.[142] 'Stories' return us relentlessly to the moments of production, to a wide cast of authors, editors, publicists, and critics. The concept of 'stories' becomes all the more important when we recognize that development or modernity are incomplete projects whose characteristics are subject to disagreement and whose impacts are unevenly felt.

When Pigg speaks of how Nepali villagers reappropriate and remake development projects to insinuate within these projects their own versions of how development should work;[143] or when Gupta describes how the leaders of the Bharatiya Kisan Union turn populist development slogans against the government;[144] or when

139. Jameson 1981.

140. Bakhtin 1981.

141. We are grateful to Rebecca Klenk for pushing us to clarify this point. She reminded us of several of the important authors who have reflected on the issue of narratives. Anagnost (1997), Basso (1996), Daniel (1996), and Stewart (1996) are divergent examples of recent studies that make sophisticated use of the narrative concept.

142. 'Discourses' have the added disability of a mysterious production and untraceable transformation.

143. Pigg 1992.

144. Gupta 1997.

Rofel tells us how Chinese factory workers reinterpret factory discipline,[145] they are describing processes that concepts such as discourse and narrative can address only inadequately. Stories allow the accommodation of complex historical contingency, multiple sites of production, and contention within presumed arenas of consent. As a construct they are far more useful to represent the incoherence that lurks at the heart of all development efforts.

CONCLUSION

This introduction situates the following essays in the context of existing works by scholars interested in theorizing the cultural politics of globalization and development. These important literatures have provided new insights to rethink the links between the global and the local, the core and the periphery. For scholars of development, the proliferation of development discourse signals a new form of international domination, a new form of governmentality. For many observers of globalization, a newly resurgent media has helped diffuse homogenous visions of modernity. In the aftermath of colonialism, these two distinct literatures argue with a common voice that localities have come to be transformed by global forces in particular and troubling ways. Other scholars, in contrast, have argued for an independent status for the local and the parochial. They have also asserted, using persuasive examples, the impress of the local on the global.

These arguments about the relationship between the local and the global help us move away from formulations that see the local and the global as distinct, and allow us to acknowledge the continuing and substantial connections across social formations and levels of analysis. This volume, starting from the conviction that there are local histories and agencies at work in any modern context, nonetheless, argues for greater attention to the region as a conceptual device to understand how the local is constructed and how supralocal, regional political–economic formations selectively empower or undermine particular local processes and phenomena. This is the reason for our insistence on the flexible concept of regional modernities and for its deployment to analyse different enactments of development. In contrast to terms like alternative modernities, our proposed alternative has a substantive content.

145. Rofel 1997.

And, in contrast to terms like local modernity, it has the virtue of focusing attention on patterns that mark relations among localities.

Representations of the relationship between the local and the supra-local, whether in the context of development or globalization, require a supple treatment. To discuss this realm of imagination and cultural construction, we have advocated the use of 'stories' in preference to discourses or narratives. Our advocacy of stories is not intended simply as call for a celebration of ambiguity and difference. Turning to a representational device such as stories is better suited to destabilize preconceived notions of authority and sequence in the practices of development and address more adequately the question of agency and the complex processes of subject formation. At the same time, it is through stories that narratives of development and change come to be constructed.

Indeed, this introduction, this volume, and its essays can also be seen as examples of how stories are told, the connections that radiate from one story into another, and the elisions that are necessary to construct narratives. Our representations of the essays that follow have been 'interested' borrowings, appropriations aimed at the production of a particular kind of coherence related to the consolidation of our critique of existing writings on globalization and development. It is only in this sense that we claim that the following essays are nested in our introduction, not in the sense of the nested relationship among the units of a Russian dolls set. The stories that our authors tell contain many other themes, several extremely powerful, that we have necessarily not examined. Take just one instance. Skaria's insights about the primitivism of development, concretized in his discussion of the Dangs, the Koknis, and the Bhils, go beyond the by now usual claims about the appropriation and manipulation of development by subalterns. To cite this example is only an invitation to explore the other stories that this volume attempts to recount.

References

Agrawal, Arun, 1996. 'Poststructuralist approaches to development: Some critical reflections.' *Peace and Change* 21(4): 464–77.

———, 1999a. *Decentralization in a Comparative Perspective: Participatory District Development Program, Nepal.* Oakland: ICS Press.

———, 1999b. *Greener Pastures: Politics, Markets and Community among a Migrant People.* Durham: Duke University Press.

Alvarez, Sonia, Evelina Dagnino, and Arturo Escobar (eds.), 1998. *Cultures of Politics/Politics of Cultures: Revisioning Latin American Social Movements*. Boulder: Westview Press.

Anagnost, Ann, 1997. *National Past-times: Narrative, Representation and Power in Modern China*. Durham: Duke University Press.

Apffel-Marglin, Frederique, and Stephen A. Marglin, 1990. *Dominating Knowledge: Development, Culture and Resistance*. Oxford: Clarendon Press.

Appadurai, Arjun, 1996. *Modernity at Large: Cultural Dimensions of Globalization*. Minneapolis: University of Minnesota Press.

———, 1998. 'Dead certainty: Ethnic violence in the era of globalization.' *Development and Change* 29(4): 905–26.

Appadurai, Arjun, and Carol Breckenridge, 1995. 'Public modernity in India.' In Carol Breckenridge (ed.), *Consuming Modernity: Public Culture in a South Asian World*. Minneapolis: University of Minnesota Press.

Applegate, Celia, 1999. 'A Europe of regions: reflections on the historiography of sub-national places in modern times.' *American Historical Review* 104(4): 1157–82.

Arendt, H. W., 1987. *Economic Development: The History of an Idea*. Chicago: University of Chicago Press.

Bakhtin, Mikhail, 1981. *The Dialogic Imagination: Four Essays*. Edited by Michael Holquist. Translated by Caryl Emerson and Michael Holquist. Austin: University of Texas Press.

Bardhan, Pranab, 1993. 'Economics of development and the development of Economics.' *Journal of Economic Perspectives* 7: 129–42.

Basso, Keith, 1996. *Wisdom Sits in Places: Landscape and Language among the Western Apache*. Albuquerque: University of New Mexico Press.

Bates, Robert, 1981. *Markets and States in Tropical Africa*. Berkeley: University of California Press.

———, 1989. *Beyond the Miracle of the Market: The Political Economy of Agrarian Development in Kenya*. Cambridge: Cambridge University Press.

Bayly, Christopher, 1998. *Origins of Nationality in South Asia: Patriotism and Ethical Government in the Making of Modern India*. New Delhi: Oxford University Press.

Berman, Marshall, 1982. *All That is Solid Melts into Air: The Experience of Modernity*. New York: Penguin.

Bernard, Mitchell, 1996. 'States, social forces and regions in historical time: toward a critical political economy of Eastern Asia.' *Third World Quarterly* 17(4): 649–65.

Berry, Sara, 1993. *No Condition is Permanent: The Social Dynamics of Agrarian Change in Sub-Saharan Africa*. Madison: University of Wisconsin Press.

Bhabha, Homi, 1998. 'Anxiety in the midst of difference.' *Political and Legal Anthropology Review* 21(1): 123–37.

Billet, Bret, 1993. *Modernization Theory and Economic Development: Discontent in the Developing World.* Westport, CT: Praeger.

Black, Jan Knippers, 1991. *Development in Theory and Practice: Bridging the Gap.* Boulder: Westview Press.

Boas, Morten and Timothy Shaw, 1999. 'The political economy of new regionalisms.' *Third World Quarterly* 20(5): 897–910.

Boas, Morten, Marianne H. Marchand, and Timothy M. Shaw, 1999. 'The weave-world: Regionalisms in the South in the new millennium.' *Third World Quarterly* 20(5): 1061–70.

Bookman, Milica Zarkovic, 1991. *The Political Economy of Discontinuous Development: Regional Disparities and Inter-regional Conflict.* New York: Praeger.

Bose, Sugata, 1997. 'Instruments and idioms of colonial and national development: India's historical experience in comparative perspective.' In Frederick Cooper and Randall Packard (eds.), *International Development and the Social Sciences: Essays on the History and Politics of Knowledge.* Berkeley: University of California Press.

Bose, Sugata and Ayesha Jalal, 1998. *Modern South Asia: History, Culture, Political Economy.* London: Routledge.

Bourdieu, Pierre, 1991. 'Identity and representation; critical reflections on the idea of region.' In John Thompson (ed.), Gino Raymond and Mathew Adamson (trans.),*Language and Symbolic Power.* Cambridge: Harvard University Press.

Breckenridge, Carol (ed.), 1995. *Consuming Modernity: Public Culture in a South Asian World.* Minneapolis: University of Minnesota Press.

Calvert, Randall L., 1995. 'The rational choice theory of social institutions: Cooperation, coordination, and communication.' In Jeffrey S. Banks and Eric A. Hanushek (eds.), *Modern Political Economy: Old Topics, New Directions.* Cambridge: Cambridge University Press.

Castells, Manuel, 1993. 'The informational economy and the new international division of labour.' In M. Carnoy, Manuel Castells, Stephen S. Cohen, and Fernando Cardoso (eds.), *The New Global Economy in the Information Age: Reflections on Our Changing World.* University Park: Pennsylvania State University Press.

——, 1996. *The Rise of the Network Society.* Cambridge: Cambridge University Press.

Chatterjee, Partha, 1986. *Nationalist Thought and the Colonial World: A Derivative Discourse?* London: Zed.

——, 1997a. *The Present History of West Bengal: Essays in Political Criticism.* Delhi: Oxford University Press.

——, 1997b. 'Beyond the nation? Or within?' *Economic and Political Weekly* 32 (1 and 2): 30–4.

Ching, Barbara and Gerald Creed, 1997. 'Recognizing Rusticity: Identity and the Power of Place.' In Barbara Ching and Gerald Creed (eds.), *Knowing Your Place: Rural Identity and Cultural Hierarchy*. New York: Routledge.

Chivallon, Christine, 1995. 'Space and identity in Maritinique: Toward a new reading of the spatial history of the peasantry.' *Environment and Planning D: Society and Space* 13: 289–309.

Clapham, Christopher, 1996. 'Introduction: Liberalization, regionalism and statehood in the new development agenda.' *Third World Quarterly* 17(4): 593–602.

Comaroff, Jean and John Comaroff, 1993. 'Introduction.' In Jean Comaroff and John Comaroff (eds.), *Modernity and its Malcontents: Ritual and Power in Postcolonial Africa*. Chicago: University of Chicago Press.

Cooper, Frederick, 1994. 'Conflict and connection: Rethinking African history.' *American Historical Review* 99(5): 1516–45.

———, 1997. 'Modernizing bureaucrats, backward Africans, and the development concept.' In Frederick Cooper and Randall Packard (eds.), *International Development and the Social Sciences: Essays on the History and Politics of Knowledge*. Berkeley: University of California Press.

Cooper, Frederick and Randall Packard, 1997. 'Introduction.' In Frederick Cooper and Randall Packard (eds.), *International Development and the Social Sciences: Essays on the History and Politics of Knowledge*. Berkeley: University of California Press.

Corbridge, Stuart, 1993. *Debt and Development*. Oxford: Blackwell.

Cowen Michael, and Robert Shenton, 1995. 'The invention of development.' In Jonathan Crush (ed.), *Power of Development*. London: Routledge.

Crush, Jonathan (ed.), 1995. *Power of Development*. London: Routledge.

Daniel, Valentine, 1996. *Charred Lullabies: Chapters in the Anthropography of Violence*. Princeton: Princeton University Press.

Deleuze, Gilles and Felix Guattarri, 1988. *A Thousand Plateaus: Capitalism and Schizophrenia*, Volume II. Translated by Brian Massumi. London: Athlone Press.

Descombes, V., 1993. *The Barometer of Modern Reason: On the Philosophies of Current Events*. Oxford: Oxford University Press.

Diawara, Manthia, 1998. 'Toward a regional imaginary in Africa.' In Frederic Jameson and Masao Miyoshi (eds.), *The Cultures of Globalization*. Durham: Duke University Press.

Dirlik, Arif, 1996. 'The global in the local.' In Rob Wilson and Wimal Dissanayake (eds.), *Global/Local: Cultural Production and the Transnational Imaginary*. Durham: Duke University Press.

Edelman, Marc, 1996. 'Reconceptualizing and reconstituting peasant struggles: Central America in the 1990s.' *Radical History Review* 65: 26–47.

Escobar, Arturo, 1984. 'Discourse and power in development: Michel Foucault and the relevance of his work to the Third World.' *Alternatives* 10: 377–400.

———, 1988. 'Power and visibility: The invention and management of development in the Third World.' *Cultural Anthropology* 4(4): 428–43.

———, 1991. 'Anthropology and the development encounter.' *American Ethnologist* 18(4): 658–82.

———, 1995. *Encountering Development: The Making and Unmaking of the Third World*. Princeton: Princeton University Press.

Esteva, Gustavo, 1992. 'Development.' In Wolfgang Sachs (ed.), *The Development Dictionary*. London: Zed.

Evans, Peter, 1996. *Embedded Autonomy*. Princeton: Princeton University Press.

Everett, Margaret, 1995. 'Memories of the future: The struggle for Bogota, Colombia.' Ph.D. thesis. New Haven: Yale University.

Featherstone, Mike (ed.), 1990. *Global Culture: Nationalism, Globalization, and Modernity*. London: Sage Publication.

———, 1996. 'Localism, globalism and cultural identity.' In Rob Wilson and Wimal Dissanayake (eds.), *Global/Local: Cultural Production and the Transnational Imaginary*. Durham: Duke University Press.

Ferguson, James, [1990] 1994. *The Anti-politics Machine: 'Development,' Depoliticization, and Bureaucratic Power in Lesotho*. Minneapolis: University of Minnesota Press.

———, 1999. *Expectations of Modernity: Myths and Meanings of Urban Life on the Zambian Copperbelt*. Berkeley: University of California Press.

Fligstein, N., 1997. '"Globalization": rhetoric and realities.' *Actes de la Recherche en Sciences Sociales* 119: 36–44.

Foucault, Michel, 1977. *The Archaeology of Knowledge*. London: Tavistock.

———, 1978. *The History of Sexuality*, Vol. 1. New York: Random House.

———, 1980. 'Truth and Power.' In Colin Gordon (ed.), Colin Gordon, Leo Marshall, John Mepham, and Kate Soper (trans.), *Power/Knowledge: Selected Interviews and Other Writings, 1972–1977*. New York: Pantheon.

———, 1983. 'The subject and power.' In Hubert Dreyfus and Paul Rabinow (eds.), *Michel Foucault: Beyond Structuralism and Hermeneutics*. Chicago: University of Chicago Press.

Fox, Richard, 1997. 'Passage from India.' In Richard Fox and Orin Starn (eds.), *Between Resistance and Revolution: Cultural Politics and Social Protest*. New Brunswick: Rutgers University Press.

Gaonkar, Dilip, 1999. 'On Alternative Modernities.' In Dilip Gaonkar (ed.), *Alter/Native Modernities*, a special issue of *Public Culture* 11(1): 1–18.

Garrett, Geoff, 1995. 'Capital mobility, trade, and the domestic politics of economic policy.' *International Organization* 49(4): 657–77.

Geschiere, Peter and Birgit Meyer, 1998. 'Introduction: Globalization and identity: Dialectics of flow and closure.' *Development and Change* 29(4): 601-16.

Gibson-Graham, J. K., 1996-7. 'Querying globalization.' *Rethinking Marxism* 9(1): 1-27.

Giddens, Anthony, 1990. *The Consequences of Modernity.* Cambridge: Polity Press.

Guha, Ranajit. 'Domination without hegemony and its historiography.' In Ranajit Guha (ed.), *Subaltern Studies VI: Writings on South Asian History and Society.* Delhi: Oxford University Press.

Gupta, Akhil, 1997. 'Agrarian populism in the development of a modern nation (India).' In Frederick Cooper and Randall Packard (eds.), *International Development and the Social Sciences: Essays on the History and Politics of Knowledge.* Berkeley: University of California Press.

———, 1998. *Postcolonial Developments: Agriculture in the Making of Modern India.* Durham, NC: Duke University Press.

Gupta, Akhil, and James Ferguson, 1992. '"Beyond culture": Space, identity and the politics of difference.' *Cultural Anthropology* 7(1): 6-23.

———, 1997. 'Culture, power, place: Ethnography at the end of an era.' In Akhil Gupta and James Ferguson (eds.), *Culture, Power, Place: Explorations in Critical Anthropology.* Durham: Duke University Press.

Habermas, Jurgen, [1985] 1996. *The Philosophical Discourse of Modernity: Twelve Lectures.* Translated by Frederick Lawrence. Cambridge: MIT Press.

Hall, Stuart, 1997. 'The local and the global: Globalization and ethnicity.' In Anthony D. King (ed.), *Culture, Globalization and the World-system: Contemporary Conditions for the Representation of Identity.* Minneapolis: University of Minnesota Press.

Hannerz, Ulf, 1992. *Cultural Complexity: Studies in the Social Organization of Meaning.* New York: Columbia University Press.

Harvey, David, 1989. *The Condition of Postmodernity: An Inquiry into the Origins of Cultural Change.* Oxford: Blackwell.

Heidegger, Martin, 1977. 'Building, Dwelling, Thinking.' In D. Krell (ed.), *Martin Heidegger: Basic Writings.* New York: Harper and Row.

Heller, Patrick, 1996. 'Social Capital as a Product of Class Mobilization and State Intervention: Industrial Workers in Kerala, India.' *World Development* 24(6): 1055-71.

Hirschman, Albert O., 1971. *A Bias for Hope: Essays on Development and Latin America.* New Haven: Yale University Press.

Hobart, Mark (ed.), 1993. *An Anthropological Critique of Development: The Growth of Ignorance.* London: Routledge.

Holmes, Douglas, 1989. *Cultural Disenchantments: Worker Peasantries in Northeast Italy.* Princeton: Princeton University Press.

Hoogvelt, Ankie, 1997. *Globalisation and the Postcolonial World: The New Political Economy of Development.* London: Macmillan.

Jameson, Frederic, 1981. *The Political Unconscious: Narrative as a Socially Symbolic Act.* Ithaca: Cornell University Press.

——, 1991. *Postmodernism, or the Cultural Logic of Late Capitalism.* London: Verso.

——, 1998. 'Notes on globalization as a philosophical issue.' In Frederic Jameson and Masao Miyoshi (eds.), *The Cultures of Globalization.* Durham: Duke University Press.

Jameson, Frederic and Masao Miyoshi (eds.), 1998. *The Cultures of Globalization.* Durham: Duke University Press.

Jansen, M. B. (ed.), 1965. *Changing Japanese Attitudes Toward Modernization.* Princeton: Princeton University Press.

Jayal, Niraja Gopal, 1999. *Democracy and the State: Welfare, Secularism and Development in Contemporary India.* Delhi: Oxford University Press.

Kaplan, Caren, 1996. *Questions of Travel: Postmodern Discourses of Displacement.* Durham: Duke University Press.

Keating, M., 1997. 'The invention of regions: Political restructuring and territorial government in Western Europe.' *Environment and Planning C-Government and Policy* 15(4): 383-98.

Kelly, John, 1998. 'Time and the global: Against the Homogeneous, Empty Communities in Contemporary Social Theory.' *Development and Change* 29(4): 839-72.

Kelly, William W., 1990. 'Regional Japan: The price of prosperity and the benefits of dependency.' *Daedalus* 119(3): 209-27.

King, Anthony (ed.), 1997. *Culture, Globalization and the World-system: Contemporary Conditions for the Representations of Identity.* Minneapolis: University of Minnesota Press.

Kitching, Gavin, 1982. *Development and Underdevelopment in Historical Perspective.* London: Methuen.

Kondo, Doreen, 1990. *Crafting Selves: Power, Gender and Discourses of Identity in a Japanese Workplace.* Chicago: University of Chicago Press.

Larsen, Neil, 1997. 'Poverties of nation, the ends of the earth, monetary subjects without money, and postcolonial theory.' *Cultural Logic* 1(1): 1-9, http://eserver.org/clogic/i-1/larsen.

Latour, Bruno, 1987. *Science in Action: How to Follow Scientists and Engineers through Society.* Cambridge: Harvard University Press.

——, 1993. *We Have Never Been Modern.* Cambridge: Harvard University Press.

Lefebvre, Henri, 1995. *Introduction to Modernity.* London: Verso.

Leftwich, Adrian, 1996. *Democracy and Development: Theory and Practice.* Cambridge: Polity Press.

Lem, Winnie, 1995. 'Identity and history: class and regional consciousness in rural Languedoc.' *Journal of Historical Sociology* 8: 198-220.

Lockwood, W. W. (ed.), 1965. *The State and Economic Enterprise in Japan: Essays in the Political Economy of Growth.* Princeton: Princeton University Press.

Ludden, David, 1992. 'India's development regime.' In Nicholas B. Dirks (ed.), *Colonialism and Culture.* Ann Arbor: Michigan University Press.

MacLeod, G., 1998. 'In what sense a region? Place, hybridity, symbolic shape, and institutional formation in (post) modern Scotland.' *Political Geography* 17(7) 833–63.

Marshall, B. K., 1967. *Capitalism and Nationalism in Prewar Japan: The Ideology of the Business Elite, 1868–1914.* Stanford: Stanford University Press.

Massey, Doreen, 1991. 'The political place of locality studies.' *Environment and Planning A* 23(2): 267–81.

———, 1994. *Space, Place and Gender.* Minneapolis: University of Minnesota Press.

Meyer, Birgit and Peter Geschiere, 1998. 'Globalization and identity: Dialectics of flows and closures.' *Development and Change,* Special Issue: 601–926.

Mitchell, Katharyne, 1996. 'In whose interest? Transnational capital and the production of multiculturalism in Canada.' In Rob Wilson and Wimal Dissanayake (eds.), *Global/Local: Cultural Production and the Transnational Imaginary.* Durham: Duke University Press.

Moore, David, 1995. 'Development discourse as hegemony: Towards an ideological history, 1945–95.' In David Moore and Gerald Schmitz (eds.), *Debating Development Discourse: Institutional and Popular Perspectives.* London: Macmillan.

Murphy, A. B., 1991. 'Regions as social constructs: The gap between theory and practice.' *Progress in Human Geography* 15(1): 22–35.

Niranjana, Tejaswini, P. Sudhir, and Vivek Dhareshwar (eds.), 1993. *Interrogating Modernity: Culture and Colonialism in India.* Calcutta: Seagull Books.

Norgaard, Richard B., 1994. *Development Betrayed: The End of Progress and a Coevolutionary Revisioning of the Future.* London: Routledge.

North, Douglass C., 1990. *Institutions, Institutional Change, and Economic Performance.* Cambridge: Cambridge University Press.

Ong, Aihwa, 1987. *Spirits of Resistance and Capitalist Discipline: Factory Women in Malaysia.* Albany: SUNY Press.

———, 1999. *Flexible Citizenship: The Cultural Logics of Transnationality.* Durham: Duke University Press.

Ortner, Sherry, 1995. 'Resistance and the problem of ethnographic refusal.' *Comparative Studies in Society and History* 37(1): 173–93.

Ostrom, Elinor, 1990. *Governing the Commons: The Evolution of Institutions for Collective Action.* Cambridge: Cambridge University Press.

Paasi, Anssi, 1991. 'Deconstructing regions: Notes on the scales of spatial life.' *Environment and Planning A* 23(2): 239–56.

Parajuli, P., 1991. 'Power and knowledge in development discourse: New social movements and the state in India.' *International Social Science Journal* 127: 173–90.

Peet, Richard and Michael Watts, 1996. 'Liberation ecology: Development, sustainability, and environment in the age of market triumphalism.' In Richard Peet and Michael Watts (eds.), *Liberation Ecologies: Environment, Development, Social Movements*. London: Routledge.

Pigg, Stacy Leigh, 1992. 'Inventing social categories through place: Social representations and development in Nepal.' *Comparative Studies in Society and History* 34(3): 491–513.

Pred, A., 1985. 'Interpenetrating processes: Human agency and the becoming of the regional spatial and social-structures.' *Papers of the Regional Science Associations* 57: 7–17.

Pred, Alan and Michael Watts, 1992. *Reworking Modernity*. New Brunswick: Rutgers University Press.

Rahnema, Majid, 1992. 'Participation.' In Wolfgang Sachs (ed.), *The Development Dictionary*. London: Zed Books.

Robertson, R., 1992. *Globalization: Social Theory and Global Culture*. London: Sage Publication.

Robinson, Mark, 1998. 'Democracy, participation and public policy: The politics of institutional design.' In Mark Robinson and Gordon White (eds.), *The Democratic Developmental State: Politics and Institutional Design*. Oxford: Oxford University Press.

Rofel, Lisa, 1997. 'Rethinking modernity: Space and factory discipline in China.' In Akhil Gupta and James Ferguson (eds.), *Culture, Power, Place: Explorations in Critical Anthropology*. Durham, NC: Duke University Press.

———, 1998. *Other Modernities: Gendered Yearnings in China after Socialism*. Berkeley: University of California Press.

Ross, Andrew (ed.), 1989. *Universal Abandon: The Politics of Postmodernism*. Minneapolis: University of Minnesota Press.

Rostow, W. W., 1960. *The Stages of Economic Growth*. Cambridge: Cambridge University Press.

———, 1990. *Theorists of Economic Growth from David Hume to the Present: With a Perspective on the Next Century*. New York: Oxford University Press.

Rouse, Roger, 1991. 'Mexican migration and the social space of postmodernism.' *Diaspora* 1(1): 8–23.

Roy, Arundhati, 1999. *The Cost of Living*. New York: Modern Library.

Sachs, Wolfgang (ed.), 1992. *The Development Dictionary*. London: Zed Books.

Safa, Helen, 1990. 'Women and Industrialisation in the Caribbean.' In Sharon Stichter and Jane Parpart (eds.), *Women, Employment and the Family in the International Division of Labor.* Philadelphia: Temple University Press.

Sahlins, Marshall, 1981. *Historical Metaphors and Mythical Realities: Structure in the Early History of the Sandwich Islands Kingdom.* Ann Arbor: University of Michigan Press.

Sangren, Steven, 1995. '"Power" against ideology: A critique of Foucaultian usage.' *Cultural Anthropology* 10(1): 3–40.

Sassen, Saskia, 1998. *Globalization and its Discontents: Essays on the New Mobility of People and Money.* New York: The New Press.

Scott, James C., 1990. *Domination and the Arts of Resistance: Hidden Transcripts.* New Haven: Yale University Press.

———, 1998. *Seeing like a State: How Certain Schemes to Improve the Human Condition have Failed.* New Haven: Yale University Press.

Sewell, William H. Jr, 1992. 'A theory of structure: Duality, agency, and transformation.' *American Journal of Sociology* 98(1): 1–29.

Sivaramakrishnan, K., 1995. 'Imagining the past in present politics: Colonialism and forestry in India.' *Comparative Studies in Society and History* 37(1): 3–40.

———, 1996. 'Forests, politics, and governance in Bengal, 1794–1994.' Ph.D. thesis. New Haven: Yale University.

———, 1997. 'A limited forest conservancy in Southwest Bengal, 1864–1912.' *Journal of Asian Studies* 56(1): 75–112.

———, 1998. 'Modern forestry: Trees and development spaces in West Bengal.' In Laura Rival (ed.), *The Social Life of Trees: Anthropological Perspectives on Tree Symbolism.* Oxford and New York: Berg.

———, 1999. *Modern Forests: Statemaking and Environmental Change in Colonial Eastern India.* Delhi: Oxford University Press & Stanford: Stanford University Press.

Slater, David, 1992. 'Theories of development and the politics of the postmodern.' *Development and Change* 23: 283–319.

Soja, Edward, 1989. *Postmodern Geographies: The Reassertion of Space in Critical Social Theory.* London: Verso.

Stewart, Kathleen, 1996. *A Space on the Side of the Road: Cultural Poetics in the 'Other' America.* Princeton: Princeton University Press.

Szeman, Imre, 1997. 'Review of Arjun Appadurai, *Modernity at Large: Cultural Dimensions of Globalization* (Minneapolis: University of Minnesota Press, 1996).' *Cultural Logic* 1(1): 1–6, http://eserver.org/clogic/i-1/szeman.

Taylor, Charles, 1999. 'Two theories of modernity.' *Public Culture* 11(1): 153–74.

Thrift, Nigel, 1995. 'A hyperactive world.' In R. J. Johnston, Peter J. Taylor, and Michael J. Watts (eds.), *Geographies of Global Change:*

Remapping the World in the Late Twentieth Century. Cambridge: Blackwell.

Tsing, Anna, 1994. 'From the margins.' *Cultural Anthropology* 9(3): 279–97.

Unnithan-Kumar, Maya, 1997. *Identity, Gender, and Poverty: New Perspectives on Caste and Tribe in Rajasthan.* Oxford: Berghahn.

Veltmeyer, Henry, 1997. 'Latin America in the New World Order.' *Canadian Journal of Sociology* 22(2): 207–29.

Warf, B., 1990. 'Can the region survive postmodernism?' *Urban Geography* 11(6): 586–93.

Washbrook, David, 1997. 'The rhetoric of democracy and development in late colonial India.' In Sugata Bose and Ayesha Jalal (eds.), *Nationalism, Democracy and Development: State and Politics in India.* New Delhi: Oxford University Press.

Watts, Michael, 1992a. 'Capitalism, crises, and cultures I: Notes towards a totality of fragments.' In Allan Pred and Michael Watts (eds.), *Reworking Modernity: Capitalisms and Symbolic Discontent.* New Brunswick: Rutgers University Press.

———, 1992b. 'The shock of modernity: Petroleum, protest and fast capitalism in an industrializing society.' In Allan Pred and Michael Watts (eds.), *Reworking Modernity: Capitalisms and Symbolic Discontent.* New Brunswick: Rutgers University Press.

White, Gordon, 1998. 'Constructing a democratic developmental state?' In Mark Robinson and Gordon White (eds.), *The Democratic Developmental State: Politics and Institutional Design,* pp. 17–51. New York: Oxford University Press.

Wigen, Karen, 1999. 'Culture, power, place: the new landscapes of east Asian regionalism.' *American Historical Review* 104(4): 1183–1201.

Wilson, Rob and Wimal Dissanayake (eds.), 1996. *Global/Local: Cultural Production and the Transnational Imaginary.* Durham: Duke University Press.

PART I

Traveling Discourses

2

The Transmission of Development: Problems of Scale and Socialization

AKHIL GUPTA

It is a measure of how quickly ideas of globalization have swept through the academic world that the editors of this volume introduce it with an argument *against* what they see as the hegemony of the 'global/local' dualism in favor of the nation-state, seen as a particularly important regional formation. Twenty years ago, or perhaps even in 1990, such an argument would scarcely have been necessary, since development was seen, despite its patently transnational aspects, as primarily a national enterprise. Thus, it was the policies of national states that were held responsible for the success or failure of the development project, and even radical theorists of imperialism saw in the workings of multilateral institutions the not-so-hidden hand of national governments, primarily that of the United States. We should not forget that it was against these ideas of a hegemonic, taken-for-granted, naturalized nation-state assumed to be the motor and subject of development that the importance of 'local' appropriations and resistances was first formulated. Similarly, it was the inability of ideas rooted in nation-states to explain the global convergences in development practices and discourses, the massive similarities across the globe in this giant project of social engineering which led some of the critics of development to formulate their theories of the globalization of discourses of development. Furthermore, it was to the credit of such critics that they refused to see 'development' as constituting an exceptional topic but one that was imbricated in other discourses of modernity, thus allowing for certain types of implicit connections between the Third World and Euro-America to emerge into the open.

It may well have been the case that in their efforts to show the globalization of development institutions, practices, and discourses that critics of development overstated the similarities between different instances of development. On the other hand, those who emphasized indigenous or localist resistance or rejection of development paradigms may have, in turn, overestimated the possibilities or actualities of such 'local' opposition. As the authors suggest in their Introduction, it has unfortunately been the case that other regional aggregations have been downplayed or overlooked in the opposition between the local and the global. I think that it is important that the relation between globalization and the nation-state not be seen as a zero-sum game; the ascendancy of the global in scholarly discourse should not be taken to imply that the nation-state has become less powerful or less important. On the contrary, in certain matters, such as immigration, this 'era of globalization' has seen the consolidation and increase of disciplinary powers exerted by First World states. Sivaramakrishnan and Agrawal are absolutely right in stressing this dialectic between the homogenizing and globalizing tendencies of modernist discourses, practices, and institutions such as development and the particular, historically specific, actions of 'local' agents. Furthermore, the editors are surely correct to suggest that in maintaining this dialectic, it is important to keep different scales in mind between the local and the global. They suggest that a notion of 'region' may be important in this scalar reimagination of development as a modern discourse, and they suggest furthermore that the most important example of regional modernity might be that of the nation-state.

Having said that, it remains a matter of considerable theoretical interest to know how the relationship between the global and the nation-state as region is to be understood. If modernity is understood as a regional phenomenon, such that 'variable patterns in the production of different modernities'[1] begin to emerge, we need

1. Introduction, this volume.

to know how to connect different scales to each other. If 'regional modernity' is not to be linked to 'its purely spatial connotations,' as the editors argue in their Introduction, then what is the appropriate scale to think about shifts in forms of modernity and practices of development?

The issue of scale is a vexed one for social analysis, not least because the scale of institutions, experiences, and representations may not converge with each other while impinging on any particular 'scene' or historical conjuncture.[2] In trying to understand 'development' as a regional modernity, we are necessarily involved in a project of 'mapping,' one that presumes that some scale, however relational, however free of any necessary spatial referent,[3] nonetheless, gathers together or 'condenses' the most important conjunctural moments. Yet, how exactly are we to determine what are the most important conjunctural moments? Is the setting of a particular direction in agricultural policy in New Delhi more important than peasant resistance in Uttar Pradesh? Or, is either of those more important than the everyday actions of a small farmer in a village? In studying development as a regional modernity, which of these instances can be adduced to 'fix' the spatial referent for 'region?'

My point is that if the answer is 'all of the above,' then 'development' cannot have one particular spatial referent; and if it is to have several spatial referents all at once, then it can be no more 'regional' or 'national' than it can be 'global' or 'local'; and that if it is simultaneously 'regional,' 'global,' and 'local,' then we need to say something more about when which particular scale becomes central to the analysis of development and when it recedes in importance.

The papers in this section demonstrate very nicely how different scales come into play in the analysis of particular events or institutions. Kim Berry's paper is an excellent example of an argument about regional modernities that sees Indian feminist's critique of women's role in state development as emerging out of the conditions of possibility in modernist claims to equality, the specific struggles of feminist groups, and the global conjuncture or regional conjunctures that might have led to the materialization of certain

2. Smith 1992; Swyngedouw 1997.
3. Introduction, this volume.

discursive possibilities in different ways at different sites, for example, in Indian planning and the United Nations.

The difficulty lies in abstracting from these concrete stories of development, in which the interplay of different scales can be demonstrated quite convincingly. The problem is not only that events, actions, and institutions involved in development often operate at different scales so that the articulation or relation between different scales becomes analytically central; the problem is also that such multi-scalar analysis also has to contend with the *durée* of divergent temporalities.

Modernity's scalar implications may be less clear than its temporal ones. The 'modern' announces a temporal rupture with what came before; it is the birth of something new, and the self-consciousness of this newness is a defining feature of the modern.[4] To speak of 'regional modernity,' therefore, is to join a particular idea of scale with that of time.

How can we identify a regional modernity? How do we know when temporal shifts, breaks, or ruptures occur to either establish or overturn a particular 'regional modernity?' And, how can we ascertain whether it is the nation or regional states, or districts, or villages that are the appropriate arenas for registering these shifts? In other words, what is the connection between geographical region, scale, and durée in the making of different kinds of modernities?

When we speak of 'alternative modernities' or endow modernity with a scalar dimension (global, regional, national, subnational, local), do we assume that all of these different modernities operate with the same temporal rhythms? Take, for instance, the example of development. Why, and under what circumstances, do we identify breaks and shifts in development discourses and forms of modernity? What kinds of periodizations are valid and what are their sources? Can development at different scales have the same temporal structure? The 'incoherence' of development as a discursive formation lies in the fact that every 'failure' prompts the *addition* of a new set of institutions and programs over the old ones. Thus, one gets not so much a fresh beginning as a layering of different histories, a palimpsest of projects of social engineering. Each of these projects has its own temporal rhythms, and their

---

4. Baudelaire 1986.

overlapping and partial overwriting create a truly mind-boggling juxtaposition of temporal figurations.

The articulation of space and scale with time has been a very important feature of scholarly and popular understandings of globalization.[5] Harvey traces the ability to conduct real-time transactions in financial markets across the world as an inaugural moment of the time–space compression that is the hallmark of contemporary globalization.

New technologies that have *accelerated* the flow of finances, images, goods, and ideas are often seen as the distinctive features of globalization in the late twentieth century. The 'scaling up' of economic (and, by implication, social) life implied by 'globalization' has not simply been accompanied, but has been made possible, by technologies that allow for more rapid communication and movement. If we live in a 'global village,' the implication is that what gives the world its 'village-like' character is that the speed of new technologies enables encounters across the globe that approximate the face-to-face interaction of social transactions in a village.

Time, in other words, mediates the experience of scale and space, making the world experientially 'smaller.' Without passing judgment on the validity of this type of popular image of globalization, it does help me make the point that other regional formations require a parallel attention to the relationship between time, scale, and space. If there is anything sociologically important about the processes that theorists of globalization have seized upon, then it clearly has implications for the temporal underpinnings of national or regional or local modernities.

However, the speed of transactions and transfers is not the only way that temporal concerns affect nation-states. Another issue in which ideas of time have been central is that of the modularity of development discourse. Development as a project is defined by the export of 'best practices' from one locale to another. The agents of this transfer are varied, ranging from multilateral institutions like the World Bank to national governments that send delegations to 'learn' how a particular technique has succeeded in another nation-state to NGOs. The assumption, shared almost universally by practitioners of development, is that a program or project that 'succeeds' in one setting can be transferred, with some adaptations,

5. Harvey 1990; Friedman 2000.

to another place with a different history, culture, and social organization. Nor, is this assumption of modularity limited to development; it may be a constitutive feature of nationalism[6] and an important aspect of modernity itself.

But what does the modularity of development mean in practice? In order to understand this, we need to pay careful attention, as Daniel Klingensmith does in his paper, to the *transmission* of development ideas, blueprints, and projects. The exact mechanisms by which an idea, a project, a program, or an institution is transferred from one context to another may have significant implications for how it functions, and more importantly, for what it means to all those affected by it. It is significant that the architects of the Damodar Valley Corporation kept pointing out that their project was 'India's TVA.' Why did they feel that it was necessary to refer to the Tennessee Valley Authority as a model? Why were the leaders of the TVA recruited as advisers to the Damodar Valley Corporation, despite their almost total lack of knowledge about India and Indian conditions?

Klingensmith's paper does a fine job of showing how the transmission of development ideas has always contained an element of tutelage and emulation, and that US advisers and Indian leaders conceived of US 'help' very much in those terms. The portability of 'development' as a set of discourses, institutions, and practices has been predicated on a particular conception of emulation that very successfully reproduced a hierarchical order in the world of 'independent' nation-states after decolonization.

Klingensmith points out that the success of 'development' lies in its ability to be appropriated for very different ends by different groups struggling to gain political power. The reception of development ideas and blueprints may alter what appears on the surface to be a modular phenomenon, as similar institutional structures and organizational mechanisms may mean something quite different in another historical, cultural and social context.[7] Thus, 'incompleteness' and 'failure,' far from being shortcomings of development, may serve as the very conditions of its continuous regeneration.

Rebecca Klenk's fascinating paper reminds us that the transmission of development occurs not just across space but across time

6. Anderson [1983] 1991.
7. Cooper and Packard 1997.

as well. Development, like nationalism or colonialism, recruits and socializes new subjects. Although there is now a substantial literature on the creation of national and colonial subjects, a parallel interest in the formation of subjects through and in development has not yet come to pass. Without such a project, we cannot understand the power that development has in people's lives, nor how 'development subjectivity' is transmitted inter-generationally.

The formation of the subject of development may be traced to the repeated, enduring, routine experiences of development institutions, ideologies, and practices, which imbue the experience of a way of life in a particular setting with a certain hue. This is a crucial area for further research because we know so little about the manner in which subjects are recruited into the development project: scholars often assume that people are already subjected to development discourse, or that they resist it from a space that is uncolonized by it.

Klenk's paper on the role of education is thus important for several reasons: (a) development even in modernization theory was not just about economics, but about political and social transformation, namely, about the creation of a modern subject; (b) within the narrow frame of economic development, the development of human capital was seen as the central developmentalist objective of national (and nationalist) states; and (c) the development of the modern subject had to do with a range of domains: everything from hygiene to voting was reconfigured according to scientific reason and modern techniques of the self.

The relation of subject formation to socialization has not received the attention it deserves, particularly if one is careful neither to reduce it to an originary moment of interpellation,[8] nor simply to the *reproduction* of the social order on the other, particularly through the experience of schooling.[9] One particularly good example of the kind of project of subject constitution that I am referring to is Berry's essay which attempts to demonstrate that 'women' were constituted as a category through specific movements and the practices of non-governmental organizations (NGOs) rather than as a pre-given social entity.

8. Althusser 1971.
9. Bourdieu 1977; Bourdieu and Passeron 1977; Willis 1981.

Any effort to link subject formation to socialization via development projects and ideologies has to confront the question of methodology. In her contribution, Klenk suggests that one way to access the reflexive monitoring and shaping of self by subjects is through the elicitation of life narratives. These are 'stories of development' in both senses of the phrase: the story of the development of the subject as a subject of development. This is one way in which the story of an individual life can be connected to the story of development. However, I do not think that life narratives offer us some magical solution to the problem of subject formation as the very act of eliciting and ordering a life narrative presupposes the use of certain stories of development. Life narratives function, rather, as another important set of data on how subjects themselves order and organize the stories of their lives and posit its connections with the stories of development and modernity.

Klenk demonstrates how Lakshmi Ashram socialized young women to be modern subjects of the nation, and, very importantly, *for* the nation, and educated them in an idiom that espoused ideas of development that were Gandhian, unconventional, and sometimes anti-conventional. Klenk follows the lives of women who graduated from this school to examine how the project of the remaking of self through education has fared. The Gandhian project of refashioning the self began with the premise that decolonizing consciousness was a necessary precursor to national liberation;[10] in the post-Independence period, this was reformulated to be a necessary precursor to 'true development.'

How exactly do subjects' connect the development of their own lives with the development of localities, regions, and the nation? This continues to be an important and understudied problem, and is particularly germane to analysts who employ a concept such as 'regional modernity:' How are regional modernities to be connected to the shaping of subjectivity?

One of the legacies of modernity is the construction of the free, rational citizen of bourgeois ideology—the individual. Once we have this notion of the individual agent, then 'collective action' becomes an analytical and political problem. Even when ideas of agency are formulated as a critique of the individual, they often

10. Nandy 1983.

retain this modernist residual. How can a more complex understanding of subjectivity, in which subjects are seen as historically and culturally created, with its attendant implications for notions of volition, will, and self, be connected to ideas of regional modernities? In other words, how can regional modernities themselves be understood as creating not just localities, but also certain types of subjects? The problem here is that of articulating the life stories of individuals with stories of development and stories of regional modernity.

In speaking thus of 'development' and 'regional modernities' interchangeably, we have so far glossed another critical issue. Most of the papers take it for granted that development represents, or stands in for, modernity. What, then, is the exact connection between developmentalist and modernist discourses? Vijay Prashad reminds us that modernity consists of many different and contradictory discourses, of which development is only one. Prashad points to the contradictions within Indian modernity, where different kinds of rights clash with each other: the human right to shelter, guaranteed by the Constitution of India versus the right to own private property.

Prashad's paper raises the larger issue of how to make connections between particular development conjunctures and different regional modernities. A more explicit treatment of this question will lead to a clearer account of why certain discourses of development are modernist and how other forms of modernity may modify, encourage, or contradict development discourses. This is a tall order, and no volume can do justice to it, but it is useful to remind ourselves not to slip too easily from a discussion of modernities to one of development.

The papers in this section all attempt to grapple with the specific reformulations and reformations of 'development' in particular institutional and geographical locations. At the same time that they draw upon the ambitious theorization of modernity presented in Sivaramakrishnan's and Agrawal's Introduction, they also attempt to illustrate what that necessarily abstract formulation would mean for the analysis of particular development projects, organizations, or problems. I thus see these papers as providing concrete examples of 'regional modernities' but also helping to extend and clarify that concept through the careful analysis of particular projects and locations. Taken as a whole, the papers in this section offer a rich, complex, and theoretically compelling portrait of development as a form of regional modernity. They raise many important questions that all of us who are interested in development discourses, processes, and institutions would do well to heed.

References

Althusser, Louis, 1971. 'Ideology and ideological state apparatuses.' In *Lenin and Philosophy and Other Essays*. Translated by Ben Brewster. New York: Monthly Review Press.

Anderson, Benedict R., [1983] 1991. *Imagined Communities: Reflections on the Origin and Spread of Nationalism*, Revised and extended edition. New York: Verso.

Baudelaire, Charles, 1986. *The Painter of Modern Life and Other Essays*. Translated and edited by Jonathan Mayne. New York: Da Capo Press.

Bourdieu, Pierre, 1977. *Outline of a Theory of Practice*. Translated by Richard Nice. New York: Cambridge University Press.

Bourdieu, Pierre and Jean-Claude Passeron, 1977. *Reproduction in Education, Society and Culture*. Translated by Richard Nice. Beverly Hills: Sage Publications.

Cooper, Frederick and Randall Packard, 1997. 'Introduction.' In Frederick Cooper and Randall Packard (eds.), *International Development and the Social Sciences: Essays on the History and Politics of Knowledge*. Berkeley: University of California Press.

Friedman, Thomas L., 2000. *The Lexus and the Olive Tree*, Revised edition. New York: Farrar, Straus, Giroux.

Harvey, David, 1990. *The Condition of Postmodernity: An Enquiry Into the Origins of Cultural Change*. New York: Blackwell.

Nandy, Ashis, 1983. *The Intimate Enemy: Loss and Recovery of Self Under Colonialism*. New Delhi: Oxford University Press.

Smith, Neil, 1990. 'Contours of a Spatialized Politics: Homeless Vehicles and the Production of Geographical Scale.' *Social Text* (33): 54–81.

Swyngedouw, Erik, 1997. 'Neither Global nor Local: 'Glocalization' and the Politics of Scale.' In Kevin R. Cox (ed.), *Spaces of Globalization: Reasserting the Power of the Local*. New York: The Guilford Press.

Willis, Paul E., 1981. *Learning to Labor: How Working Class Kids Get Working Class Jobs*. New York: Columbia University Press.

3

Developing Women: The Traffic in Ideas about Women and their Needs in Kangra, India

KIM BERRY

INTRODUCTION

The Changar area of Kangra, in the northwestern Indian state of Himachal Pradesh, is locally referred to as a backward region. The dirt roads carved into the highly erosive hill slopes of the Changar provide unreliable linkages to the markets and jobs in nearby Kangra Valley and to the highways connecting the region to the metropolitan centers in the plains. For five months of the year, travel to and from the Changar is limited to transportation by foot and donkey, as the pounding monsoon rains carve gorges and gullies in the fragile roads, which then take months to repair. Many hamlets are located one or more hours' walk from even these unpredictable byways. People joke that only the '11 Number' bus is reliable, eleven referring to a person's legs which, stick-like, mimic the numbers one-one. This relative isolation leads most able-bodied men to migrate to urban centers for work, returning once or twice a year for family celebrations and harvests. Many women become de facto heads of household and bear the responsibility for the largely subsistence agriculture which constitutes their annual cycles of work.

Yet the geographic marginality of the Changar, affecting work, transport, and access to goods and services, has never isolated it from more distant cultures and political economies. Sivaramakrishnan and Agrawal argue that, '[l]ocalities are produced as nodes in the flows of people and ideas, and are thoroughly socially constructed.'[1] The local, then, is always an amalgam. Through practices of migration, trade, pilgrimage, military service, marriage, and celebration, people have flowed into and out of the Changar region of Kangra, providing rich context for the imagination of self, place, and other. In the last two decades, with the introduction of electricity, temporary roads, and other development services, the interchange between Changar residents and regional, national, and transnational political economies has intensified. Schools shape future citizens of India, the proliferation of television brings national and international themes and events into homes, and corporate advertisements, encouraging commodified lifestyles, shape local desires and needs. Politicians vie for votes, spreading the messages of their political parties and bringing select ideas and needs of local people into regional and state politics. Furthermore there are government health centers, agricultural offices, creches, and population clinics, which inform and are informed by local peoples' routines of work and interpretations of their bodies. The Changar village women's organizations, created some twelve years ago, are simply one of many institutions through which local people are shaped by and shape national and international interpretations of their lives and needs.

Through an analysis of the *mahila mandals* (village women's organizations) of the Changar region of Kangra, I trace the multiple and often contradictory ideas about women and development in one locale. This chapter is an analysis of the traffic in ideas about who Changar women are and of what their needs consist. The concept of regional modernity, elaborated upon in the introduction to this volume, sheds light on the practices and politics of the flow of these ideas. By forwarding a concept which is founded upon the analysis of the production of modernities, and in particular of the mediating impact of regions on the specific character of modernities, the authors enable us not only to thoroughly deconstruct oppositions between local and global, but also to focus on agency,

1. Sivaramakrishna and Agrawal, this volume.

interpretation, and practices of the production of subjectivities, locales, regions, and global spaces. My analysis of the traffic in ideas about Changar women's development engages with some of these themes, and focuses on the following key issues: (a) the importance of regionality, particularly of the history of colonial rule and of nationalist movements and nation-building, in producing ideas about rural Indian women and their needs; (b) the politics through which some ideas are privileged within policies and programs for women's development, while other ideas are marginalized; and (c) the relationship between ideas about women's development and the production of new subjectivities.

In any discussion of women and their needs it is first necessary to interrogate the 'group called women.'[2] Within the Changar area of district Kangra, although women are in the majority, with so many men living and working in urban centers, and although women's work is more similar than different, even across caste and class divides, simply being a woman in a generic sense has little to do with the rhythms of work and friendship, speech and gesture, movement and rest, which comprise days and constitute lives. Within Changar daily life a commonality as women is visible in dress and adornment, repertoires of gestures, types of work, and forms of celebration. But differences of kinship, caste, age, education, and class provide the substance of these practices: the *styles* of dress and adornment, the *quantity* of work, the authority specific women have over others, the gestures of respect, deference, and equality, the inclusion and exclusion of persons in rituals and celebration, and the genres of song and dance. The constant and minute positionings along kinship lines within households, and caste and class lines across households, produce multiple differentiations which give texture to daily routines and depth to friendships and relations of deference. Even women's rituals and the accompanying songs, dances, and play which join women in a common bond of difference from men also sift out differences among them: through the exclusion of women of other castes and clans, the authority of elders and deference of juniors, and the divergent genres of song and dance of the young and old. Within Changar hamlets, subject positions that mark differences among women (of kinship, caste, age, education, and class)

2. Cassell 1977.

have, in general, a greater salience than a positioning specifically as women.

The subject position 'woman,' while receding into the background during many daily routines of the Changar, emerges as a primary subject position within modernist discourses and programs of nationalism and development. The meanings of this subject position are highly contested and are formed within the processes of the production of a specifically Indian modernity. The conflict over the meanings of the subject position 'woman' is evident when we analyse which norms, attributes, values, ideas of appropriate work, spheres of influence, and responsibility become the basis for institutional policies and programs for Indian women's development and which norms, attributes, etc., are ignored or rendered invisible. Within the Changar area of Kangra district, multiple and conflicting ideas about women and their needs circulate through development programs, non-governmental organizations, and *mahila mandals*, spanning the spectrum from housewife to one who possesses spiritual power for social transformation.

Yet, to simply call attention to this multiplicity of ideas about women is inadequate. For, ideas about women and their needs are created out of and are nested within unequal power relations. Fraser, writing about welfare in the US, focuses on the conflict which emerges within the social arena over what constitutes needs, who defines them, and the resulting political effects. She argues for a fully political analysis of the discourse of needs:

From this perspective, needs talk appears as a site of struggle where groups with unequal discursive (and non-discursive) resources compete to establish as hegemonic their respective interpretations of legitimate social needs. Dominant groups articulate need interpretations intended to exclude, defuse, and/or co-opt counter-interpretations. Subordinate or oppositional groups, on the other hand, articulate need interpretations intended to challenge, displace, and/or modify dominant ones.[3]

Fraser's emphasis on *unequal* resources is crucial for engaging in a thoroughly political analysis of the traffic in ideas about women's development. By attending to the unequal resources for shaping ideas about who rural women are and of what their needs consist, we can analyse which ideas travel far and become institutionalized

3. Fraser 1989: 166.

in policies and programs for women's development, and which ideas are marginalized, remaining simply as stories of development within specific locales.

Finally, we must attend to the subjective effects of development. Changar women, through engagement with programs for their development, are positioned by others and position themselves in relation to the subject position 'woman.' In so doing, they engage in new ways of imagining themselves and positioning themselves in relation to others. New desires are created and/or realized, and new actions become possible. In other words, the positioning of self and other is not simply a dance of pre-constituted parts of a supposedly concrete identity; rather through positioning oneself in new ways, new subjectivities are created.[4]

In the following pages I explore the traffic in ideas about women's needs in the Changar area of Kangra district, tearing apart the interweaving themes of regionality in the production of particular ideas about rural Changar women and their needs, the politics of unequal resources which affects the force with which ideas travel, and the production of new subjectivities as rural women mediate and create ideas about their lives and needs. I explore three primary centers of production of ideas about rural women and their needs: the local government block development office, the non-governmental organization SUTRA (Social Uplift Through Rural Action), and rural Changar women themselves.

BLOCK DEVELOPMENT PROGRAMS AND THE RESILIENCE OF THE HOUSEWIFE

Only a handful of women in the Changar area of Kangra district are full-time homemakers. Married to men who have been posted to the region as government servants (such as schoolmaster, electrical board worker, and veterinarian), these women have no land to farm and no need for further income in the household. The vast majority of Changar women work full-time as farmers on marginal subsistence fields, and some poorer (and predominantly *dalit*) women work as farm laborers and craftspersons. Yet, despite this fact—blatantly obvious to anyone who walks through the

---

4. See Klenk, this volume, for rich accounts of the effects of a Gandhian education on shaping women's subjectivities.

hamlets which dot the dry hills of the Changar region—the government block development office workers represented women as housewives and promoted programs to craft them into improved mothers and wives.[5] The *mukhiya sevika* (supervisor of women's programs) promoted programs for training girls to sew and for teaching women how to produce pickles, jams, dried vegetables, and other products which could be produced within the confines of the home. The health programs for women all focused on maternal and child health, never addressing the health issues of injuries from scythes, back problems, and muscle strains which are a primary concern of farming women. Even the local literacy program for women, coordinated by the mukhiya sevika, promoted the idea that literate women make better mothers and wives.

The dissonance between local government development workers' representation of women and the routines of the majority of Changar women's lives is striking—and the history of these development programs for women is even more so. Indian women had been positioned as housewives within programs for their development which began in the early 1950s through the auspices of the Community Development Program (CDP). Yet, even in the early years following Independence, when Prime Minister Jawaharlal Nehru ushered in the Community Development Era, the majority of rural Indian women were farmers, craftspersons, and laborers; only elite women lived and worked within the confines of the home. The origins of this development model for women did not emerge out of the daily realities of the majority of rural Indian women's lives, but rather from the programs of the US Agricultural Extension Service.

The US model of agricultural development, which India adopted, originated in the late nineteenth century as a program to persuade American farmers to shift from subsistence to capitalist methods of agricultural production. These initial agricultural programs in the United States were directed solely at men, and they largely failed to encourage farmers to make significant capital investments in their farms. By the early 1900s the US Department of Agriculture had established programs for rural American women in scientific

5. The ethnographic material which I present in the remainder of this paper is based on field research that I conducted in Himachal Pradesh during 1992 and 1993.

principles of homemaking. This approach did not reflect the gender division of labor in many US farming households at that time, but rather imposed urban middle-class gender relations upon rural families. US agricultural officials reasoned that if women were convinced by home economists that they needed to buy commodities for the betterment of their family life, then they would encourage their husbands to adopt capitalist methods of agriculture. Women extension agents organized homemakers' clubs in which groups of US farming women were introduced to the latest home appliances, middle-class values of good taste in home decoration and clothing, and principles of scientific and rationalized housewifery. When these early programs to persuade women and men did not meet with success, the 4H club was established to transform US children into 'the future farmers and homemakers of tomorrow.' By the 1950s this new gender division of labor was firmly in place among the upper and middle classes in rural America. Although sharecropping and subsistence farming women were not so easily transformed into housewives, this elite model of gender relations was nonetheless the dominant sign of upward mobility.

Upon achieving Independence, Nehru's government adopted this US-based model of home economics for women's programs in the community development movement in India, thereby making the housewife the subject of and for rural Indian women's development. This was despite the fact that the majority of rural women in India did not have the time or interest to learn scientific principles of housekeeping. There were several reasons for Nehru's decision. The first was Nehru's firm commitment to Western models of modernity while the second was the powerful resources of the United States: US governmental and non-governmental organizations provided significant funding for the nascent Community Development Program, and US officials lobbied hard for the adoption of the family approach to agriculture, arguing that programs for women and children were central to the success of agricultural development programs as a whole. And finally, and perhaps most significantly, this model of agricultural development found fertile ground within modern nationalist ideas about gender in India. For, the positioning of women as housewives resonated with two dominant and complementary views of gender relations: indigenous elite discourses linking family honor with women's confinement to the home; and the hybrid gender discourses of nationalism in which women were associated with the sphere of the home as the protectors of a supposedly pure Indian tradition.[6]

While the US Agricultural Extension Service served as the model for the Indian Community Development Program, these US programs for rural development were not simply transferred to India. Indian development officers reinterpreted programs for women's development to fit not only the practicalities of Indian rural homemaking contexts, but also to articulate with the production of a national identity.[7] The names of women development workers and organizations for women's development were also translated: the equivalent of the US women's extension agent was named *gram sevika* (village-level woman worker), her supervisor was named mukhiya sevika, and the 'Homemakers' Club' through which US Agricultural Extension Agents disseminated their information, was renamed mahila mandal. Over time, Indian development officers transformed the US-based home economics curriculum for training of village women workers and altered their job charts to fit Indian homemaking contexts. Programs for improved mud-brick stoves (*chullahs*) replaced programs for electric and gas ranges, emphasis was placed on sanitation and insect control through DDT spraying, and more attention was paid to immunization campaigns and to family planning. Programs for home decoration and crafts focused on indigenous arts such as *kolam*, and the dissemination of regional forms of embroidery. And, CDP publications circulated stories of model village women workers who provided technical and scientific guidance in home management along with a nationalist interpretation of Indian tradition.

6. Chatterjee (1990, 1993) argues that this nationalist discourse emerged from the contradiction which elite Indians faced, namely their acknowledgment of the political and economic dominance of the West and their desire to assert the superiority of Indian tradition. Their response was to bifurcate India into an outer male realm in which Western materialist values dominated, and an inner female realm of spirituality in which an imagined essence of India was preserved.

7. See Berry (1997) for a detailed analysis of the conflicts within India over the adoption and representation of the US model of women and development in India. See also Klingensmith, this volume, for his discussion of 'the communicative aspects of development' in relation to India's embrace of the TVA model.

The core of the US Agricultural Extension program, however, in which development officials targeted men as farmers and women as housewives, remained the same—and it had powerful political effects. Most significantly, these early programs disenfranchised farming women from the inputs, technologies, and information of farming and simultaneously enfranchised landholding men, thereby creating new gendered inequalities and reinforcing old ones. Since the US model of development favored wealthy farmers over poor, this capitalist model of agricultural development also increased class inequities, and ignored issues of land rights, land redistribution, and agricultural wages.

This model of development remained the dominant force influencing programs for rural women for several decades. By the mid-1970s critiques of this model began to influence national level policies. A convergence of research and reports within India along with international attention to the 'status of women' created a context for reassessment of the CDPs and the creation of new directions for women's development in India.[8] Through participation in the United Nations declaration of International Women's Year in 1975 and the numerous transnational events to follow, Indian governmental and non-governmental designees joined with representatives from around the world in producing critiques of development programs for women. This new international discourse of women and development (itself a result of the flow of ideas from specific locales to transnational spaces and back again to locales) created opportunities for, and legitimated efforts of, government officials, feminist scholars and activists, and NGO workers within India to produce numerous studies and policy statements in which approaches to women and development were re-examined and re-formulated.[9]

8. See the report issued by the Commission on the Status of Women in India titled *Towards Equality* (commissioned in 1971 and completed on the eve of the UN International Women's Year of 1975) as the most comprehensive critique of the conceptualization of women as simply mothers and wives.

9. See, for example, the National Plan of Action for Women (1976), National Perspective Plan for Women 1988–2000 (India Ministry of Human Resource Development 1988), The National Commission on Self-employed Women and Women in Informal Sector Report entitled *Shram Shakti* (labor power) (1988).

Policy makers within the Government of India, influenced by reports which detailed the decline in women's participation in the workforce since Independence, over the next several decades developed programs supporting women as craftspersons and entrepreneurs—including training programs for women in 'non-traditional' sectors. These new programs marked a radical divergence from the representation and targeting of women as homemakers and consumers.[10] And yet, this new focus on women's development continued to assert that 'women' constituted a salient category with distinct needs. A new discourse of womanhood replaced a prior one, but in so doing gaps and omissions were inevitable. In particular, the view of women as housewives and women as producers both render women's subsistence work invisible.[11]

While the central government's programs for women's development meandered away from the housewife as the subject of women's development, in the Changar block development office, the housewife remained at the center of development initiatives. Gupta's analysis of the state is useful here in reminding us that local offices of the state are 'more discrete and fragmentary' than unitary, while simultaneously arguing that 'it is precisely through the practices of such local institutions that a translocal institution such as the state comes to be imagined.'[12] In the context of local government offices, the vagaries of personality, class, caste, and kin identity shape the interpretation and implementation of central government mandated programs.

In the Changar area of Kangra district the mukhiya sevika mediated new government programs positioning women as producers by promoting income-generating activities that could be

10. The Government of India's Fifth Five-Year Plan (1974–8) marked the first shift from welfare to economic development-related activities. By the Eighth Five-Year Plan (1990–5) the authors self-consciously addressed the shift in the subject of women's development advocating a more holistic view of women's lives and work. Programs targeting women as economic producers include Development of Women and Children of Rural Areas, Support to Training and Employment Projects, and Rashtriya Mahila Kosh.

11. See Luthra (this volume) for a thorough discussion of the discourse of women as income generators in general, and the effect of this discourse on eliding many women's very productive (though often subsistence) work lives.

12. Gupta 1995: 384.

performed within the confines of the home and which emerged from their roles as wives and mothers; her advocacy of pickle-making activities exemplified this trend. She had been trained during the era in which home science was professed as the path for women's development. And, the American-imported model of the housewife also coincided with the local elite value that links a family's honor with women's confinement to the home—not a practical option for the vast majority of households in the Changar, but a dominant value, nonetheless. This value was reinforced and reflected through nationalist representations of women as mothers of the nation, the representations of housewives and mothers in television advertisements and programs, and in the lives of wives of government employees living in the area.

SUTRA—*SHAKTI* AND WOMEN'S COLLECTIVE ACTION

Changar mahila mandals were formed by women leaders from the area who were supported by a young NGO called ERA (Society for Environmental and Rural Awakening—now disbanded), a sister organization of the well-established NGO SUTRA. Changar women leaders attended trainings and workshops at SUTRA, and they brought their neighbors to the SUTRA campus for the annual *mela* (festival) of mahila mandals' members. Through these training programs, workshops, and melas, Changar women were introduced to ideas about women and their needs which were rooted in SUTRA's hybrid feminist discourse.

SUTRA, founded in 1985 and directed by Subhash Mendhapurkar, originally served as a mainstream development organization which sought to distribute various development goods and services. It began targeting their work with women not out of conscious design, but in response to their observations that, in general, local women were more enthusiastic about the development projects than were men. Rural women challenged the director of SUTRA on their exclusion from agricultural development programs, raising questions about why women did not have access to bank loans and directing the organization's attention to issues of the collective good such as schools, water, and government corruption. In response to these questions and demands, SUTRA helped women to demand their fair share of government goods and subsidies.

A formative moment in SUTRA occurred when a local woman raised the issue of alcoholism and the related problems of squandered incomes and wife abuse.[13] This issue was immediately embraced as a core concern by the other rural women in the meeting. In a matter of several months a mass anti-alcohol campaign began, culminating eight months later in a protest march across mountainous paths to petition the state government for changes in the liquor licensing laws. Although their demands were not met by the government, SUTRA was transformed. More women joined SUTRA, local women leaders were identified, and the first instances of contestatory action had begun.

Janet Price, a British feminist who lived and worked on the SUTRA campus for several years during, and following, the anti-alcohol campaign, called for training programs for local women leaders that would address internalized aspects of gender oppression, such as women's self-image. The director along with Janet Price, Giti Thadani, a Sanskrit scholar from Delhi, and Madhu Sarin, a board member of SUTRA, crafted a training program for local women leaders. The ten-day training interweaves themes of Western and Indian feminisms with radical reinterpretations of India's past to craft a hybrid feminist discourse.

On the first day of the training, SUTRA staff members show slides of pre-Aryan goddesses, resplendent in their naked and fertile bodies, standing proud and alone in their strength. In contrast to the gaudily clothed deities found in small, local temples throughout this mountainous state, these ancient stone goddesses stand naked, with heads erect. As the slides click by, staff members frame the images with commentary on *shakti*, feminine spiritual power. These symbols of shakti are a condensed visual representation of the discourse which informs the activities of SUTRA.

SUTRA's commentary on shakti emerged from Thadani's feminist re-reading of ancient Sanskrit texts. Scouring lesser known passages and volumes of the *Puranas*, she uncovered empowering representations of womanhood. Through radical reimaginings of the past, she proclaimed a view of shakti as located in woman's power to give birth, and represented menstruation, commonly seen as shameful and polluting, as the sign of woman's shakti. As the director and staff argue, it is women's power to give birth

13. Mendhapurkar 1991.

which endows them with the power to change society and change their lives.[14]

At SUTRA the deployment of the concept of shakti occurs within a specifically contestatory framework: shakti is not simply to be worshipped, but it is to be understood as the source of power for combating all forms of oppression against women The 10-day trainings at SUTRA for grassroots women leaders teach these women to think critically about society, to identify restrictions on women's lives, and to fight for equal rights and equal responsibilities for men and women in the home and society. SUTRA staff members encourage participants to fight for women's honor, which is interpreted as fighting all instances of oppression against women. Although the discourse of shakti emerges out of a reinterpretation of ancient texts, the deployment of this concept is firmly grounded in the critical issues of Himachali women's lives.

SUTRA's radical discourse of womanhood has emerged out of an engagement with extra-local discourses and local practices—grounded in Himachali women's critiques of state alcohol policy and male alcoholism and informed by feminist discourses within and beyond India. In turn, SUTRA's hybrid feminist discourse of shakti and history of fostering Himachali women's collective action shapes feminist discourses within the nation and beyond: the staff and director of SUTRA attend global forums on women and development and on women's movements in which they share their history through conversation and publications; stories of Himachali women's collective action now circulate in books on Indian women's movements which are taught in US classrooms; and by foregrounding the concept of shakti they have contributed to the emergence of shakti as a symbol of feminism around the globe.[15]

14. Stuart Hall (1991) discusses the moment within the formation of contestatory collective identities in which there is an effort to ground identities in stories of homelands, origins, and the past. At SUTRA, the place of grounding is not an imagined homeland, but a reclaimed body where menstruation is the source of woman's power. Like stories of imagined homelands, the stories of woman's shakti rooted in a past of goddess worship enable the formation of affective solidarity across differences which otherwise might be divisive.

15. See Luthra, this volume, for her discussion of NGOs as representing 'an important arena of globalization.'

SUTRA's survival as an institution is dependent upon working within the context of national and transnational programs for women's development. It receives government funding through a variety of programs, and it has been very active in transforming some of these programs through government lobbying, often in concert with other progressive NGOs. One such case is the Awareness Generation Program (AGP), a government scheme devised in 1979–80 by the Central Social Welfare Board to train rural women in 'public cooperation.' There were three major components of this program as devised by the government: to encourage women to become sterilized under the family planning program; to teach proper response to air raids; and to encourage women's participation in small savings schemes. Rural women were targeted by this program as problematic citizens at worst, and ignorant citizens at best, who needed to be persuaded to cooperate with national objectives. Population control was a particularly high priority for the government of India, with tremendous international as well as national pressure to curb the fertility rate. Rural women were seen not as mothers (that symbolic amalgam of the physical, emotional, and communal/national), but as biological reproducers whose potential fertility jeopardized national and international interests.

In 1985–6, SUTRA joined with other NGOs to review the AGP program. The committee recommended that the program should abandon its focus on public cooperation and instead strive to develop awareness about women's rights, atrocities against women, and government development schemes. In SUTRA's AGP training program, women leaders were first introduced to SUTRA's feminist discourse and were then trained to demand goods and services from their local block development office—irrespective of whether the programs were designed for women specifically. SUTRA advocated mahila mandals as the local institution through which such demands can be legitimately made, as once these organizations become registered with the local mukhiya sevika, mahila mandals become official legal bodies. By teaching practical skills of collective action (such as which government offices control which goods and services, how to fill out government forms, how to write petitions, how to stage protests, and who are the best officials with whom to file grievances about local government officers) the staff and director of SUTRA provided women with the framework for collectively defining their own needs and the skills to demand that those needs be met by the government. Furthermore, in trainings, the demand for community development services is presented in a politicized light: first, development issues such as access to clean water, roads, and health care are asserted as rights for which communities must fight; second, mahila mandals' struggles to meet community development needs are presented as an avenue for gaining local legitimacy from men who might otherwise be opposed to the formation of mahila mandals; and third, these issues are presented as a training for fighting more difficult battles which men of the community might oppose (such as organizing to close liquor shops, helping women leaders to become elected members of the panchayat council, and protesting wife abuse).

SUTRA's efforts to transform government programs have not always met with success. For instance, when the Himachal Pradesh government decided to create a post of para-veterinarians to improve the health of livestock in the state, SUTRA led a campaign to guarantee women's rights to these positions. The staff and director, along with a consortium of mahila mandals from across the state, argued that women—as farmers—have historically cared for the livestock and have the most in-depth knowledge of their health as well as folk remedies for treating illness. However, their efforts were stymied as the communalist BJP government ultimately ruled that reservation for women in these posts was not a desirable goal—for, in their view of gender relations, women (understood to be dependent wives and mothers) did not need access to paid employment.

SUTRA challenges many dominant ideas about who rural women are and of what their needs consist. By understanding women not as mothers and wives, but as full persons who are productive members of society (as farmers, laborers, and active agents for social change), they challenge elite values (often reproduced in local government offices) that locate women in the home as dependent members of society. In addition, SUTRA challenges the current women and development paradigm with its single-minded focus on income-generation activities for women. Acknowledging that many women work for about 16–20 hours daily managing farms and households, but also that some women are desperate for paid employment, SUTRA proffers a multi-stranded approach which focuses on the creation of arenas in which women can define their own needs and learn the skills of democratic protest to achieve them. Yet, despite SUTRA's radical critique of dominant discourses of and programs for women's development, SUTRA's work (as is true for all organizations for women's development) is based on the assertion that the identity as women is salient. For SUTRA, this assertion comes from a political critique of gender oppression, and this assertion is accompanied by a dedication to enabling Himachali women to join together and form a collective identity across the numerous differences, which divide them in daily locales. In other words, SUTRA focuses not only on meeting women's needs, but also on producing feminist subjects who define and meet their needs through collective action.

CHANGAR WOMEN—FROM COMMUNITY AND FAMILY TO WOMEN

Changar mahila mandal members make sense of their lives and form their identities within the network of ideas that emerge from a diversity of sites of production, including not only routines of work, relations of kinship and friendship, ritual, and celebration, but also television, schools, political parties, SUTRA, and the block development office. Changar mahila mandal members' views of who they are and of what their needs consist are local only in the sense invoked in the introduction to this volume—as thoroughly socially constructed and as a node in the flows of people and ideas. Mahila mandal members are operating within a dynamic context of ideas about who they are and who they should become. We can best see them not only as subjected to others' ideas about rural Indian women, but also as subjects who are interpreting and making meaning of their lives within the context of programs to develop them.

By focusing on Changar mahila mandal members as subjects in this second sense, we can explore ideas which they are constructing and disseminating about their lives and needs. We can ask how far and with what influence do these ideas travel: which of their ideas are taken up and become woven into the fabric of discourses of women and development? Which of their ideas are marginalized and remain as stories of development which have force only within circumscribed locales? Furthermore, we can inquire about how mahila mandal members' subjectivities are shaped by their encounters with discourses and programs for their development. In what ways are their desires, needs, and sense of themselves and the possibilities of their lives transformed through their engagement with policies, programs, and discourses targeting them as rural Indian women?

Mahila mandal members gathered and discussed their needs in a variety of locales: hamlet-level meetings, multi-hamlet meetings for special trainings and events (such as on women's health issues or literacy camps organized by the block office or SUTRA), development activities (such as building schools or installing bridges across the Neugal river), melas (organized by SUTRA), and protests (organized by mahila mandal members in order to demand development goods from the state). Through speeches and actions in these various forums mahila mandal members communicated to government officials, community members, and NGO workers their understanding of their lives and needs. Yet, despite the variety of contexts through which they expressed their ideas, Changar mahila mandal members only indirectly shaped the formation of policies and programs for rural Indian women's development. For, due to lack of access to the necessary resources, they themselves were not crafting policies, writing articles, or representing their lives and issues in national and transnational contexts.

In particular, the relationship between Changar mahila mandal members and block development programs for developing women was, most often, characterized by dissonance. The location of women as housewives was relevant only to a few local elite women and to some daughters of mahila mandal members who were educated up to Class 10. For these girls, the idea that they would be housewives resonated with images of romantic love which suffused the films they watched on television and the film songs which they sang over and over, local elite goals of marriage to a government servant (providing job security and the hope for a lower middle-class devoid of the reliance on subsistence agriculture), as well as discourses of womanhood promoted by teachers within their schools.

For the rest of the mahila mandal members block development office programs which sought to make them improved mothers and wives were simply irrelevant. Yet, mahila mandal members generally were not stymied by this dissonance between local government discourses of womanhood and the realities of their lives. Rather, they used their participation in block development office sponsored events to fulfil their own goals. For example, at a literacy meeting mahila mandal members sat and talked among themselves, taking the opportunity to greet friends and relatives who they had not seen recently and to catch up on each others' news. With some difficulty government officials quieted the women so that the speakers could be heard. When the meeting finished, numerous mahila mandal leaders surrounded the block development officer and presented him with petitions and lists of development demands for roads, schools, bridges, hospitals and other development goods (for the block development officer and not the mukhiya sevika controlled the funds for such development projects). These meetings were seen as the best opportunity to submit their requests to the block development officer who otherwise could be quite difficult to reach in the office.

Given the workload of subsistence farming in primarily female-headed households, the income-generating programs for women espoused by the block development office were largely irrelevant for most Changar women. Farming, a topic central to many mahila mandal members, was still considered by the government to be a male domain. The mukhiya sevika had no jurisdiction over programs and funding for farming. When the male agricultural officer was invited by Changar mahila mandal members to speak at a gathering, he addressed his speech not to the hundreds of women farmers in front of him, but to the handful of men sitting on the sidelines. Women's attempts to present themselves as farmers in need of technical advice and input were marginalized. Changar mahila mandal members' ideas about their lives and needs, in this and other instances, did not travel far in government offices.[16]

It was principally through their engagement with SUTRA that mahila mandal members' stories of themselves, their needs, and struggles traveled and become woven into discourses of feminism and women and development. These stories were necessarily mediated as they flowed from SUTRA into Himachali, national, and transnational arenas: SUTRA re-presented local women's protests and actions through the lens of their feminist philosophy, and in some instances this representation diverged sharply from

16. Here, one can imagine that a different mukhiya sevika could have been a conduit for disseminating mahila mandal members' views of themselves and their needs, working to interpret government programs (as SUTRA did) to fit more with local realities of diverse women's lives.

mahila mandal members' own self-presentation. In short, SUTRA positioned these mahila mandal members as women, largely eliding other positions they occupied (clan [*khandan*], kinship, and caste). Changar women's own self-presentation—predominant within the remote hills of the Changar—was at times not incorporated in larger discourses of women and development.

When mahila mandal members joined together in meetings to discuss their needs, the focus of their discussions was more often on family and community than on gender. There were important exceptions to this generalization, including reports by leaders fresh from their visit to SUTRA on current issues within Indian women's movements (such as the campaign against Norplant and new initiatives to help fight dowry death) and enlivened discussion of the unjust attacks that they had faced from their men when they had engaged in instances of collective action (in these cases local men who opposed the mahila mandal members positioned them specifically as women who they claimed had stepped beyond the bounds of proper womanly behavior; the mahila mandal members responded specifically as women, strongly defending their rights to work for the collective good). However, in the routines of mahila mandal activity, these women positioned themselves not specifically as women but as community members working to better their lives. And, their interpretation of bettering their lives had as much to do with local values of maintaining family honor as it did with improving local amenities and decreasing gender oppression.

In numerous examples of collective action which went uncontested by male members of the community—such as cleaning communal springs, holding eye camps, building village paths, and raising funds for a new school—Changar mahila mandal members represented their activity as stemming from their position as members of the community. When they told stories of their collective work they would recount the involvement of other community members such as young men, and in no way position themselves as women who were working for the larger good. While SUTRA, in response to local women's stories of their lives and needs, had expanded their concept of women's needs to include such community projects, SUTRA retold these stories of community work and highlighted mahila mandal members' position, as 'women' working to fulfil local needs.

Women of the Changar have also used mahila mandals as arenas for resolving conflicts over issues of harassment and rape, and in so doing they employ a hybrid mix of SUTRA's and local conceptions of honor. Before the establishment of mahila mandals in the Changar, such cases would be brought before the panchayat. As panchayats are comprised of five or more hamlets, the issue would spread throughout many members of the community. The girl's honor as well as the boy's/man's would be destroyed, and the girl would be unable to find a husband in a nearby area. Such dire consequences for attempting to achieve justice in cases of harassment discouraged people from bringing cases to panchayat councils, and aggressors went unpunished. Mahila mandals in the Changar provide an alternative venue for pursuing such cases, for they are located within hamlets which are usually comprised of members of the same clan. Although the mahila mandal cannot impose binding punishments for rape or harassment, such as jail sentences, they can place blame, extract apologies, and threaten future police action if harassment continues While the punishment of boys and men who harass girls is consonant with SUTRA's emphasis on fighting for women's honor, local concerns for the entire *family's* honor (both the boy's and the girl's) also shape the processes through which cases are tried and punishments are meted out. Furthermore, while at SUTRA such cases of harassment are generalized as women's collective issues, in local contexts they often remain framed as a specific girl's/woman's and family's honor. Action is taken by mahila mandal members not as women, but as specifically positioned relatives and/or neighbors.

While in many cases of harassment the focus is on both family honor and gender oppression, extreme cases of oppression are taken up by local women as a collective women's issue—fully consonant with SUTRA's feminist discourse. In response to the first dowry death in the Changar, women from across hamlets (and therefore across caste and clan) staged a three-day demonstration outside the hospital in which a girl lay dying of severe burns. The mahila mandal members shut down the bazaar and forced a police inquiry into the case. The women interpreted this issue as not simply a family matter, but a concern of all women. They used methods of protest that they had role-played at SUTRA, and they framed the tragedy within a feminist discourse of oppression against women.

As Changar women's ideas were mediated by SUTRA, their subjectivities were also transformed through their participation in SUTRA trainings and melas and through their experiences of collective action in the Changar. While staying at the SUTRA campus, mahila mandal members were positioned specifically as women, and differences among them were downplayed or ignored. Mahila mandal members and leaders addressed each other as 'women' or 'mothers, sisters, and daughters' in speeches, held hands across caste boundaries, and slept and ate in communal rooms irrespective of differences among them. As mahila mandal members espoused the politicized representations of women and women's duty, and as they engaged in contested instances of collective action in their communities, they embraced a new subject position—that of the politicized woman. Acting from this new subject position, they produced new ways of imagining their lives. They contested gendered boundaries limiting movement and regulating speech (such as joining together across boundaries of caste, clan, and kin position to work and/or protest collectively in public spaces, or telling stories at melas in front of men from the community of the abuse they suffered as they worked for the collective good). And, as they countered opposition from family and or community members from their collective actions, the philosophy of women's shakti was further enforced: at melas they gave speeches and sang songs in which they proclaimed that their shakti enabled them to sustain the criticism and violence they face when they attempted to better their lives and the lives of their community.

For some members this new position as a politicized woman may only be meaningful within specific instances of gendered contestation. For others, such as leaders of mahila mandals, it may be woven more densely into the fabric of daily life.[17] Yet, even for grassroots women leaders, this new position is always negotiated alongside of a multiplicity of others. For, in most daily hamlet contexts, differences among women structured daily interactions of work and leisure. The salience of an identity specifically as women shifted according to the dynamic context of interaction—

17. See Berry (1997) for an expanded discussion of subject positions, subjectivity, and mahila mandal members' dynamic engagement with multiple discourses of womanhood (especially chs 3 and 8).

emerging in the foreground of large gatherings of mahila mandal members at the SUTRA campus and during instances of collective action, and receding to the background in daily hamlet contexts. Even in single-caste hamlet mahila mandal meetings, differences among women rather than a commonality as women prevailed: elder women dominated the conversation, and rules of kinship shaped how women greeted each other, where they sat, who spoke and the weight their words carried. Rules of caste purity were studiously maintained by many upper-caste women, and concerns for familial honor generally predominated over concerns about gender oppression. New subjectivities, produced within the context of collective action mediated by SUTRA's feminist discourse, must therefore not be seen as univocal. Rather, Changar mahila mandal members embraced a new subject position and negotiated this position along with prior ones.

CONCLUSION

Changar mahila mandals are sites in which ideas about women and their needs circulate, ideas which are the product of a distinctively Indian modernity. As Changar women mediate these representations of their lives—rejecting some, reinterpreting others—they produce new subjectivities. Particularly through their embrace of a distinctively Indian and modern subject position of a politicized woman (infused with SUTRA's reinterpretation of women's shakti and women's duty), Changar mahila mandal members imagine new desires and needs, as well as a new sense of themselves and the possibilities of their lives.

Changar mahila mandal members' ideas about their lives and needs are thus formed within the context of a flow of ideas and people, mediated by governmental and NGO actors, and informed by locale-specific daily practices, nationalist projects, transnational institutions, and feminisms. Their ideas travel far beyond hamlet contexts, particularly through SUTRA's work in state, national, and even transnational development arenas. Yet, in the inevitable representation of these ideas, omissions and transformations occur.

The issues of who has the power to represent others' ideas, and who has the power to promote particular models of development, are central to understanding the *politics* of the traffic in ideas about women's development. Changar women do not have the resources (nor can we assume the interest) to define for the nation (much less the world) who women are and of what their needs consist. In dramatic contrast, the US Department of Agriculture was able to not only transform gender and class relations within the rural United States through their agricultural development programs, but also to promote this model of development around the globe. India adopted this model, recast it, and redeployed it for particular projects of nation-building and development. In the Changar, mahila mandal members mediated this and other projects for their development, and in so doing they shaped their subjectivities. While attention to practices of mediation, the multi-directional flow of ideas, and the production of subjectivities is critical for understanding the traffic in ideas about women and their needs, so is an attention to inequalities. For, some ideas travel far with significant force, while others are marginalized, their movement confined to specific locales.

References

Banerjee, Sumanta, 1990. 'Marginalization of women's popular culture in nineteenth century Bengal'. In Sangari and Vaid (eds.), *Recasting Women: Essays in Indian Colonial History*. New Brunswick: Rutgers University Press.

Berry, Kim, 1997. 'When women get together: The politics of collective action and difference in village women's organizations of Kangra, India.' Ph.D. thesis, Cornell University.

Cassell, Joan, 1977. *A Group Called Women: Sisterhood and Symbolism in the Feminist Movement*. Prospect Heights, Illinois: Waveland Press, Inc.

Chakravarti, Uma, 1990. 'Whatever happened to the vedic dasi? Orientalism, nationalism and a script for the past.' In Sangari and Vaid (eds.), *Recasting Women: Essays in Indian Colonial History*. New Brunswick: Rutgers University Press.

Chatterjee, Partha, 1993. *The Nation and Its Fragments: Colonial and Post-Colonial Histories*. Princeton, NJ: Princeton University Press.

———, 1990. 'The Nationalist resolution of the women's question.' In Sangari and Vaid (eds.), *Recasting Women: Essays in Indian Colonial History*. New Brunswick: Rutgers University Press.

Fraser, Nancy, 1989. *Unruly Practices: Power, Discourse, and Gender in Contemporary Social Theory*. Minneapolis: University of Minnesota.

Gupta, Akhil, 1995. 'Blurred boundaries: The discourse of corruption, the culture of politics, and the imagined state.' *American Ethnologist* 22(2): 375–402.

Hall, Stuart, 1991. 'Old and new identities: Old and new ethnicities.' In King (ed.), *Culture, Globalization and the World System: Contemporary Conditions for the Representation of Identity.* Binghamton: SUNY Press.

India Department of Women and Child Development, 1993. *Policies and Programmes for the Advancement of Women in India.* New Delhi: The Women's Bureau of the Department.

India Ministry of Education and Social Welfare, 1974. *Towards Equality: Report of the Committee on the Status of Women in India.* New Delhi: Department of Social Welfare.

India Ministry of Human Resource Development, 1988. *National Perspective Plan for Women, 1988–2000 AD: Report of the Core Group Set Up by the Department of Women and Child Development, Ministry of Human Resource Development, Government of India.* New Delhi: Department of Women and Child Development.

India Planning Commission, 1974. *Fifth Five Year Plan, 1974–1978.* New Delhi: Planning Commission.

———, 1990. *Eighth Five Year Plan, 1990–95.* New Delhi: Planning Commission.

Mendhapurkar, Subhash, 1991. *SUTRA: A Perspective.* HP, India: SUTRA.

National Commission on Self Employed Women and Women in Informal Sector, 1988. *Shramshakti: Report of the National Commission on Self Employed Women and Women in the Informal Sector.* New Delhi: The Commission.

Sangari, Kumkum, and Sudesh Vaid, 1990. 'Recasting women: An introduction.' In Sangari and Vaid (eds.), *Recasting Women: Essays in Indian Colonial History.* New Brunswick: Rutgers University Press.

4

'Difficult Work': Becoming Developed

REBECCA KLENK

DIFFICULT WORK

Another thing, Rebecca, that you should listen to from me: in these Kumaon hills working is very, very difficult. You need ten times the energy and ten times the strength within yourself. When I became head of this institution, I had to move around, to be ready to go anywhere. I was trying my best, you know? Dashing here and there, going everywhere. But people didn't understand me, they thought that perhaps I was not a good girl. Because I was talking to men, I was going by myself, I was asking for money for this project and that project. Some people admired my strength. Some did not understand me. That was very difficult![1]

Sixty-year-old Radha[2] and I sat together upon a *khadi* rug at her low desk as she remembered the struggles of her early days as director-secretary of Lakshmi Ashram, some thirty years ago. Her early childhood passed in a small, off-road village. As a teenager she came to teach in the ashram during its first decade. 'So,' I interjected, 'you changed peoples' minds about what a Kumaoni woman

---

1. Except for Radha's comments, all direct quotations are translated from Hindi into English. Radha's comments were in a mixture of English and Hindi, and are translated completely into English.

2. Except for public figures who asked that I use their real names, all names used below are pseudonyms.

could do....' She laughed while she recalled the turmoil she had faced as a young, unmarried woman when she suddenly was put in charge of the rural institution:

I tell you this because as an anthropologist, you should understand that working like this in these areas—especially for a person from the same area—is not easy. It is difficult, it is very difficult. But I think when one is challenged, then strength comes up from inside, you know? So, this came and then I could do it.

Lakshmi Ashram is about half an hour by footpath from the nearest roadside bazaar, in the middle hills of Almora district in the Kumaon division of the Himalayan state of Uttaranchal, North India.[3] During my fieldwork, I learned from women and girls involved with the Gandhian experiment in education there that 'education' and 'development' have the potential to transform one's life, that realizing this potential is always very difficult work, especially for rural women and girls, and that—most importantly— such a realization is predicated upon one's 'strength coming up from inside.'

This chapter complements and complicates recent scholarship on development and modernity.[4] I retain the insight that development is a historically specific project structured by myriad power asymmetries, and combine this with a concept of 'modernities,' in the plural, to highlight the idea that there are ways of being modern other than those which have characterized Euro-America.[5] In India and elsewhere, development processes and discourses have been central to the ways that regional modernities are taking shape.[6] My fieldwork in rural Uttaranchal revealed that various discourses of development have long since blended into the 'common sense'

3. The state of Uttaranchal was created in 2000. Before then, the region was part of Uttar Pradesh and referred to as 'Uttarakhand.'

4. For a review of this scholarship, see Sivaramakrishnan and Agrawal, this volume.

5. For related discussions of situated and multiple modernities, see for instance: Appadurai 1991, 1996; Berman [1982] 1988; essays in Breckenridge 1995; Chatterjee 1997; Gupta 1998; Hall et al. 1996; Ivy 1995; Pigg 1995, 1996; Sivaramakrishnan and Agrawal, this volume.

6. See Gupta (1998) for a detailed analysis of the centrality of development to experiences of modernity in India, as well as the theoretical discussion by Sivaramakrishnan and Agrawal in this volume.

of stories and everyday talk. Therefore, by examining how people constituted as the supposed 'targets' of development creatively receive, negotiate, and re-present development's categories to make sense of their day-to-day experiences, it is possible to learn something new about what the microprocesses of development and the desire to become developed mean in a specific context. This requires close attention to how becoming 'developed' and 'modern' is associated with gendered shifts in subjectivity when people participate in particular development initiatives.

Here, I explore how gendered subjects are produced by regional modernities in a specific development context. Focusing on connections between stories of self and development, I explore two types of contradictions: those that arise when women's subjectivities shift as they become educated and those produced when one model of development clashes with another. In so doing, my aim is to attend to some of the multiple vocalities and processes through which consequences a culturally-specific, gendered development initiative—Lakshmi Ashram—have been realized. Rather than treat this Gandhian institution as a 'local' site of pure Indian 'tradition' uninflected by modernity and development, I explore how graduates were being Gandhian on their own terms.[7] Returning to Radha's comments, this chapter explores the negotiation of 'difficult work,' that is to say, the negotiation of global development processes within local practices and discursive spaces that generate their own modernities. It examines what it means to be developed and the role of education in realizing this condition by focusing on the negotiation of development in a particular educational context.[8] Along with other contributors to this volume, I argue that lived experience is never entirely colonized within the spaces of such transnational discursive formations as 'development.'

SCHOOLING THE NATION: LAKSHMI ASHRAM

In order to understand graduates' stories, it is first necessary to situate their experiences and the educational mission of Lakshmi

7. Thanks to an anonymous reviewer's comments for prompting me to make my point explicit in this way.

8. In so doing, this chapter aims to analyse shifting, localized productions and experiences of modernity in the context of shifting and sometimes contradictory productions of modernity at state and transnational levels.

Ashram in the context of the contradictory aims posed by Gandhian and Nehruvian programs to reconstruct the Indian nation-state and train its citizen subjects. The development of 'human capital' through the education of modern subjects has been central to transnational processes and discourses of development. Education may, of course, serve other ends. In colonial India, some prominent nationalists emphasized that the decolonization of the consciousness of Indian national citizen subjects through education would be crucial for national liberation. Prior to Independence, nationalists had different ideas about how far and in what direction this decolonization would need go. Since Independence, virtually every Education Commission report has identified education as the most important forum for developing a modern, unified Indian nation by shaping the national culture of its citizens. Yet, recent studies of state-issued textbooks reveal that contradictory narratives of what constitutes 'India' are embedded in an ideology that promotes industrial modernization as the only legitimate paradigm of development.[9] These contradictory narratives contained in textbooks intended for schoolchildren are shaped by a larger contradiction that characterized nationalist debates over the reconstruction of the postcolonial Indian state: Nehru's vision of rapid industrialization as the basis of the developmentalist state, versus Gandhi's vision of revived village-level economies as the cornerstone of national development.

These competing visions for a postcolonial modernity that would be specifically Indian have continued to fuel debates over national integration and economic planning since Independence. From the Second Five Year Plan onwards, rapid industrialization (with an emphasis on heavy industry) has been a guiding agenda for economic development, despite the fact that most of India's population is involved in agriculture. Government school syllabi and textbooks have been and continue to be designed to articulate with the Indian developmentalist state's plans for rapid industrialization, despite the poor fit of this model with economies and day-to-day life in most of rural India. Indeed, the irrelevance of

9. See especially Advani 1996. Several studies have analysed the hegemonic processes of state-designed and controlled education in India, and how such education fails poor, rural schoolchildren and those from marginalized groups, including: Advani 1996; Erevelles 1998; Jeffery and Jeffery 1994; Newman 1989; Rajabalasubramanian 1997; Scarse 1993; Sahni 1994.

both colonial and postcolonial government school syllabi for the day-to-day lives of most rural Indian students has been recognized since the early days of the nationalist movement, and continues to be cited as a primary source of the so-called failure of government education. This raises a question, however: If textbooks and government school syllabi do not present viable alternatives for rural communities, then how do rural students make sense and use of education?

Critical perspectives on education, nationalism, and modernity are in the foreground of historical and contemporary debates in India regarding alternative education programs for rural students—most notably, Gandhi's *naii taaliim* scheme—and the education of girls and women. Gandhi's naii taaliim scheme challenged the objectives of the Nehruvian developmentalist state by locating 'education' in rural daily life rather than in textbooks and the classroom.[10] Meanwhile, as I discuss in more detail below, official controversy over the education of girls and women has used 'women' as a ground for discussing tradition and modernity in the postcolonial nation.[11] It is in the context of the competing visions of modernity in India that frame these debates, together

10. The Hindi term *naii taaliim* literally means 'new education.' 'Basic Education' is the English term used in India for naii taaliim. Gandhi's program for naii taaliim, proposed in 1937, was an experiment with education that would make it relevant to village life, and a direct interrogation of colonial education systems in India (see Gandhi 1951). Gandhi believed that village-level, village-relevant education would be essential for the sort of village regeneration that would facilitate real *swaraj*. Naii taaliim schools were meant to be vocational, integrated into village life, and self-financing. Children would not learn primarily from textbooks, but rather from daily work and training in crafts, such as producing khadi. Naii taaliim would emphasize the all-round development of pupils, including not only intellectual development, but also the development of the heart and spirit. This, in the Gandhian dream for post-swaraj India, would be 'true national education,' that is, education for national swaraj not only at the political level, but more importantly, at the level of the national citizen–subject him/herself (see Fox 1989).

11. For example, in her analysis of the debates on *sati* (widow burning) in colonial India, Lata Mani (1987) has shown that women became the ground upon which colonial and indigenous elites in nineteenth century India waged battles of modernity and tradition. Indian womanhood continues to be a key symbolic construction in local and national debates on development planning.

with the question raised above regarding how rural students make sense and use of their education, that the mission of Lakshmi Ashram and the stories that women and girls tell of their studies and experiences there become particularly interesting. Their stories speak to the ways that their subjectivities were transformed by education, but such transformations often put ashram graduates at odds with local ideas about gender, sexuality, and appropriate roles for women. It is these moments of tension that sometimes became moments of agency in graduates' lives.

Preceding the proliferation of non-governmental organizations (NGOs) in India, Lakshmi Ashram is a small, unique, 'alternative-to-development'[12] institution established with the aim of creating a new kind of womanhood and realizing Gandhi's dream of *gram swaraj* (*graam svaraajy*, or village self-sufficiency) in postcolonial Uttarakhand. With Gandhi's encouragement and enthusiastic co-operation from local nationalists, Lakshmi Ashram was founded in 1946 by Sarala Devi, one of Gandhi's British followers.[13] It was first housed in a donated building and designed to be largely self-sustaining.[14] At the time of its founding, the ashram became a

12. The emphasis on an 'alternative-to-development' as opposed to 'alternative development' agenda is generally intended as a direct critique of the 'Western' design and orientation of many economic development paradigms popular in India. These terms are frequently contrasted in talk of development planning among NGO workers and Gandhian leaders in Uttaranchal. The terms are sometimes used to invoke a specifically anti-modern and sometimes anti-Western rhetoric that draws heavily on Gandhi's notions of anti-modernity.

13. Not to be confused, as she sometimes is, with Gandhi's better-known British follower, Mirabehn (formerly Madeline Slade). Sarala Devi's major published works include *Vyaavahaarik Vedaant: Ek Aatmakathaa* (1979), *Sanrakshana ya Vinaasha (Paryaavaraniiy Paristhiti: Ek Chunautii)* (1981), and *Revive Our Dying Planet: An Ecological, Socio-economical and Cultural Appeal* (1982).

14. Initial funding for Lakshmi Ashram came from Gandhi Smarak Nidhi. However, in accordance with naii taaliim philosophy, the ashram was designed to be largely self-supporting. All daily work was done by the students and teachers, including handicraft and food production, and keeping a dairy. Minimal school fees were used to purchase essential items such as school supplies, kerosene, homeopathic medicines, khadi cloth, agricultural implements and tools, etc. Students made their own clothing, and the ashram ran a khadi shop and a homeopathic dispensary.

central node in a network of *sarvoday* projects and institutions that was developing throughout Kumaon and Garhwal. This locally rooted network continued to be influential during the 1990s in the designing and implementation of alternative development (or, again, alternative-to-development) schemes in this region. The network was deeply influenced by and closely articulated with Vinoba Bhave's ashram-based sarvoday experiments after Gandhi's assassination in 1948. Sarala kept the ashram in close contact with this network, and made a point of sending her students all over India to work and study with village-based Gandhian activists at other Gandhian institutions.

The ashram was set up as a naii taaliim program where girls would receive an academic education along Gandhian lines and be trained to become social activists (*samaaj sevikaa*) who would with self-confidence (*antimvishvaas*) work to become self-reliant (*svaavalambii*) and to uplift (*uthaan, sudhaarnaa*) their village sisters. This political agenda was embraced by most, if not all, of the parents of first generation students. Most of these parents were active nationalists themselves and saw the ashram as a place where their daughters would be trained to become rural leaders. Some, however, saw the ashram as a place where girls would be trained to do the same work that they did at home while receiving an academic education. Such parents were often particularly surprised by the changes in their daughters. In the words of a graduate,

For those Freedom Fighters active in the struggle for Independence, the ashram was a team engaged in building the nation through education, a

---

All of this work, with the exception of the dispensary, continued in the 1990s. A detailed consideration of the complex and changing financial situation of the ashram and its extension projects is beyond the scope of this chapter. However, in 1969, after the class background of ashram students had begun to change, the ashram decided to accept donations from an informal Danish group (Lakshmi Ashrams Venner, or 'Friends of Lakshmi Ashram') to support student scholarships. In the 1990s nearly all ashram students were funded by Danish scholarships. Although members of Lakshmi Ashrams Venner visited regularly, they did not take a formal part in ashram management. Other small projects were funded by small domestic grants and occasional grants from international donor agencies, but otherwise the ashram continued to be partially self-sustaining in the 1990s. The funding situation at the ashram was therefore modestly transnational and rather unusual.

place where the backbone of mountain life, the women and girls, would receive an education useful in their own lives. For others the ashram was a place where girls were brought up the same way as they were at home, at the same time having an opportunity to study.[15]

In 1946, there existed virtually no options for the education of rural girls in Uttarakhand beyond primary school.[16] The first group of girls entered the ashram just as the Independence movement was about to triumph in the hills and throughout India. The establishment of the ashram was consequently an exciting moment during extremely heady days for local nationalists, who embraced it as a decisive contribution by Uttarakhand to the cause of national *swaraj* (independence or home rule for India). This points to the construction of local identities: Uttarakhand would participate in the emancipatory project of hegemonic nationalism, but not exactly on the terms provided for the region by metropolitan nationalist discourse. That is, Uttarakhand, led by its womanhood, would participate not as a marginal region of 'backward' *kisaan log* (farmers),[17] but as an integrated component of the nation in its own right and a model of gram swaraj, or village self-sufficiency.

Lakshmi Ashram's mission was scripted on many levels by wider interlocking national and transnational debates on the education of women and the Indianizing of education in nationalist and feminist circles. Some Independence-era Indian feminists, educators, and Gandhi himself debated the importance of girls' education within a framework of 'domestic socialization' for the sake of the nation. The contribution of women to the stability, orderliness, and discipline of their families would be crucial for creating a stable, orderly society.[18] Debates on the importance of

15. This quote is translated from an essay written in Hindi by an ashram graduate whom I call Priti in the next section. She wrote the essay for the Danish group that provides donations, Lakshmi Ashrams Venner.

16. Although some rural girls from educated families were being taught beyond this level at home, most were not educated or attended school only through class two. Lakshmi Ashram was the first institution specifically designed to educate rural girls in the region.

17. See Chanana 1988: 100.

18. This refers to Nehru's initiation of the Community Development Program in the early 1950s. See Berry's chapter, this volume, for an excellent discussion of these programs in which she traces 'crafting housewives' in discourses of development from the United States to India.

girls' education informed, and were informed by, a transnational discourse on development in which the 'housewife' became the over-determined subject of and for a 'home science' model of rural development, despite the fact that most rural women in India (and elsewhere) were farmers, artisans, and laborers, not housewives.[19] Educating activists at the ashram was a Gandhian project and a modernizing, developmentalist project in the Nehruvian sense. Educating activists meant training scientific housewife–agriculturalists to become modern citizen–subjects of the new nation, who would then lead their families and villages in reconstructing rural society through scientific hygiene, household and farm management, contentment with material simplicity, personal spiritual discipline, handicraft production, and selfless devotion to the Gandhian dream of real swaraj.

However, the commitment of the ashram to a Gandhian program for educating women and girls is ironic in important ways. While the program was (and continued to be, in many respects) designed as a basic education school that would emphasize Gandhian thought, Gandhi's preferred (paternal) mode of female education—male tutelage—was completely de-emphasized, and many of his patriarchal ideas about womanhood and domesticity, woman's location in the household, and appropriate women's roles were undone. Something of Gandhi's essentialization of womanhood was certainly central to the ashram program, yet its students were overtly encouraged to become decision-makers and to take on controlling roles outside of the household. The roles opened up for women and girls by ashram schooling may well not have been to Gandhi's liking, and most of the women Gandhians

19. There are two rather different generations of ashram students. Many of the women and girls in the first groups of ashram students and teachers came from relatively elite rural families committed to Gandhian ideology and to educating their daughters (and consequently were usually able to pay minimal school fees before the era of Danish donations). With the expansion of government education in the region, access to school was no longer an issue for families concerned about educating daughters. Most of the students there in the 1990s came from extremely poor, sometimes landless families and were often without two living parents (and most were dependent upon scholarships funded by Lakshmi Ashrams Venner). Some were from particularly remote villages where access to school continued to be a problem for girls. Very few were sent by Gandhian parents for ideological reasons.

who have been involved with the ashram program were not exactly being Gandhian on Gandhi's terms. While Gandhi's reformulations of womanhood ensured that patriarchy would not break down in the postcolonial nation, ashram education, in some respects, critiqued patriarchy in ways that Gandhi would neither have anticipated nor intended. In its critique of some dimensions of male authority within the patriarchal extended family, the ashram program was clearly feminist. At the same time, in its mission to produce modern citizen–subjects and its valorization of scientific ways of knowing, education at Lakshmi Ashram was explicitly developmentalist and modernizing in the Nehruvian sense. Yet, by rejecting the government syllabus in favor of a Gandhian naii taaliim program, education at the ashram also questioned the modernizing objectives of the newly independent developmentalist state.

When Sarala left the ashram in 1967, Radha took up the post of director–secretary and ashram teachers voted to introduce the government academic syllabus into the program so that girls could sit for government board exams. Many graduates had written back to the ashram saying that they were having trouble finding employment. They said that although they were educated and skilled, their achievement was not recognized by wider society because they did not hold government board certificates of graduation. In keeping with Gandhian ideas, students were trained to be critical of paid employment (especially government service) as a meaningful and moral way of life. Yet, upon leaving the ashram many found that the unconventional paths that they had been prepared for were not viable without employment. Many graduates were vociferous in insisting that the ashram give up the naii taaliim academic program and replace it with the government academic syllabus.

There was much internal controversy over the introduction of the government syllabus, and ambivalence about the decision to incorporate it into the program continued to linger in the 1990s. Ashram students usually passed their board exams, sometimes after a few sittings, but seldom received outstanding marks. In this respect, their achievement was similar to that of their peers in rural government schools of the region. The rest of the curriculum continued to be designed to produce students who interrogate the worthiness of rapid industrial modernization as a national, regional, and personal goal. Unlike early students, students who attended the ashram after the government syllabus was introduced had to negotiate this curricular paradox as they prepared to sit for board exams while simultaneously being taught to criticize government development paradigms and education schemes, and to stand up and speak out for what they believe in. This seemingly highly localized conflict is of significance because it points to the ways in which participants in development held 'education' accountable to the multiple subject positions they occupied, and to the material politics of their lives.

Negotiating the unusual education at the ashram as a resident is one matter; using the training received during a childhood there after one leaves is another matter entirely. A significant number of early graduates and some recent graduates have gone on to lead remarkable lives. Some have refused or postponed marriage; others have refused to allow their families to give dowry and some women have arranged their own marriages. Several have devoted themselves to work and social activism in the region, sometimes establishing their own small institutions or businesses, and often taking on unconventional leadership roles in regional social movements. Yet, many students found it challenging to return 'home' when they graduated. What does it mean to be a young woman who has been taught to imagine a different story for her life than the ones that she was told in her village? How did graduates remember their ashram years? How did they store such memories into their later lives? The next section examines contradictions that arose when graduates negotiated their transformed subjectivities in not always supportive local environments upon leaving the ashram. Although education at the ashram was designed to produce young women that fit a Gandhian model of development, the stories told by graduates complicated this.

EDUCATING ACTIVISTS: *SAHII VIKAAS*[20]

Lakshmi Ashram's current principal and Radha's sister, Kamala, who came to the ashram in the mid-1950s, contrasted ashram girls to village girls for me this way:

20. True development.

Our girls are quite different from village girls.... When they go outside, people say that our girls never hesitate to do any sort of work. They are not shy and ashamed, they are not reluctant to work for outsiders. Our girls learn this from their education here.... Say there is a village girl, a student. What can become of her? The education she has received [from the government syllabus], from first class through tenth, this is illiteracy, this word–knowledge. In addition to this, other things are crucial. One should do some labor, okay? Right along with this girls should do some [social] work in Kumaon, so that they may become self-reliant (svaavalambii), stand on their own feet.

Kamala's generalizations were not unusual. They provide a kind of ideal for the sort of woman that the ashram is meant to produce. Most ashram residents perceived of themselves as—and were often described by outsiders as—different from village women and girls. The Gandhian ideology of 'true swaraj' beginning in the hearts and minds of India's national citizen subjects continued to inform thinking about the location of what some ashram teachers called *sahii vikaas*. This vikaas began not 'out there' in capitalist networks, roads, and buildings, but in a profoundly interior space. In this representation, one became developed by blossoming from within rather than by being transformed from without by income generation schemes, government school education, and so on.[21]

Do students and graduates themselves talk about 'standing on their own feet' after leaving the ashram? When I would ask older Class 10 girls at the ashram in the mid-1990s if they felt themselves to be different from their sisters in their home villages, I was usually answered with an emphatic *yes*: 'Oh, it is completely different here, you know that.' I would be reminded, 'Here, we learn how to speak nicely and look nice and stay clean.' 'We are

---

21. This is not to imply that ashram students, teachers, and graduates did not consider capitalist networks, roads, buildings, income generation schemes, government school education, etc. to be important features of development; they did consider these to be quite important. However, several emphasized to me that these did not constitute true development.

This 'anti-modern' representation that engages a specifically modern mode of interiority seems to be a rather vivid example of Akhil Gupta's argument that '[t]o search for premodern or antimodern critiques of development...is to occupy a space of opposition created by modernity's representation of itself.' (1998: 38)

not afraid to speak.' 'We do not feel so much shame (*sharm*).' 'My parents are happy because I am learning to do some things and getting educated also.' 'The village people speak well of us when we go home because we are developed.' Priti, a 35-year old ashram graduate, described the shock of her first return trip to her small, off-road village home as a young girl, after nearly a full year at the ashram:

I thought, these girls are my friends! I used to cut grass with them, I used to speak with them about everything, and now they hesitate to come near me. They were ashamed, because I was becoming educated and they had not gone to school. This did not trouble me, but it troubled them. I was so lonely! I wanted to go back to the ashram, quickly! All they talked about was marriage, and I had no wish to marry. I wanted to do some work myself, in the way that I read about in books of Gandhian philosophy in the ashram library.[22]

Many graduates carried the self-confidence—or strength coming up from inside—schooled into them as a kind of powerful talisman against times of hardship. Graduates often had different attitudes towards the program at Lakshmi Ashram, and their points of disjuncture illustrate that participants in development often hold diverse interpretations of one model of development. Some have dedicated themselves to endeavoring to realize the utopian goals of ashram education. For others, the expectations and Gandhian ideology of their school days became exacting yardsticks against which they never seem to measure up. Still others were stunned by this-worldly contradictions when they left the ashram, and some rebelled against what they experienced as distressing hypocrisy at the heart of the Gandhian program in wider society. For many, conjunctions of such contradictions encountered in life after school became crucial turning points. For most, ashram experiences seemed to become reference points for negotiating and narrating their later lives. There is much at stake in relying upon strength coming up from inside to navigate and interrogate one's experiences. I will now explore stories in which women negotiated contradictions in their lives after graduation, sometimes

22. This quote is also translated and reproduced from Priti's Hindi essay written for the Danish group that provides donations for the ashram, Lakshmi Ashrams Venner.

interweaving conflicting modes of thinking about their educational experiences. The stories told by Meena and Priti focus on contradictions that arose because their subjectivities had shifted during their education, while those told by Basanti and Deena emphasize contradictions that arose when one model of development clashed with another.

Nineteen-year-old Meena was sent to the ashram by her father when she was a small child. She left after finishing her Class 8 government boards and returned home to a large Bhotiya[23] village to marry at the age of 17. There, she lived with her husband and did farming work on his family's land. Together with an elderly ashram graduate for whom Meena had been like a daughter and my research assistant, Nalini, I visited her at home. They had not seen each other for years. Initially it seemed as though all was well in Meena's life, but one evening—after the elderly graduate had gone to sleep and at the insistence of her cousin—she became more frank with Nalini and me. She said that her husband was prone to violent drinking binges. Her second child, a son, had died unaccountably in infancy, a tragedy for which she was blamed. Her mother-in-law treated her poorly. Her first child was a healthy daughter. When we met she was in her third pregnancy, and concerned that her life could take an even deeper turn for the worse if she gave birth to another girl. Her in-laws wanted a boy. Also, while most ashram students and their parents expressed pride in the skills girls learned, Meena's relatives were disappointed that she did not have the carpet weaving skills of most Bhotiya women her age. Forthright, articulate, quite confident, critical of her mother-in-law's abuse and ardent desire for sons, intolerant of her husband's behavior, poorly trained in a crucial skill, and vexed by her location in the household, Meena's life was riddled with contradictions. She explained to us that

I sometimes think that if I hadn't gone to the ashram, but rather had remained here then it would be fine; I'd know how to do everything, like this I think. Because people here, even very little girls, know [how to weave carpets]. I alone don't know how to do it. (...) in my heart I want to leave, but because of these children, I cannot go.

23. Bhotiya are people of Tibetan origin living in well-established communities in Uttaranchal.

Meena explained to us that if she left, she would have to leave her 'husband's child' behind because if a woman left her husband, their children were not hers to take. Later on that evening, she told us that she would consider taking her little one with her if she left. The next morning Meena shocked us and everyone else by gathering up her strength, her daughter, and some clothing, and declaring that she was going to get on the bus with us and stay at the elderly graduate's place for a while. Here, a disjuncture in being developed both caused her turmoil and provided a solution: Meena 'stood on her own feet' and left.

Now recall Priti, the 35-year-old graduate who began to experience contradictions produced by becoming developed during her first childhood visit home. Priti was born to a Brahmin farming family from a village in the valley below the ashram. Her father sent her to the ashram as a little girl, after she had attended a local government primary school. During a conversation with local men in a roadside bazaar, her father had heard about an ashram up in the hills just above the valley where they sat talking, an ashram where one of the men whom he was sitting with had sent his daughter, and where another man wanted to send his daughter. Priti's father was intrigued by the program at Lakshmi Ashram, and decided to go have a look at the ashram for himself. He liked what he saw, and he decided to send Priti there. Priti finished the ashram program and continued to work there while she studied independently for her MA, an educational level which she probably would not have reached had she remained at home in her village. She missed her family while she was at the ashram, but her visits continued to become more strained as the years passed, 'I was lonely there!' she explained, 'All the girls my age were already married, and all the women spoke only about my marriage, saying that I was getting so old, it was time for me to marry!'

Priti became an outspoken woman who wore only khadi saris, got married when she was 22 years old to a Gandhian social worker who had trained her to knit and weave at the ashram, and became the mother of two sons. When we met, she lived in a house not far from the ashram and worked there as a teacher. 'After so many wonderful years in the ashram, I never thought that I would go back to the village!' she explained to me,

The way village people think is just totally different, no? And the people, they need this ashram, I thought, the work of this ashram is necessary for our society, so I will stay in the ashram and work. Like this, I thought. But it is not easy. Now I am trying to form a new organization, so that our work can be of more direct benefit to the village people through small projects.

She was somewhat critical of the ashram while I was there because it did not seem to be as meaningfully integrated into local village society as she remembered it to be when she was a girl, and she felt that its works should be of more direct benefit to the immediate area. Together with her husband and women in the local area, she was working on projects to reintegrate the ashram into the immediate area.

Although village life became rather awkward for Priti as her subjectivity shifted, as an adult she romanticized her childhood home affectionately. When a Danish woman who organized donations for the ashram requested teachers to send brief essays about their experiences for a translated informative booklet, Priti remained awake late for many evenings, long after her family had gone to sleep, writing page after page, the whole story of her life. She wrote, 'In the situation I find myself in these days [working as a teacher at the ashram], lacking complete satisfaction, I feel a certain emptiness. In searching for a clue to this emptiness, I reached the conclusion that I must respect my past.' Then she described a beautiful, thick jungle that surrounded her childhood village, and there she began her story. Her story was longer than that of anyone else asked to contribute to the Danish booklet, and her idyllic childhood memories had been edited in the version that appeared in the final booklet. This is perhaps due to the point of the project, which was to show how Lakshmi Ashram changes women's lives for the better in tangible ways, not to document the complex and creative ambivalence of women's experiences with education and development or the challenges of occupying multiple subject positions in day-to-day life.

Fifty-seven-year-old Basanti's experiences provide a contrast to Meena and Priti's stories. Rather than placing contradictions produced by a shifting subjectivity in the foreground of her stories, she emphasized contradictions produced by her experiences with conflicting models of development. She was one among the group of graduates mentioned earlier who became critical of Sarala Devi's naii taaliim syllabus after leaving the ashram. She came to the ashram as a widow in her early twenties. She had grown up in a small, off-road village doing farming work with her Kshatriya family, and had attended school irregularly through Class 2. At 14 her marriage was arranged, then she went to live in her in-law's home where she continued to do farming and housework. When her husband passed away eight years later, her elder brother-in-law (a Gandhian) decided that she must become educated. Although she protested, he sent her to the ashram for training. She remained in the ashram for 20 years, and then went to work with a small NGO in the hills. She described changes within herself to me this way:

Before I came to the ashram I was shy, afraid, and always ashamed. From coming here, from living here, from seeing society, then I did very good work. I opened nursery schools in villages. Sarala behn went into the valleys for women's meetings, and I sometimes went with her. I watched, I listened. So my life, which had seemed like hell, no? Suddenly changed into another life. A lot of change came!... Life took a new turn, it was a new world.

I received an education. After this, I got to train so many others. Also, wherever I go, I talk to anyone and everyone, I give speeches, no? Wherever I go, I speak on (relevant) topics. Whatever work is to be done, I do it with courage. I learned so many things here: sewing...practical agriculture and how to look after the cow-shed properly. All these changes and ideas happened. They were so many! And wonderful.

However, because Basanti was there during Sarala Devi's days, she studied under her village-relevant, naii taaliim syllabus and was not able to sit for government board exams. Despite her academic achievement, she held no board certificates. She was critical of her education because it was not recognized in wider society. She saw the controversial introduction of the government syllabus into the ashram program as progress, and felt that rural girls were benefiting from government education. In fact, although some ashram and government schoolteachers were critical of the government syllabus and corruption within the government educational system, students and parents seldom questioned the benefit of some government schooling for girls. Most saw it as a sure sign that the hills were developing. Ashram residents and graduates criticized the government syllabus while describing the benefits of government schooling in terms of character development and the tactical use of board certificates to open doors for employment and perhaps university. As Basanti put it, 'if girls keep on studying then their future will be made bright; they will become intelligent and devote time to making their children honorable.' An educated girl, I was often told, was less likely to be married at a young age, and more likely to find employment and be able to make her own decisions.

Basanti was not alone in her criticism of Sarala Devi's village-relevant naii taaliim syllabus. Many elderly graduates praised its rigor and relevance to hill life, and some seemed to feel that the ashram program of the old days was superior to the new program. Yet, most early graduates had found themselves to be at a tactical disadvantage at some point in their lives because they lacked government board certificates. Deena, a 42-year-old graduate from a small, off-road, Brahmin village who was sent to the ashram by her elder brother when she was eight, described her life as utterly rerouted by the ashram. Like Basanti, she emphasized contradictions that she negotiated when different models of development clashed in her experiences after graduation. After leaving the ashram, she became a writer and a lecturer in Hindi at a government university. However, if she had remained in her village, she probably would have received little schooling. She had some warm memories of the ashram, yet told me that she was resentful that she was not able to sit for government board exams because,

There was no certificate, so we weren't able to go anywhere outside after education there.... If we should do further studies, then there was no way. If we wanted to do outside work, if we wanted to do outside service [become employed], then there was no way. So, I had no notion of outside service [employment] at that time; I did not even desire it. But I wished to study very much!

There was another thing I didn't like, that there was no English there. Outside, well, in every place it was a very English environment.... Hindi is necessary, English is also just as necessary. We did not want to be made English, but we wanted to know English. We didn't, so for this reason we also sometimes felt a lack.

Without board certificates, she was unable to apply for admission to a government university. Rather, the ashram sent her to a Gandhian institute in Gujarat for further studies. There she became critical of some aspects of the Gandhian program as a viable 'alternative to development.'

Some of the Gandhians that are around today, for them my respect is very little.... Some put on shows of becoming Gandhians...but they do not behave within these ideas.... Nowadays they want every type of facility in their own lives, but they want others to lead simple lives.

Deena emphasized that her critique did not apply to all Gandhians or to Gandhians at Lakshmi Ashram, but was rather directed at some aspects of the Gandhian program in wider society. Deena explained to me that in Gujarat she

became disgusted with some of those people.... I reacted in this way because of khadi. Khadi was completely compulsory there.... People used to say that from khadi, poor people's stomachs are filled.... But in Gujarat, where production is the greatest, I saw that even there, there was class discrimination. There is the manager class...they went around in cars, had magnificent homes, pomp and show, such was their *sevaa* (selfless service). But those who spun, who knit, the labor class, their living conditions were not very good...[Yet,] he who wears khadi considers himself to be special...and he also seems special to society. I don't want to be 'special' in this way.

...So I adopted [my current] lifestyle, that I am who I am and this is okay. I like this kind of life, so I will not claim to like a simple, austere life. Yes, that simplicity that I desire, I shall bring into my life. But if one should speak of khadi, of simplicity, and desire luxury for oneself, I don't like that.

Deena negotiated these contradictions in her late twenties with decisions that reconfigured her life: she stopped wearing only khadi[24] and gave up plans to devote her life exclusively to Gandhian *samaaj sevaa* (selfless service for society). She stayed on with a family in Gujarat, studied for her Ph.D., then returned to the hills to teach in a government university. There, having refused more than a decade of demands by her family that she marry, she requested that her marriage be arranged. She composed a detailed list of qualifications for her groom, and drew attractive responses despite her unconventional requirements and age. Through all of this, intermingled with her critiques both of the old naii taaliim syllabus and Sarala Devi's rigid rules, Deena emphasized that she definitely considered the personal courage that she developed at the ashram to be absolutely crucial for her own empowerment.

24. Deena explained that she did not so much 'give up' khadi as 'take on another cloth.' She wore both mill and khadi saris.

She also considered this to be the main benefit of ashram education for girls studying there in the 1990s, and felt that courage was not instilled in rural girls by government schools.

SAHII VIKAAS, RECONSIDERED

These women were not exactly being Gandhian on Gandhi's terms. Ashram education has encouraged some rural women to take on more controversial roles than the spaces of hegemonic nationalism and government education anticipated for them. Furthermore, ashram graduates often went on to shock the very male relatives who sent them there with their later choices and behavior. Their stories suggest that discourses of development are complexly received, domesticated, contested, and re-presented as they travel to particular locations where they enter into new narratives of modernity.[25] Ethnography reveals fissures and ambiguities in situations where contradictory discourses are sometimes interconnected in specific experiences and stories of development. In this particular 'local' context, 'education' and its lack were frequently used as a sort of trope for 'modernity' and 'backwardness.' It was also 'education' that became a potent site where ashram graduates negotiated interlocking, often conflicting, notions of gender and development in their lives. These shifting processes of gendered subjectivity formation are inflected by generation. Many of the narratives included above reveal overt tension when first generation graduates embraced an education that questioned the objectives of the developmentalist state while simultaneously criticizing the fact that such an education had not prepared them to take advantage of new employment and educational opportunities for women. These narrative tensions are significant because they index a reworking of the categories of development discourse through the experiences of graduates seeking jobs and academic degrees. In this case, ashram graduates, who are constituted as the supposedly passive 'targets' of development, have themselves transformed development. They have done so by holding 'education' accountable to the material realities of the multiple subject positions that they occupy.

25. For related discussions of traveling discourses and regional modernity, see chapters by Berry, Klingensmith, and Prashad in this volume.

The stories which Radha, Kamala, Meena, Priti, Basanti, and Deena told reveal that the negotiation of development discourses with a global reach within the local spaces of their lives is 'difficult work' that can lead to moments of agency and to profoundly unsettling paradoxes. Their stories illustrate that becoming developed entails complex, gendered shifts in subjectivity that can lead to experiences of personal and institutional contradiction. Yet, their stories often narrated moments of poignant contradiction as moments of agency; that is to say, as moments in which one experiences one's capacity to generate new types of meaning.[26] This type of agency is not limited to—or constituted through—graduates as individuals. It is rather constituted through the ashram and other institutions, households, the patriarchal extended family, travel, social movements, and a historical figure.[27] Education in this specific context is key to becoming 'developed' and 'modern' insofar as that education is of certain tactical use in wider society and insofar as it nurtures strength coming up from inside. Yet, strength coming up from inside may transform into an unanticipated excess that has potential both to reinvigorate and to destabilize 'development' from within when women call upon it to interrogate their personal lives, their educational experiences, a particular configuration of the nation-state, and their place on its 'periphery.'

ACKNOWLEDGMENTS

I would like to thank everyone at Lakshmi Ashram as well as my research assistant, Nalini Pandey, for making this chapter possible. This chapter took shape, in part, during three panel presentations and related discussions: thanks to Arun Agrawal, Sangeeta Luthra, and K. Sivaramakrishnan for including me on a panel for the 26th Annual Conference on South Asia at the University of Wisconsin-Madison; thanks to Cecilia Coale Van Hollen for including me on a panel for the American Anthropological Association Meetings in Washington DC; and thanks to Arun Agrawal and K. Sivaramakrishnan for including me on a panel at a Yale University

26. For a discussion of agency, 'the habit of habit change,' and 'agentive moments' that I draw upon here, see Daniel (1996: 189-91).

27 That is, in the lives of ashram graduates, Gandhi sometimes became a ground for moments of agency. For a discussion of agency that I draw upon here, see Keane (1997).

mini-conference. Finally, thanks to Kim Berry, Kathryn Forbes, David Hopkins, Stacy Pigg, and Cecilia Coale Van Hollen for their comments on various versions of this chapter, and thanks especially to Akhil Gupta and Daniel Klingensmith for their comments on two different versions of this chapter. All errors and shortcomings are, of course, my own.

References

Advani, Shalini, 1996. 'Educating the national imagination.' *Economic and Political Weekly* 31: 2077–82.

Appadurai, Arjun, 1991. 'Global ethnoscapes: Notes and queries for a transnational anthropology.' In Richard Fox (ed.), *Recapturing Anthropology: Working in the Present*. Santa Fe: School of American Research Press.

———, 1996. *Modernity at Large: Cultural Dimensions of Globalization.* Minneapolis: University of Minnesota Press.

Berman, Marshall, [1982] 1988. *All That is Solid Melts into Air: The Experience of Modernity.* New York: Penguin.

Breckenridge, Carol (ed.), 1995. *Consuming Modernity: Public Culture in a South Asian World.* Minneapolis: University of Minnesota Press.

Chanana, Karuna, 1988. 'Social change or social reform: The education of women in pre-Independence India.' In Karuna Chanana (ed.), *Socialization, Education and Women: Explorations in Gender Identity.* New Delhi: Orient Longman.

Chatterjee, Partha, 1997. 'Our Modernity.' In *The Present History of West Bengal: Essays in Political Criticism.* Delhi: Oxford University Press.

Daniel, E. Valentine, 1996. *Charred Lullabies: Chapters in an Anthropography of Violence.* Princeton: Princeton University Press.

Devi, Sarala, 1979. *Vyaavahaarik Vedaant: Ek Aatmakathaa.* New Delhi: Gandhi Shanti Pratishthaan.

———, 1981. *Sanrakshana ya Vinaasha (Paryaavaraniiy Paristhiti: Ek Chunautii).* Nainital: Gyanoday Prakashan.

———, 1982. *Revive Our Dying Planet: An Ecological, Socio-economical and Cultural Appeal.* Nainital: Gyanoday Prakashan.

Erevelles, Nirmala, 1998. 'Bodies that do not matter: Social policy, education, and the politics of difference.' Ph.D. thesis. Syracuse University.

Fox, Richard, 1989. *Gandhian Utopia: Experiments with Culture.* Boston: Beacon Press.

Gandhi, M. K., 1938. *Hind Swaraj or Indian Home Rule.* Ahmedabad: Navajivan Publishing House.

————, 1951. *Basic Education*. Ahmedabad: Navjivan Publishing House.

Gupta, Akhil, 1998. *Postcolonial Developments: Agriculture in the Making of Modern India*. Durham: Duke University Press.

Hall, Stuart, David Held, Don Hubert, and Kenneth Thompson (eds.), 1996. *Modernity: An Introduction to Modern Societies*. Oxford: Blackwell Publishers.

Ivy, Marilyn, 1995. *Discourses of the Vanishing: Modernity, Phantasm, Japan*. Chicago: University of Chicago Press.

Jeffery, Patricia and Roger Jeffery, 1994. 'Killing my heart's desire: Education and female autonomy in rural north India.' In Nita Kumar (ed.), *Women as Subjects: South Asian Histories*. New Delhi: Stree.

Keane, Webb, 1997. *Signs of Recognition: Powers and Hazards of Representation in an Indonesian Society*. Berkeley: University of California Press.

Mani, Lata, 1987. 'Contentious traditions: The debate on sati in colonial India.' *Cultural Critique* (17): 119–56.

Newman, R. S., 1989. *Grassroots Education in India: A Challenge for Policymakers*. Bangalore: Sterling Publishers.

Pigg, Stacy, 1995. 'Acronyms and effacement: Traditional medical practitioners (TMP) in international health development.' *Social Science and Medicine* 41(1): 47–68.

————, 1996. 'The credible and the credulous: The question of "villagers' beliefs" in Nepal.' *Cultural Anthropology* 11(2): 160–201.

Rajabalasubramanian, Aruna, 1997. '"Deliver us from darkness": Formal education and lower class children in Tamil Nadu.' Ph.D. thesis. Syracuse: Syracuse University.

Sahni, Urvashi Malhotra, 1994. 'Building circles of mutuality: A sociocultural analysis of literacy in a rural classroom in India'. Ph.D. thesis. Berkeley: University of California.

Scarse, Timothy J., 1993. *Image, Ideology and Inequality: Cultural Domination, Hegemony and Schooling in India*. New Delhi: Sage Publications.

5

Building India's 'Modern Temples': Indians and Americans in the Damodar Valley Corporation, 1945–60

DANIEL KLINGENSMITH[1]

TEMPLES OF THE NEW AGE

Since Independence, the Government of India has invested enormous amounts of political and economic capital in large dam
projects. By the early 1980s, fully 15 percent of total government
expenditure since Independence had gone to the construction of
dams, and the power lines and irrigation canals which distributed
their benefits.[2] The percentage of the yearly budget devoted to
these was even higher in the 1950s and 1960s. More recently, the
government has insisted on forging ahead with a series of dams on

1. In writing this essay I have received help and encouragement from many
people, including especially Henry Hart, who revisited his research on the
TVA-DVC connection for my benefit; Sangeeta Luthra, who recruited me
for the panel on development at the South Asia Conference in Madison, WI
(1997), where an early draft of this paper was presented; Arun Agarawal and
K. Sivaramakrishnan, who invited me to participate in a mini-conference on
development and regional modernities (New Haven, CT, 1998) where I had
a further opportunity to present these ideas; and Rebecca Klenk, who read
various drafts patiently and closely.
2. Thukral 1992: 3.

the Narmada river, despite considerable opposition. The same projects for which millions of people were uprooted became central sites in the celebration of the nation and its march toward full modernity—most famously when Jawaharlal Nehru dedicated the first phase of the Bhakra-Nangal Dam in 1954 and spoke of it and other such projects as India's modern secular temples.

India's was not the only government to pour its resources into river valley development projects. After the Second World War, many of the world's modernizing states embarked on significant, and in a few cases, gargantuan dam-building programs, often meant to be the keystone of a radical transformation of environments, economies, and even of individual and national characters. Dams were to speed along development toward a society of more affluent, secure, and rational individuals; their most ardent votaries saw in them a means by which modernity might be realized for all members of society. They, indeed, constituted the first 'fashion' in the newly-emerging complex of disciplines, discourses, and political practices that constituted the field of 'development.'

This enthusiasm had roots, in part, in the perceived successes of the great New Deal water projects in the United States, and particularly that of the Tennessee Valley Authority (TVA). During the depression of the 1930s, TVA undertook almost two dozen dams, and a good deal else, in the Tennessee basin of the American South.[3] Its supporters claimed a wider significance for the agency; to them it proved that economic individualism could be reconciled with rational land use, that state planning could heal the environmental ravages of the past and lay the basis for a clean prosperity for the future, that expert, technocratic management need not

3. TVA was established in 1933, and given very broad authority to address the social, economic and environmental situation in the Tennessee Valley. It dammed the Tennessee to provide flood control, power generation, and navigation. It promoted new kinds of forest usage and the agricultural transformation of the valley. It greatly increased the industrialization of the area, and in promoting the industrial and domestic consumption of the electricity which it produced, it took the lead in the New Deal's transformation of American electrical energy use. In later years, it has become more than anything else a simple power company, America's largest electrical utility, and has contributed to serious environmental degradation in its service area and beyond by burning surface-mined coal in obsolescent thermal plants, thus leading both to ravaged landscapes and to air pollution.

conflict with decentralized control and public participation, that its approach to economy and environment could bring comfort, convenience, prosperity, and moral improvement for all, that in a world threatened by totalitarianism from the left and the right, it represented (as proclaimed in the title of a panegyric on the agency by David Lilienthal, its most famous publicist) 'Democracy on the March.'[4] Partly due to the adroitness with which Lilienthal and others linked its particular situation to the larger problems of world reconstruction and decolonization after the war, TVA became a template for modernization, a symbol of progress and development, well known to liberal intellectuals around the world. In the late 1940s, many governments were interested in building their own 'TVAs.'[5]

Nowhere was there more talk of emulating TVA in the late 1940s than in India. The DVC, or Damodar Valley Corporation—'India's TVA'—claimed the honor of being the first enterprise to pattern itself after TVA and to apply its lessons to a river basin outside the US. The establishment of the DVC was hailed throughout America, Europe, and the rest of the decolonizing world as proof that the East was finally ready for modernity and democracy, just in time to halt the coming of a communist social revolution that was presumed to feed on 'backwardness.' TVA itself helped to train Indian employees of the DVC, and recruited Americans, especially from its own ranks, to fill key advisory and supervisory positions in India. Meantime, it gloried in the publicity that came with being the blueprint for a foundational project in one of the first of the 'new nations.' In India, especially in West Bengal, which it served along with southern Bihar,[6] the DVC was the object at first of great pride in some quarters, regarded as evidence that India could leap to the very forefront of economic modernism. Later, it became the focus of just as much anxiety and cynicism, once the achievements promised by its early political

4. Lilienthal 1953.

5. Klingensmith, forthcoming.

6. The DVC built four dams in the Damodar river basin in southern Bihar (now Jharkhand), to service a watershed stretching from the Chotanagpur plateau to the alluvial plains of southwestern Bengal to the Hoogli south of Calcutta. It also built several power stations, irrigation canals, and various other kinds of infrastructure in the valley, which is one of the most heavily industrialized areas of India.

backers failed to materialize. Though eventually it came to be seen as a failure, its conceptual influence on subsequent Indian river management remains important.[7]

In this paper, I want to analyse and contextualize this early example of development borrowing, this relationship of what was construed as American 'tutelage' and Indian 'emulation,' a construction that I will argue masked sharp divergences in program design and function. The stories of Indians and Americans who worked to build the DVC directly speaks to issues of authority and hegemony in development knowledge and practice, and to the multiple and often conflicting material and discursive possibilities development has provided. Moreover, the DVC as 'India's TVA' repays careful attention because it dates back to the early days of the idea of development, as the specifically postwar and postcolonial incarnation of the long-running tropes of enlightenment and progress. Although it is important to bear in mind that if one attends only to the official, authoritative discourse of development, one will have missed much that is important, nonetheless, their significance is great. What I seek to demonstrate and to explain here is the disjuncture between, on the one hand, the rhetorical characterization of development as a universalizing process that proceeds via the implementation of 'models,' and, on the other hand, the reality in which so-called models like TVA are appropriated only partially, and very selectively, for ends which cannot easily be subsumed under the heading of 'emulation.'[8]

At first sight, the relationship between TVA and DVC (and, more broadly, the 'developed' and the 'developing') might seem easily summed up by the phrase 'knowhow, showhow,' occasionally used in the 1950s by American agricultural advisors in India.[9] What this informal expression conveyed was the notion that Americans knew how to produce affluence for themselves, and that

7. In some respects (e.g., the construction of a network of reservoirs behind dams, placed throughout a watershed—'total watershed management') the controversial project for the Narmada is a descendent of the DVC, and more remotely of the TVA.

8. Here, I will not be much concerned with the political economy of dams in India as such. Thukral (1992) and especially Singh (1997) address this directly and cogently in the Indian context. McCully (1996) presents these issues in an international and comparative context.

9. Sen 1989: 104.

development was a simple matter of teaching American techniques to the rest of the world. Of course, it was conceded that it would take a very long time, indeed, for developing nations to be able to afford all the affluence of the West, but eventually they would accumulate enough capital to make possible some facsimile of it. Meantime, the pressing need was for immediate Western technical assistance, so that a start could be made. More than anything else, according to the emerging development community of the 1940s and 1950s, India (and Africa, Latin America and the rest of Asia) needed instruction in modern ways of doing things.

In some respects this formulation still pervades thinking about development issues both in the development community and (with a different valuation) in a good deal of the criticism of development. One critical approach toward much of conventional development practice has charged that, as it were, far too many development projects have in fact rested on the implicit assumption that 'knowhow, showhow' is at some level the essence of development aid. This principle leads to the imposition of costly, alien, high technologies on societies that have neither been able to use them efficiently nor to afford them, an imposition coming at the expense of cheap, local, low technological solutions that might better address fundamental, social and economic problems. Since these technologies are not appropriate, the argument goes, 'technology transfer' only results in the creation or reproduction of the very poverty that development is supposed to wipe out—hence providing fresh tasks and thus legitimation for the developmentalist state. The attempt to impose modernity authorizes technocracy, privileging the perspective of the trained, modernizing expert, and making all perspectives outside the worldview of the technocrat symptomatic of the pathology of 'backwardness' that must be 'cured.'[10]

While in many respects this analysis is a useful starting point, nonetheless it oversimplifies things. Rather than seeing development as a homogenizing process that creates a homogenized modernity, I seek to draw attention to the way in which signifiers of development and modernity circulate and take on new significance in new settings. The deployment of seemingly the same literal and

10. I am generalizing here from critiques made by Ferguson (1990), Marglin and Marglin (1990), Sachs (1992), and Escobar (1995). For a more nuanced discussion of these authors and others, see the introduction to this volume.

symbolic vocabulary of development in two different places can give a false sense of homogenization. I argue here that it is useful to attend to the varied and significant inflections of this vocabulary in diverse constructions of development and modernity, differences which suggest that, in place of a homogenized, singular, stable modernity, it might be better to theorize what Sivaramakrishnan and Agarawal call, in their introduction to this volume, 'regional modernities.'

At the same time, the fact that the vocabulary of development seems at first glance to circulate without any change in inflection also requires some analysis. The story of the DVC's relationship to TVA is suggestive because what was claimed by both Indians and Americans to be an undertaking of emulation and instruction was actually something different, and much less coherent. While 'India's TVA' has been described as a vast undertaking in inappropriate technology, it was in fact never actually a copy as such—even a bad copy—of TVA, however much those who built it claimed that it was. In a variety of important respects it made no attempt to follow its supposed model; it answered to a different constellation of authorities; had a different and altogether more remote relationship with its target population, no part of which it ever made much effort to cultivate; it got its money differently and spent it on different priorities; and it distributed its water and power differently.[11] In reality, the chief similarity between the two was somewhat superficial: both built networks of dams and power stations, and were originally intended to be independent of central government bureaucracies. The modularity of TVA as a development model was rhetorical rather than practical.

This rhetoric needs some explaining. For, despite all these differences, both Americans and Indians working to build the DVC in the 1950s persistently and publicly claimed to be building 'India's

11. TVA answered to the President of the United States, and enjoyed a great deal of autonomy from the rest of the government in making policies and undertaking new projects. DVC projects were under the close scrutiny of the Government of India and the state governments of Bihar and West Bengal, any one of which could (and often did) veto proposals from the DVC board. Although formally independent of any particular government department, DVC had to follow standard Government of India financial and personnel policies, unlike TVA. These differences were crucial in determining each organization's ultimate political viability.

TVA,' making a great deal of the new agency's Tennessee connection and of India's commitment to 'American' methods. Why, if they were actually building something significantly different? The answer, I think, lies in what kind of claims this rhetoric communicated—claims about one's proximity to full modernity (*imagined* as a unitary, stable condition), about the ethical life of one's nation and oneself, and about the position of nation and individual in history, understood as a march of progress. Such claims were political. Invocations of TVA and 'American methods' generated both opportunities for the disciplining of agrarian society, and for the simultaneous undermining of that discipline, for building authority and legitimacy and for disputing claims to authority and legitimacy—all in the name of development. These claims to power were not the same for the Americans and Indians involved, however, and not the same for all Americans or for all Indians. 'Building India's TVA' was an activity that took on different meanings and proceeded differently depending on the context.

CIVILIZING MISSIONS

A few words, first, on the Americans. Nearly two dozen one-time TVA employees had worked in India or consulted with Indian authorities at some point by 1961, most with some connection to the Damodar Valley Corporation (DVC).[12] Among these were Arthur Morgan, TVA's first chairman, and David Lilienthal, his bureaucratic rival who in the late 1930s successfully campaigned to have Morgan fired and who succeeded him after a few years. Morgan had hoped to make TVA a regional government that would steer its people to economic self-sufficiency, new modes of citizenship, a return to artisanal craftsmanship, and new ways of caring for the land. Like many of the nineteenth century Anglo-American reformers he admired, he hoped to build this utopia by means of new forms of discipline and surveillance of everyday life. Lilienthal scorned this 'basket weaving,' and campaigned, much more successfully, for a TVA dedicated to heavy industrialization of the South and the creation of a new, capital intensive agriculture. In so doing, Lilienthal and his allies tied the TVA to elite groups in the Tennessee Valley and to broader national constituencies, belying their claim that TVA was apolitical. Their struggle pro-

12. TVA 1961.

foundly influenced TVA's sense of itself and the values it stood for, with Lilienthal's 1944 bestseller, *TVA: Democracy on the March*, becoming the classic statement (much read among Indian planners) of a self-describedly anti-romantic, 'hard-headed' approach to development. Both Morgan and Lilienthal went to India in the late 1940s and early 1950s to promote their versions of development, and the advice of each was sought for DVC. While Morgan's careful, more specific advice was based on considerably more technical expertise (he was an engineer, Lilienthal a lawyer and publicist), and was much valued by DVC's management,[13] Lilienthal's more optimistic account of what development could accomplish, especially with regard to industrialization, carried more weight in Delhi. Lilienthal's opinions were widely circulated in the English press, while Morgan's idea was taken up chiefly by the Gandhian Navajivan Press.[14] Not all foreign advisors got the same reception.

In terms of practical service, however, the two most important TVA employees to serve the DVC were William Voorduin and Andrew Komora. When the Government of India (at that time still under British control) asked for a TVA engineer to consult on the possible development of the Damodar in 1944, Lilienthal dispatched Voorduin. He stayed on for four years, drafting the overall plan for the development of the Damodar, and eventually becoming chairman of the government's Central Technical Power Board. Voorduin's plan was ambitious, calling for eight dams, a diversion barrage, irrigation, canals, and at least one thermal power station. At TVA, Voorduin had been a pioneer in his field, a self-described 'system design engineer.' The network of dams, power lines, irrigation canals, and power stations he designed for the Damodar in its basic conceptions strongly resembled the work he and his colleagues had done at TVA—it aimed at total development of an entire watershed, using a number of multiple-function medium-sized dams and reservoirs (though no more than half the scheme was ever implemented).[15] Voorduin in fact went on to make a

13. Sen 1989.

14. Klingensmith, forthcoming.

15. This has prompted some of the DVC's defenders to insist that the reason it has been a disappointment is that it was never allowed to implement the full plan, and that half a project may not be much better than none. Most notably, only four of the dams were actually constructed.

career out of reproducing TVA-like schemes for various developing countries, most notably Iran, as an employee of his old TVA bosses, Lilienthal and Gordon Clapp.[16]

About Voorduin there is little documentary evidence other than the bare record of his career and the technical memoranda he drew up for his projects. There is somewhat more available regarding Andrew Komora, the DVC's first chief engineer, who served from 1950 to 1959. Komora was instrumental in maintaining TVA's relationship with what it regarded as its Indian protege, and was regarded in Knoxville as TVA's man in India—as such, a combination of technical advisor, teacher, and missionary. Early in his tenure, TVA's chairman told him: 'I pray that you are well-fortified with patience and the desire to teach! They will expect both but admit it with respect to neither.'[17]

Komora took his responsibilities as a teacher very seriously. He was the organization's highest technical authority, and as such in a position to make important decisions on basic techniques. He tried hard to instruct his employers how to go about large-scale construction in the modern world:

One of the biggest jobs is the introduction of modern machinery and its use in high-speed construction. The younger men seem to grasp and absorb the ideas much quicker and better than do the older men. The older men seem to want to persist in the 'head basket' idea and I have seen plenty of it in action.[18]

In establishing the construction plant and procedures for the Maithon dam, Komora combined his missionary zeal with a technical rationalization, on the grounds of efficiency, of what was actually an inefficient use of resources. The DVC under his guidance imported a great deal of heavy machinery, despite having plenty of skilled, cheap labor readily at hand. He thereby established a system for converting quarry bedrock into concrete for the dam without human hands ever touching it. His rationale was that his process enabled him to build the concrete portion of the dam much faster than a more labor-intensive regime could allow, thus providing flood control and electricity benefits as much as

16. Klingensmith, forthcoming.
17. TVA 1950. Records, General Managers Files, Box 69; Administrative Records, Folder 'DVC.' East Point, Georgia, National Archives.
18. Ibid.

one full year earlier. On these grounds, he rejected the use of local masonry techniques and manual labor, the 'head basket' idea (so called because materials were transported manually by workers with head baskets). But the project ultimately lost something by his insistence on heavy equipment: it was very costly to acquire and maintain, and since the DVC had a hard time getting and retaining personnel capable of running it, it could not actually be used very efficiently.[19]

If Komora's rationale for designing such a high-tech construction process was flawed, technical rationalization was perhaps not the only consideration in his mind in designing it. As Henry Hart, a former TVA employee and later political scientist who knew and interviewed him at the time has put it, Komora simply could not imagine how domestic technologies and processes could possibly be an appropriate or effective alternative, nor how they could be implemented. To him the idea of, for example, thousands of women laborers carrying concrete up the scaffolding to the top of a dam was 'obscene.'[20] Voorduin's calculated, putatively value-neutral technical utilitarianism had called for the reproduction of TVA on the Damodar; Komora's involved a reproduction of TVA's techniques. Both engineers in different ways reproduced something of their own and their institution's implicit values regarding what kind of landscape, and what kind of labor, might be appropriate. The point here is not that their calculations were mistaken, or insufficiently rational, but that in both cases those calculations also expressed and reproduced meaning and moral commitment. In Komora's approach to his construction job, the dividing line between sentiment and utility was blurred.

Komora's work at the DVC can be understood in the context of a different kind of construction, an ideological construction of nation and self. His letters home suggest that Komora was rather self-conscious about being an American (not merely a Westerner) in a newly-decolonized land: that is, about being the representative of a nation that he and his peers might have described as the most advanced on earth (without, perhaps, feeling much need to explain

19. Hart 1961; Klingensmith, forthcoming.
20. See Klingensmith, forthcoming. Komora was not interested in the creative mix of indigenous and foreign technologies or machine and manual production attempted at some other Indian dam projects.

the criteria by which advancement was measured); and of a society which many of them also considered 'the first new nation,' i.e. itself a former colony, which had struck the very first anti-colonial blow, and which therefore, was unquestionably on the side of liberty, democracy, and progress in India and all former colonies, values trampled on by the old colonialism and Soviet communism alike. To them America's position imposed responsibilities on its representatives abroad: they had to be 'well-fortified with patience and the desire to teach.' The desire to teach, because India and the rest of the decolonizing world desperately needed American help if prosperity were to be achieved and (according to a linkage commonly made then as now) freedom thereby maintained; patience, because although Americans in some respects were now taking up the 'White man's burden' of helping others to civilization, any hint of old-style colonialist authoritarianism would constitute an insult to natural nationalist sensibilities that could set the whole enterprise of development back.[21]

For Komora and Voorduin, and other TVA employees in India, and the emerging American development community more generally, the claim that they were helping Indians build their own TVA on the Damodar was a validation of a universalizing brand of American nationalism, one which featured Americans, and themselves in particular, at the vanguard of progress and freedom. They would be the teachers of the hitherto oppressed peoples of the world. Komora stuck to this construction of his own activity in India even after he had been on the job for several years, by which point his Indian employers, much though they might express their commitment to 'the TVA idea,' had gone a long way toward building something else.

THE USES OF DEVELOPMENT 'MODELS'

Indian development rhetoric in the same period was no less fervent. However, with regard to the rhetoric surrounding emulation of the West, i.e. to the ways in which the experience of development tutelage was expressed, there was a certain amount of ambivalence. Indian politicians and engineers of the 1950s were careful to emphasize that science and technology were universal, not simply

21. Klingensmith, forthcoming.

'American,' and that 'unified river valley development' was a field in which India could accomplish feats that would outstrip those of other countries.[22] On the other hand, TVA seems to have derived some part of its glamour simply from the fact that it was American, and more specifically from the 'progressive' America of the New Deal and Roosevelt. The United States as a land of science, affluence, and progress (but also of racial discrimination, alienation, and extremes of wealth and poverty) looms large in the rhetoric of modernization in late colonial and post-Independence India.[23]

In the rhetoric of emulation, there was also some degree of calculation. Throughout the early days of the DVC, when both Indians and Americans were rhapsodizing about what TVA would teach India, the political masters and even the designers of the new agency were careful about what parts of their American model they were adopting (and adapting), careful about what they would and would not 'learn' from their new teachers, and careful of whom they would and would not flatter by describing their policies as American-inspired.[24]

To be sure, one of the highest early functionaries of the DVC was enthusiastically committed to the 'TVA idea': Sudhir Sen, its first Secretary, devoutly wanted to adopt wholesale its holistic land and water use approaches, its commitment to dams, its encouragement of industrialization, and its rural planning. After a few months of training in Knoxville in 1948, Sen devoted the rest of his career to TVA-style development, first with the DVC, and later for the United Nations. Incidentally, it is worth noting that Sen,

22. Ironically, however, there was little attempt to play up such pioneering engineers as Sir Ganga Ram and Sir M. Viswesvaraya, who had made contributions to dam-building techniques that were of international importance. Nor, was there any mention of the influence that the colonial irrigation service (with a good number of Indian engineers by the later 19th century) had on the US Bureau of Reclamation, a premier dam-building institution which had itself influenced TVA.

23. See, for example, Nehru's *Glimpses of World History* and *Discovery of India*; Kanwar Sain, *America Through Indian Eyes* (Sain was a dam engineer), and articles by M. N. Saha in his journal *Science and Culture*. (Saha was the earliest advocate of 'TVA on the Damodar.')

24. Not everyone was necessarily pro-DVC, as we shall see, or pro-dam. One sharp critic of the DVC was Kapil Dev Bhattacharya, whose criticisms are summarized in Roy (1985).

like many other Indian readers of Lilienthal's book about TVA (including many senior civil engineers and economists, as well as the prime minister), never seems to have been particularly engaged by what Lilienthal promoted as his central (and nowadays largely discredited) claim: that TVA represented 'democracy on the march,' development with the direct participation of its beneficiaries. What was more enthralling to them was the claim that TVA represented a technocratic, scientific, and apolitical approach to progress.[25]

Ironically, Sen, the DVC officer most faithfully committed to the project of emulating a specific model of development, ultimately failed politically in carrying out his project in the face of bureaucratic and political maneuvering at various levels, despite his training, intelligence, and commitment. He was not able to create a 'TVA on the Damodar' after all. He ultimately resigned, realizing that the project would never be, from his own point of view, more than 'a mutilated success,' if that.[26] His colleagues often invoked TVA as the justification for their organization and its various projects, but they were much less personally invested in it and its philosophy as a literal model. TVA had prided itself on its special autonomy from most of the rest of the US federal government and its bureaucratic procedures: it was thereby given (for better or worse) considerably more flexibility and independence.

Lilienthal and his allies had recognized the need to cultivate support from constituencies who could be mobilized on the organization's behalf, and under them TVA celebrated its connection to groups that it labeled 'the grassroots' and who later critics have recognized as local elites. This enabled TVA to pressure state governments in its service region to cooperate, and gave it occasional opportunities to defy rival state and federal bureaucracies. The DVC board, on the other hand, was dominated by ICS officers, who sought to run the organization on ICS lines and who were generally complacent at the prospect of interference from Delhi, Calcutta, and Patna, places where they had either just served or would soon serve. They saw little need to build support among at least some part of the local population they served, even its elite, as TVA had done, and consequently had no available constituency

25. See Klingensmith, forthcoming.
26. Sen 1989: 55-6.

to mobilize on the occasions when they did wish to avoid interference from other state and central agencies and interests.[27]

This interference was continual. The political and bureaucratic
establishments that set up and funded DVC—the central government and the state governments of Bihar and West Bengal—were
always careful not to allow it too much independence, and each
allowed the others a veto over the doings of the agency.[28] Very
quickly, state and central bureaucracies persuaded their ministers
to strip the DVC of functions which impinged on their own
domains, while politicians brought under state government domination those functions (e.g., the supply of power) through which
political capital might be made, and rents generated.[29] Any possibility that the DVC might genuinely achieve some kind of social
transformation via development was thus closed off by the Bihar
and West Bengal legislative assemblies, and indirectly by the elites
that dominated them. Political elites in the two states were not
averse to the electricity and irrigation water DVC was providing
by the mid-1950s, but they were not about to let control of these
resources rest in hands which they could not force, much less go
along with Sen's far-reaching ideas for land reform. Once the
DVC's dam-building program no longer served their interests, it
was halted, and the unfinished portion of Voorduin's plan (which
insisted that rationalized, cost-efficient development called for four
more dams in addition to the four completed) was thereafter
relegated to a never completed 'second phase.'

The fate of the DVC's irrigation program suggests that the
project generated opportunities for appropriations and negotiations, both discursive and material, from a variety of quarters.
Many actors might acknowledge the value of 'scientific' planning,
as per the TVA model, without agreeing to what that might mean.
Sen did most of the investigations for the irrigation system
Voorduin designed, calculating that this aspect of the program
would pay for itself if all cultivators paid an irrigation levy of
Rs 8 per acre.[30] Once the flow of irrigation water began in the
1950s, however, the DVC found that peasant cultivators were
unwilling to pay for it. Many were quite willing to use it, however,

27. Klingensmith, forthcoming.
28. Franda 1968.
29. Ibid.
30. See Klingensmith, forthcoming; Franda 1968.

breaching DVC channels or digging their own illegal channels and, in effect, stealing the water for use not in the extra cropping Sen had envisaged but simply to make existing cultivation easier.[31] The DVC asked the West Bengal government to enforce collection of the betterment levy. Local level politicians in the West Bengal Congress Party, however, realized how deeply unpopular the levy was and the possible political consequences of enforcing it. For several years the party, and hence the government, dragged its feet on the issue of collection. As the chairman of the Burdwan District Congress Committee observed

Of course, we were not going to stand by and see the people of Burdwan paying these fantastic rates—that is why we had fought against the British for so many years. This is a social service state and we were going to see to it that the people of Burdwan received irrigation from the government...after all, that is the only way food production will ever be increased and our country will escape from its miserable condition.[32]

Meanwhile, in fact, both opposition parties and the Congress actively campaigned against the DVC's irrigation levy—garnering political support for themselves, in the name of 'real' development, by condemning the demands of a government development agency both sides had helped to create. Eventually, the West Bengal government forced the DVC to relinquish to it full control over irrigation facilities.

The results of this sort of interference were an abandonment of any holistic, coherent, or environmentally sound principle of development, and the conversion of what was supposed to be a semi-autonomous agency serving many different purposes into, finally, a generator of power for distribution by state electricity boards. All this happened at the same time that DVC officials and state and central ministers spoke proudly of their organization as one which was chiefly different from its American predecessor only insofar as it was accomplishing, with less money and less time, even more herculean tasks. If building a 'TVA on the Damodar' was not a practical priority, it remained a point of celebration well into the 1960s.[33]

31. Franda 1968: 106–10.
32. Ibid.: 110.
33. Klingensmith, forthcoming.

I must emphasize here that my point is not that India's development community or its politicians 'got it wrong,' nor that had they followed their professed model more closely the outcome would have been more desirable. The TVA's own record in the provision of efficient, apolitical, environmentally sound economic benefits leaves much to be desired. Moreover, there is good reason to doubt whether Voorduin's plan could really have succeeded even according to its own criteria. A growing body of literature throws doubt on the whole enterprise of development via large dams. I am arguing, rather, that the bureaucratic and political authorities in charge of developing the Damodar were not about to *copy* anything, merely on the advice of foreign engineers and economists. No sooner was Voorduin's design for the DVC complete than various different parties in Bihar, Bengal, and Delhi were contesting it or revising it to suit their own purposes. In this atmosphere of contention and political trading, Sudhir Sen and other enthusiasts had little chance to implement their TVA training.

There was, however, something to be gained by invoking that model, if one could tie it to other concerns. On the one hand, the emerging community of development and foreign aid policy makers in the US, and to a lesser extent in Canada and Britain, thought very highly of TVA, as did the World Bank, which gave two important loans to the DVC. One must wonder whether the compliments paid to TVA by some of those responsible for infrastructure development in India were wholly disinterested. Other projects besides the Damodar were occasionally given the TVA label in those years, even when they were decidedly different in their aims and execution. At the same time, thanks to David Lilienthal's book, and accounts by British Fabian socialists as well as by Indian authors like M. N. Saha, TVA enjoyed a reputation among English-speaking lay readers in India as the key to development, as the very latest thing from the most advanced nation in the world. Some politicians, like Nehru, seem to have been genuinely (if quite uncritically) enthusiastic about its dams; others, perhaps, realized that a certain amount of political mileage could be obtained by claiming that they were building an Indian TVA. But if some used this rhetoric insincerely, it was only possible because it resonated with larger public concerns.[34]

34. Klingensmith, forthcoming.

DEVELOPMENT AS SIGNIFICATION

Ultimately, TVA was not a viable 'blueprint' for development—none of the dozens of river projects around the world which were in the 1950s described as new TVAs were actually faithful reproductions, not even in the United States. It was, however, a highly effective signifier of development, one which could be seen to stand for a variety of things, depending on one's perspective, because by the late 1940s it had been represented on several successive occasions by Americans, Indians, and others. It denoted work on behalf of the world's poor, and at the same time, 'American-style' affluence; the restoration of nature or, alternatively, the human triumph over nature; popular control over public planning or, on the other hand, the triumph of the scientific expert and the manager over the politician; 'creeping socialism' to some and the expansion of opportunities for capitalist growth to others; attention to the rural population which, in both Indian and American nationalist discourses, were occasionally taken as the very core of the nation. But at the same time the transformation of the selfsame population was also seen as the impediment that held the nation back from full realization as a futuristic, highly industrialized society.

As a signifier, it was deployed and invoked and juxtaposed, appearing in pamphlets, political speeches, newspaper articles, educational films, cartoons, and dedication ceremonies, tied to other ideas central to the Indian state's construction of itself and its mission: the nation, progress, 'the scientific temper.' 'India's TVA' was to be taken as a sign that India had shaken off both colonial overlordship and superstitious tradition, and was moving forward, catching up, even exceeding, the West. The 'modern temples' Jawaharlal Nehru spoke of were temples at which Indian nationalism and modernist science came together, holy places where India's equality with the West was rendered, literally, concrete.

The nationalist project had a distinctly middle-class orientation, and it is not surprising that so much of the conceptualization, ceremony, and propaganda surrounding Indian dams should seem to have been more clearly directed toward the concerns of the managerial, technocratic elite who had inherited the colonial state, than to the laborers who built the dams or the peasants who were supposed to benefit from them. These others had experienced colonialism and its challenges to subjectivity differently. This is not to say that development did not present rhetorical and material opportunities for them, as well as threats. As the essays by Klenk, Berry, and Prashad elsewhere in this volume suggest, it will aid understanding to disaggregate the much too large categories of the 'objects' of or the 'recipients' of development, bearing in mind that constructions of modernity are nuanced within regions as well as between them. Furthermore, it needs to be emphasized that peasants, tribals, laborers, and others seen as recipients of development are not 'blank slates' any more than the bureaucracies that undertake development projects of external origin.

The larger project of development was less central to the construction of American nationhood in the 1950s and 1960s than it was in the formation of postcolonial nationalisms, but it ought not to be underestimated. It fit into a discourse of Cold War liberalism, the 'loyal opposition' to early Cold War militarism, and economic conservativism.[35] This discourse was part of a claim to political legitimacy at home as much as a way of describing the world. Indeed, much of the neo-New Deal rhetoric of the Kennedy and Johnson years is a reworking of international developmentalist themes. The New Deal of the 1930s reverberated in the foreign aid rhetoric of the 1950s, which in turn informed the domestic public policy of the 1960s. At each phase, new formulations of development justified new kinds of power and intervention against rival claims, and a continuum was established between the underdeveloped of the Third World and the underdeveloped of American inner cities and rural backwaters. This should not be seen, however, as a sign of the ever-expanding reach of a homogenizing discourse; just as the tropes and the models of New Deal liberalism underwent considerable changes, first as 'remembered' by Old New Dealers abroad, and then by those in the postcolonial world who invoked American experiences, so too did the elements of development discourse mutate when they 'returned' to America.

I want to emphasize two related points. The first concerns authority and intellectual hegemony in development. I have argued here that the 'knowhow, showhow' principle does not adequately describe the history of development borrowing. This is not to say that there is not implicit and explicit authority and hierarchy in development knowledge—the history of Western-inspired

35. Klingensmith, forthcoming.

development gambits shows otherwise (TVA was only the first of a series that continues into the present era of 'restructuring'). But, as in many relationships of hegemony, we may find agency on the part of the 'subordinate,' not simply in rejectionist dissent, but in appropriations, 'corruptions,' and manipulations, all enacted within the boundaries of a discursive universe. Development models (like colonial education policies, missionary endeavors, or social reforms) can be appropriated and turned, to some extent, to the different purposes of either the elites of the countries they are supposed to change, or, possibly, others who find themselves cornered by the status quo. Transnational politics, including development politics as much as colonial politics, can be thought of as in one sense a process of collaboration (albeit hierarchical collaboration) between certain social classes of two or more different societies, each using its contacts with foreign sources of power and prestige in a struggle with domestic rivals for power and authority. There is no need, however, to assume that because the various parties to such collaborative relationships use some of the same symbolic language, they therefore mean the same thing by it, or have the same agendas and goals. The fact that developmentalist and other modernist discourses travel does not preclude them being incorporated in new ways in different 'regional modernities.'

The second, related point is that it is worthwhile to attend to the communicative aspects of development, that is to the various uses of this symbolic language, to regard development projects as signifiers as much as means toward the generation of wealth or the extraction of surplus. In general, the dam projects of the 1950s and 1960s communicated, made outwardly visible, the modernity and the historic missions of nations and selves, at least to some. But as symbols they could be invested with different further meanings, depending on the context of their builders and viewers: they could prove to Americans (but only to some Americans, I must emphasize) that they belonged to a nation with a historic mission to the world's oppressed, and to Indians (but only some Indians) that they belonged to a nation rapidly reasserting an ancient equality with the rest of the world. Furthermore, they were part of a larger collection of signifiers (including things like irrigation canals and mechanized construction plants, and much more) that could serve the needs of a variety of different actors, all struggling over the specifics of development and modernity but using many of the same images, metaphors, and words in different ways. 'Genuine development' meant one thing to Sudhir Sen as he designed a financially-rationalized irrigation system, and another thing for the West Bengal politicians who won votes by refusing to enforce its logic, and a third thing to Andrew Komora, seeking to educate his Indian colleagues out of 'the head-basket idea.' Indeed, viewed this way, 'development' appears as a much more shifting and less stable idea than any of its practitioners will admit. It is hard to say what exactly it means, and what it excludes, outside of particular contexts. Development, and likewise the 'modernity' that it is supposed to bring into existence, are constructs and tropes, rather than things, and as such can be invested with various, even contradictory, meanings.[36]

Development may not have reached its putative goals at the DVC or elsewhere in India, nor for that matter in the Tennessee Valley, where TVA has also been marked by a disconnect between an ideology of technocratic efficiency and a far messier, less satisfactory, practical outcome. But as a signifying practice, development transactions like the Indian 'borrowing' of New Deal techniques outlined above have collectively formed a new kind of transnational politics, because such transactions have provided a rich vocabulary through which rival claimants to resources, power, and authority can advance their claims. This vocabulary has especially linked social classes of distinct, separate regions of the world in ways of speaking about the world and their role in it that allow both commonality and communication, on the one hand, and a certain amount of flexibility and independence, on the other. Like any vocabulary, the symbolic and literal vocabularies of development are open to appropriation and redefinition for new kinds of ideological projects. The durability of development in the postwar, postcolonial world lies not in the extent to which it constitutes a vision that has been realized, but in the wide variety of political and ideological possibilities into the service of which it can be pressed.

36. The ways in which discourses of development and modernity 'travel' are illustrated, for example, in Kim Berry's essay (this volume), which addresses the resituation of programs for agricultural development and the production of housewives, originally of American provenance, in Himachal Pradesh, and Rebecca Klenk's essay (this volume), which shows how a women's education program in Kumaun reformulated Gandhian and developmentalist ideas to meet needs not well-addressed by either.

References

Alvares, Claude, 1991. *Decolonizing History: Technology and Culture in India, China and the West, 1492 to the Present Day.* Goa: The Other India Press.

Escobar, Arturo, 1995. *Encountering Development: The Making and Unmaking of the Third World.* Princeton: Princeton University Press.

Ferguson, James, 1990. *The Anti Politics Machine.* Minneapolis: University of Minnesota Press.

Franda, Marcus, 1968. *West Bengal and the Federalizing Process in India.* Princeton: Princeton University Press.

Hart, Henry C., 1961. *Administrative Aspects of River Valley Development.* London: Asia Publishing House.

———, 1956. *New India's Rivers.* Bombay: Orient Longman.

Klingensmith, Daniel, forthcoming. *Nation and World in Concrete and Steel.* New Delhi: Oxford University Press.

Lilienthal, David, [1944] 1953. *TVA: Democracy on the March.* New York: Harper Brothers.

Ludden, David, 1992. 'India's development state.' In Nicholas Dirks (ed.), *Colonialism and Culture.* Ann Arbor: University of Michigan Press.

Marglin, Frederique Apffel and Steven Apffel Marglin, 1990. *Dominating Knowledge: Development, Culture and Resistance.* Oxford: Clarendon Press.

McCully, Patrick, 1996. *Silenced Rivers: The Ecology and Politics of Large Dams.* London: Zed Books.

Roy, Dunnu, 1985. 'The politics of the environment.' In Centre for Science and Environment, *The State of India's Environment 1983-1984.* Delhi.

Sachs, Wolfgang (ed.), 1992. *The Development Dictionary: A Guide to Knowledge as Power.* London: Zed Books.

Sen, Sudhir, 1989. *Wanderings: In Search of Solutions of the Problem of Poverty.* Madras: Macmillan.

Singh, Satyajit, 1997. *Taming the Waters: The Political Economy of Large Dams in India.* New Delhi: Oxford University Press.

Tennessee Valley Authority, 1961. *TVA: Symbol of Valley Resource Development.* Knoxville: TVA.

Thukral, Enakshi Ganguly, 1992. *Big Dams, Displaced People: Rivers of Sorrow, Rivers of Change.* New Delhi: Sage Publications.

Tomlinson, B. R., 1993. *The Economy of Modern India, 1860-1970.* Cambridge: Cambridge University Press.

6

'Shelter' in Modern Delhi

VIJAY PRASHAD

The United Nations confirmed the International Declaration of Human Rights on 10 December 1948. A unanimous convention, it was accepted by India and championed by Nehru. The 25th article of the convention provides each person with the 'right to a standard of living adequate for the health and well-being of himself and of his family, including food, clothing, housing and medical care and necessary social services, and the right to security in the event of unemployment, sickness, disability, widowhood, old age or other lack of livelihood in circumstances beyond his control.' The sexist idea of the 'family wage' notwithstanding, this is a tremendous document. In many ways, it sets the tone for a global sentiment towards the rights of persons, something that we might call the prejudice of democracy. The hopefulness of the anti-fascist victory and the process of decolonization in Asia and Africa enabled many of the new nations to set forth tasks for 'development' that stand in stark contrast to the kind of 'realism' enacted today under the regime of Structural Adjustment and of Habitat II (which, in July 1996, reduced housing from a human right of all people to an important charge of modern states).

The managers of the new Indian Republic evinced keen interest in the condition of the masses from the 1940s (even in the bourgeois–landlord Bombay Plan of 1944).[1] The state commissioned

1. Prashad 1996: 39–43.

studies of the living and working conditions of the working poor and it turned some resources to the alleviation of these conditions. In terms of housing, for instance, the state realized the gravity of the problem from the late 1940s, and by the 1970s a series of reports revealed some alarming facts. The Working Group on Slums, set up by the Planning Commission before the aborted Fifth Plan (1974-9), reported that in metropolitan and major cities (population above 500,000), about 20-5 percent of the population lives in slums. At the same time, the Centre for Monitoring the Indian Economy reported a figure of between 25-35 percent as slum residents. But there was widespread concern that reports and good-will alone could not solve the problem of shelter. Issues of land rent, capital, and wages, coupled with a callousness towards the working poor and a belief that they have a different threshold of pain, revealed that the problem of shelter could not be resolved within the confines of the political and economic structure. The popular media was alert to this structural vice:

Today the Jhuggi-Jhonpri problem is not one of housing and homeless. Indulgence towards them has not only provided a shield for the unscrupulous land speculators but has also enabled commercial concerns to take advantage of the authorities lack of concern about land rights.... The homeless in Delhi, whose number is progressively increasing, deserve every consideration, but if they are a pawn in the hands of middlemen and unscrupulous among the officials and politicians, it is time that they were segregated. They must no longer be exploited by politicians, junior officials and others who benefit because of their helplessness.[2]

If certain structural features emerged for discussion by the 1960s, the policies in the 1970s failed to pursue solutions in line with those features. Instead of struggling against speculation in land, the state went after those who live in poverty. In the early 1980s, I. K. Gujral noted that

The housing situation [in Delhi] is tragic. With land prices skyrocketing, even the middle class is unable to afford the steep rise in house rents. Unauthorised colonies, *jhuggies* and pavement dwellers, now account for nearly 60 percent of the existing population. For much of this callous indifference and the elitist approach the policy guardians can be blamed.[3]

Gujral blames the 'policy guardians' due to the strong sentiment that the state's policy of forced relocation (exemplified at Turkman

2. *Hindustan Times*, 24 June 1967.
3. Gujral 1984.

Gate in 1976) failed to grasp the dynamic that enabled certain people to demand astronomical tribute from land that they possess for historical reasons. There is a tendency to assume that if the guardians provide better laws to regulate the ground rent on shelter, perhaps the problems will be solved or, at any rate, will not be as severe as at present. However, the structural contradiction between 'rent' (as a form of value extraction by rentiers) and 'wages' (as remuneration to workers for their reproduction, but minus the value extracted by various types of capitalists—industrial, commercial, agricultural) does not allow regulation itself to solve the crises of our cities. This phenomenon is made more acute when the rentiers (sometimes called developers or contractors) who dominate the land market act in concert with industrial capitalists.[4] This essay assumes the existence of this structural dynamic, one that prevents an easy solution to the housing question.

Rather than delve into either the constitution of the crisis or in solutions to the crisis, I will explore the politics of the crisis. That is, this essay maps out the ways in which the 'housing question,' as a problem, is constituted within Indian modernity as an argument between, at least, those who called for a devolution of power to provide human rights and those who felt that the only right worthy of protection was that of private property. One strand of the state's leaders in the 1950s departed from the colonial disinterest in the production of citizenry. Rather than simply be interested in the condition of the masses in an imperial way, they sought to devolve power to slum localities so that the working poor may, with state resources, craft their human rights. I want to show how that brief window reveals alternative and defeated possibilities that might help us with today's dilemmas. Before I attempt to do so I want to offer a brief detour into the tangle of modernity and the question of its regionalness. This is a necessary preface since it allows me to clarify how I use 'modernity' as well as show the importance of 'democracy' to the construction of the 'housing question' in the 1950s and after.

GENERIC MODERNITY

In 1959–60, a set of US scholars gathered at the University of Chicago under the aegis of the Committee for the Comparative

4. Marx 1991, vol. 3: 908.

Study of New Nations. Milton Singer, Clifford Geertz, Edward Shils and others comprised this influential collective who oversaw the publication of a series of books including *Old Societies and New States*.[5] In the volume, the Africanist Lloyd Fallers offered a useful discussion on the study of modernization. The processes of political and economic modernization, he argued, 'are the products of the interaction between the forces of generic modernity' and 'the traditional societies and cultures upon which, and within which, modernity works.'[6] 'Generic modernity' appears here as 'Westernization' or a process that *sui generis* occurs in Europe along the lines sketched by US Weberians.[7] When the non-West gets 'modern,' then, it does not simply copy the process set in motion by the 'West.' However, it articulates with the 'West' and finds its own dynamic in accordance with its past. In India, for example, Fallers notes (following Milton Singer) that 'the Indian tradition of diversity and syncretism' enabled 'Indian modernizers to innovate while retaining a deep sense of national identity and continuity.'[8] If we are to construct a theory of 'regional modernity,' there is a need to first start with essays such as Fallers, since they offer the very best of modernization thought and they also seek out regional variations in modernity (despite their own romanticization of the mess of contradictions in Indian life).

Modernization thought in its many manifestations is not as crude as some believe. There are significant problems with it, but it can hardly be entirely associated with the types of simplistic analyses offered by Rostow, among others.[9] Much of the Chicago version of modernization theory suffers from its belief that the 'West' is a coherent entity, that it moves to a form of modernity

5. Geertz 1963; Johnson 1967.

6. Fallers 1963: 160.

7. Notably, Talcott Parsons 1940 and 1960. This approach appears to be 'theoretical' and not grounded in any 'area,' whereas its own presuppositions and narratives reveal that its propositions follow from a caricature of early modern European history (a caricature, that is, because they fail to acknowledge the birth of imperialism and its impact on modernity). Fallers (1963: 160–1) notes that 'modern Western society [the 'generically modern'], including its stratification system, is what it is in part because of the special character of the late medieval European society and culture out of which it grew.'

8. Fallers 1963: 199; Singer 1956.

9. Rostow 1971.

by itself, and that its model is then available (after the fact) for articulation with local traditions (that are themselves formed *sui generis*). For one, the 'West' as an entity refers to northwestern Europe, and its proto-industrialization relied upon the crucible of imperial expansion both into the Americas (from whence it raised specie) and into Eastern Europe (which became the agrarian heartland).[10] The Weberian fascination with the culture of the self-willed entrepreneur ignored this dimension of the imperial creation of Europe (a myth revived by Bill Warren in his theory of imperialism).[11] In chronological terms, we locate the emergence of the 'modern' in that event known as the Enlightenment (eighteenth century). 'Enlightenment is man's release from his self-incurred tutelage,' wrote Kant.[12] He counseled his peers to 'Dare to Know' (*Sapere Aude*) and to 'have courage to use your own reason.' Kant's unfettered individual is the bourgeois citizen, whose own production relied upon the extraction of values from territories other than Europe. But modernity is more than chronology; it is also a condition of being. Kant and d'Alembert, among others, demonstrate an impatience with unreason and barbarism. They manifest a desire to walk away from the 'sluggish state.'[13] Here are conjoined ideas of progress and freedom, but this is a bourgeois sort of freedom since it relies upon the unfreedom of property (that is, private property in the means of production) and luxury for skill development. The idea of the 'modern,' therefore, is not the gift of Europe to the world, but it bears within it the empire. Modernity, then, is the bourgeois condition spawned in the context of imperialism.

Europe's self-image as modern in itself and of modernization as Europeanization was not accepted without criticism by anti-colonial nationalists, however bourgeois their views.[14] Few nationalists absorbed the model in an uncritical fashion (and the recent critiques of these nationalists fail to trace the subtle manipulations offered to what is generically seen as 'modernity'). There is little, therefore, that is generically modern. Those components of it

10. Wallerstein 1972; Wolff 1994.
11. Ahmad 1996.
12. Kant [1874] 1990.
13. d'Alembert 1759.
14. The autobiographies of Nehru (1942) and Nkrumah (1957) are to the point.

sketched by the modernization theorists hardly stood the test of their own sociological insights.[15] Many turned to the details of the 'new nations' to find their own logic and their own cultural modes of dealing with the modern. There is, however, one element that continues to interrupt the search for difference in the details (what is called area studies). This is the impact of the idea of democracy and the process of democratization. The modern, as unfettered or radical freedom, is grounded in a bourgeois possibility, but it offers the hope of something more. It is this that conjoins with various traditions of radical freedom to produce the anti-colonial movements. The modern, as a contradictory entity, offers intimations of freedom grasped by people from around the world. That is, even when unfreedom is begun as a condition (slavery by the Europeans in the New World or bondage relations in Bihar), it must be justified in relation to democratic rights.[16] Modernity is not inherently democratic, but its contradictory manifestations requires that one consider the democratic each time one makes an enunciation about the contemporary condition of being. The question of the right to the city can only be legible if we grant this theoretical claim.

In these few ways, the project of 'regional modernity' is not entirely novel. It too seeks to find the forms in which South Asia forges its modern. However, it departs from one fundamental premise and therefore sets itself apart from modernization theory. It abandons the belief that the 'modern' is created in Europe isolated from imperialism and then exported to the rest of the world. Rather, both Europe and the rest of the world formed each other in struggle (with European maritime power and, soon, military power in dominance). The production of 'imperial modernity' proffered us the 'universal contradictions' of capitalism.[17] Given the persistence of the 'universal contradictions' (capitalism), the project of regional modernity must avoid the essentialized turn to cultural logic of regions (what is generally called indigenism). Rather, we need to locate the different and conflictual class cultures (who draw their sustenance from older cultural traditions, from forms of European tradition as well as from the structures

---

15. The work of Clifford Geertz (1963) is significant here.
16. Patterson 1982: 340; Prakash 1990: 1–12.
17. Nicholas 1970: 18.

of capitalism), for these class cultures determine the historical creation of modernity in the subcontinent. In the précis on housing in Delhi below, the contradictions of rent and wages (one such universal contradiction) structure the cultural dilemmas faced by the managers of the city and its residents from at least the 1930s onwards.

THE HOUSING QUESTION

The 'housing question' was posed in the newspapers of the European working class in the 1870s. The question of the life of the poor only entered the purview of the elite during the 1832 cholera epidemic after which such unenlightened policies as the Small Tenements Recovery Act (1838 in England) appeared on the books (landlords, with minimal notice, could evict poor tenants who lived in tenements). In the 1870s, as a result of the movement of workers, *Volksstaat* carried an exchange between the Proudhonist Mülberger and Engels. While Mülberger championed the right of all workers to own their own homes, Engels countered that such a slogan was useful, but meaningless, if one failed to grasp its impossibility in the current social climate. Why is there a housing shortage? Here is Engels:

[The housing shortage] cannot fail to be present in a society in which the great labouring masses are exclusively dependent upon wages, that is to say, upon the quantity of means of subsistence necessary for their existence and for the propagation of their kind; in which improvements of the machinery, etc., continually throw masses of workers out of employment; in which violent and regularly recurring industrial fluctuations determine on the one hand the existence of a large reserve army of unemployed workers, and on the other hand drive the mass of the workers from time to time on to the streets unemployed; in which the workers are crowded together in masses in the big towns at a quicker rate than dwellings come into existence for them under the prevailing conditions; in which, therefore, there must always be tenants even for the most infamous pigsties; and in which finally the house-owner in his capacity as capitalist has not only the right but, by reason of competition, to a certain extent also the duty of ruthlessly making as much out of his property in house rent as he possibly can. In such a society, the housing shortage is no accident.[18]

18. Engels [1872] 1979: 43–4.

Moral outrage against homelessness, Engels emphasized, is important, but it fails to grasp the logic of the shortage, one built into the bone of the system. The workers' movement attempted to create workers' colonies, but many of these failed due to an insufficient grasp of the stranglehold of the political economy. Each of the innovations of the state remained wedded to the policy of class quarantine. Either the workers are housed in settlements besides industrial units or else they are expelled from the city to its outreaches. In both cases, the workers live in areas far from the homes of the bourgeoisie (although the segregation is rarely planned).[19]

There was no 'housing question' of this nature in the colony. The aftermath of the cholera of 1832 exacerbated the fear of the racialized native and the colony's cities bifurcated social space into 'White Town' and 'Black Town.' Reports on the latter concentrated on strategies to minimize its danger and to segregate it from the health of the former.[20] When the British took Delhi in 1857–8, they took control of what might be described as an experiment in urbanity. Shah Jahan's city was built to correspond to various cosmological rules and its population was settled to reflect the sociological vision of the Mughals (with nobles settled by the fort and artisans by the city wall, a form of status segregation). This careful Mughal logic, one made manifest by Abu-l Fazl's 'social contract' in 1596,[21] was demolished by the British in the decade after 1857. Revenge was high on the list and the British desecrated the city and expelled many of its residents outside its walls. The Civil Lines, already home to the Resident from 1803, was now expanded and it became the political center of the region. The strict separation between Black Town and White Town was now enforced, a logic that found its way into the making of New Delhi between 1911 and the 1930s.

In the 1930s, the managers of the New Imperial Capital took another look at the old city. They felt that it was a public health nuisance and they pledged to either refashion it or to isolate it further. Hume's 1936 Report is a landmark, since it identified 'congestion' as the principal problem of the city and urged the

19. Daunton 1990; Shapiro 1985.
20. Ross and Telkamp 1985.
21. Habib 1996: 169.

administration to remove substantial sections of the population out of the walls and further away from the new capital. That many of the poor already lived in the Western Extension Area (WEA, started in 1926) was noted by the Report. The WEA was built to house certain artisans (in the main dalits) who were offered accommodation on the basis of their caste by the British planners (hence, the Reghar Chamars lived in Reghar Basti and plied their trade as artisans of leather). Now, Hume called for the 'improvement of Basti Reghar to convert it into a better class residential site' and for the provision of 'poor class accommodation' at some distance from the city (in Tirpaulia).[22]

The colonial supervisors analysed and planned Delhi as a bifurcated organism. One part of this was seen as healthy, White Town, and it was to be the area that secured the city's resources and new technologies of urbanity (such as water flush latrines). The Delhi *rais*, as early as the 1870s, complained that their city, the Black Town, or the unhealthy part, was a victim of colonial discrimination: 'the arrangements of the city [Shahjahanabad] are day by day less attended to, and while some parts of it are well cleaned and lighted others are totally deprived of these benefits which is highly unjust. As octroi tax is collected from all the inhabitants alike, there is no reason why the benefits of the Municipality should not be equally extended to all.'[23] The point of urban planning, until the 1950s, was to lift up the healthy Delhi (White Town) at the expense of the unhealthy Delhi (Black Town). To further protect the former, the colonial overseers designed and maintained a cordon sanitaire (the grassy zone south of Delhi and Turkman Gate, what used to be called Jatwara Kalan).

In the mid-1950s, the tenor of planning changed and remained different for a few brief years. On 1 April 1956, Nehru journeyed through Delhi at the insistence of Brijkrishen Chandiwala, eminent Gandhian and head of the Bharat Sevak Sangh (founded in Delhi in 1952). In a confidential note to various ministries on 14 April, Nehru noted that 'it is our bounden duty to take this matter [the condition of slums] in hand positively and effectively.'[24] The

22. Hume 1936, vol. 1: 39.

23. Prashad 1994: 253.

24. J. Nehru, Note of 14 April 1956, file no. 28, Chandiwala Papers, Nehru Memorial Museum and Library.

language of 'effectiveness' did not imply a Haussmannish solution (that is, to demolish the homes and push the workers from the city by force). Nehru was clear that 'people cannot be driven out of their bastis. They will have to be provided some accommodation while new buildings etc., are put up.' Told of police action against the slums in Karol Bagh, Nehru explained that 'police eviction in this way should be avoided at this stage and the place should be examined as to what we can make of it. We must adopt a human approach to this problem.' Ten days later, Chandiwala (who had Nehru's ear) informed him of rumors that landlords had begun to evict tenants in the slums in order to benefit from a rise in land prices. Act fast, Chandiwala pleaded, or else the entire purpose of the humanist approach would be lost.[25]

For a brief moment, the 'housing question' emerged with an eye to power relations. The principal aim was not to remove the poor from the city, but to devolve power to the poor so that they might reconstruct their social ecology. There was little interest in transformation of the class inequalities, but there was a sentiment that the devolution of power and self-initiative of the poor would produce a new kind of urban life. Nehru, in his 14 April 1956 note, was explicit on this point and he made it twice: 'Many of these people said that if they were given a loan, they could do much themselves' and 'In some of these *katras*, the residents told me that if Government acquired that land from the present owners, they would form a cooperative and build their houses according to specifications. They are prepared to do this immediately.'[26] In a letter to member of Parliament Radha Raman in 1958, Nehru noted the two paths open to his government. The government could remove the residents to temporary camps, destroy the slums and then resettle the residents in newly built homes. This was an executive decision from above. Or else, there is the approach 'broadly on the lines of community development where the community in question is made responsible' after the provision, by government, of sufficient power and resources.[27] One need not be naive about these statements. After all, at this same time, Nehru's

25. BKC to JN, 25 April 1956, file no. 29, Chandiwala Papers.

26. Nehru to various ministers, confidential letter, 14 April 1956, file no. 21, Chandiwala Papers.

27. Nehru to Radha Raman, 4 August 1958, file no. 190, Chandiwala Papers and Nehru's foreword to Samaj 1958.

administration opened fire on a sanitation workers' strike and he was himself getting ready to overthrow the communist ministry in Kerala. Nevertheless, for this brief moment, bourgeois nationalism conceptualized a strategy for urban community redevelopment in terms of devolution of power and development by locality. Of this, the Kadam Sharif Pilot Project, launched in 1956, is exemplary.

The Bharat Sewak Samaj (BSS) along with requisite government agencies created a plan on the basis of a set of conferences held under the chairmanship of Nehru in 1956. They listed three tasks. The first item on the agenda was to push for enactment of the Slum Act, inclusion of the slum areas under the authority of the Delhi Development Authority (DDA) and the creation of a 'Competent Authority' (such as the DDA, but with extra power) to oversee the question of the slums. Once the legal dimension was on the table, the BSS felt that the state should create homes for those who are to be relocated. Chandiwala contacted the Delhi Improvement Trust to build homes at Idgah, Jhilmila-Tahirpur, Jangpura and Kilokri. Alongside the legal and construction work, BSS asked the local authorities to inform the populace of its activities, notably by the publication of the interim General Plan from the Town Planning Office. BSS did not just ask for social justice, but its tasks put the administration on a timetable and in a spot. Even this plan, however, was at some distance from the mood of devolution of power to the masses.

By early 1960, the guardians of the state transformed the 'housing question' from a concern over relations of power and production to a concern over the presence of the poor within the city. When the 'policy guardians' began to debate the 'Slum Act' (1957 law to establish the DDA), the drift of the deliberations favored the class culture of the landlords over the slum-dwellers. In a note to Swaran Singh (minister for works, housing and supply), Chandiwala noted that the landlords will not 'swallow the decisions [to buy their property at low rates] lying down.' Rather than confront the landlords, Chandiwala proposed that the state act through them. He suggested that the state oblige landlords to 'provide the specified improvements in their property in the specified time and charge rent at the fixed rate from the existing tenants, who will not be allowed to be evicted without the permission of the said authority.' If the landlord breaks this trust, the land can be acquired.[28] Two years later, Chandiwala was even more despondent. The gazetted rent was too high for most of the slum dwellers who faced eviction for non-payment of these rents. The entire project seemed doomed to failure.

The vice of landlordism reared its head as the problem of 'housing' was quickly transformed into a problem of 'slums.' The Delhi administration conducted a census of 'squatters' in June–July 1960 in order to relocate some and regularize others. On 22 January 1964, the Ad Hoc Slum Clearance Committee met and decided to remove 'squatters' from the city. To do so, the Committee asked the municipality to make 'squatting' on public land cognizable (imprisonment for three years). In 1967–8, the Delhi Development Authority put its entire muscle behind the principle that urban planning was to mean the removal of 'squatters.' The DDA cleared Yamuna Bazar, Hanuman Temple, Prasadnagar, Idgah, Patelnagar, Kela Godown, Gurdwara Moti Bagh, Kotla Ferozshah, Tilak Bridge, Ghata Masjid, Phool Walon-ki-Sair and other localities. The improvements made by the state on the 'rehabilitated land' valorized the price of the land and this once again '"flushed" out [the working poor] into slum katras and such other slum areas.'[29] The events at Turkman Gate on 19 April 1978 fit into a pattern that started with the Yamuna Bazar clearance on 17 June 1967, whose pattern was set by Indira Gandhi (who told the Rajya Sabha on 8 January 1976 that slum clearance was 'not operation demolition, but operation resettlement') and Bhagat (who told the Rajya Sabha on 15 January 1976 that the government was moving people 'for resettlement purposes only. We are not removing people for the sake of fun'). On 20 August 1974, both Congress and Jana Sangh asked for the Defence of India Rule and MISA against those who lived in slums! The idea of 'resettlement' from the 1960 Squatter Resettlement Scheme (but already in the 1956 meetings) came to mean the removal of the poor outside the confines of the city. At the end of the Emergency, Mohammed Rafi's voice intoned the sense of betrayal felt by the bulk of those whose faith in nation-state construction was slowly being tarnished. 'Nasha daulat ka aisa bhi

28. Chandiwala to Swaran Singh, 14 June 1956, file no. 58, Chandiwala Papers.
29. Trivedi 1980: 92.

kya,' he sang the words of Majrooh, 'ke tujhe kuch bhi yaad nahi. Kya hua tera vada, woh kasam, woh irada' (*So intoxicated by wealth that you cannot remember anything. What happened to your promise, that vow, those hopes?*)[30]

During the 1950s, the concept of 'vested interests' referred to those bound by monetary ties to property and power, such as landlords and capitalists. By 1967, the Delhi state apparatus used the concept to refer to those 'urban peasants' whose labors kept the city together. The lieutenant governor sent out instructions to the effect that 'a political slant is now sought to be given to every operation and strong resistance is being put up by vested interests. It is, therefore, absolutely necessary to strengthen the demolition-cum-clearance machinery and to make available its assistance to all the departments concerned.'[31] The 'vested interests' here are those 'squatters' whose attempts to draw in the political parties to prevent their wholesale eviction become the problem, rather than those landowners and local officials who benefit both by retaining the slums (from which they derive inflated rents and bribes) or by removing them (by which process they receive state monies and cleared land for 'development').

The planning structure failed both because of the form that it took (planning from above) and for the decisions taken by the planners. On the latter problem, the Delhi Improvement Trust located the resettlement colonies far from the location of the slums. These distant homes came with inadequate facilities and the design of these homes prevented the continuation of the class culture of those who had to now live here (the homes alienated one family from the next and demanded unfamiliar forms of privacy).[32] Of those offered housing in the newly-constructed houses (far from their residences), Chandiwala had this to say:

some people who had moved on to these quarters, formerly, have returned to the Jamuna side again. The reason is that they cannot afford to live at this distance. It is apparent also that adequate provision of drinking water is not made in the colony. With regard to other localities, it has

30. 'Hum Kissise Kum Nahi' (1977).

31. File no. F 50 (6)/67-L & B, 27 July 1967, Delhi State Archives.

32. 'The urban renewal programmes also became targets of severe attack, and got politicized on the ground that they tend to replace lively and humane neighbourhoods with multiple unit monoliths that lack humanity, scale and any sense of community or architectural distinction.' (Mehta 1991: 24).

come to our notice that quarters have been allotted to un-authorised persons and subletting is going on there on a large scale.[33]

Many of the new colonies failed to address questions of gender, since women still had to walk a fair distance for water and to collect resources for the maintenance of the family. The city planning did not address issues of social justice, bent as it was to see its mission in terms of pragmatism (getting the job done). When the state did take an interest in social engineering, it did so without forethought. For example, the new colonies spatially disrupted cultural aspects of the working class (for the planners saw these as anachronistic and pre-modern). There was little interest in the cultural features of everyday life that would have facilitated normative planning of the workers' *mohallas*.

The 'policy guardians' could not grasp the class culture of the working poor, something that followed from, but was not caused by the centralized and bureaucratic form of planning. When the DDA Act came to the Lok Sabha in September 1957, four MPs studied it and offered the following critique: 'the underlying principle of the Bill was that the initiative for town planning would be derived from the top, rather than be allowed to emerge from the bottom.'[34] One can decentralize decision-making and remain within the framework of elite culture. Decentralization is a necessary, but not sufficient, criterion for the transformation of the cityscape. To decentralize is often to miss the gains from endeavors that are bigger than the locality. Nevertheless, there are experiments underfoot (viz., the *panchayati* regime) that energize the contradiction between the project of commodification and of democracy.

Confronted by the problem of creating consent amongst the 'squatters' evicted by the state and set up at the fringe of the city, the political establishment produced spectacular images of progress rather than social development itself. For example, in 1976 the resettlement colony of Khichripur was flooded due to poor drainage and rains. Bhagat, both MP of the area and minister of state for works and housing, visited the site and asked why a pump had not been set up to drain the water. A civil servant explained that it was futile to set up a pump since the area was lodged in a deep depression. 'Never mind all that,' barked Bhagat, 'These people

33. Chandiwala to Nehru, 10 April 1958, file no. 138, Chandiwala Papers.
34. Pillai 1991: 42.

expect me to take some action. They must see a pump working here.'[35] In many instances, the bourgeois–democratic government acts without a desire to either resolve the problem or to transform the situation, but it acts simply to act, so that it gives the impression that it is doing something. In some instances, this is able to produce a certain amount of support amongst the oppressed (evidence of which is the low incidence of protest and the very common placement of pictures of politicians, such as the Gandhi family, on the wall—pictures of people who may not have acted in the best interests of the dislocated, but whose spectacular acts generated a considerable amount of favor). When the political elite felt it could count on this support (purchased at such low cost), it squandered the brief moment of innovation and retreated into the sloth of the status quo.

THE RIGHT TO THE CITY

The 'development' of urban Delhi from the 1930s to the 1961 Master Plan and beyond occurred in the pith of a 'universal contradiction': that between the commodified city (in which land values and private profit in the main determine questions of 'shelter') and the democratic city (in which the populace's social needs configure the production of space).[36] Both cities exist simultaneously in Delhi, as the policy guardians and the residents struggle between their two logics. The fight over the city, the right to the city, is a battle over the terrain we deem as the 'social.'[37] To configure the 'social,' planning is offered in place of the anarchic development of urban life governed by the logic of 'unplanned' expansion. Not to plan is a form of planning, since to neglect the workers' domain of reproduction is a sure means to condemn workers' housing to slum conditions. It is convenient to offer culturalist statements of the peasant character of the slum dwellers and their comfort in the urban villages. However, what this avoids is the sustained protests from the slums, either in the space of theft of power lines, political barter for water and sanitation facilities, or militant fights against the police and landlords. The right to the

35. Dayal and Bose 1977: 27.
36. Deutsche in Wallis 1991: 60.
37. The general argument in Lefebvre 1968.

city is expressed occasionally, since this instinct is still being elaborated by organizations of the workers' neighborhoods (galvanized by the recent anti-worker attempt to buy up this land for speculation).

The Nehru–Chandiwala phase proposed a form of city life that both acknowledged the presence of the working poor and attempted to provide space for them for the present and the future. That is, the new housing (as seen by Chandiwala and Nehru) was to be designed to facilitate current class configurations, but it was not to freeze those class stratifications into wood and mortar. Planning, in this mode, was to build from the cultures of the competing classes, but it was not to sacrifice social change to an imagined expediency of the moment. When this planning was reduced to 'slum clearance' and 'resettlement,' the right to the city was ceded to the landlords and the wealthy. The extension of Delhi into the West (by the new refugees from Pakistan in the 1950s) and into the East (by the new middle class, especially journalists, teachers, and corporate middle management in the 1980s) followed this procedure. With the increase in land rent in the city, 'gentrification' is on the agenda as slums are being torn down and servants quarters are being rented.[38] The working poor must once again travel from the city's margins. Current planning (as in the High Court judgment on 'pollution')[39] could benefit from a consideration of the

38. This is precisely the context for the murder of Sunit Khatau in 1994 (*Frontline*, 3 June 1994) and of Datta Samant in 1997 (*Frontline*, 7 February 1997). As the Mumbai mills are being sent to the dustheap of history by the owners, the workers' housing is coming under dispute and owners (such as Khatau) and union leaders (such as Samant) emerge as victims in a criminalized land market. 'Criminalisation is no longer invisible,' wrote Vivek Monteiro, 'It has expanded vertically and horizontally. It has diversified and multiplied and spread to all areas of the economy. What was earlier an occupational hazard for unions has become an environment hazard for citizens.' (*Frontline*, 7 February 1997)

39. The High Court's recent decisions plainly show how its interests do not intersect with those of working people. To claim that the main agents of pollution are the industries that employ a considerable proportion of the working poor is to narrow the idea of pollution itself. Recent research shows that an important agent in polluting Delhi is the automobile (*Frontline*, 7 March 1997) and that the shift to unleaded petrol is no panacea to these statistics. In fact, unleaded petrol produces an increased amount of carcinogenic polyaromatic hydrocarbons such as benzpyrene (*Frontline*, 2 June 1995).

1950s, a time when the policy guardians recognized the contradictions of our regional modernity. Now, these contradictions are
flattened as the guardians offer 'solutions' that simply turn the
brunt of the contradictions over to the working poor.

Delhi is not alone in the condemnation of the working poor to
the furnace at what is called 'the end of history.' If the 1948
Declaration on Human Rights enframed a kind of political work,
the recent curtailment of its vision to an interest only in habeas
corpus enframes another kind of reality—one that cannot seem to
support the idea that employment, housing, and cultural diversity
are human rights. Certain that its provisions in the realm of housing
have come to nothing, the UN called for a conference on the topic
that was held in Vancouver in 1976 and is now called Habitat I.
This conference reaffirmed the belief that housing is a human right
and that, therefore, states that fail to provide housing for citizens
can be taken to court.[40] Twenty years later, in response to the
failure of states to produce housing and of the spectre of future
homelessness, the UN convened Habitat II in Istanbul. Fidel Castro
asked the delegates to reaffirm the declaration that housing is an
essential right. This did not happen. The final document backed
away from the 1948 declaration to argue that states must make an
attempt towards the 'full and progressive realisation of the right to
adequate housing as provided for in international instruments.'[41]
The new language implies that a state cannot be held accountable
for homelessness and that it must only hold onto the principle that
housing is important. This did not please all present at Habitat II
nor did it please those who have struggled for years to ensure that
'human rights' does not remain at the level of juridical rights. 'We
shall continue to hold meetings,' an impassioned Castro said at
Habitat II, 'we shall continue striving and proclaiming our truths
to the world; by and large, we are the world and the world does
not yield to masters nor to suicidal policies; the world does not
accept that a majority of selfish, insane and irresponsible people
lead it to annihilation.' Meanwhile, in Delhi, working people
resolutely refuse to abdicate their rights to the city nor to their
history of defense in the face of the encroachment of the elite.

40. As noted in the Vancouver Action Plan, 31 May–11 June 1976, UN
Conference on Human Settlements.
41. *Frontline*, 12 July 1996.

References

Ahmad, Aijaz, 1996. 'Imperialism and progress.' In *Lineages of the Present. Political Essays*. New Delhi: Tulika.

Daunton, M. J. (ed.), 1990. *Housing the Workers, 1850–1914: A Comparative Perspective*. London: Leicester University Press.

Dayal, John and Ajoy Bose, 1977. *For Reasons of State: Delhi Under Emergency*. Delhi: S. S. Publications.

Deutsche, Rosalyn, 1991. 'Alternative space.' In Brian Wallis (ed.), *If You Lived Here*. Seattle: Bay Press.

Engels, Fredrich, [1872] 1979. *The Housing Question* Moscow: Progress.

Fallers, Lloyd, 1963. 'Equality, modernity, and democracy in new states.' In Clifford Geertz (ed.), *Old Societies and New States: The Quest for Modernity in Asia and Africa*. London: Free Press of Glencoe.

Geertz, Clifford (ed.), 1963. *Old Societies and New States: The Quest for Modernity in Asia and Africa*. London: Free Press of Glencoe.

Gujral, I. K., 1984. 'Has Delhi a future?' *Design* (January–March).

Habib, Irfan, 1996. 'Reason and science in medieval India.' In D. N. Jha (ed.), *Society and Ideology in India: Essays in Honour of Professor R. S. Sharma*. New Delhi: Munshiram Manoharlal.

Hume, A. P., 1936. *Report on the Relief of Congestion in Delhi*. Simla: GOI Press, volume I.

Johnson, Harry G., 1967. *Economic Nationalism in Old and New States*. Chicago: University of Chicago Press.

Kant, Immanuel, [1874] 1990. *What Is Enlightenment?* New York: Macmillan; London: Collier Macmillan.

Lefebvre, Henri, 1968. *Le Droit à la Ville*. Paris: Editions Anthropos.

Marx, Karl, 1991. *Capital* (volume 3). London: Penguin.

Mehta, Ajay, 1991. *The Politics of Urban Redevelopment. A Study of Old Delhi*. New Delhi: Sage Publications.

Nehru, J., 1958. 'Foreword.' In Bharat Sevak Samaj, *Slums of Old Delhi: Report on the Socio-Economic Survey of the Slum Dwellers of Old Delhi City*. New Delhi: Atma Ram.

Nicholas, Martin, 1970. 'The universal contradiction.' *New Left Review*, 59 (January–February): 18.

Parsons, Talcott, 1940. 'An analytical approach to the theory of social stratification.' *American Journal of Sociology* 45.

———, 1960. *Structure and Process in Modern Societies*. New York: The Free Press of Glencoe.

Patterson, Orlando, 1982. *Slavery and Social Death*. Cambridge: Harvard University Press.

Pillai, Laksmi, 1991. *Decision Making in a Public Organisation: A Study of Delhi Development Authority*. New Delhi: IIPA.

Prakash, Gyan, 1990. *Bonded Histories*. Cambridge: Cambridge University Press.

Prashad, V., 1994. 'Native dirt/imperial ordure: The cholera of 1832 and the morbid resolutions of modernity.' *Journal of Historical Sociology* 7(3): 253.

———, 1996. 'Emergency assessments.' *Social Scientist* (280–1): 39–43.

Ross, R. and G. Telkamp (eds.), 1985. *Colonial Cities: Essays on Urbanism in a Colonial Context*. Dordrecth: Nijhoff.

Rostow, W. W., 1971. *The Stages of Economic Growth: A Non-communist Manifesto*. Cambridge: Cambridge University Press.

Shapiro, Ann-Louise, 1985. *Housing the Poor of Paris, 1850–1902*. Madison: University of Wisconsin Press.

Singer, Milton, 1956. 'Cultural values in India's economic development.' *Annals of the American Academy of Political and Social Science* 305.

Trivedi, Harish, 1980. *Housing and Community in Old Delhi*. New Delhi: Atma Ram.

Wallerstein, I., 1972. 'Three paths of national development in sixteenth century Europe.' *Studies in Comparative International Development* VII (Summer 1972).

Wolff, L., 1994. *Inventing Eastern Europe: The Map of Civilization on the Mind of the Enlightenment*. Stanford: Stanford University Press.

PART II

Development Situations

7

Beyond Blackmail: Multivalent Modernities and the Cultural Politics of Development in India[1]

DONALD S. MOORE

> [T]he places of social space...may be intercalated, combined, superimposed—they may even sometimes collide. Consequently the local (or 'punctual', in the sense of 'determined by a particular "point"') does not disappear, for it is never absorbed by the regional, national or even worldwide level. The national and regional levels take in innumerable 'places'; national space embraces the regions; and world space does not merely subsume national spaces, but even (for the time being at least) precipitates the formation of new national spaces through a remarkable process of fission.
>
> —*Henri Lefebvre*[2]

1. Neither my own academic training nor embodied spatial practices have interpellated me as a South Asianist. My comments are those of an interested interlocutor with 'regional' experience mapped to other geographical imaginaries, especially those routed through southern Africa. I hope that South Asianists will forgive my trespasses, and thank those, including the four contributors, whose inspired work has helped tame a modest terrain within the vast territories of my ignorance. While I do not wish to implicate them as accessories, I do gratefully acknowledge sustained conversations with Arun Agrawal, Amita Baviskar, Shubhra Gururani, Ousmane Kane, Saba Mahmood, Anand Pandian, Raka Ray, K. Sivaramakrishnan, James C. Scott, Ajay Skaria and especially Lawrence Cohen. Their insights and work have shaped my thinking about alternative modernities within and beyond South Asia.

2. Lefebvre [1974] 1991: 88.

At the time when Lord Hardinge laid the foundation stone of the Hindu University, there was a darbar. There were rajas and maharajas of course, but Pandit Malaviyaji specially invited me also to attend it, and I did so.

I was distressed to see the maharajahs bedecked like women—silk *pyjamas* and silk *achkans*, pearl necklaces round their necks, bracelets on their wrists, pearl and diamond tassels on their turbans and, besides all this, swords with golden hilts hanging from their waist-bands.

I discovered that these were insignia not of their royalty, but of their slavery. I had thought that they must be wearing these badges of impotence of their own free will, but I was told that it was obligatory for these Rajas to wear all their costly jewels at such functions. I also gathered that some of them had a positive dislike for wearing these jewels, and that they never wore them except on occasions like the darbar.

—*M. K. Gandhi*[3]

Recent formulations of modernity and development often fall into the trap of what Foucault, referring to the Enlightenment, termed its 'blackmail'—the compulsion to be either 'for' or 'against' an elaborate historical formation and its radically heterogeneous legacies. Refusing the Faustian bargain, Foucault argued that modernity, which he understood as an attitude and ethos more than a historical epoch, has since its formation struggled with counter-modernity.[4] As one of the editors' opening epigrams suggests,

3. Gandhi [1927/1929] 1993: 230.

4. See Foucault 1997: 310, 312-13. Hall (1988: 164) offers a related helpful formulation of 'regressive modernization' richly elaborated in the context of Britain's Thatcherism. As Hall stresses, 'there is no serious political project in Britain today which is not also about constructing a politics and an image of what *modernity* would be like for our people.' Elsewhere, Hall (1992a: 15) argues: 'Essential to the idea of modernity is the belief that everything is destined to be speeded up, dissolved, displaced, transformed, reshaped. It is the shift—materially and culturally—into this new conception of social life which is the real transition to modernity.' Many analysts have stressed the radical unevenness and heterogeneity of these processes as well as the myriad contradictions they engender. Recently, Roy (2001: 2) has eloquently argued: 'As Indian citizens we subsist on a regular diet of caste massacres and nuclear tests, mosque breakings and fashion shows, church burnings and expanding cell phone networks, bonded labor and the digital revolution, female infanticide

Goethe's geist animates this collection as an injunction: to tarry and to dwell upon histories of the present.[5] Recent attempts to map the contours of 'alternative modernities' beyond the West's sovereign space have provincialized Europe and its privileged position in authorizing a single, unilineal unfolding of Universal History. As several critics have noted, Foucault's own formulation of modernity was foundationally constituted within the borders of the West, an imagined geography that writes the Rest as a disarticulated appendage of Europe's body politics. His analytic of power largely excluded Europe's constitutive outside, occluding the histories and geographies of imperialism that remain critically formative to modernity and its alternatives. The contributors assembled in this volume articulate a counter-position. Their contemporary emphasis on disjuncture and difference further challenges any formulation of a seamless global uniformity—modernity—that eclipses cultural heterogeneity, historical specificity, and geographical differentiation.[6] This book furthers this effort by

---

and the Nasdaq crash, husbands who continue to burn their wives for dowry and our delectable stockpile of Miss Worlds.' Her perspective on the dark side of the Enlightenment project and the recent glow of globalization is well captured in her reflections on the plight of the working poor: 'every night I walk past road gangs of emaciated laborers digging a trench to lay fiber-optic cables to speed up our digital revolution. In the bitter winter cold, they work by the light of a few candles.'

5. The editors quote Goethe's famous passage: *Verweile doch, du bist so schoen,* which they translate as 'Tarry awhile. You are so beautiful.' I detect an echo, whether intentional or not, of Zizek's (1993: 220) *Tarrying with the Negative,* where he subjects 'the Western gaze upon the East' to scrutiny. As I tarried to reflect on the editors' invocation from *Faust,* I noted the semantic resonances among *verweilen* (to linger, to stop, to stay; but also, figuratively, to dwell on) and *verweben,* to interweave.

6. Chakrabarty's (2000: 43) project of 'Provincializing Europe' is *not* a project of cultural relativism, but rather one of elaborating the historical processes through with the 'reason' of Enlightenment rationalism 'was not always self-evident to everyone, [and] has been made to look obvious far beyond the ground where it originated.' In a related yet distinct formulation, West (1999: 57) emphasizes the 'colonial provinciality' of North American cultural formations that melded flourishing democracy with the trans-Atlantic slave trade and naturalized ideologies of racism. For West, the historical product represents the 'ignoble paradox of modernity' (p. 54). See Appadurai (1992) for an influential elaboration of 'disjuncture and difference' in the global

emphasizing the specific practices, performances, and projects to which 'development' and 'modernity' have been harnessed in diverse Indian contexts. Together, the authors effectively counter ethnographic anemia—a trenchant theoretical tendency in recent writings on development, modernity, and globalization that are critically examined in the editors' Introduction—while also attending to the historical sedimentations that shape contemporary cultural politics.[7]

The contributors to this section on the cultural politics of locality carefully attend to *the discursive practices of alternative modernities* in diverse development encounters.[8] In so doing, they echo the editors' and Haraway's recognition that 'Stories are means

---

cultural economy. In the past decade, scholars have articulated a compelling vision of vernacular and alternative modernities in contrast to a singular universal European monolith. Despite differences in emphasis and approach, there remains considerable affinity between those who have elaborated alternative modernities among different historical geographies and geographical imaginaries. For a sense of this burgeoning field, see: for west Africa (Geschiere 1997; Mbembe 2000; Piot 1999); for southern Africa (Comaroff and Comaroff 1997; Ferguson 1998; Worby 1997); for China (Anagnost 1997; Jones 2001; Litzinger 2000; Liu 1999; Rofel 1998); for Latin America (Coronil 1997; Nelson 1999; de la Cadena 2000; Lomnitz 2001; and Whitten *et al.* 1997); for the African diaspora (Diawara 1998; Gilroy 1993; Hall 1992b; Hanchard 2001); and among diasporic and 'immigrant' communities in transnational processes (Chuh and Shimakawa 2001; Kaplan *et al.* 1999; Lowe 1996; Ong 1999). On South Asian diasporas, with particular attention to the cultural politics of nation and difference that animate visions of modernity, see Axel (2001), Brah (1996), Grewal (1996), Kumar (2000), and Prashad (2000). For explicit formulations of 'alternative modernities,' see Appadurai (1991), Comaroff and Comaroff (1993), Gaonkar (2001), Feenberg (1995), Mitchell (2000), and Watts (forthcoming). I point to this range of positions to emphasize that, despite critical affinities, there is no single, shared 'alternative' formulation.

7. For generative explorations of modernity and development in India, see Bose (1997), Bose and Jalal (1999), Ranjit Guha (1997), Ludden (1992) and Thesis Eleven (1994). Chatterjee (1998a: 14) offers an especially cogent and compelling formulation for Indian contexts: 'the various cultural forms of Western modernity were put through a nationalist sieve and only selectively adopted, and then combined with the reconstituted elements of what was claimed to be indigenous tradition.'

8. See Grillo and Stirrat (1997) and Peters (2000) for ethnographic attempts to elaborate these development encounters.

to ways of living,'[9] the contention that 'the lens of storytelling' raises aesthetic, ethical, and political stakes. Like Haraway, the contributors' chapters fuse material and semiotic processes in their own stories. In so doing, they necessarily contest the construction of other stories whose telling remains entrenched in uncritical visions of a stable, universal, and placeless modernity seen to unfold in the shadow of Europe's Enlightenment. In what follows, I engage convergences among the four chapters around three overlapping themes critical to an understanding of regional modernities: visions of temporality and history; geographical imaginaries and translocal linkages; and the integration of political economy and cultural politics. The articulated effect is to move from an implicit understanding of 'Europe and the People without History'[10] to the project of 'Provincializing Europe'[11] where histories, spatialities, and modernities are conceived as emerging through imperial assemblages.[12] As Gilroy provocatively argues, 'thinking of modernity as a region rather than a period'[13] opens up questions of translocal histories radically attentive to the imperial scales *produced* through the entanglements of peoples, places, and cultural practices. Perhaps 'regional modernities' offers an enframing, an alternative storytelling practice, that enables a greater appreciation for the *work* these translocal and transcultural processes perform. At the same time, this analytic foregrounds the contingent terrain on which historical agents ground experiences, and dwell in places animated with storied lives.[14]

9. Haraway 1989: 8.

10. See Wolf 1982.

11. See Chakrabarty 2000.

12. For perspectives that analyse the geographically specific historical sedimentations of capitalist political economy while critiquing a single universal logic of capital and modernity, see Asad (1987), Donham (1999), Hart (forthcoming), Lowe and Lloyd (1997), and Radhakrishnan (2000). See Cooper and Stoler (1997) and Catherine Hall (2000) for excellent elaborations of the cultural politics of difference within imperial formations. Farred (2001) offers a contemporary political vision of this project that seeks to rework these imperial legacies. Lewis and Wigen (1997) offer a sharp critique of the Eurocentric 'metageography' that shapes many prevalent visions of regions.

13. Gilroy 2000: 95.

14. The notion of experience as a ground need not entail a pre-given subject which receives and possesses those experiences (see Das and Kleinman 2001: 5). Similarly, the presence of cultural practices that animate a place need not

The four chapters offer complementary visions that recognize the constitutive role of Indian alterity in European understandings of rule, development, and progress. At the same time, they explore the manifest modalities of power that entangled South Asian and European practices of subjection, articulations of agency, and understandings of moral duty and political right.[15] Chatterjee's critique of normative liberal political theory shares affinities with this project of provincializing Europe, echoing the editors' interruption of a unilineal teleology, the inexorable, universal unfolding of modernization. He challenges us 'to find an adequate conceptual language to describe the non-Western career of the modern state not as a distortion or lack, which is what inevitably happens in a modernisation narrative, but as the history of different modernities shaped by practices and institutions that the universalist claims of Western political theory have failed to encompass.'[16] Cohen answers the challenge with a stunningly brilliant ethnography of embodied knowledge and practices that route through India yet are never incarcerated within its national boundaries.[17] He offers an eloquent ethnography of critical assemblage, excavating the historically and culturally *contingent* articulations of cultural practices that animate alternative modernities that shape the terrain and imaginary of national territory. By querying the prevailing narratives of history and progress about India, his analytic opens a new field of conceptual vision, never foundering in the furrows of modernization's teleology nor the territorial trap of a naturalized nation–space.

---

entail a humanistic definition of place as an abstract space rendered constitutively meaningful through culture. For a critique of an entrenched, unenlivened analytic of space, and its relationship to conceptualizations of place, see Lefebvre (1992) and Massey (1994).

15. Parry's (1998: 11) reflections on research exploring imperial rule in colonial India underscores these entangled formations: 'What struck me when I was immersed in the dusty volumes written by Anglo-Indians and their metropolitan allies was an exorbitantly florid rhetoric replete with boasts about the British as a governing race, and claims to a destiny, sometimes secular and sometimes divine, ordaining them to bring technological progress, the reform of social practices and rational government, in short modernity, to a benighted people.'

16. Chatterjee 1998b: 279.

17. Cohen 1998.

This book's contributors follow Cohen and Chatterjee's crucial moves, offering compelling analyses of alternative histories, spatialities, and the modernities they form. The chapters ground stories of development and modernity in compelling accounts of colonial and postcolonial governmentality, those political technologies of rule that constituted governable subjects by seeking to influence and transform their conduct. This ensemble of practices, procedures, and reproduced rationalities have cultivated conduct, regulated populations, and promoted their welfare—often in the name of a universal discourse of improvement.

If, as the editors argue, development has been a signal index of modernity, then a crucial task becomes to situate development practices in the wider fields of power that have constituted subjects, manufactured regimes of rule, and engendered forms of resistance among those *subjected* to development. As Bourdieu suggests, 'To change the world, one has to change the ways of making the world, that is, the vision of the world and the practical operations by which groups are produced and reproduced.'[18] For this reason, he argues that '[r]egionalist discourse is a *performative discourse* which aims to impose as legitimate a new definition of the frontiers and to get people to know and recognize the *region* that is thus delimited in opposition to the dominant definition.'[19] The strength of this volume emerges from contributors' ethnographically and historically specific stories which *ground* their regional reflections. The moral and political geography their work envisions resonates with Marx's Eleventh Thesis on Feuerbach: 'Philosophers' have only interpreted the world in various ways; the point is to change it.'[20] Rather than asserting an authentic site of autonomous insurrection beyond development, nor conceiving of Indian subjects as docile bodies in the service of European modernity's inexorable unfolding in the colonial periphery, these four chapters emphasize forms of agency that embody the *situated practices* of alternative modernities.

Yet, they also attend carefully to the *historical sedimentations* of colonial regimes of rule, political economic relations, and disciplinary practices that shape the terrain of postcolonial development

18. Bourdieu 1990: 137.
19. Bourdieu 1991: 223.
20. Marx [1845] 1983: 158.

politics. Like the editors, the contributors follow Ferguson's call to 'reconfigure the intellectual field in such a way as to restore global inequality to its status as "problem" without reintroducing the teleologies of and ethnocentrisms of the development metanarrative.'[21] Future alternatives for academic and development projects will emerge out of cultural imaginaries and practices situated in heterogenous and multi-local politics, not a universal monolith of modernity. To encourage alternative practices of development, in Chakrabarty's provincializing project, 'pluralizes the history of power in global modernity.'[22] This move also appreciates the historical sedimentations of cultural practices and political economic relations that have global, regional, and local routes. The four chapters offer illuminating perspectives on the hybrid histories, geographical imaginaries, and spatial practices of development and modernity *routed* through, but not rooted in, India's nation–space.[23]

OTHER TIMES, HYBRID HISTORIES

Ajay Skaria highlights the importance of temporality and historical process in his analysis of the distinctive political rationalities represented in what has become the annual Dangs *darbar* in Gujarat, an institution that emerged out of the colonial encounter yet was selectively assembled from precolonial customs. He foregrounds shifts in the meanings and practices of an enduring institutional form, offering a genealogy of colonial governmentality through the exploration of this particular ritual of ruling.[24] By

21. Ferguson 1998: 249.

22. Chakrabarty 2000: 14.

23. On 'hybrid histories,' see Skaria (1999). On the geographical assemblage of India as a nation-state, see Edney (1997).

24. Foucault's (1979: 20) analytic of governmentality focuses on the 'ensemble formed by the institutions, procedures, analyses and reflections, the calculations and tactics that allow the exercise of [a] very specific albeit complex form of power' constituting governable subjects in nineteenth-century Europe. Others have stressed the imperial contexts productive of these political technologies (see Pels 1997; Scott 1995; Stoler 1995). The project of provincializing Foucault's Europe has often articulated with demonstrating the alternative modernities and counter-modernities engendered in what Pratt (1992) terms the 'contact zone' of imperial encounter. For helpful elaborations

emphasizing the *historicity* of the darbar, Skaria is able to demonstrate the *distinctiveness* of precolonial and early colonial forms of political power.[25] Prior to British rule, the darbar was a site where authority, alliances, and rights were negotiated among Dangi Bhil chiefs and Gaekwadi officials, who staked claims to 'shared sovereignties' in the region. It was also a site suffused with the performance of a distinct Bhil cultural identity symbolically associated with wildness, in contrast to the more sedentary and 'cultivated' plains settlements. The militarized presence of British colonial officials, who conducted punitive expeditions in the 1820s and 1830s against raids by Dangi Bhil chiefs, transformed the relationship between the darbar and political power. Key to this transformation, Skaria argues, was the consolidation of a colonial developmental regime with its regularization of rule, the fixing of levy payments in the hopes of ending raiding parties, and the leasing of forests for teak to build British naval ships. British rule thus harnessed the darbar's rituals for both commercial and administrative purposes. Despite its declining administrative significance

---

of a Foucauldian notion of governmentality in India, see Agrawal (2001), Chatterjee (1998b), and Prakash (1999). Pandian (2001) offers a compelling analysis of sovereign power and 'predatory care' in the culture of rule surrounding imperial hunting rituals in Mughal and British India.

25. While my ignorance of Hindi, Urdu, and Persian makes any assertion of shared etymological roots problematic, I do want to note the sonic resonance of *darbar* (a court, royal gathering, assembly, or audience) and *darkar* (need). The official recognition of 'needs' often involves ritual performances before altars of authority where a regime of ruling acknowledges the legitimacy of subjects' social claims. Like social needs, political authority is enacted in particular sites of assemblage, and the micro-practices that transport its technologies of rule travel widely beyond those contexts of explicitly performative enunciation. This is certainly *not* to suggest that there are social and cultural spaces 'beyond' power, but rather to ask how different kinds of sites, practices, and contexts become articulated together within a political technology of rule. It is also to appreciate the importance of processes through which subjects stake claims to needs; in turn, government officials recognize these as legitimate or inappropriate. Yet, these expectations and evaluations also shape the very enunciation of popular claims to legitimate needs and rights in a robustly recursive relationship. The cultural politics of custom—including those of legitimate social needs—are of course highly contested on multiple fronts and by multiple actors, subaltern and dominant.

in the late nineteenth century, the darbar remained a critical site where British officials and Dangi chiefs subjected to colonial rule enacted identities and authority. Attention to the historicity of a particular institutional form, the darbar, signals the importance of historical processes at work in Gujarat that shaped the regional contours of colonial governmentality.

Skaria contends that the darbar also represented the British affirmation of Dangi primitivism, locating the wild tribes in an Other Time.[26] Because Dangis, in the precolonial period, had cultivated an image of wildness in contrast to their more sedentary neighbors whom they raided, the 'savage slot'[27] they occupied was shaped by the dictates of British rule yet also animated by subaltern agency. Skaria thus adds historical and regional specificity to Visvanathan's assertion that '[m]odernity was a vision of conquest. Every structure of conquest needs a calendar as a liturgy of its power. To acquire one it has to capture or rewrite time.'[28] The particular manifestations of colonial primitivism in Gujarat, however, suggest that this fashioning of temporality reflected Dangi initiative as well as British attitudes toward their imperial responsibility to rule races located in a prior evolutionary stage. Dirks[29] argues that 'for Hegel...caste fails to establish a relationship with history, and India remains plunged in a dreamlike state that necessitates its subjection to Europe.'[30] For British administrators, the hill tribes, like the forested landscape of a

26. Fabian (1983) explores the linkages among temporality and cultural alterity in the anthropological imaginary. Spencer (1995) offers a helpful perspective on anthropological constructions of South Asian culture, differentiating between what he terms evolutionary, positivist, and romantic forms of occidentalism. See Haraway (1989) and Neumann (1997) for thoughtful discussions of 'ambivalent primitivism.' They trace out cultural logics, with particular attention to colonial practices in Africa, that placed primitives in a time before the modern yet in ambivalent relationships to nature, conceiving primitive subjects as both protector and destroyer of environmental resources. Skaria (1999) elaborates resonant patterns in Gujarat.

27. Trouillot 1991.

28. Visvanathan 1997: 20.

29. Dirks 2001: 52.

30. See Dirks (2001) for an elaboration of the cultural politics of caste, and its entanglement with colonial constructions of civil society, cultural identities, and political rights. Bayly (1995) and Robb (1995) offer illuminating perspectives on the connections among race and caste.

nature without history, were not yet cultivated or tamed. Their wild nature required molding into a modernist teleology of progress. A dis-course of *improvement* bound nature and culture, and European administrators sought to manage the welfare of emerging targets of technical interventions: the national population, the environment, and the relationships that linked bodies, collectivities, and landscapes.[31]

Here, debates around the darbar signal the regional resonance of the more widespread salience of Victorian evolutionary discourses throughout the British empire. Frederick Lugard's influential 'Dual Mandate' for British indirect rule drew on colonial experience in India and Africa to argue for the 'sacred trust' of colonial officials who undertook the 'grave responsibility of..."bringing forth" to a higher plane...the backward races.' Europeans were responsible for developing 'the bounties with which nature has so abundantly endowed the tropics' precisely because subject races were 'so pathetically dependent on their guidance.'[32] An imperial civilizing mission legitimated violence in the name of improving, taming, and managing the presumed wildness of both nature and culture in the tropics.[33] A racial rule

31. On imperial discourses of improvement that linked nature and culture, see Dirks (1992), Drayton (2000), Grove (1995), and Prakash (1999). For an elaboration of the imperial traffic between nature and culture with particular attention to race and the politics of difference, see Moore, Pandian, and Kosek (forthcoming). Foucault's formulation of biopower has been especially productive in linking bodies, landscapes, and populations within imperial racial formations and in exploring their contemporary legacies.

32. Lugard (1926: 58); see also his (1922) extremely influential elaboration of the Dual Mandate in British colonial contexts. Significantly, Lugard draws on both Indian and African experiences. He invokes the racialized cultural project of a colonial civilizing mission, at once moral and political, as the 'White man's task' (1926). This formulation shared resonant affinities with Rudyard Kipling's infamous imperialist poem 'The white man's burden,' published in 1899 in London amidst the US–Philippines war. While an analysis of the global circuits of trade, travel, and empire that linked South Asia and Africa are beyond the scope of my chapter, I point readers to several projects that have explored the historical conceptual traffic between these two 'regions,' including taking up the traveling theory that has spanned continents. See, in particular, Ahmed and Kane 2000; Cooper 1994; Crush 1994; Engels and Marks 1994; Moore 1998; Ranger 1992.

33. See Arnold 1996; Dirks 1992.

of colonial difference[34] targeted those whose welfare would be managed on behalf of Europeans and 'natives.' Lugard's civilizing rulers would be custodians of the 'common good' for European empire, for colonial subject races, and thus for a universal invocation of humanity. They would manage nature and culture on behalf of metropole and periphery, effectively doubling his dual mandate. Europeans, representing a singular history as universal, thus invoked both the moral duty and political right to rule colonial subjects understood as racially and culturally different. Part of the colonial project of improvement was tutelage in the time of the European modern and its affiliated practices, beliefs, and understandings.

In India, as elsewhere, distinctively modern modalities of power made colonial subjects into 'conscripts' of Western civilization.[35] Marshalling colonial subjects toward the time of modernity required cultivating the civilized habits of bourgeois metropolitan culture deemed necessary to escape the backwardness of a ahistorical tradition, a cultural alterity beyond the pale of modern reason.[36] Mehta's examination of nineteenth-century British liberal strategies of imperialism incisively excavates the constitutive *exclusions* of liberal modes of rule that sought to govern without the consent of those whose cultural alterity precluded their exercise of universal reason.[37] By placing 'natives' in proximity to an ahistorical nature, British administrators sought to exclude them from political representation as citizens of a modern polity. In the early nineteenth century, when Dangi Bhil raids provoked punitive expeditions by an increasing British administrative presence in Gujarat, a colonial grid of intelligibility strained to contain the cultural politics of

34. Chatterjee 1993.

35. Asad 1992.

36. The historical depths of European 'traditions' could also be marshalled against claims for self-rule in the colonies. Parry (1998: 60) examines Lord Curzon's 1905 address at the Convocation of Calcutta University. He conceived of 'Asiatics' as the legitimate wards of British rule because they lacked the basic attributes required for self-rule; and he criticized their 'moral weakness.' In turn, Curzon grounds an imperial ethics of truth in the deep history of Europe, contrasting it to the shallow performance of guile in India: 'undoubtedly truth took a higher place in the moral codes of the West before it had been similarly honoured in the East, where craftiness and diplomatic wile have always been held in much repute.'

37. Mehta 1999.

wildness. For British officials, the Bhil 'wild tribes' defied colonial reason even as they demanded ruling recognition of masculinist respect. Dangi chiefs in the late eighteenth century enacted claims of being wild or *jangli*, embodying tokens of wildness in the orchestrated rituals of the darbar. By the late 1820s, British administrators attempted to domesticate this wildness: they regulated the payment of fixed levies to discipline the political maneuvers that once animated raiding and the Bhil extraction of payments through the cultural idiom of *giras*, a negotiable, if contested, levy demanded from Gaekwadi villages by Dangi Bhil chiefs. Skaria suggests that when colonial rationality refused to recognize this alternative mode of politics, officials either sought to 'civilize' Bhil wildness or placed it beyond European rationality. In the latter case, 'inscrutability' becomes a means through which cultural identities were denied the 'minimal conditions requisite for political inclusion,' what Mehta terms the 'anthropological minimum'[38] required for liberal political inclusion.[39]

Yet, if these liberal exclusions were widely prevalent throughout colonial India and the British empire, the particular institutional forms they instantiated remained diverse, dynamic, and unstable.[40]

38. Mehta 1999: 68, 52.

39. Sartre's ([1956] 2001: 41) blistering critique of French colonial policy in Algeria criticized the French Republic's maintenance of 'kinglets who derive their power solely from it and who govern on its behalf. In a word, it *fabricates* "natives" by a double movement which separates them from their archaic community by giving them or maintaining in them, *in the solitutude of liberal individualism*, a mentality whose archaism can only be perpetuated in relation to the archaism of the society.' The Algerian 'native,' a product of colonial modernity, is in this cultural logic relegated to a time before the modern. For Sartre, colonialism as a historically specific system fabricated the 'native' as an archaic relic of a time before the Universal History of Europe's Reason, an unfolding of developmental progress. This time warp's logic, the historical product of colonialism, manufactures the archaic as a timeless cultural tradition that proceeds the moment of its own historical inauguration. In this sense, the archaic, as a distinct cultural category, temporally coincides with the time of the modern; yet the former remains represented as an essential feature that pre-exists the 'arrival' of European modernity and its civilizing mission in the colonies.

40. Pels (2000: 83) offers a rigorous exploration of the resonances as well as disparities among 'the imperially marginal ethnographic tradition of Indian aboriginality' and London-based ethnologies. He attends not only to the politics of location that shaped representations of Indian aboriginality in the

Skaria responds to the editors' challenge to attend carefully to
genealogies of power that are geographically and historically specific, where *regions matter* in the formation of sites both spatial
and institutional.[41] His analysis resonates sharply with those who
emphasize the discursive practices of 'ambivalent primitivism,' a
product of multivalent modernities. Despite enduring relations of
power and social inequality, these charged forms of primitivism
emerged from the cracks of the colonial crucible and their postcolonial legacies of race, nation, and cultural difference.[42]

For this reason, the postcolonial darbar cannot be understood
as simply the continuation of colonial primitivism. Rather, Skaria
suggests, since Independence, the darbar affirms the rational rule
of the bureaucratic state, enacting a vision of the national–popular
that hinges on the 'yoking together' of two different times, that
of a naturalized popular primitivism and the triumphalist, historically modern nation-state.[43] Far from reproducing the binaries of
tradition/modernity and nature/history, Skaria's analysis suggest
the ways that culturally and historically specific visions of modernity rely on 'selective traditions.'[44] Moreover, neither the commercial agendas nor administrative optics of colonial rule animated a
unified field of vision.[45] Rather, they unfolded across a 'contact

---

colonial, ethnographic, and ethnological archives but also to critical historical
shifts that scuttle the notion of a single, seamless discursive formation of
imperial alterity.

41. For a contrapuntal construction of alternative modernities in South
Asia that challenges both British and Hindu hegemonic histories and geographies, see Jalal (2000), especially her chapter 'Between Region and Nation.'

42. For perspectives on 'ambivalent primitivism' that haunt the cultural
politics of race, nature, and difference, see Baviskar (1997), Povinelli (1999),
Taussig (1987), and Tsing (1999). Cohen's (1998: 140) brilliant examination of
imperial discourses of memory and body politics in India provides an
insightful analysis of Sir Henry Maine's influential 1866 address in Calcutta:
'Maine worried that memory as imperial pedagogy had rather paradoxically
encouraged a forgetting of the savage and corrupt Indian past.'

43. These themes are also explored at length in Bhabha's (1990) influential
essay 'Dissemination.' Chakrabarty (2000), Srivastava (1998), and Roy (1998)
offer insightful discussions of the multiple temporalities at work in postcolonial
India.

44. Williams 1977: 115.

45. For insightful elaborations of this perspective, see Thomas (1994) and
Cooper and Stoler (1997).

zone' of competing agendas, cultural difference, and radical in-equalities of power.[46] As a result, darbars were also the site of cultural appropriation. Markets attracted bustling commercial activity and drinking subverted colonial desires for decorum. The unintended consequences of this linchpin of colonial rule speak to the competing cultural meanings and practices that converged around a single institutional form. Far from a unified rationality of rule overdetermining the practices of subaltern subjects, the multiplicity of cultural practices surrounding the darbar attest to fissures within colonial governmentality.[47]

Less explored by Skaria is the relationship between spectacles of power, institutional sites that enact and display official imagi-naries of authority, and the everyday practices that reproduce, rework, and challenge those formations. Yet, he implicitly engages recent debates that have questioned rituals of ruling as a privileged site for the production of cultural meanings.[48] The relationship between colonial imaginaries and everyday practice further animates the gendered constructions of authority and identity in Gujarat. The masculinity of the 'wild tribes,' Skaria suggests, opposed the effeminacy of the castes and required a particular form of British masculine discipline to tame. Yet, I wonder how these cultural formations were interwoven with gender and generation in the cultural constitution of authority and rights among Dangi Bhil subjects. How might the gendered practices that worked the landscape, procured livelihoods, and negotiated access to territory and resources rework the meanings of chiefly and colonial authority? And how have they, in turn, informed the gendered constructions of a national popular in postcolonial India?[49] Gandhi's reflections on the imperial society of spectacle that laid the foundations for Hindu University's

46. Pratt 1992.

47. In a similar vein, Ranajit Guha (1997: xv) has criticized both imperialist and nationalist historiography for their reliance upon a 'monistic view of colonial power relations.'

48. See, in particular, the animated debates in *Public Culture* provoked by Mbembe (1992). Anagnost (1997), Comaroff and Comaroff (1993), and Worby (1997) offer helpful discussions of the cultural politics of ritual, particularly in the context of nationalism.

49. Bose 1999; Chatterjee 1993; Cohen 1998; Das 1995; Mankekar 1993; Chatterjee and Jeganathan 2001.

opening darbar, with which I began this chapter, explicitly weaves together gender and nation. The maharajahs' emasculation emerges in their sartorial displays of feminized pyjamas and bejeweled 'badges of impotence.' The rajas, 'bedecked like women,' and with swords hung impotently as ornamental adornments to their colonial costumes, become for Gandhi a sign of having sacrificed their sovereignty to the mimicry of pomp and power. The feminization of the maharajas is not incidental—but rather constitutive—of their loss of sovereign control over India's nation-space.

The gendered inflections of authority also animate the Weberian gloss on Foucault that Skaria highlights in recent analyses of development. He engages perspectives that envision the expansion of bureaucratic state power as a necessary corollary to development's erasure of politics. As Wendy Brown reminds us, Weber's under-standing of the origins of the state had twin pillars: bands of marauding male warriors prefigured organized political institu-tions while patrimonial authority was rooted in the defence of households against these predations.[50] Gendered notions of sexu-ality, territoriality, and violence here converge, Brown argues, in the very formation of liberal notions of political authority and state power. Liberal political theory, never confused about who wears the pyjamas in the family romance, maps political potency to those who ably wield their manly swords. One finds uncanny resonances in Skaria's depiction of the mutual construction of British masculinity, the military disciplining of Dangi Bhil raids against the effeminized castes living on the plains, and the 'wild tribes' savage location in 'nature,' an Other space and time not yet within 'society' and 'history.' The darbars were a critical pre-colonial site where 'shared sovereignties' among Dangi Bhil chiefs and Gaekwadi officials were negotiated and reconfigured. Skaria underscores that what Foucault identifies as the key triad of sovereignty–discipline–government[51] in the working of political technologies needs to be destabilized, historically contextualized, and opened up as an ensemble of investigation.[52]

50. Brown 1995: 187.

51. Foucault 1979: 19.

52. For an illuminating perspective on the cultural politics of sovereignty, see Ong (2000).

REWORKING MODERNITY,
DEMANDING DEVELOPMENT

If Skaria's project is to explore the historicity of both political rationalities and institutional forms, Subir Sinha underscores the historical influences upon recent social movements in the Indian Himalayas, tracing out their connections to previous political activism in the region. Key activists in Chipko, he argues, first gained salient organizing experience in the Sarvodaya movement, strongly influenced by Gandhi's writings on the Constructive Program. Focusing primarily on positions espoused by Sundarlal Bahuguna and Chandi Prasad Bhatt, activists prominent in both the Sarvodaya and Chipko movements, Sinha argues that their politics represent not a wholesale rejection of development and modernity but rather an alternative formulation of these key-words. Activists *demanded* state assistance, development planning, and increased market integration in rural hinterlands. Rather than the 'unilineal project of domination' formulated by the 'death of development thesis', Sinha critiques alternative visions embodied in Sarvodaya and Chipko staked popular claims to development as a postcolonial political entitlement. Bhatt's insistence on development as a birthright of forest dwellers sought to make demands upon state officials to deliver the promises of modernity as a necessary condition for legitimating the construction of a postcolonial nation. Situating social movements within a historicized moral economy in the Himalayas emphasizes the cultural politics of 'custom' and selective reworkings of 'tradition' that staked claims to modernity and development.[53] Here, we find strong resonances with Skaria's chapter. Rather than locating popular movements beyond the state, Sinha follows Timothy Mitchell's assertion that 'Political subjects and their modes of resistance are formed as much *within* the organizational terrain we call the state, rather than in some wholly exterior social space.'[54]

53. See Ramachandra Guha (1997) for an exploration of these themes that emphasizes the 'vocabularies of protest' deployed by environmental movements in India. For a germinal perspective on the cultural politics of 'custom' in British colonial Africa, containing many insights that travel well, see Chanock (1985) and Berry (1992).

54. Mitchell 1991: 93.

As a result, collective struggles for social justice and environmental sustainability in the Himalayas, Sinha suggests, are best seen not as anti-state, or beyond development, but rather as alternative reworkings[55] of modernity.[56]

Echoing Skaria's concerns with temporality, Sinha views post-Independence development planning as a project that sought to bring the 'traditional' sectors of the Indian economy into the time and rationality of 'the modern.' The state, in this model, was to orchestrate capitalist forestry, balancing the strategies of accumulation and legitimation in order to maintain popular support. Planning is here seen as itself a site of political struggle where popular demands sought to shape, rather than totally reject, state interventions in rural livelihoods. Instead of locating planning as a technocratic intervention beyond the fray of politics, Sinha insists on a more malleable understanding of the planning process, emphasizing its vulnerability to popular demands that challenge state legitimacy. Cultural understandings of *rights* have been key to the political valences of planning and popular struggles to inform state projects in the Himalayas. Far from a timeless 'tradition,' however, a historicized politics of custom fused precolonial livelihood strategies, Gandhian notions of social justice and self-rule, and Nehruvian socialist ideology to fashion alternative imaginaries of development.[57]

Prakash[58] argues that Gandhi's critique of British rule relied upon a 'non-modern' cultural alternative that refused to be incarcerated

55. Cf. Pred and Watts 1992.

56. Li (1999) and Tsing (1999) provide ethnographically and historically nuanced explorations of the cultural politics of development 'demands' in Indonesia. They situate these struggles within contemporary imaginaries of nation and modernity. Baviskar (1995), Sundar (1997: 251–3), Gupta (1998), and Sivaramakrishnan (2000) offer ethnographically grounded analyses of the contentious cultural politics of development in India.

57. In what follows, I elaborate Gandhian themes rather than Nehruvian notions. For a sense of the contrapuntal tendencies in Nehru's vision of Indian modernity, see Brecher (1959: 235). Nehru invokes the 'old Hindu idea that if there is any divine essence in the world every individual possesses a bit of it…and he can develop it.' He elaborates notions of personal and societal improvement, yet finds difficulty in reconciling 'moral and spiritual standards' with 'modern life.'

58. Prakash 1995: 6–7.

in a 'pre-modern' temporality.[59] Gandhi's vision of a non-modern civilization, Prakash notes, drew upon Thoreau, Ruskin, and Tolstoy, whom Gandhi looked upon 'as one of my teachers.'[60] Ruskin's *Unto This Last* 'captured me and made me transform my life,' Gandhi declared.[61] Both conscript and critic, Gandhi was an active bricoleur who imaginatively practised alternative possibilities. His political strategy and ethical commitments relied on constructing an alternative modernity that forged a global geographical imaginary—a formation of imperial routes, radically insisting that 'the West' and 'the East' share an entangled global history. Yet, by also recognizing distinct regional histories, this vision was especially attentive to cultural difference.[62] Assertions of alternative histories challenged a universal History; claims to cultural difference mingled with articulations of transcultural enlightenment. Both arguments countered the political exclusions and modernist teleologies of liberal rule. Mehta suggests that Gandhi's political tactics sought to dislodge liberal notions of 'the political conditionalities of historical progress, writ large in terms of civilizational typologies. When Gandhi speaks of progress it is invariably as an ethical relationship that an individual or a community has with itself, with others, and with its deities.'[63] As Chakrabarty suggests in reference to Gandhi, 'Freedom from the past could... mean that the past could be treated as though it were a pool of resources, a standing reserve, on which the subject of political modernity could draw as needed in the struggle for social justice. Gandhi's attitude to the scriptures contained this sense of freedom.'[64] His challenge to liberal visions

59. Chakrabarty (2000: 39) similarly stresses the 'non-modern' idiom of alternative modernity 'that allowed Indians to fabricate a sense of community and to retrieve for themselves a subject position from which to address the British.' Gandhi figures prominently in highlighting 'the political importance of this cultural move.'

60. Gandhi 1991: 75.

61. Quoted in Arnold 2001: 54.

62. See Ramaswamy (2000) for an excellent discussion of Tamil spatial fables and the geographical imaginaries they have influenced. Chatterjee (1997) offers a representation of 'our modernity' in West Bengal. These positions emphasize competing configurations of nation, region, and modernity within and beyond India.

63. Mehta 1999: 81.

64. Chakrabarty 2000: 246.

of politics, freedom, and sovereignty entailed an assault on Eurocentric teleologies of 'progress,' a discourse of *universal* improvement that mistook Europe's historical hubris for a global civilizational history.

Gandhian politics, in this sense, attempted to disarticulate political and ethical notions of progress from the civilizing mission of liberal rule and the horizon of modernity those regimes inaugurated. Dirks argues that Gandhi spoke 'for many in his attempt to fashion a middle ground between revivalist traditionalism and reformist modernism,'[65] suggesting the multiple temporalities animating Gandhi's political vision. Young echoes this insight: 'Gandhi's philosophy was based on a critique of modernity and technology, but *satyagraha*, his form of resistance to colonial power was, as he himself acknowledged, dependent for its success on free access to communication around the world by means of media technology and it was this which enabled him to exert political pressure simultaneously at local and international levels. In this respect, his counter-modernity proved to be the most modern of all those of anti-colonial activists.'[66] Gandhi's politics and ethics entangled imperial geographies in his experiments with regimes of historical truth. He writes of a moment of danger, but also of recognition, tarrying on a 'desolate veld' in South Africa in 1913 during a non-violent march where he led miners to protest the discriminatory laws subjecting 'Asian' bodies and populations to a racialized regime of ruling.[67] On this march across a conjunctural terrain of history, he realizes that many colonial officials 'knew that not only had arrest no terrors for us but on the other hand we hailed it as the gateway of liberty. They, therefore, allowed us all legitimate freedom and thankfully sought our aid in conveniently and expeditiously effecting arrests.'[68]

65. Dirks 2001: 235.
66. Young 2001: 334.
67. Gandhi 1956: 93.
68. While I cannot here explore the linkages, I want to signal the articulations of power, freedom, and liberalism that circuit through Gandhi's anti-colonial politics, Mehta's (1999) historical study of British imperial discourse, and Rose's (1999) influential elaboration of governmentality and modern power in late liberalism. Part of Gandhi's brilliance was to appreciate these connections and rearticulate them through the prism of a counter-modernity of social justice, which, of course, contained its own exclusions

Non-sovereign subjects were nonetheless effective agents of history, laboring in conditions not of their choosing.

Gandhi's non-violent vision of satyagraha, which emerged from his experiences in South Africa, wove together the force of truth, love, and the ethics of cultivating the ensouled body through acts of self-suffering. The spinning-wheel that produced *khadi* was also a *charkha* of cultivation—a technology of self as well as a rejection of industrial manufacturing technologies and the forms of hegemony they perpetuated. Thus, *swaraj* necessarily bound self-rule to the freedom of embodied practice and national autonomy. To assert this sovereignty of self, community, and nation required refusing imperial imperatives. Gandhi's 'plea for the spinning-wheel' echoed Ruskin, simultaneously making a 'plea for recognizing the dignity of labor.'[69] The ethics of this subject spun a politics of work, self-sufficiency, and anti-colonial nationalism out of Gandhi's radical refusal of Enlightenment blackmail. His experience with labor politics, legal rulings, and assaults on civil liberties in South Africa informed his vision of social justice in South Asia. Translocal routes gave traction to an anti-colonial politics that torched Indian's colonial shame as well as their foreign-manufactured silk pyjamas.[70]

Drawing from related yet distinct experiences of colonial subjection on two continents, Gandhi's anti-imperial new clothes adorned an emergent body politic that articulated resistance to colonial rule as a moral duty of 'non-cooperation with evil.'[71] He underscored that 'on the political field the struggle on behalf of the people mostly consists in opposing error in the shape of unjust laws,' and insisted that satyagraha 'is civil in the sense that it is not criminal.'[72] Gandhi's ethical and political good sense would challenge the illegitimate state's common sense definition of law. In this sense, he anticipated Gramsci's reflections, penned in an Italian prison where he was unjustly incarcerated several decades

---

perpetuated in the ethics of a self, community, and nation. Jalal (2000), among others, offers an illuminating discussion of the often contentious cultural politics of exclusion surrounding interpretations of satyagraha, with particular attention to invocations of Islamic identities.

69. Gandhi quoted in Arnold 2001: 127.

70. 'In burning my foreign clothes,' Gandhi told Tagore, 'I burn my shame' (Gandhi quoted in Arnold 2001: 129).

71. Ibid.: 131.

72. Gandhi 1951: 6–7.

later: '"popular beliefs" and similar ideas are themselves material forces'[73] for social transformation. Like Gandhi, Gramsci elaborated a politics that positioned itself on a contested terrain while recognizing the critical 'front of cultural struggle, and constructed the doctrine of hegemony as a complement to the theory of the State-as-force.'[74] Arguably, Gandhian tactics succeeded in South Africa insofar as they outed the illiberal excesses of *force* that subjected Asians to an unjust racialized regime of rule. Effective resistance to colonial rule in South Africa and India, despite its differences, hinged critically on working through, rather than outside, modes of imperial *power*. This project included exposing illiberal and unjust uses of force, turning liberalism against its own ruling pretensions. In short, Gandhi's tactical invocation of 'nonmodern' cultural practices emerged through the historically and geographically specific articulations of alternative modernities.[75]

73. Gramsci 1971: 165.

74. Ibid.: 56.

75. See also Visvanathan's (1997: 212–44) 'Reinventing Gandhi' for a complementary perspective. Prakash (1999) offers a helpful reading of the relations among Gandhian and Nehruvian visions of Indian community and polity and their alternative formulations of temporality and modernity. Significantly, both Prakash (1999: 125) and Nandy (1995: 181–5) ground Gandhi's tactical maneuvers in body politics that highlight the situated practices *embodying* alternative modernities. Prakash links these explicitly to a Foucauldian analytic of biopower and governmentality. Nandy (1995: 183) sees in Gandhi's vegetarianism 'a site for the location of alternative worldviews' and a dialogue with 'the other West of occult philosophy, theosophy, various versions of socialism, and anti-vivisectionism.' Crucially, Gandhi's experiences beyond the nation-space of India—formatively in South Africa—shaped his understanding of the violence of racism and medical technologies that disciplined populations in spatially segregated communities in part through the invocation of public hygiene and the policing of sanitation. Arguably, Gandhi's critique of colonial body politics—its attempt to improve and police bodies, populations, and nations—emerged translocally through the imperial routes he traveled. The grounding of Gandhian ethics and politics through the body thus emerges through the *production* of a global scale that spans continents and moves through regional histories. These scales—body and global—are relationally produced, not structurally fixed. Das (1995: 190) brings up the gendered practices of community, identity, and embodiment that have marked bodies with the memories of suffering in post-Partition India. She argues that 'the body is the surface on which the political programmes of both the state and industrial capital are inscribed.'

In India, romanticized visions that essentialize a timeless cultural tradition among hill people whose harmony with 'nature' is ruptured with the advent of capitalism and colonialism in the region may unintentionally locate postcolonial subjects in a premodern temporality, the pristine time of use-values unsullied by the commoditizing imperative of modern markets. The same move, however, as Skaria cautions against in a slightly different context, may also locate subalterns in an Other Time, undermining the historical recognition of 'modern' rights within the nation-state.[76] Sinha counters this tendency by insisting that hill peoples inhabit a modern temporality *and* craft their agency within a political space that is not 'beyond' development, modernity, or the state. Sarvodaya activists could thus argue for greater marketing opportunities for cooperatives to be spearheaded by state incentives as well as micro-dams for irrigation projects. Their arguments hinged not on locating a pristine 'nature' beyond the reach of the market and production politics but rather on how 'nature' was to be developed, who was to control those projects, and how benefits were to be distributed. Social movements also had to contend with the historical legacies of colonial forestry policies that had greatly curtailed access to critical productive resources by criminalizing the customary uses of forest products.[77] The complex traffic between 'culture' and 'nature' in the Himalayas weaves itself through a history interlaced with the imperatives of capitalist accumulation, hill peoples' livelihood strategies, and popular challenges to state legitimacy.[78] As Stuart Hall argues, 'there is no whole, authentic, autonomous 'popular culture' which lies outside the field of force of the relations of cultural power and domination.'[79] Environmental imaginaries, like popular

76. See Willems-Braun (1997) for an insightful exploration of these themes in the context of First Nation politics, commercial forestry, and environmentalism in British Columbia, Canada.

77. Guha 1989; Gururani 2000.

78. See Rangan 2000. On the regional differences that have shaped the landscape of postcolonial forestry initiatives, including those of joint management, compare Agrawal (2001), Gururani (n.d.), Sivaramakrishnan (1998), and Sundar (2000).

79. Hall's 1981: 232. perspective shares considerable affinity with Foucault's (1978: 95) insistence that 'resistance is never in a position of exteriority in relation to power.'

culture, must also negotiate the forcefields of history, culture, and power.

Sinha's analysis of social movements in the Himalayas thus locates subaltern agency neither in an authentic insurrectionary space beyond state power, nor a radically disjunctive time before modernity, nor a teleological moment after development. Rather than a post-development imaginary, Sinha suggests, Sarvodaya and Chipko represent alternative reworkings of modernity, state power, and development understood as a political entitlement required for the legitimation of Indian nationalism.[80] A key question remains the kinds of rights-bearing subjects who stake these claims and their relationship to the unstable hyphen joining nation and state. Sinha argues that colonial forestry regulations epitomized in the 1927 Forest Act represented a significant shift from community to individual rights. Yet, there is little sense of how socio-economic differentiation within collective movements informed the political struggles of Sarvodaya or Chipko. On the one hand is the issue of how to conceive of 'social movements' as historical agents, the extent to which their participants can be seen to share a single interest and intentionality. On the other hand is the cultural politics of community: how understandings of shared rights, entitlements, and identity are mapped onto claims to territory and resources; how idioms of 'tradition' demarcate boundaries of group inclusion and exclusion; and how social relations of cooperation, negotiation, and conflict rework those boundaries. In short, how might one think of community as *process*, with shifting sedimentations, rather than as an assumed social and territorial entity.

Struggles for authority, legitimacy, and accountability *within* social movements and communities may also reveal salient features of development and modernity, including a range of understandings of state power. If social movements are composed of differentiated historical agents whose interests are shaped by political struggle, 'the state' can also be opened up, seen to be less a single entity with structurally determined interests and more an ensemble

80. For an eloquent formulation of 'post-development' imaginaries, see Escobar (1992). Rahnema and Bawtree (1997) offer their perspective on the emergence of a post-development 'field' of sorts. The editors of this volume provide a critical elaboration of these positions.

of practices, institutions, and policies with powerful discursive and material effects. Within a single state apparatus, then, the practices of 'planning,' 'administration,' accumulation, and regulation may thus contradict or compete with one other, articulating in uneven ways with transnational development initiatives. The relative instability of this configuration in particular historical moments may increase the 'vulnerability' to social movements' claims for 'legitimacy' that Sinha underscores. Insofar as popular demands for the state delivery of 'development' reinscribe the sovereignty of a unified Indian nation-state, however, do they also cut against the goals of social movements struggling for greater control over livelihoods and landscapes?

If the relationship between key activists and members of a social movement differentiated by gender, class, generation, and other differences remains a question, so too does the relationship between the writing of two prominent leaders and the particular forms of activism participants within movements enacted. Here, what is the relationship between these textual representations of authority and entitlement and the livelihood struggles of women and men in the Himalayas? Sinha takes us in the direction of problematizing planning, seeing it as a site vulnerable to demands of accountability animating the project of state legitimation, here conceived as a historically contingent process. Yet, if planning is seen as both a complex assemblage of labor processes as well as discursive practices, what might more ethnographic and historical attention to the *practices* of planning reveal? In turn, this query underscores the translocal linkages that shape claims for social justice and environmental sustainability in the region. These same linkages also enabled contractors to hire migrant laborers to undercut local labor cooperatives. The 'local,' in Sinha's analysis, is shot through with translocal connections that shape its politics, configurations of authority, and relations to state power.

CASTE-ING NETS, NATIONALIST TIDES

Ajantha Subramanian's exploration of the cultural politics of modernization in Kanyakumari foregrounds articulations of a localized cultural identity in relation to class, caste, and the shifting terrain of nationalist politics. Rather than seeing development as a uniform monolith inscribing docile bodies, she stresses how it has been reworked in regionally distinct forms through the competing crucibles of Dravidianism, Hindu nationalism, and environmentalism. This ethnographic perspective underscores Escobar's call for greater attention to how 'development operates both as an arena of cultural contestation and identity construction.'[81] A great strength of Subramanian's exploration of 'Mukkuvar Modernity' is to combine an analysis of the cultural construction of multiple identities and interests, tracing their convergence and contestations through historically shifting alliances, with attention to the nested relations among locality, region, nation, and the global. Rather than conceiving of these notions as fixed scales or definitively defined boundaries, she demonstrates how geographical imaginaries animate the cultural politics of modernity.

Since state policy in Tamil Nadu constructed a category of 'active fisherman' as a target of development, Subramanian argues that fisherpeoples experienced modernization through the idiom of caste. Far from a vision of caste as timeless cultural essence, she demonstrates how political favoritism, the support of Catholic clergy, and the concentration of mechanized fishing crafts in a single village effectively carved out a hierarchy of difference within a single caste. 'Modern' Mukkuvars, she argues, embraced technological 'progress' in the fishing industry as a 'means to caste and religious minority empowerment.' The cultural politics of caste thus defied any facile opposition of 'tradition' and 'modernity' in a uniform development discourse. In turn, the lived experience of Mukkavar modernity became informed by electoral politics, shifting class alliances, union coalitions, and the appeal of Dravidian articulations of Tamil nationalism emerging in the late 1960s. The salience of these complex historical layerings of caste, class, and nationalism help explain why, by the 1990s, middle-class Mukkuvars from Colachel, a village that greatly benefited from the state mechanization of the fisheries industry that began in the late 1950s, embraced Hindu nationalist rhetoric. Here, a localized construction of community interest among trawler owners in Colachel invoked Hindu nationalism as a means to criticize the Catholic clergy, from whom they felt increasingly alienated, and artisanal fishers, whose militant union politics had torched boats and fomented confrontations at sea.

81. Escobar 1995: 15.

While Subramanian stresses the highly localized articulations of Mukkavar middle-class identity in Colachel, she explicitly counters a vision of the 'local' as a cultural site hermetically-sealed from the influences of a global political economy. Liberalization of the Indian economy enabled the rise of export-oriented fishing as well as joint ventures between Indian-owned companies and a foreign industrial fleet capable of deep-sea fishing. This shift in the livelihoods of Kanyakumari's fisherpeople's integration into global capitalism also expanded the political vision of the National Fishworkers Forum, the unions' umbrella body sharply critical of trawler fishing. Here, populist critiques of capital-intensive development strategies benefited from the support of Catholic clergy advocating the cultural rights of the poor, as well as anti-imperial sentiments that resonated with the claims of Hindu cultural nationalism. The politicization of 'culture' as a shared affinity of Hindu nationalism and pro-nativist artisanal fishers in Kanyakumari enabled alliances that cut across caste and religion. New nets were cast amidst the shifting tides of nationalism. In the late twentieth century, cultural politics reworked what Gandhi's anti-colonial tactics of non-cooperation had interwoven with khadi spun on the anti-industrial artisan's icon, the charkha. Competing constructions of community, identity, and interest emerged out of historical struggle, cobbling together relatively durable, yet shifting, political coalitions.

Bricoleurs fashioned their coalitions through political fabric that articulated richly textured patterns of translocal, transcultural, and relational routes converging on the shores of Kanyakumari. As Ramaswamy suggests, Kanyakumari's geographical location as the land's end of the Indian peninsula figures prominently in 'spatial fabulations' of an imagined Tamil homeland of Lemuria.[82] Historical geographies entangle with fabulist geographical imaginaries of cultural nationalism that span a sea of stories. Much like Rushdie's protagonist, Haroun, I am a visitor unfamiliar with these imaginative and historical landscapes, who asks for forgiveness because 'I'm going to need a little help with the geography.'[83] Fortunately, Subramanian provides that critical cartography, emphasizing a politics of regional contingency. She convincingly

82. Ramaswamy 2000.
83. Rushdie 1990: 79.

demonstrates how modernization and development shape these cultural struggles yet do not overdetermine them. Much like van der Veer's influential analysis of 'religious nationalism,'[84] she asks how differing practices of religiosity and cultural identity become articulated in the 'new discursive space of nationalism.'[85]

Rather than assuming historical continuity or spatial uniformity, her perspective conceives culture as a site of contestation. A finely-differentiated array of historical actors clash and cooperate, producing both social conflict and cultural identities. Even within competing groups, internal tensions caution against assuming a monolithic understanding of a single social agent with a uniform intentionality. Catholic clergy, alarmed by the Communist Party's success in neighboring Kerala, supported the Congress Party in the late 1950s and backed the mechanization of the fishing sector. In a later historical moment, however, members of the same Church also invoked liberation theology, arguing for social and economic justice in the age of market liberalization. They forged alliances with nativists, anti-imperialists, and Hindu cultural nationalists. How the fragments of an Indian nation would be stitched together, and the cultural identities that formation would legitimize, remain key to understanding development politics in Kanyakumari and elsewhere. Bengali writer Mahasweta Devi's imaginary map of India[86] offers a resonant chord. A character ponders the wonders of Blueprint Development in Pirtha, a place of promised projects in an area where 'the tribals know nothing, everything about them is backward, most barbaric.' Devi's character Puran elaborates: 'In the Pirtha *package*, you get a *sample of tribal India*. Incredible.' Subramanian suggests that alternative modernities emerge through contentious cultural struggles over the valences of authenticity and their deployment in relation to discourses of both tradition and planned development.

Struggles over the 'artisanal' as a sign of authentic indigenousness suggest affinities with Skaria's exploration of 'primitivism' and the ambivalence of Sarvodaya activists to modernization through

---

84. van der Veer 1994: xiv.

85. See Aravamudan (2001) and Viswanathan (1998) for insightful discussions of the articulation of religion, modernity, and communities of faith in South Asia and within its relational histories of people and place.

86. Devi 1995: 171.

planning, which Sinha sees as an orchestrated effort to bring the primitive into modern temporality. In each of these cases, attempts to locate subjects in a temporality radically disjunctive from the modern relied also on depictions of their relationship to an ahistorical 'nature.' The 'wild tribes' of Gujarat lived in and of nature, in a British colonial imaginary, dwelling neither in the time of the modern nor in the reach of civilized society. Kipling's poem, 'The white man's burden,' imposed a masculinist and racialized duty on imperialists to 'serve your captive's need,' subjecting a civilizing mission on 'fluttering folk and wild' who were 'half devil and half child.'[87] Romanticized visions of Himalayan forest dwellers living in harmony with nature until the corrupting arrival of capitalism and colonialism similarly map an essentialized cultural identity onto a nature without history. Significantly, in these enduring visions being criticized, modernity arrives from the outside to a culture without history, a locality where timeless tradition unfolds in harmony with nature.[88] The authors' critical reworking of this formulation insists that nature's history become viewed as a crucial component of the cultural politics of modernity.[89]

GOVERNMENTALIZING NGOS, ENTREPRENEURIAL INITIATIVES

Sangeeta Luthra's 'Educating Entrepreneurs' shifts the interrogation of modernity, offering an institutional ethnography at the interface of so-called grassroots NGOs (non-governmental organizations) and *mahila mandals,* or women's circles, in New Delhi. She provides a nuanced portrait that opens up the black box of specific NGOs, adding faces and voices to an entity far too often explained away in development accounts by reference to their organizational structure.[90] Like Subramanian's attention to class differentiation, Luthra explores how these are refracted within NGOs' internal hierarchies, and how they shape visions of

87. See Kipling [1899] 1941: 136–7.
88. See Asad (1987) for an insightful critique of this position.
89. Cf. Coronil 1997.
90. For exceptions to this tendency, see Bornstein (2001) and Ray's (1999) excellent formulation of the political fields in which women's movements have been articulated in India.

entrepreneurial rationality, industriousness, and the cultural construction of risk. She does so by focusing on contemporary microenterprise initiatives aimed at women, strongly influenced by—yet distinct from—World Bank models. The work of Action India and similar NGOs is contrasted with SEWA, the Self-Employed Women's Association, influential enough in national and international arenas to inform policy of the International Labor Organization. Luthra seeks to map this heterogeneity of development practices that persist despite the hegemony of privatization and 'market fundamentalism.'

Income generating projects have tended to follow a pattern of 'blueprint development,'[91] using assumed notions of entrepreneurial incentive and commoditization to inculcate gendered dispositions toward generating profits. The experience of a women's grain cooperative, whose members feared risking money loaned to it by the NGO Action India, suggest an astute resistance to market capture that requires capital-intensive investments from poor women. Perceptions of risk emanated not from a backward economic rationality that was not-yet-modern in its market orientation, but rather from the disenfranchized class experiences of women whose economic security nets were severely strained. If the middle-class NGO workers tended to essentialize targeted lower class women 'clients' as anti-modern in their economic rationality, they also reproduced class distinctions within an NGO's internal hierarchy. In one program, while higher echelon NGO staff enjoyed secure salaries, non-formal teachers were asked to work in a fee-for-service model, a plan that generated considerable hostility. This hyper-commoditization of education, disciplining teachers through competetive market incentives, violated norms of social trust and a moral economy that differentiated among different modalities of wealth, cultural capital, and exchange.

Opposition to income generating projects in other instances underscores the cultural construction of wealth, vividly illustrated by Luthra's tale of Devi, a woman who feared the impact of entrepreneurial imperatives on her herbal medicinal 'craft.' A major concern was that an economistic logic focused on profit would eclipse alternative valuations of her specialized knowledge and the potency of her prepared medicinal herbs. Devi's concern, like

91. Roe 1991.

aspects of Gandhi's anti-imperial position in an earlier moment, saw the non-artisanal production process as a *devalorization* of the specialized knowledge associated with preparing ayurvedic and herbal medicines. For Devi, entrepreneurial initiatives threatened to devalue the medicine's potency (*shakti*), reducing it solely to an instrument of earnings (*kamai*). Neo-Smithian models that emphasize market exchange as a motor of economic development are notoriously ill-equipped to handle the 'cultural topographies of wealth'[92] that morally compromise particular transactions and hence counter a 'pure economic' system of universal commodity exchange. While market fundamentalism focuses on exchange, neglecting the social relations of production, SEWA's initiatives highlight production politics, arguing that the key to women's empowerment is in their gaining greater control over their working conditions. Rather than subordinating a gendered labor process to neo-liberalism's market imperatives, SEWA has rallied around improved working conditions as a political right reliant upon changing social relations.

One of SEWA's strategies has been to reveal the class and gender inflections woven into the very definitions of 'work' and 'labor,' showing their cultural construction. Denaturalizing these categories may open them up to being refashioned in ways that increase women's control over their livelihood practices. Despite being situated in several relations of subalternity, these women may wear the pyjamas while at the same time turning swords into gendered plowshares. While presumably refusing Gandhi's gendering of anti-imperial agency embodied in the masculine nobility of maharajas, the mahila mandals—collective women's groups in slum communities—have fused visions of feminism and Freireian conscientization, articulating an explicit agenda of 'empowerment.' A critical insight across these cases remains how NGOs, in seeking to discipline the conduct and rationality of targeted subjects of development, might better be understood within the context of *governmentality*.[93] To place the 'N' in NGOs under scrutiny is also to ask how specific projects and programs serve particular

92. Ferguson 1992.
93. For a helpful elaboration of governmentality along these lines, and which attends specifically to entrepreneurial practices in the context of neo-liberalism, see Rose (1999).

political interests. Rather than conceiving of those interests as objectively given, adhering in fixed locations of subjects who share a single structural relationship to state or capital, Luthra queries the limits of both the state and economism. She also fruitfully elaborates the 'situated knowledges'[94] of women differentially placed in unequal relations of class, caste, education, and cosmopolitan mobility.

Despite market fundamentalism, embodied in the missionary zealotry of neo-liberalism's faith in the miracle of the market, she reveals discrepant practices and resistant reworkings that shape the gendered landscape of 'development' and 'empowerment' in New Delhi. Liberal feminism, with its emphasis on individual liberties and which leaves many assumptions of bourgeois social theory intact, implies a radically different rights-bearing subject than the collective historical agent of the empowerment perspective she charts.[95] Yet, these differing understandings of entitlement would not, I presume, map so easily onto two separate spheres of individual and collective interest. The contradictory dynamics of the interpretive struggles Luthra traces out accord with Nancy Fraser's assertion that oppositional political understandings of 'needs' often crystallize emergent social identities within a constructed community of interest.[96] The stakes in these interpretive struggles are not solely symbolic, but rather have profound implications for the livelihood strategies and everyday practices of social agents.

Arundhati Roy's eloquent critique of the pursuit of national 'development' in the Narmada valley depicts big dams as 'weapons of mass destruction,' 'weapons governments use to control their own people.'[97] In the crucible of development's cultural politics, 'Power is fortified not just by what it destroys, but also by what it creates.' She weaves a Foucauldian thread into a more Marxian populism. Alvares' contentiously characterizes Gandhi's 1909 *Hind Swaraj* as an 'epochal anti-development work.'[98] In it, Gandhi critiques technologies perpetuated in the name of Western

94. Haraway 1989: 183–202.
95. See Mahmood (2001) for a trenchant critique of these tendencies to champion a liberal secular subject within a range of feminist positions often depicted as radical.
96. Fraser 1989.
97. Roy 1999: 80.
98. Alvares 1992: 131.

progress that come 'tarred with the brush of violence' because he has 'seen the wreckage that lies at the end of this road.'[99] Here, Gandhi's specifically Indian vision of alternative modernity may unintentionally echo Marx's travel advisory for those pursuing capitalist modernity's promised telos: 'the road to hell is paved with good intentions.'[100]

The Mahatma's non-violent ethics sought to turn even the most vicious and racist imperial ambitions to alliance in a quest for global peace and justice. In 1938, he argued that 'The Jews of Germany can offer *satyagraha* under infinitely better auspices than the Indians of South Africa.' Yet, his universal humanist aspirations encountered the brutal crucible of historical contingency forged in the ovens of Germany's genocidal modernity and exclusionary nationalism. Gandhi urged a path of non-violent resistance: 'If I were a Jew and were born in Germany and earned my livelihood there, I would claim Germany as my home even as the tallest gentile German might, and challenge him to shoot me or cast me in the dungeon.'[101] Addressing a letter to his 'Good Friend' Adolf Hitler in July of 1939, Gandhi tells his fellow-vegetarian that 'you are the one person in the world who can prevent a war which may reduce humanity to the savage state.' Gandhi signs his missive, 'Your Sincere Friend,' and relates other friends' urging to write to Hitler 'for the sake of humanity.'[102] Recall that the modernity Hitler envisioned from his Landsberg prison term tarried on Goethe's disgust at the prospect of marriage between Christians and Jews, whose beauty neither German reflected upon. In *Mein Kampf*, Goethe's 'voice of the blood and of reason' countered those laws Hitler proclaimed unjust, representing instead a national spirit that 'instinctively saw in the Jew a foreign element' excluded from a common humanity.[103]

99. Gandhi quoted in Alvares 1992: 131.

100. Marx [1867] 1990: 298.

101. M. K. Gandhi quoted in Mehta 1976: 166.

102. M. K. Gandhi, 23 July 1939, letter to Adolf Hitler; reproduced in Ruhe 2001: 151.

103. Hitler [1925] 1943: 312. The Holocaust, as Arendt ([1951] 1968) and Bauman (1989) have famously argued, was not an aberrant offshoot of modern power, but rather constitutive of modernity. Their insights are among many that alert us to the racialized forms of violence that underwrote the so-called 'civilizing process.'

One of the constitutive exclusions that liberal regimes of power produce is the ruling project of seeking to foreclose the articulation of radically conflicting visions of modernity—Gandhian, Marxian, or otherwise—that rework development practices and their discursive effects. Roy and Luthra's critique of liberal politics that claims to speak for the 'common good' here join Mehta's genealogy of the constitutive exclusions of liberal discourses in nineteenth century India. Each chapter charts the imperial legacies of forms of power that have been productive of identities, regimes of ruling, and what Foucault terms a 'plurality of resistances, each of them a special case... by definition, they can only exist in the strategic field of power relations.'[104] Foucault's generative insight, the spirit of which animates several contributions to this volume, emphasizes a *relational* understanding of power that does not romanticize resistance as an authentic insurrectionary site of originary insurgency, a 'single locus of great Refusal.'[105] My assertion is not that Skaria, Sinha, Subramanian, and Luthra are (or should become) Foucauldians, but rather to recognize an affinity among their common concerns and collective good sense. They share an emphasis on how relational forms of power, resistance, and identity have become constitutive of India's alternative modernities within affiliated, yet distinct, development politics.[106] Moreover, they make tangible Chambers' assertion that 'Rendering someone else's modernity problematic, plural and porous is also to render one's own modernity less secure.'[107] In their collective ethos, the chapters provincialize Foucault as well as Europe.

ARTICULATING ASSEMBLAGES, RELATIONAL ROUTES

By foregrounding the heterogeneity of practices that shape, reproduce, and rework formations of development and modernity in India, these four essays offer insights that extend beyond the specific

104. Foucault 1978: 96.

105. Ibid.: 95–6.

106. For elaborations of the relational forms of subalternity that figure prominently in South Asian articulations of nation and alternative modernities, see Visweswaran (1996). For an ethnographically-grounded attempt to grapple with the cross-cutting fields of power and resistance in subaltern struggles in a particular southern African locality, see Moore (1998).

107. Chambers 2001: 2.

contexts they explore. First and foremost, the authors refuse a predominant tendency in recent writings on globalization to map the economic onto the 'global' and the cultural onto the 'local.' Regional modernities and critical localities are thus conceived as having necessarily relational histories. Places, as Doreen Massey has powerfully argued, are fruitfully conceived as nodal points of connection, linkage, and process rather than as 'introverted'[108] sites hermetically sealed from external influences. 'If regions are the product of historically contingent, multi-dimensional "coherences" that make a particular geo-social space stand out in relief (while simultaneously blurring others),' Deshpande argues, 'then it is clear that communalism, globalisation and...other forces...are, individually and jointly, rearranging the regional map of India.'[109] These regional reworkings, historically contingent and culturally specific, may indeed mimic Clifford's call for theoretical tools that 'conjure with new localizations.'[110] This collection conjures with translocalizations, too, revealing the kinds of 'discrepant cosmopolitanism' Clifford charts across the power-saturated and uneven routes of global travel, political economy, and diaspora.[111] Understanding places as nodal points, as relational rather than essential, opens up the possibility of analysing historical *routes* rather than insisting on the authenticity of a *rooted* culture, identity, and tradition.

Moreover, appeals to 'culture' or 'the local' against the outside predations of imperialism and capitalism, the twin juggernauts in many visions of globalization, are neither necessarily progressive nor reactionary. Resonating with Subramanian's analysis, Watts

108. Massey 1994.
109. Deshpande 2001: 211.
110. Clifford 1997: 37.
111. I am aware of the disputed deployments of the term 'diaspora,' and their competing political resonances. I share the concern of those who fear the term's uncritical use will occlude the radical power asymmetries and histories of violence that created forced migrations and geographical dispersal. Said (2001: 442), for instance, explicitly rejects the term to describe the historical dispersion of Palestinians, preferring to use the Arabic term *shatat* (dispersion). While these debates remain beyond my chapter's scope, I find especially compelling Gilroy's (2000: 123) elaboration of the term's conceptual and political advantages for specific 'outer-national' relational networks and their transcultural forms.

argues that 'there is surely nothing necessarily anti-capitalist or particularly progressive about cultural identity: calls to localism can produce Hindu facism as easily as Andean Indian co-operatives.'[112] Rather than the unexplored celebrations of 'local culture' characterizing much anti-development writing, these four authors insist on exploring how 'culture' is historically constructed and politically deployed in specific contexts, emphasizing agency instead of assuming discursive determination. The authors echo this move, countering a tendency to analyse development through the manichean opposition of power and resistance.[113] Contextualized analyses of practice and process offer an antidote to reliance on structural binaries or recourse to a single, overarching theoretical punchline. They stress *contingencies*, which are anything but free-floating systems of signification, but rather distinct formations that emerge from historical, geographical, social, and cultural relations.[114]

If the authors share a steadfast refusal of the problematic binary mapping of local/cultural and global/economic, they also refute the analytical separation of political economy and cultural struggle. In Gujarat, darbars enacted a colonial imaginary of authority at the same time that they enabled the collection of levies serving British administrative agendas. Gandhi's perspective on the darbar that celebrates the founding of Hindu University conceives the spectacle as demonstrating insignias of Indian 'slavery' rather than selective sovereignties, obligatory displays of ostentatious wealth against the maharajahs' subjected wishes. State planning, in the context of struggles in the Himalayas, is a site of politics at the intersection of capitalist accumulation and nationalist legitimation. An understanding of conflicts over the mechanization of the fishing industry in Kanyakumari requires attention to class, caste, shifts in the global political economy, and alliances among pro-nativists and cultural nationalists. Articulations of nationalism emerge from these contrapuntal formations. And, women's negotiation with micro-enterprise initiatives in New Delhi are mediated through class experience and through the cultural construction of work and

112. Watts 1999: 91.
113. See Baviskar (1995) for a critique.
114. See the chapters in Gaonkar (2001) for insightful elaborations of contingent formations of alternative modernities.

wealth. In each case, struggles that are far too often, in contemporary social theory, assumed to be 'merely cultural'[115] are shown to have critical material impacts upon landscapes and livelihoods. In this view, development and modernity are reworked through struggles that are *simultaneously* material and symbolic.

The fusion of cultural politics and political economy suggests that visions of regional modernity require a theory of *articulation*. Here, I have in mind not the clunky, economistic articulation of 1970s structural Marxism and the modes of production debates. Rather, as Hall notes, articulation carries within it the twin concepts of joining and enunciation. An articulation both brings together disparate elements and, in the process of assemblage, gives that constellation a particular form and potential force.[116] The shape of this *formation*, the effectiveness of the linkages established among its elements, and the impact it will have on cultural, social, and political processes is historically contingent, not able to be 'read' off from an underlying structural logic.[117] A critical question becomes how contingent constellations come together in particular historical contexts, the heterogeneity of practices and cultural forms they authorize—in other words, what novel forms emerge from this provisional 'unity'—and how these linkages inform political subjectivities and cultural identities. Thus conceived, articulation offers a means for understanding emergent assemblages of institutions, apparatuses, practices, and discourses. Nodal points of intersection give shape to formations that are reworked through historical agency rather than structurally determined. The distance of this vision from Althusserian structuralism is most clear not simply in the rejection, as the editors note, of the economic as the determinative 'last instance,' but also in the proliferation of sites that constitute subjects. Rather than positing the state as overdetermining subject formation, the authors envision identities enacted through popular struggles for social justice, interpellated

115. Butler 1998.

116. Hall 1986.

117. By emphasizing the 'formations of modernity,' Hall (1992a: 7) stresses that the former term covers '*both* the activities of emergence, and their outcomes or results: both process *and* structure.' 'Formation' thus shares affinities with my emphasis upon emergent assemblages, a thematic fruitfully explored in Rabinow (1999).

by transnational NGOs, and reconfigured by shifting alliances among class, caste, Catholicism, and Hinduism. Structural determination is here supplanted by a politics of profound contingency, open-ended historical processes without guarantees.[118]

For this reason, the cultural politics of modernity and development unfold across what Gramsci termed the 'terrain of the "conjunctural."'[119] The multivalent meanings of modernity require not blanket assertions of discursive determination but rather finegrained ethnographic and historical analyses that contextualize this keyword's diverse forms, practices, and institutions. A growing number of critics argue that while ethnocentrism, imperialism, and universalism continue to haunt the development project, the historical agency of popular struggles has also appropriated from that project the articulation of political entitlements, staking claims to social justice and challenging structures of inequality.[120] Lisa Lowe seizes a spirit of affinity, reanimating Marx's Theses on Feuerbach with a cultural politics of difference while mapping an alternative formulation of modernity:

the ample evidence that capitalism works unevenly in different regions and locales has led us to the conclusion that neither exploitation nor the emergence of the political subject can be thought only in terms of single collectivity, teleology, or narrative development, and, therefore, that the practice and the terrain of the *political* must be imagined differently.[121]

These analysts appreciate the dangers of romanticizing resistance or neglecting the productive and social inequalities that cut across any formation of 'community' or 'the popular.' Subaltern appropriations of 'development,' Gupta emphasizes in his analysis of agrarian populism in India, contain their own 'exclusions and repressions.'[122] There is no necessary relation between these selective deployments and progressive politics, social justice,

118. See Li (2000) and Moore (1999) for ethnographically-grounded elaborations of 'articulation' in the cultural politics of development. Watts (1999) provides an insightful perspectives on articulation within the geographical imaginaries of national development.

119. Gramsci 1971: 178.

120. Cooper and Stoler 1997; Cooper and Packard 1997; Li 1998.

121. Lowe 2001: 11.

122. Gupta 1997: 321.

transformation of productive inequalities, or the dismantling of disenfranchizing social hierarchies. Counter-hegemony remains hard work.

Here, the theoretical and political status of *appropriation* might be enhanced if understood as a particular kind of *articulation,* a *contingent constellation* of discursive practices and formations. How selective appropriations, such as the liberal notions of universal human rights, are deployed and harnessed in the service of political projects is an empirical question open to critical inquiry, not foreclosed by theoretical fashion. These historically specific articulations do not unfold mechanistically, but rather require cultural *work* on the part of situated *agents* who are simultaneously nonsovereign *subjects*.[123] A critical challenge remains mapping the strategies and tactics that surround these reworkings, charting their often unanticipated consequences, and exploring diverse participants' understanding of their multivalent meanings. From this perspective, interests and identities are understood not as fixed structural locations, but rather as emerging through historical struggles that shape the landscape of contemporary cultural politics. Regional modernities animate these shifting sedimentations of identities, interests, and entitlements, while the heterogeneity of practices elaborated in these four chapters challenge formulations of a unitary, homogeneous development discourse. By offering rich relational histories of South Asian regions, they open up possibilities for an alternative ethos of modernity. The authors' emphasis on *cultural politics, practice,* and *process* refuses the tired binary oppositions of global/local, economic/cultural, power/resistance, and modernity/tradition. Collectively, these moves constitute a forceful refusal of blackmail, substituting in its place a productive mix of critical history and effective ethnography.

123. Das (2000: 222) offers a resonant 'formulation of the subject, a complex agency made up of divided and fractured subject positions.' In turn, this echoes Butler's (1997: 17) assertion: 'That agency is implicated in subordination is not the sign of a fatal self-contradiction at the core of the subject' nor 'a pristine notion of the subject, derived from some classical liberal–humanist formation, whose agency is always and only opposed to power.' Bhabha (1994: 186) elaborates a formulation of 'the contingency of the subject as agent.' See Moore (1998) and Mahmood (2001) for anthropological explorations of this nonsovereign terrain shaped by the embodied and situated practices of historical agents.

References

Agrawal, Arun, 2001. 'State formation in community spaces? Decentralization of control over forests in the Kumaon Himalaya, India.' *Journal of Asian Studies* 60(1): 9–40.

Ahmed, Imtiaz and Ousmane Kane (eds.), 2000. 'Editor's Note.' *Identity, Culture and Politics* 1(1): vi–viii.

Alvarez, Claude, 1992. *Science, Development, and Violence.* New Delhi: Oxford University Press.

Anagnost, Ann, 1997. *National Past-Times: Narrative, Representation, and Power in Modern China.* Durham: Duke University Press.

Appadurai, Arjun, 1990. 'Disjuncture and difference in the global cultural economy.' *Public Culture* 2(2): 1–24.

———, 1991. 'Global ethnoscapes: Notes and queries for a transnational anthropology.' In Richard Fox (ed.), *Recapturing Anthropology.* Santa Fe: School of American Research Press.

Aravamudan, Srinivas, 2001. 'Guru English.' *Social Text* 66: 19–44.

Arendt, Hannah, [1951] 1968. *Imperialism. Part Two of the Origins of Totalitarianism.* New York: Harcourt Brace Jovanovich.

Arnold, David, 1996. *The Problem of Nature.* Oxford: Blackwell.

———, 2001. *Gandhi.* London: Longman.

Asad, Talal, 1987. 'Are there histories of people without Europe?' *Comparative Studies in Society and History* 29(3): 594–607.

———, 1992. 'Conscripts of western civilization.' In Christine Ward Gailey (ed.), *Civilization in Crisis*, vol. 1. Gainesville: University of Florida Press.

Axel, Brian Keith, 2001. *The Nation's Tortured Body.* Durham: Duke University Press.

Bauman, Zygmunt, 1989. *Modernity and the Holocaust.* Ithaca: Cornell University Press.

Baviskar, Amita, 1995. *In the Belly of the River: Tribal Conflicts over Development in the Narmada Valley.* Delhi: Oxford University Press.

———, 1997. 'Tribal politics and discourses of environmentalism.' *Contributions to Indian Sociology* 31(2): 195–223.

Bayly, Susan, 1995. 'Caste and "race" in the colonial ethnography of India.' In Peter Robb (ed.), *The Concept of Race in South Asia.* New Delhi: Oxford University Press.

Berry, Sara, 1992. *No Condition is Permanent.* Madison: University of Wisconsin Press.

Bhabha, Homi (ed.), 1990. 'Disesemination: Time, narrative, and the margins of the modern nation.' In Homi Bhabha (ed.), *Nation and Narration.* London: Routledge.

———, 1994. *The Location of Culture.* London: Routledge.

Bornstein, Erica, 2001. 'Child sponsorship, evangelism, and belonging in the work of world vision Zimbabwe.' *American Ethnologist* 28(3): 595–622.

Bose, Sugata, 1997. 'Instruments and idioms of colonial and national development: India's historical experience in comparative perspective.' In Frederick Cooper and Randall Packard (eds.), *International Development and the Social Sciences*. Berkeley: University of California Press.

———, 1999. 'Nation as mother. Representations and contestation of "India" in Bengali literature and culture.' In Sugata Bose and Ayesha Jalal (eds.), *Nationalism, Democracy and Development: State and Politics in India*. New Delhi: Oxford University Press.

Bose, Sugata and Ayesha Jalal (eds.), 1999. *Nationalism, Democracy and Development: State and Politics in India*. New Delhi: Oxford University Press.

Bourdieu, Pierre, 1990. *In Other Worlds*. Translated by Matthew Adamson. Stanford: Stanford University Press.

———, 1991. 'Identity and representation: Elements for a critical reflection on the idea of region.' In *Language and Symbolic Power*. Translated by Gino Raymond and Matthew Adamson. Cambridge: Harvard University Press.

Brah, Avtar, 1996. *Cartographies of Diaspora*. New York: Routledge.

Brecher, Michael, 1959. *Nehru: A Political Biography*. Boston: Beacon Press.

Brown, Wendy, 1995. *States of Injury*. Princeton: Princeton University Press.

Butler, Judith, 1997. *The Psychic Life of Power*. Stanford: Stanford University Press.

———, 1998. 'Merely Cultural.' *New Left Review* 227: 33–44.

Chakrabarty, Dipesh, 2000. *Provincializing Europe*. Princeton: Princeton University Press.

Chambers, Ian, 2001. *Culture After Humanism*. New York: Routledge.

Chanock, Martin, 1985. *Law, Custom, and Social Order: The Colonial Experience in Malawi and Zambia*. Cambridge: Cambridge University Press.

Chatterjee, Partha, 1993. *The Nation and Its Fragments*. Princeton: Princeton University Press.

———, 1997. 'Our modernity.' In *The Present History of West Bengal*. New Delhi: Oxford University Press.

———, 1998a. 'Introduction.' In Partha Chatterjee (ed.), *Wages of Freedom: Fifty Years of the Indian Nation-State*. New Delhi: Oxford University Press.

———, 1998b. 'Community in the East.' *Economic and Political Weekly* 31(6): 277–82.

Chatterjee, Partha and Pradeep Jenganathan (eds.), 2001. *Subaltern Studies IX: Community, Gender and Violence*. New York: Columbia University Press.

Chuh, Kandice and Karen Shimakawa (eds.), 2001. *Orientations: Mapping Studies in the Asian Diaspora*. Durham: Duke University Press.

Clifford, James, 1997. *Routes: Travel and Translation in the Late Twentieth Century*. Cambridge: Harvard University Press.

Cohen, Lawrence, 1998. No Aging in India: *Alzheimer's The Bad Family, and Other Modern Things*. Berkeley: University of California Press.

Comaroff, Jean and John Comaroff (eds.), 1993.*Modernity and Its Malcontents*. Chicago: University of Chicago Press.

Comaroff, John and Jean Comaroff, 1997. *Of Revolution and Revelation, The Dialectics of Modernity on a South African Frontier*, vol. 2. Chicago: University of Chicago Press.

Cooper, Fred, 1994. 'Conflict and connection: Rethinking colonial African history.' *American Historical Review* 99(5): 1516–45.

Cooper, Frederick and Ann Stoler (eds.), 1997. *Tensions of Empire*. Berkeley: University of California Press.

Cooper, Frederick and Randall Packard (eds.), 1997. 'Introduction.' In *International Development and the Social Sciences*. Berkeley: University of California Press.

Coronil, Fernando, 1997. *The Magical State: Nature, Money, and Modernity in Venezeula*. Chicago: University of Chicago Press.

Crush, Jonathan, 1994. 'Post-colonialism, de-colonization, and geography.' In Anne Goldlewska and Neil Smith (eds.), *Geography and Empire*. Oxford: Blacwell.

Das, Veena, 1995. *Critical Events*. Delhi: Oxford University Press.

———, 1998. 'The act of witnessing: Violence, poisonous knowledge, and subjectivity.' In Veena Das *et al.* (eds.), *Violence and Suffering*. Berkeley: University of California Press.

———, 2000. 'The act of witnessing: Violence, poisonous knowledge, and subjectivity.' In Veena Das, Arthur Kleinman, Mamphela Remphele, and Pamela Reynolds (eds.), *Violence and Subjectivity*. Berkeley: University of California Press.

Das, Veena and Arthur Kleinman, 2001. 'Introduction.' In Veena Das *et al.* (eds.), *Remaking a World*. Berkeley: University of California Press.

de la Cadena, Marisol, 2000. *Indigenous Mestizos: The Politics of Race and Culture in Cuzco, 1919–1991*. Durham: Duke University Press.

Deshpande, Satish, 2001. 'Hegemonic spatial strategies: The nation-space and Hindu communalism in twentieth-century India.' In Partha Chatterjee and Pradeep Jenganathan (eds.), *Subaltern Studies XI: Community, Gender and Violence*. New York: Columbia University Press, pp. 167–211.

Devi, Mahasweta, 1995. *Imaginary Maps*. Translated by Gayatri Chakravorty Spivak. New York: Routledge.

Diawara, Manthia, 1998. *In Search of Africa*. Cambridge: Harvard University Press.

Dirks, Nicholas, 1992. 'Introduction: Colonialism and culture.' In Nicholas Dirks (ed.), *Colonialism and Culture*. Ann Arbor: University of Michigan Press.

———, 2001. *Castes of Mind*. Princeton: Princeton University Press.

Donham, Donald L., 1999. *Marxist Modern*. Berkeley: University of California Press.

Drayton, Richard, 2000. *Nature's Government: Science, Imperial Britain, and the 'Improvement' of the World*. New Haven: Yale University Press.

Edney, Matthew, 1997. *Mapping an Empire*. Chicago: University of Chicago Press.

Engels, Dagmar and Shula Marks (eds.), 1994. *Contesting Colonial Hegemony: State and Society in Africa and India*. New York: St. Martin's Press.

Escobar, Arturo, 1992. 'Imagining a post-development era? Critical thought, development and social movements.' *Social Text* 31/32: 20–56.

———, 1995. *Encountering Development*. Princeton: Princeton University Press.

Fabian, Johannes, 1983. *Time and the Other: How Anthropology Makes its Object*. New York: Columbia University Press.

Farred, Grant, 2001. 'A thriving postcolonialism: Toward an anti-postcolonial discourse.' *Nepantla* 2(2): 229–46.

Feenberg, A., 1995. 'Alternative modernity: Playing the Japanese game of culture.' *Cultural Critique* 29 (Winter): 107–38.

Ferguson, James, 1992. 'The cultural topography of wealth: Commodity paths and the structure of property in rural Lesotho.' *American Anthropologist* 94(1): 55–73.

———, [1990] 1994. *The Anti-Politics Machine: 'Development', Depoliticization, and Bureaucratic Power in the Third World*. Minneapolis: University of Minnesota Press.

———, 1998. *Expectations of Modernity: Myths and Meanings of Urban Life on the Zambian Copperbelt*. Berkeley: University of California Press.

Foucault, Michel, 1978. *History of Sexuality*. New York: Vintage Books.

———, 1979. 'On governmentality'. *Ideology and Consciousness* 6 (Autumn): 5–21.

———, 1997. 'What is Enlightenment?' In Paul Rabinow (ed.), *Michel Foucault: Ethics, Subjectivity and Truth. Essential Works of Foucault, 1954–1984*, vol. 1. New York: Free Press.

Fraser, Nancy, 1989. *Unruly Practices*. New York: Routledge.

Gandhi, Mohandas K., 1951. *Non-Violent Resistance (Satyagraha)*. New York: Schocken Books.

———, 1956. *The Gandhi Reader*. Homer A. Jack (ed.), New York: Grove Press.

———, 1991. *The Essential Writings of Mahatma Gandhi*. Raghavan Iyer (ed.), Delhi: Oxford University Press.

———, [1927/1929] 1993. *An Autobiography: The Story of My Experiments with Truth*. Boston: Beacon Press.

Gaonkar, Dilip Parameshwar (ed.), 2001. *Alternative Modernities*. Durham: Duke University Press.

Geschiere, Peter, 1997. *The Modernity of Witchcraft: Politics and the Occult in Postcolonial Africa*. Charlottesville: University Press of Virginia.

Gilroy, Paul, 1993. *The Black Atlantic*. Cambridge: Harvard University Press.

———, 2000. *Between Camps: Nature, Cultures and the Allure of Race*. London: Penguin.

Goankar, Dilip Parameshwar (ed.), 2001. *Alternative Modernities*. Durham: Duke University Press.

Gramsci, Antonio, 1971. *Selections from the Prison Notebooks*. Edited by Quintin Hoare and Geoffrey Nowell Smith. New York: International Publishers.

Grewal, Inderpal, 1996. *Home and Harem*. Durham: Duke University Press.

Grillo, R. D. and R. L. Stirrat (eds.), 1997. *Discourses of Development*. Oxford: Berg.

Grove, Richard, 1995. *Green Imperialism: Colonial Expansion, Tropical Island Edens, and the Origins of Environmentalism, 1600–1860*. Cambridge: Cambridge University Press.

Guha, Ramachandra, 1989. *The Unquiet Woods*. New Delhi: Oxford University Press.

———, 1997. 'The environmentalism of the poor.' In Richard Fox and Orin Starn (eds.), *Between Resistance and Revolution: Cultural Politics and Social Protest*. New Brunswick: Rutgers University Press.

Guha, Ranajit, 1997. 'Introduction.' In Ranajit Guha (ed.), *A Subaltern Studies Reader, 1986–1995*. Minneapolis: University of Minnesota Press.

———, 1997. *Dominance Without Hegemony: History and Power in Colonial India*. Cambridge: Harvard University Press.

Gupta, Akhil, 1997. 'Agrarian populism in the development of a modern nation (India).' In Frederick Cooper and Randall Packard (eds.), *International Development and the Social Sciences*. Berkeley: University of California Press.

————, 1998. *Postcolonial Developments*. Durham: Duke University Press.

Gururani, Shubhra, 2000. 'Regimes of control, strategies of access: politics of forest use in the Uttrakhand Himalaya, India.' In Arun Agrawal and K. Sivaramakrishnan (eds.), *Agrarian Environments*. Durham: Duke University Press.

————, n.d. 'Administrative communities in the making: State inscriptions in the forests of the Indian Himalayas.' Manuscript.

Hall, Catherine (ed.), 2000. *Cultures of Empire*. Manchester: Manchester University Press.

Hall, Stuart, 1981. 'Notes on deconstructing the popular.' In Raphael Samuel (ed.), *People's History and Socialist Theory*. London: Kegan Paul.

————, 1986. 'On postmodernism and articulation. Lawrence Grossberg interviews Stuart Hall.' *Journal of Communication Inquiry* 10(2): 45–60.

————, 1988. *The Hard Road to Renewal: Thatcherism and the Crisis of the Left*. London: Verso.

————, 1992a. 'Introduction.' In Stuart Hall and Bram Gieben (eds.), *Formations of Modernity*. Cambridge: Polity Press.

————, 1992b. 'The West and the rest: Discourse and power.' In Stuart Hall and Bram Gieben (eds.), *Formations of Modernity*. Cambridge: Polity Press.

Hanchard, Michael, 2001. 'Afro-Modernity: Temporality, politics, and the African diaspora.' In Dilip Parameshwar Gaonkar (ed.), *Alternative Modernities*. Durham: Duke University Press.

Haraway, Donna, 1989. *Primate Visions*. New York: Routledge.

Hart, Gillian, forthcoming. *Disabling Globalization: Places of Power in Post-Apartheid South Africa*. Berkeley: University of California Press.

Hitler, Adolf, [1925] 1943. *Mein Kampf*. Translated by Ralph Manheim. Boston: Houghton and Mifflin.

Jalal, Ayesha, 2000. *Self and Sovereignty: Individual and Community in South Asian Islam since 1850*. New York: Routledge.

Jones, Andrew F., 2001. *Yellow Music: Media Culture and Colonial Modernity in the Chinese Jazz Age*. Durham: Duke University Press.

Kaplan, Caren, Norma Alarcon, and Minoo Moallem (eds.), 1999. *Between Woman and Nation: Nationalisms, Transnational Feminisms, and the State*. Durham: Duke University Press.

Kipling, Rudyard, [1899] 1941. 'The white man's burden.' In T. S. Eliot (ed.), *A Choice of Kipling's Verse*. London: Faber and Faber.

Kumar, Amitava, 2000. *Passport Photos*. Berkeley: University of California Press.

Lefebvre, Henri, [1974] 1991. *The Production of Space*. Translated by Donald Nicholson-Smith. Oxford: Blackwell.

Lewis, Martin W. and Karen E. Wigen, 1997. *The Myth of Continents*. Berkeley: University of California Press.

Liu, Lydia (ed.), 1999. *Tokens of Exchange: The Problem of Translation in Global Circulations*. Durham: Duke University Press.

Litzinger, Ralph, 2000. *Other Chinas: The Yao and the Politics of National Belonging*. Durham: Duke University Press.

Li, Tania Murray, 1999. 'Marginality, power, and production.' In *Transforming the Indonesia Uplands: Marginality, Power and Production*. Amsterdam: Harwood Academic.

———, 2000. 'Articulating indigenous identity in Indonesia: Resource politics and the tribal slot.' *Comparative Studies in Society and History* 42(1): 149–79.

Lomnitz, Claudio, 2001. 'Modes of citizenship in Mexico.' In Dilip Parameshwar Gaonkar (ed.), *Alternative Modernities*. Durham: Duke University Press.

Lowe, Lisa, 1996. *Immigrant Acts*. Durham: Duke University Press.

———, 2001. 'Utopia and modernity: Some observations from the border.' *Rethinking Marxism* 13(2): 10–18.

Lowe, Lisa and David Lloyd (eds.), 1997. *The Politics of Culture in the Shadow of Capital*. Durham: Duke University Press.

Ludden, David, 1992. 'India's development regime.' In Nicholas Dirks (ed.), *Colonialism and Culture*. Ann Arbor: University of Michigan Press.

Lugard, Frederick, 1922. *The Dual Mandate in British Tropical Africa*. Edinburgh: W. Blackwood and Sons.

———, 1926. 'The White Man's Task in Tropical Africa.' *Foreign Affairs* 5(1): 57–68.

Mahmood, Saba, 2001. 'Feminist theory, embodiment, and the docile agent: Some reflections on the Egyptian Islamic revival.' *Cultural Anthropology* 16(2): 202–36.

Mankekar, Purnima, 1993. 'National texts and gendered lives: An ethnography television viewers in a north Indian city.' *American Ethnologist* 20(3): 543–63.

———, 1999. *Screening Culture, Viewing Politics*. Durham: Duke University Press.

Marx, Karl, [1845] 1983. 'Theses on Feuerbach.' In Eugene Kamenka (ed.), *The Portable Marx*. New York: Penguin.

———, [1867] 1990. *Capital, Volume One*. Translated by Ben Fowkes. London: Penguin.

Massey, Doreen, 1994. *Space, Place, and Gender*. Minneapolis: University of Minnesota Press.

Mbembe, Achille, 1992. 'The banality of power and the aesthetics of vulgarity in the postcolony.' *Public Culture* 4(2): 1–30.

———, 2000. *On the Postcolony*. Berkeley: University of California Press.

Mehta, Uday Singh, 1999. *Liberalism and Empire: A Study in Nineteenth-century British Liberal Thought.* Chicago: University of Chicago Press.

Mehta, Ved, 1976. *Mahatma Gandhi and His Apostles.* New York: Penguin.

Mitchell, Timothy, 1991. 'The limits of the state: Beyond statist approaches and their critics.' *American Political Science Review* 85(1): 77–96.

Mitchell, Timothy (ed.), 2000. *Questions of Modernity.* Minneapolis: University of Minnesota Press.

Moore, Donald S., 1998. 'Subaltern struggles and the politics of place: Remapping resistance in Zimbabwe's Eastern Highlands.' *Cultural Anthropology* 13(3): 1–38.

——, 1999. 'The crucible of cultural politics: Reworking "development" in Zimbabwe's Eastern Highlands.' *American Ethnologist* 26(3): 654–89.

Moore, Donald S., Anand Pandian, and Jake Kosek (eds.), forthcoming. *Race, Nature, and the Politics of Difference.* Durham: Duke University Press.

Nandy, Ashis, 1995. *The Savage Freud and Other Essays on Possible and Retrievable Selves.* Princeton: Princeton University Press.

Nelson, Diane M., 1999. *A Finger in the Wound: Body Politics in Quincentennial Guatemala.* Berkeley: University of California Press.

Neumann, Roderick, 1997. 'Primitive ideas: Protected buffer area zones and the politics of land in Africa.' *Development and Change* 28(3): 559–82.

Ong, Aihwa, 1999. *Flexible Citizenship: The Cultural Logics of Transnationality.* Durham: Duke University Press.

——, 2000. 'Graduated sovereignty in South-East Asia.' *Theory, Culture and Society* 17(4): 55–75.

Pandian, Anand S., 1998. 'Predatory care: The imperial hunt in Mughal and British India.' *Journal of Historical Sociology* 14(1): 79–107.

Parry, Benita, 1998. *Delusions and Discoveries.* London: Verso.

Pels, Peter, 1996. 'The anthropology of colonialism: Culture, history, and the emergence of western governmentality.' *Annual Review of Anthropology* 26: 163–83.

——, 2000. 'The rise and fall of the Indian aborigines: Orientalism, Anglicanism, and the emergence of an ethnology of India, 1833–69.' In Peter Pels and Oscar Salemink (eds.), *Colonial Subjects.* Ann Arbor: University of Michigan Press.

Peters, Pauline (ed.), 2000. *Development Encounters.* Cambridge: Harvard University Press.

Piot, Charles, 1999. *Remotely Global.* Chicago: University of Chicago Press.

Povinelli, Elizabeth, 1999. 'Settler modernity and quest for an indigenous tradition.' *Public Culture* 11(1): 19–48.

Prakash, Gyan, 1995. 'Introduction: After colonialism: Imperial histories and postcolonial displacements.' In Gyan Prakash (ed.), *After Colonialism*. Princeton: Princeton University Press.

———, 1999. *Another Reason*. Princeton: Princeton University Press.

Prashad, Vijay, 2000. *The Karma of Brown Folk*. Minneapolis: University of Minnesota Press.

Pred, Allan and Michael Watts, 1992. *Reworking Modernity*. New Brunswick: Rutgers University Press.

Pratt, Mary Louise, 1992. *Imperial Eyes: Travel Writing and Transculturation*. New York: Routledge.

———, 1992. 'Belly-up: More on the postcolony.' *Public Culture* 5(1): 47–145.

Rabinow, Paul, 1999. *French DNA*. Chicago: University of Chicago Press.

Radhakrishnan, R., 2000. 'Postermodernism and the rest of the world.' In Fawzia Afzal-Khan and Kalpana Seshadri-Crooks (eds.), *The Pre-Occupation of Postcolonial Studies*. Durham: Duke University Press.

Rahnema, Majid and Victoria Bawtree (eds.), 1997. *The Post-Development Reader*. London: Zed.

Ramaswamy, Sumathi, 1998. 'History at land's end: Lemuria in Tamil spatial fables.' *Journal of Asian Studies* 59(3): 575–602.

Rangan, Haripriya, 2000. *Of Myths and Movements: Rewriting Chipko into Himalayan History*. London: Verso.

Ranger, Terence, 1992. 'Power, religion and community: The Matobo case.' In Partha Chatterjee and Gyandendra Pandey (eds.), *Subaltern Studies VII*. New Delhi: Oxford University Press.

Ray, Raka, 1999. *Fields of Protest: Women's Movements in India*. Minneapolis: University of Minnesota Press.

Robb, Peter, 1995. *The Concept of Race in South Asia*. New Delhi: Oxford University Press.

Roe, Emory, 1991. 'Development narratives, or making the best of blueprint development.' *World Development* 19(4): 287–300.

Rofel, Lisa, 1998. *Other Modernities: Gendered Yearnings in China after Socialism*. Berkeley: University of California Press.

Rose, Nikolas, 1999. *Powers of Freedom*. Cambridge: Cambridge University Press.

Roy, Arundhati, 1998. *The Cost of Living*. New York: Penguin.

———, 2001. *Power Politics*. Boston: South End Press.

Roy, Parama, 1998. *Indian Traffic*. Berkeley: University of California Press.

Ruhe, Peter, 2001. *Gandhi*. London: Phaedon.

Rushdie, Salman, 1990. *Haroun and the Sea of Stories*. London: Granta Books.

Said, Edward, 2001. *Power, Politics and Culture.* New York: Pantheon Books.

Sartre, Jean-Paul, [1956] 2001. 'Colonialism is a system.' In *Colonialism and Neocolonialism.* New York: Routledge.

Scott, David, 1995. 'Colonial governmentality.' *Social Text* 43: 191–220.

Sivaramakrishnan, K., 1998. 'Modern forestry: Trees and development spaces in south-west Bengal.' In Laura Rival (ed.), *The Social Life of Trees.* Oxford: Berg.

———, 2000. 'Crafting the public sphere in the forests of West Bengal: Democracy, development, and political action.' *American Ethnologist* 27(2): 431–61.

Skaria, Ajay, 1999. *Hybrid Histories.* New Delhi: Oxford University Press.

Spencer, Jonathan, 1995. 'Occidentalism in the East: The uses of the West in the politics and anthropology of South Asia.' In James Carrier (ed.), *Occidentalism: Images of the West.* Oxford: Clarendon Press.

Srivastava, Sanjay, 1998. *Constructing Post-Colonial India.* New York: Routledge.

Stoler, Ann Laura, 1995. *Race and the Education of Desire Foucault's History of Sexuality and the Colonial Order of Things.* Durham: Duke University Press.

Sundar, Nandini, 1997. *Subalterns and Sovereigns.* New Delhi: Oxford University Press.

———, 2000. 'Unpacking the "joint" in joint forest management.' *Development and Change* 31(1): 255–79

Taussig, Michael, 1987. *Shamanism, Colonialism, and the Wildman.* Chicago: University of Chicago Press.

Thesis Eleven, 1994. 'Special issue: India and modernity: Decentering western perspectives.' 39.

Thomas, Nicholas, 1994. *Colonialism's Culture: Anthropology, Travel, and Government.* Princeton: Princeton University Press.

Trouillot, Michel-Rolph, 1991. 'Anthropology and the savage slot: The poetics and politics of otherness.' In Richard Fox (ed.), *Recapturing Anthropology.* Santa Fe: School of American Research Press.

Tsing, Anna Lowenhaupt, 1999. 'Becoming a tribal elder and other green development fantasies.' In Tania Murray Li (ed.), *Transforming the Indonesia Uplands.* Amsterdam: Harwood Academic.

Van der Veer, Peter, 1994. *Religious Nationalism: Hindus and Muslims in India.* Berkeley: University of California Press.

Visweswaran, Kamala, 1996. 'Small speeches, subaltern gender: Nationalist ideology and its historiography.' In Shahid Amin and Dipesh Chakrabarty (eds.), *Subaltern Studies IX.* New Delhi: Oxford University Press.

Visvanathan, Shiv, 1997. *A Carnival for Science: Essays on Science, Technology and Development.* New Delhi: Oxford University Press.

Viswanathan, Gauri, 1998. *Outside the Fold: Conversion, Modernity, and Belief.* Princeton: Princeton University Press.

Watts, Michael, 1999. 'Collective wish images: Geographical imaginaries and post-development.' In Doreen Massey and John Allen (eds.), *Human Geography Today.* Cambridge: Polity Press.

———, forthcoming. 'Alternative modern: Toward a cultural geography of development.' In Steve Pile, Nigel Thrift and Kay Anderson (eds.), *Handbook of Cultural Geography.* London: Sage Publications.

West, Cornel, 1999. *The Cornel West Reader.* New York: Basic Civitas Books.

Whitten, Norman, D. S. Whitten, and A. Chango, 1997. 'Return of the Yumbo: The indigenous caminata from Amazonia to Andean Quito.' *American Ethnologist* 24(2): 355–91.

Willems-Braun, Bruce, 1997. 'Buried epistemologies: The politics of nature in (post) colonial British Columbia.' *Annals of the Association of American Geographers* 87(1): 3–31.

Williams, Raymond, 1977. *Marxism and Literature.* New York: Oxford University Press.

Wolf, Eric, 1982. *Europe and the People without History.* Berkeley: University of California Press.

Worby, Eric, 1997. 'Tyranny, parody, and ethnic polarity: Ritual engagements with the state in northwestern Zimbabwe.' *Journal of Southern African Studies* 24(3): 561–79.

Young, Robert J. C., 2001. *Postcolonialism.* Oxford: Blackwell.

Zizek, Slavoj, 1993. *Tarrying with the Negative.* Durham: Duke University Press.

8

Development, Nationalism, and the Time of the Primitive: The Dangs Darbar

AJAY SKARIA

Around mid-March every year, a *darbar* is held in Ahwa, the district headquarters of Dangs in Gujarat, India. At the darbar, the former Dangi chiefs, their relatives, and the village headmen are paid their annual political pensions; the forest department presents prizes to those villagers who have protected the forests around their village from fire; and local Gandhian leaders lament the addiction of Dangis to liquor, and exhort them to stay away from these evil habits. By some estimates, nearly half the district's population visits Ahwa during the darbar week, partially to visit the annual market and fair which accompanies the darbar.

The Dangs' darbar has been an annual fixture since the mid-nineteenth century, and it possibly existed earlier too. More broadly, as we know, British darbars were amongst the most prominent of all colonial rituals, staged repeatedly in many parts of India. I would like to explore here how the British darbar, and indeed ritual more broadly as a modern topos, emerges from the distinctive historicism of colonial rule.

In the process, perhaps we can also explore what is involved in the discourse of development. Over the last few years, a very powerful critique of development has emerged. What makes this critique so interesting and suggestive is that it is not simply anti-development, as many of the earlier critiques were, but that it tries rather to understand development as a regime of power. It has argued that development is connected with the growth and consolidation of a distinctive kind of rationality, and the extension of this rationality through bureaucratic state power, with the instrument effects of suspending politics in the name of professional expertise.[1] In what follows, I would like to extend this critique by focusing on the curious relationship of development with its object—the primitive. In talking of the primitive, I refer to that figure which is posited by historicist thought to be in a time before that of the modern. To the extent that the discourse of development identified itself with the modern and claimed progress or growth as a goal, it produced the primitive as the object that required and called forth development. It is the strand of development discourse that tries to make the primitive modern that we usually pick on and name as development. But there is also another strand, perhaps as pervasive, which affirms the primitive. This moment of affirmation usually produces primitivism. But especially in nationalist thought, there is also another—intimately linked and yet radically different—affirmation that threatens always to dismantle the figure of the primitive itself, and thus undo both historicist thought and the discourse of development. Indeed, such a threat is perhaps crucial to the very constitution of nationalist thought.

I

Consider first the early nineteenth century annual meetings between the many small chiefs of Dangs, a small hilly and forested region of around 650 square miles, and officials of the neighboring kingdom of Baroda, one of the most powerful in the subcontinent. Principally two communities, the Bhils and the Koknis, inhabited nineteenth century Dangs. Bhil chiefs held political power in the region, each important group controlling a tract within the Dangs.[2] In the mid-eighteenth century, Bhil chiefs had played a crucial role in helping the Maratha chiefs associated with the Gaekwad

1. See Ferguson [1990] 1994.
2. Government of Bombay 1880: 598f.

family establish what eventually became the kingdom of Baroda. The first capital of the Gaekwadi kingdom, Songadh, was on the outskirts of Dangs, though later the capital was moved to Baroda in the north.[3]

In the early nineteenth century, the *killedar* or fort commandant of Songadh met the chiefs at least once a year, usually at Songadh. The meetings were crucial to sustaining relations between the Gaekwads and the chiefs. At the meetings, the commandant paid a range of dues, which the chiefs considered to be their right. Disputes with the chiefs—over raids that they had made onto territory where the Gaekwads possessed authority, or over payments—were also settled. In turn, the chiefs paid the dues that Gaekwadi officials had on some villages, and made presents. The alliances with the various chiefs were affirmed or, less often, repudiated. On these occasions, Gaekwadi representatives provided, 'for purposes of state, cushions, pillows, floor cloth and other articles, as well as Lamp and Light, with oil for the same.'[4] They also provided the food and liquor for the occasions.

The ways in which we understand meetings such as these reveal much about our understandings of power. It is tempting to think of the meetings between the killedar and the chiefs as symptomatic of the partiality of Gaekwadi power, as involving attempts by centralized states, in this context of partial power, to slowly control and subordinate forest polities such as those represented by the Bhil chiefs. Such a reading may be described as almost classically developmentalist. Here, power itself is taken to be of a relatively constant nature, of essentially the same nature whether precolonial, colonial or postcolonial—the changes that we discern are primarily in the extent of this power. Our task as historians becomes that of specifying the continuities, disruptions, and transformations of this constant power. Missing out on the distinctiveness of precolonial and non-modern forms of power, such a perspective—pervasive amongst colonial officials, and still broadly accepted amongst scholars[5]—is premised on an implicit narrative which traces the development and growth of this constant power from then through to the present.

3. Bomanji 1903; Wink 1986: 117–22.
4. Cited in Skaria 1999: 181.
5. See Bayly 1983, 1996; Mann 1983–96.

How then does one think of the distinctiveness of such authority? It is tempting to slip into the converse position, and think of darbars as the enactment of power as spectacle. It could be argued, in other words, that rather than producing an inevitable and inescapable power which would extend into Dangs, the meetings staged Gaekwadi authority as a visible intensity; that power was produced here by the dramatic spectacle of Gaekwadi authority rather than the extensive reach of its officials. Such arguments sometimes claim legitimacy from and affinity with Foucault, depending on a somewhat misplaced reading of his *Discipline and Punish.* They have been made often in the context of differentiating pre-modern regimes from modern ones; the former have been seen variably as theater states, or as exercising power through spectacular authority; the latter have been seen as more regulatory, capillary, and everyday in their workings. From such a perspective, occasions such as precolonial darbars seem to be characterized by incorporation and the exchange of substances, while their colonial successors seem marked by subordination and contractual relations. Perhaps, such perspectives can be thought of as attempts to be outside the developmentalist paradigm, in that they try to specify a space and set of practices outside the discourse of development and its forms of power. As such, these arguments are not so much wrong as too preliminary, for they accept that conceit of modernity and see all that preceded it—the pre-modern or, if you will, precolonial—as sharing, in their relation to it, some crucial affinity. In this sense, as Ranajit Guha has suggested in a related context, such a perspective allows dominant values to determine the criteria of the historic.[6] The effect of such lumping is to oversimplify the contradictions of power by reducing them to an arbitrary singularity—in this case, to that between the modern and the pre-modern, or the colonial and the precolonial.

What is needed, in other words, are more attentive genealogies of specific regional regimes of power. As has been argued at length elsewhere,[7] in the forested and hilly regions of late eighteenth and early nineteenth-century western India, this regime was about a politics organized around wildness and its antinomies. In their politics, the Dangi chiefs enacted a claim to being wild or *jangli.*

6. Guha 1996.
7. Skaria 1999.

This claim to being jangli was in an agonistic and even antagonistic relationship with the forms of political power wielded by plains powers like the Gaekwads. *Giras* and raids were two crucial and intertwined modalities of the politics of wildness. In the early nineteenth century, revenue and political authority was shared between the Dangi Bhil chiefs and the Gaekwads along the frontier villages.[8] The chiefs often raided Gaekwadi villages, carrying away cattle, grain, or cash. These raids were often retaliation for the non-payment of a direct and sometimes substantial levy called giras. At other times, they were attempts to increase existing claims or establish new claims to giras. Accompanying giras were other payments like *bhet*, a small gift of Rs 2 or 3, and *sirpav*, usually a turban, from the villagers. Sometimes, they were also gifted an expensive *shela* or shawl. Together, shela, sirpav, bhet, and giras were an assertion by the chiefs of their partial authority over these Gaekwadi villages. The raids of the Bhil chiefs enacted their claims to being jangli or wild; giras payments were implicitly an affirmation by the Gaekwads of Dangi wildness. And, because Gaekwadi officials too were involved in this politics of wildness, they did not treat raids as unambiguous acts of hostility; indeed, they saw the payment of giras by them as a valuable dimension of their relations with Dangi chiefs.[9]

In a very constitutive sense, the darbar was a privileged site for the enactment of the politics of wildness. It was the occasion when giras payments, crucial to the enactment of wildness, were distributed; it was also the occasion when Gaekwadi officials negotiated with Dangi chiefs to avoid raids by the latter. In some other ways too, a politics of wildness was enacted at the darbar. Oral traditions around since at least the early twentieth century emphasize how, at these meetings, Gaekwadi officials were gifted five pots of water from Bokarvihir, five baskets of the umbar fruit from Donumbria, five baskets of the *tembrun* fruit from Divantembrun and five baskets of the *payar* fruit from Kahapayar.[10] It is surely suggestive that so many items sent were wild, and associated with forests: after all, it would have been quite possible to send the shawls, sets of clothes, or turbans that were more conventional gifts amongst both

8. Bomanji 1903.
9. Skaria 1999: 124–52.
10. Khanapurkar 1944: 106; Skaria 1999: 127.

the chiefs and Gaekwadi officials. By deliberately choosing products that carried connotations of being jangli, were the chiefs
representing themselves as wild? Because the darbar was so constitutive of the modality by which Gaekwadi officials and Dangi
chiefs interacted, both were quite committed to the occasion.
In the 1830s, when the British took over giras payments from
Gaekwadi officials, the latter were left with no ostensible reason
for continuing the darbar. But rather than discontinue it, they took
to paying an additional unauthorized giras to the chiefs as a way
of continuing the darbar.[11]

II

My effort so far has been to identify the singularities of that which
preceded colonial rule in the forested regions of western India,
rather than understanding these as a particular manifestation of
the precolonial and the premodern. With the consolidation of
colonial power, the darbar continued in what was apparently
much the same form. At the annual meetings held by the British
from the 1830s or 1840s, presents and provisions were given to
the chiefs and their followers. Giras and other payments were
also distributed.

But while in some ways the very same darbar continued, with
many of the same gestures, dues, and ceremonies, its meanings had
changed radically from Gaekwadi to British times; it was part of
new forms of power rather than a continuation of old ones. Most
importantly, the politics of wildness was marginalized. Soon after
the British took over the neighboring district of Khandesh from
the Peshwas following the settlement of 1818, they found themselves harried by the raids of Dangi Bhil chiefs. To the British, the
raids appeared as criminal acts of aggression on territory over
which they held singular authority. A series of punitive expeditions
through the 1820s and 1830s finally put an end to raids. These
expeditions demonstrated to the Bhil chiefs that the British refused
to treat the raids as part of the process of negotiating and sharing
authority, and that colonial officials would retaliate with a ferocity
quite unlike their Maratha predecessors. Also, by 1826, the British
had identified the irregular payment of giras (an irregularity which
was central to its nature as means of negotiating authority) by

11. Skaria 1999: 141.

Gaekwadi officials as the main reason for the raids. Giras payments were investigated, pegged at a fixed annual amount, taken over by the British, and made regularly to the chiefs in the hope of halting raids. Involved in all of this was an extirpation of the old practices of wildness. While giras and other payments continued to be made at the darbar, their connotations now were very different.[12]

Those connotations are best understood in the context of the historicism that was constitutive of colonial rule. It is characteristic of this historicism that, assuming a unified and linear process of development, it placed the 'people' it dealt with in a time behind that of the colonizers, a time that was more backward, primitive, and natural. Colonial rule thus assigned to itself the task of bringing these 'people' into its time; it is thus that development—the development of the colonized, necessarily primitive by the very fact of being colonized—emerges as the self-proclaimed mission of colonial rule.

While all Indians were backward by the very fact of being colonized, those like Dangis, who came to be classified as tribes, were considered even more primitive than the castes. Thus, the 'civilizing mission' was carried out especially enthusiastically by British officials when amongst the wild tribes. Under the steadying influence of a British officer, it was envisioned that tribes would abandon their shifting cultivation, hunting, and fishing, take to settled agriculture, and become steady, yeomen cultivators. One of the tasks of the Khandesh Bhil Agency was to extend loans to tribes in order to make them take up settled agriculture.[13]

Just as colonial officials civilized and developed the tribes, so did the forest department civilize and develop the forests. Dangi forests had been leased in 1843 for their valuable teak, especially suited for British naval shipbuilding. As has been pointed out, colonial forestry was in many ways 'an industrial science...informed by a conception of the "rational" use of natural resources intrinsic to industrial capitalism.' As part of the articulation of a Cartesian scientificity, plantations were set out in straight lines, an almost geometrical order was imposed on forests, and they were converted into industrial resources that had to be rationally utilized.[14]

12. Ibid.: 154–7.
13. Gordon 1994.
14. Guha 1985: 1949.

Developing the forests and the tribes were intimately connected tasks. Thus, forest department taxonomies regulated Dangi social practices in keeping with the extent of 'damage' they caused to 'valuable timber' such as teak. By such criteria, most Dangi modes of subsistence were harmful. Their shifting cultivation involved firing the forests, lopping trees, and clearing wooded patches—all of which were seen as either killing trees or at least preventing the production of long straight boles of timber because of the knots and twists they caused. The regular migration to new spots for cultivation was also seen as inimical to the production of large timber, since new houses had to be built and new land cleared for cultivation at the freshly chosen site. Hunting, similarly, was considered objectionable because it usually involved firing. All these Dangi activities, had to be modified and preferably done away with; at the very least, they had to be excluded from forests.[15]

The darbar was a privileged site for the enactment of this developmentalist project. One of the principal reasons for regularizing a system of annual meetings was the need to make the forest lease payments in an appropriate manner. The two major sets of nineteenth-century rules restricting Dangi use of the forests were announced at the annual meetings of 1849 and 1855. At the annual meetings, the chiefs were exhorted to abide by forest department restrictions, and some chiefs were even fined for not reducing the popular use of teak for subsistence in their territories. And, the civilizing mission was very directly involved: the meetings were also thought of as necessary 'for the purpose of enquiring into any complaints brought forward and of encouraging them in any attempt at civilization which more frequent intercourse might induce.'[16]

III

From what I have said so far, it might seem that in the discourse of development, tribals or forests can exist only as moments of resistance to be overcome, as resources to be transformed. The persuasiveness of such arguments may derive from their convergence with that well-established trope in social theory, associated

15. Skaria 1998.

16. Graham to Blanc, 18.4.1839. Dangs District Records, Daftar 1, File 3, Gujarat State Archives, Baroda.

most of all with Hegel and Weber, which sees the growth of modern society as the growth of rationality, the state or bureaucracy as a particularly important locus of that rationality. In recent times, these arguments have also been associated with a dissatisfyingly straightforward reading of Foucault—should one say an elision of Foucault with a particular strand of Weber?—where development is regarded as erasing politics while simultaneously pursuing the very political task of expanding bureaucratic state power.[17]

One way, perhaps the dominant way right now, of objecting to such an argument is to point to how development and colonial knowledge are appropriated and reworked by local communities, how they inflect it with their own agendas. By pointing to how such reworking was constitutive of development, we hope to displace the argument that development discourses radically remake the local and the regional in the image of instrumental rationality.[18]

Such reworking at the margins was certainly a notable theme at the Dangs' darbars. The British darbar had become central to Dangis because of colonial power. It was at the darbar that a significant proportion of the annual income of many Bhils was distributed; that local hierarchies were remade, and many disputes were adjudicated. But Dangi interpretations of the darbar differed fundamentally from, and often displaced, British meanings of the occasion. There was the appropriation of British power: for many chiefs, the occasion was about the affirmation of their authority rather than of British authority. The chiefs also tried to regulate the giving of presents by the British so that it accorded with the hierarchies that they were interested in sustaining. Similarly, complaints to the British at darbars were often attempts to pursue feuds by involving the British rather than an appeal to colonial legality: colonial officials learnt at annual meetings about 'crimes' principally because of the complaints made by the rivals of 'criminals.'

Further, for many Dangis, the darbar had nothing to do with colonial power. Of the two thousand or more men and women (between 6 to 11 percent of the region's population) who attended

---

17. Cf. Ferguson [1990] 1994.
18. For an analysis of this argument, see Sivaramakrishnan and Agrawal, this volume.

the occasion, only the male Bhil *bhauband* were directly involved with colonial enactment of power, receiving a share of the lease payments. Both for them and certainly for the others who attended the occasion, an important attraction must have been the large market, the most important in the year. In 1875, it was reported that the village on the outskirts of the Dangs where the darbar was held was 'filled with Banias and other creditors of the chiefs waiting to be paid.' These banias, principally from the nearby market towns of Mulher and Songadh, also ran the temporary stalls that constituted the market. They sold everything from salt, cloth, shawls, and turbans to horses. The considerable payments made on the occasion to the chiefs were widely redistributed amongst senior bhauband, other Bhils, and important Koknis. The resultant widespread abundance of cash made the darbar the lynchpin of many Dangis' annual commercial transactions. The money was used to settle old debts and purchase additional goods. For the rest of the year, merchants extended credit annually on the security of the British lease payments.[19]

Like money, food, including meat, was plentiful, supplied by the British for all those who attended. In a society where seasonal scarcity sometimes forced even minor chiefs onto frugal diets below subsistence levels, this fact alone must have been significant, especially since the darbar was held around March or April, when stocks of grain would have run low. To make matters better still, liquor too was available. 'On Bazaar day, it is hardly an exaggeration to say that the whole population, men women and children are drunk.'[20] The darbar was convened at a particularly opportune time for such activity. It was held around the time of Shimga, the principal festival of the Dangis, normally celebrated with much drinking. Those who attended came from different villages, having already suspended their various agricultural and non-agricultural subsistence activities—there was little shortage of time for drinking. Abundant food, liquor, and a market-fair: this attractive combination must have accounted for the large crowds that milled to the

19. KPAAR, 1874–5, BA.PD. 1875. vol. 115, Compilation 244; McIver to Coll., Kh., 28.4.1899, BRO.DDR.DN 5. FN 26; FDO to Coll., Kh., 1.9.1891, BA.RD. 1892. vol. 144, Compilation 948.

20. Ashburner to Secy., GoB, 31.3.1873, BA.RD. 1873. vol. 87, Compilation 2039; McIver to Coll., Kh., 28.4.1899, BRO.DDR.DN 5. FN 26.

darbar. Surely, for the bulk of those who attended the darbar, revelry was more important than internal disputes, resistance, or the affirmation of colonial power.

Then there was resistance, some of it at a popular level. The chiefs and Dangis' drinking and revelry undermined the colonial staging of the darbar as a solemn and dignified occasion. British officials regularly upbraided the chiefs, fined them for being drunk, and in later decades exhorted them to abjure liquor. The chiefs also used the darbars to oppose British measures such as the creation of new forest reserves, grazing restrictions, or the ban on killing witches. Persistent collective resistance was visible at several darbars in the 1880s and 1890s, when forest officials tried to push through a new set of restrictions that would have dramatically increased their surveillance and control of the region.

IV

To point, in this manner, to how the developmentalist project (or, as the case maybe, science or other forms of colonial knowledge) is hybridized and inflected with local meanings, is of course important. But we should not be too quick to assume that such appropriations have an aporetic relationship with development. For, there is a certain time of the primitive involved in development that has affinities with this regional and local—which, perhaps, even produces the figures of the local and the regional as points of resistance to the extension of bureaucratic power.

Consider a curious paradox. For the nineteenth century, the darbar can still be understood by pointing to its administrative importance, given the relatively limited reach of the colonial state. Dangs was sometimes described as 'an unknown country.'[21] The annual meeting was virtually the only annual occasion when a British official visited the region, as when the collector adjudicated on feuds, disputes or successions, or when he tried to persuade the chiefs to accept more stringent forest restrictions. But by the early twentieth century at least, such an argument cannot

21. Annual Report of the Khandesh Political Agent, 1874–5, Maharastra State Archives, Bombay (MSA), Political Department (PD), 1875, vol. 115, Compilation 244.

hold. In the years following 1901, when a British demarcation of the region was authorized and colonial authority was extended in far-reaching ways. The region was now divided into Reserved and Protected forests. Dangis were now regularly tried for violating newly imposed forest laws; cultivation was entirely and success-fully prohibited in that half of the Dangs which had been declared Reserved forest; and even in the protected forests, cultivation practices were forcibly recast so as to do less 'damage' to teak. Administratively, the darbar was now marginal: a diwan was now based permanently in the Dangs, and a police force was set up for the region. By this time, one might be tempted to say, there was a shift to new forms of government, forms which sought to exercise a more regular, capillary, and everyday authority over the region.

Officials still claimed that the darbars 'enable the administration to keep in touch with the wants of the people.'[22] But there is little doubt that annual meetings became less important as a means of administering the region. This declining administrative importance was indexed in the fate of reports on them. While there are detailed reports on the meetings till the mid-1850s, these thin out in later decades. From the 1860s, already, they are usually confined to a routinized paragraph. Interaction with the Dangis was now a more routinized affair, distributed across the year instead of being concentrated in one event. Disputes, proposals, or successions were no longer decided at the darbar; even the money was paid in installments rather than at the meetings.

And yet, paradoxically, the darbar flourished. Indeed, so impor-tant was the darbar to the British that it was held twice a year from the late nineteenth century. There was even a nomenclatural index of the elaboration of the meetings. From around 1870, officials slowly stopped referring to the occasion as an annual meeting, and commenced calling it the Dangs Darbar. This novel framing also required appropriate forms of behavior: now, more than before, the collector met the chiefs 'solemnly in Darbar.'[23] By the late nineteenth century, the ceremonials surrounding the occasion had been lovingly filigreed,[24] and that genre of British

22. Dangs Administration Report, 1944–6, IOL.V. 10.1050.

23. MSA, PD, 1888, vol. 115, Compilation 1683. See also: Cumine to Commissioner, Northern Division, 9.7.1895, MSA, PD, 1895. vol. 314, Compilation 948.

24. Hardiman 1994.

ritual for which colonial officials had such flair, the oriental darbar, was well in place.

Even an additional darbar was instituted. After the demarcation, Kokni cultivators—the Koknis and the Bhils were the two major communities in the Dangs—became very important in the colonial scheme of things. They were seen as more 'civilized' and less wasteful of timber. Kokni village headmen could supply the forest department with labor power, and assist in afforestation or fire-protection. And so, it came to be that a new darbar (a third one) was instituted for Kokni patils, where 'a silver bangle or other suitable present' was given to each of the patils who helped the department. Such presents, it was claimed, would be 'well understood and appreciated in the Dangs where so many giras allowances exist.'[25]

Put another way, the consolidation of those very forms of power that potentially made the darbar superfluous was accompanied by the elaboration of the darbar. Nor, as we know, was Dangs exceptional in this regard. The nineteenth and early twentieth century saw a furious expansion of state rituals, precisely at the time when forms of everyday power made these occasions irrelevant as a means of creating authority in the older sense. In Britain, for example, the period saw the elaboration of royal rituals, and similar rituals developed elsewhere in Europe during the time.

How do we understand this paradox of the proliferation of superfluous ritual? One response has been to view it as part of the invention of tradition. Such invention, Hobsbawm famously suggested, has been taking place at a particularly rapid pace in the last two hundred years as a result of the urge to create symbols of continuity in the midst of a rapid transformation of society.[26] Yet, to point to the invented nature of tradition is to underscore, may one say, the fact that the past, which appears to inhabit the present, and be affirmed within the present, is actually produced in the present rather than having been extruded into it from a time before? But the very constructivism that makes it such a powerful riposte to the notion that traditions in the present are continuous with the past also makes it the oppositional mirror image of that

25. See the correspondence in MSA, Revenue Department (RD), 1907, vol. 126, Compilation 632; and MSA, RD, 1902, vol. 107, Compilation 949 Part II.

26. Hobsbawm 1983: 1.

historicism which it contests. That is to say, instead of a continuing and unfolding past, it emphasizes a continuing present as the locus of the production of tradition. But it fails to recognize the production of the distinctive time that has made possible its particular way of separating past and present, a way that it shares with the perspective it criticizes.

Nor is it adequate to simply deny the paradox, and to point to the ways in which ritual is really about power. This curious response, though not wrong, refuses to acknowledge the paradoxical separation of ritual and power save as an error or misrecognition. It would be far more interesting rather to explore the ways in which this separation comes to be instituted and made real. Inherent to this relatively new conviction about the separability, and therefore potential superfluity, of ritual was its relationship to the time of development, that is to say, to historicist time. On the one hand, rituals were seen as the form in which power had been wielded in former times, times before 'men become enlightened.'[27] As such, the time of ritual could not be the time of modern power; it could only provide rehearsals of a power already constituted within the time of development; in this sense, within a developmentalist vision, ritual was necessarily separate from power.

On the other hand, ritual was considered necessary for dealing with the time of the primitive. Increasingly, there was faith in its persuasiveness for those groups who inhabited an earlier time—the colonized East, and the popular in Europe—its easily roused and pacified rabble. In the colonial portmanteau of persuasive symbols and rituals, we know, the darbar had an especially important role to play, for the Oriental mind was seen as peculiarly susceptible to its elaborate ceremony. As a British viceroy of India, Lytton, remarked, 'the further East you go, the greater becomes the importance of a bit of bunting.'[28] The popular, it seemed to colonial officials, mistook the simulacra of power for the real; empty pomp created real power. In this sense, perhaps occasions like modern darbars sought to effect the goals of development by creating a medium and language appropriate to the primitive time of the wild tribes and the colonized.

27. Cannadine 1983.
28. Cohn 1983: 192.

Often, this engagement produced primitivism—that distinctive discourse which insisted on pervasiveness and inescapability of historicist time, and simultaneously sought to affirm the primitive produced by that time. Thus, in British understandings, there was often a celebration of wild tribes, especially of their masculinity as opposed to the effeminacy of the castes. The former were ascribed a number of qualities regarded as masculine—nobility, honesty, loyalty, and rugged independence amongst them. It was because of the effeminacy of plains castes that the Bhils had been restive and resorted to raids in precolonial times. British gazetteers often claimed that precolonial relations between Bhils and the surrounding Maratha plains states had been one of unremitting hostility. Left to themselves, upper-caste native officials, whether in princely states or British territory, were prone to be cruel to the Bhils, to deceive them, or to resort to treachery. This celebration of the wild tribes was deeply tied to the affirmation of colonialism itself. In British accounts, it was often the demonstration of colonial masculinity that persuaded the Bhils to halt raids. Bhil Agents, the British officials responsible for looking after the forest communities, conformed closely to British conceptions of what was involved in being particularly masculine—they had to be capable of hard riding, very good at sports and hunting, and so on. And, because they were like public school boys, Bhils were believed to recognize British gentlemanliness. They had 'reverence' and 'affection' for the British, they had 'unbounded confidence in European Gentlemen, whose character they think they understand.'[29] Perennial boys because of their primitive nature, and likeable boys at that, the Bhils and the wild tribes made ideal subjects. The nobility of the Bhils provided British officials a means of thinking about themselves, of locating the essence of imperial masculinity.[30]

The overlaps between colonial understandings of wild tribes and of forests are striking (as, in a related context, were the similarities between castes and agricultural wastes).[31] Just as the Bhils were before civilization, the forests were in colonial understanding before cultivation (and therefore civilization). The large forests in

29. BA.PD. 1858. vol. 95. Compilation 734.
30. Skaria 1997.
31. See Gidwani 1992.

the hills were also invested with the time of the primitive. True, here too, malaria killed, and the weather was hardly very prepossessing from the point of view of the British. Yet, the forests were the abode of the wild tribes, where they had their 'wild inhospitable mountain homes'[32] and that itself already made the forests more attractive. The nobility, simplicity, and sense of honor of the wild tribes refigured these forests and made them a more masculine and friendly place—repeatedly, officials remarked on how while their provisions had been stolen from camp in the plains, in the forests there was no such worry.

The colonial affirmation of the primitive, while most spectacularly visible in the British celebration of the masculine tribes, was also involved in British orientalism, if in less dramatic ways. True, Orientalist scholarship claimed to be classicist (in the sense that the classic is that which claims to be unmarked by or indifferent to evolutionary time; it is that which is located in an eternal present) rather than primitivist. Yet, as Said's argument suggests, Orientalism could never be classicist: it was inevitably about locating the Orient in a time behind that of the West, and in certain contexts affirming that time. Similarly, there is the trope of the contented countryside—of the peasant who, though from another time, was happy with British rule, and would not rebel unless instigated to by outside agitators. Such tropes suggest that the affirmation of the primitive was constitutive of colonial thought not just in dealing with the wild tribes, but with the colonized more broadly.

If primitivism was so pervasive, then perhaps this was because the peasants and the tribes represented a moment of danger to historicist thought. By insisting on and even celebrating their subsumption within the time of the primitive, colonial officials emphatically rejected the apprehension that the wild tribes did not actually belong to the time of the primitive, that they were outside historicist time itself, and represented an other time. By affirming Dangis as primitives, colonial officials affirmed the pervasiveness of colonialism's developmental time; they insisted that there could be no other time. Rendered this way, the radical difference represented by Dangi cultural and political practices could be conceived of as past, and then invoked back into the present as the primitive, and as primitivism.

32. BA.PD. 1858. vol. 95. Compilation 734. Cf. also MacKenzie 1988: 191f.

V

In independent India, state ritual has been extensively transformed. Darbars, like much other ritual associated with the colonial state, did not fit into the nationalist vision. Already, the Indian language press had been critical of the 1877 imperial assembly, and early twentieth century nationalists were even more hostile to florid British rituals.[33] This was not only because the intimations of exoticism and backwardness carried by the darbar were anathema to a movement which claimed modernity. More importantly, perhaps, the British claim to have the consent of the popular rested in part on institutions like the darbar, and such a claim was a direct challenge to the nationalist claim to be the popular. Predictably, state-organized darbars soon became virtually extinct in independent India.

Why, then, does the postcolonial state continue to stage the Dangs darbar? In part, because of a primitivism very akin to that of colonial officials. The Dangis are, in the argot of development, 'Scheduled Tribes,' the wild and exotic Other of mainstream indigenous Indian discourse. As most government officials would point out, the darbar is very important to the Dangis, who think very differently from us, which is why it cannot be done away with. That is to say, because groups like the Dangis are at the margins of dominant Indian notions of nationhood, because the metonym of the national–popular operates less forcefully for them, because they inhabit a different time, rituals like the darbar can be deployed for them with less compunction. Unthreatening, exotic Others, fascinated by bits of bunting: perhaps the darbar persists because the Scheduled Tribes are in national–popular discourse the laggards who require the darbar to be made modern and brought into the unfolding narrative of the nation, and whose time can be affirmed and celebrated? Indeed, tourism brochures for the state of Gujarat tout the Dangs darbar as an event that must be attended.

The overwhelming dominance of the Indian state at the darbar is also perhaps symptomatic of the way in which the Dangs darbar is part of a nationalist primitivism. Soon after Independence, the Indian government made explicit its sovereignty over the region by doubling the payments to the chiefs, and designating them as political pensions instead of lease dues. Around the same time, the

33. Cohn 1983.

different darbars were collapsed into one tightly trussed occasion, shorn of many of its older features: gone were the provisions, the rose water, the shawls, and the turbans. At a darbar I attended, the chiefs were seated on one corner of the dais, but they were certainly not the focus of attention. The center of the dais was occupied by forest officials, the Dangs district collector, and the invitees. Even the money was not distributed to the chiefs in public. They merely sat (all 14 of them) along one side, and the Amala raja glowered while little girls (the daughters of government officials at Ahwa) sang a prayer, and young women (the wives of government officials) presented bouquets of flowers to VIPs (very important persons, mainly senior government officials). All these changes are indicative of the transformation of the darbar into an official function, a ritual that is about the administrative hierarchies of the modern state, especially that gargantuan version of the modern state that accompanies the development of forms of everyday power. Thus, it is that the principal actors in the official function are state functionaries, normally bureaucrats, and elected representatives holding positions of state power. The audience too is composed principally—not necessarily in terms of numbers but in terms of the targeted group—of lower level state functionaries and bureaucrats. Here, then, two different times are yoked together, that of development and of the primitive, and the dominance of the former is clear.

Yet, it would be hasty to assume that nationalist primitivism is little different from its colonial predecessor. The double bind of the relationship between the nation-state and the popular at work in nationalist primitivism threatens, far more seriously and systematically than under colonial rule, to undo the time of the primitive itself. True, in a modified continuation of colonial rule, the popular—whether as peasant, tribal, or the poor—now emerges as the distinctive object of nationalist development. The ascription of primitiveness to it is evinced in its repeated casting as natural, as in Nehru's lyrical evocations of the Indian peasant's deep connections to the land. As such, one strand of the relationship between the nation-state and the popular involves the insistence that the latter needs to be remade. This project of development is carried out in the name of the nation; indeed, the nation claims development as its very rationale for existence.[34]

34. Chatterjee 1993.

Nevertheless, the Indian nation-state shares that distinctive ventriloquism of modernity where the nation-state has to speak not simply in the name of the popular or for the popular but as the popular. That is to say, the nation-state is presented and understood as the embodiment of the people. At meetings that Nehru addressed during the Independence struggle—the struggle, in a sense, for the Indian nation to realize itself as a nation-state—he would explain to crowds that India was not so much lands, rivers, or forests as 'the people of India.' 'You are part of this *Bharat Mata*, I told them, you are in a manner yourselves Bharat Mata, and as the idea slowly soaked into their brains, their eyes would light up as though they had made a great discovery.'[35] It was this claim to embody the popular, to fold within itself the particularity of that popular, which allowed the abstract and universal time of development to be reworked so that it represented India. Without this claim (and Indian culture and Indian history emerge as categories out of the efforts to sustain it) to be the popular, India could not be produced as a nation. The primitivism of development is mainstream nationalism's way of staging the resultant relationship of the nation-state with the popular. Such a primitivism claims to inhabit the popular but denies substantive equality to it; it renders the popular into an object that needs to be developed and educated so that the popular can truly acquire agency and become the nation. In this sense, a claim to inhabiting the time of the primitive is constitutive of the nation-state.

Yet, the intimacy of the connection between the national and the popular also threatens primitivism. To become the popular, to speak as the popular: this move sometimes undid the time of primitivism itself, and created the possibility that the nation could be constituted by another time and politics. In this other time, the popular was a substantive equal, and as such could not be the primitive, or the object of development. Mainstream nationalism gestured towards this other time in its anti-historicist insistence on a universal rather than limited adult suffrage. On the conceptual fringes of this mainstream nationalism, figures such as Gandhi, Indulal Yagnik, and Babasaheb Ambedkar sought to produce the popular as a substantive equal. In the case of Gandhi and Yagnik, I have argued elsewhere, their affirmation of the popular led to a

35. Nehru 1984: 60.

politics of neighborliness that was quite hostile to the insistence of mainstream nationalism that the primitive be made to transcend its time and place through development.[36] Within such a politics, indeed, there was no conceptual space for development and its historicism.

VI

In these crucial senses, development cannot only be thought of in the ways it represents itself: as a force of history, as an attempt to transform the natural–popular into the historical by bringing about modernity and progress. Nor, can it be thought of in terms of its instrument effects of extending bureaucratic power, of depoliticizing poverty by claiming that it has technical solutions. Development is all of that, of course. But, especially in nationalist thought, the popular is not only that which development would like to erase; it is also that which development has to embody. This is, of course an impossibility, for if it did then development itself would be abolished. It is the attempt of developmentalist thought to affirm the popular without abolishing itself that produces the nationalist time of the primitive. In this sense, development is not the same as progress: it both affirms and denies progress through its peculiar relationship with the popular. It is, perhaps, only with the death of progress that the discourse of development becomes possible. Developmentalist thought does not simply extend a distinctive bureaucratic rationality; it has also to insist on the deathlessness of the primitive in order to sustain its claim to be a nation. And, this claim to the deathlessness of the primitive, in turn, always threatens to transmute into a completely different radical politics that rejects the very time that sustains both development and the primitive.

References

Bayly, C. A., 1983. *Rulers, Townsmen and Bazaars: North Indian Society in the Age of British Expansion, 1770–1870*. Cambridge: Cambridge University Press.

———, 1996. *Empire and Information: Intelligence Gathering and Social Communication in North India, 1780–1870*. Cambridge: Cambridge University Press.

36. Skaria 2002.

Bomanji, K. R., 1903. *The Dangs Boundary Dispute*, Part I. Bombay.

Cannadine, David, 1983. 'The context, performance and meaning of ritual: the British monarchy and the "invention of tradition", c. 1820–1977.' In Eric Hobsbawm and Terence Ranger (eds.), *The Invention of Tradition*. Cambridge: Cambridge University Press.

Chatterjee, Partha, 1993. *The Nation and its Fragments.* Princeton: Princeton University Press.

Cohn, Bernard, 1983. 'Representing authority in Victorian India.' In Eric Hobsbawm and Terence Ranger (eds.), *The Invention of Tradition*. Cambridge: Cambridge University Press.

Ferguson, James, [1990] 1994. *The Anti-politics Machine: 'Development,' Depoliticization and Bureaucratic Power in Lesotho*. Minneapolis: University of Minnesota Press.

Gidwani, Vinay, 1992. '"Waste" and the permanent settlement in Bengal.' *Economic and Political Weekly* 27(4).

Gordon, Stewart, 1994. 'Bhils and the idea of a criminal tribe in nineteenth century India.' In Stewart Gordon, *Marathas, Marauders and State Formation*. New Delhi: Oxford University Press.

Government of Baroda, 1891. *Selections from the Records of the Baroda Government*, no. 10, vol. 1,*Dang Case*. Baroda: Government of Baroda Press.

Government of Bombay, 1880. *Gazetteer of the Bombay Presidency*, vol. 12, *Khandesh*. Bombay: Government of Bombay Press.

Guha, Ramachandra, 1985. 'Scientific forestry and social change.' *Economic and Political Weekly* 20 (Special Number).

Guha, Ranajit, 1996. 'The small voice of history.' In Dipesh Chakrabarty and Shahid Amin (eds.), *Subaltern Studies IX: Writings on South Asian History and Society*. New Delhi: Oxford University Press.

———, 1982. 'The prose of counter-insurgency.' In Ranajit Guha (ed.), *Subaltern Studies I*. New Delhi: Oxford University Press.

Hardiman, David, 1994. 'Power in the forests: the Dangs, 1820–1940.' In David Arnold and David Hardiman (eds.),*Subaltern Studies, Vol. VIII*. New Delhi: Oxford University Press.

Hobsbawm. Eric, 1983. 'Introduction: Inventing traditions.' In Eric Hobsbawm and Terence Ranger (eds.), *The Invention of Tradition*. Cambridge: Cambridge University Press.

Khanapurkar, D. P., 1944. 'The Aborigines of South Gujarat.' Ph.D. thesis, University of Bombay.

MacKenzie, J. M., 1988. *The Empire of Nature: Hunting, Conservation and British Imperialism*. Manchester: Manchester University Press.

Mann, Michael, 1986-93. *Sources of Social Power*, 2 vols. Cambridge: Cambridge University Press.

Nehru, Jawaharlal, 1984. *The Discovery of India*. New Delhi: Oxford University Press.

Skaria, Ajay, 1997. 'Shades of wildness: tribe, caste and gender in western India.' *Journal of Asian Studies* 56(3).

———, 1998. 'From desiccationism to scientific forestry: the Dangs, 1840s–1920s.' In Richard Grove, Satpal Sangwan and Vinita Damodaran (eds.), *Nature and the Orient: The Environmental History of South and Southeast Asia.* New Delhi: Oxford University Press.

———, 1999. *Hybrid Histories: Forests, Frontiers, and Wildness in Western India.* New Delhi: Oxford University Press.

———, 2001. 'Homeless in Gujarat and India.' *Indian Economic and Social History Review.*

Wink, Andre, 1986. *Land and Sovereignty in India: Agrarian Society and Politics under the Eighteenth Century Maratha Svarajya.* Cambridge: Cambridge University Press.

9

Educating Entrepreneurs, Organizing for Social Justice: NGO[1] Development Strategies in New Delhi Bastis[2]

SANGEETA LUTHRA

NGOs, DEVELOPMENT, AND GLOBALIZATION

Since the mid-1980s grassroots non-governmental organizations (NGOs) have been widely celebrated as the best hope for development, and particularly poverty alleviation, in the Third World. The popularity of NGOs has been attributed to their intimate knowledge of and connection to the communities and localities in which they work. They have been extolled by both the political left and right for being more accountable, more efficient, more innovative, more democratic, more participatory, and more empowering than

1. The abbreviation 'NGO' stands for 'non-governmental organization' and will be used as such throughout this paper. A popular term in India for such organizations is also 'Volag' which stands for 'voluntary agency' or 'voluntary organization.' I decided to use 'NGO' because the organizations I observed used this phrase to describe themselves particularly in reference to a larger national and international development community.

2. The word *basti* means settlement, neighborhood, or community and it is often used by NGOs to refer to the squatters' settlements in and around New Delhi.

their governmental bureaucratic counterparts.[3] In addition, they have been associated with progressive social movements like environmentalism, feminism, and human rights, and as deftly combining development work with political activism—what D. L. Sheth[4] has described in an essay of the same title as 'alternative development as political practice.'

By their supporters on the left, they are seen as the Robin Hoods of development—empowering the poor and weak to take what is rightfully theirs.[5] And, from the perspective of the right, they are viewed as efficient microenterprises relatively uncorrupted by temptations of political and bureaucratic power.[6] Although much of the praise for NGOs is well deserved, this paper seeks to complicate both of these images—the Robin Hood, subaltern image and the clean-cut 'social entrepreneur' image.

In the 1970s and 1980s, NGOs played an important role in formulating critiques of the highly centralized, growth-centered development approaches of international agencies and many national governments, and were instrumental in getting those agencies to rethink their development priorities.[7] However, the success of NGO efforts to lobby for alternative definitions of development (measurable partially in the popularity of such discourses as 'participatory' and 'sustainable' development) has had its costs. NGOs are faced with a troubling paradox. They must balance their growing links to the international development community

3. In the last few years, the success of NGOs to live up to their promise has been under serious scrutiny. S. Akbar Zaidi (1999: 204–4) paints a picture of dismal failure by the NGO movement to achieve the large-scale reform of development that had been hoped for.

4. Sheth 1987.

5. See Bhatt 1989; Kothari 1984; Pandey 1991; Sethi 1984, 1985; Sethi and Kothari 1985; PRIA 1991; and Tandon 1986.

6. See Gulhati et al. 1995; Reilly quoted in Carroll 1992; and Smith 1990.

7. See Pietila 1990; Sheth 1984, 1987. Of course, there have been attempts to rethink growth-centered development from within mainstream development agencies, in particular within the United Nations agencies and the World Bank. Kate Young (1993) discusses this in the context of the Women in Development debate, and Martha Finnemore (1997) presents an analysis of the rethinking of development in terms of poverty alleviation by the World Bank.

with the need to continue the critique of hegemonic development discourses. In other words, they are balancing a growing cosmopolitanism while maintaining connections to specific locales. The latter is particularly important since NGOs, or specifically grassroots NGOs, have been often characterized as essentially 'local' institutions. This characterization purports not just an infrastructural relationship to a specific locale but also an epistemological, social, and political relationship with those communities that are the targets of development programs. In this way, the NGO identity is grounded in a regional modernity that is both cosmopolitan and parochial and enables the 'imagining' of communities like 'Third World women' or 'indigenous peoples.'[8] Furthermore, NGOs create important institutional nodes in development networks that stretch from rural grassroots organizations to international development agencies, thus constituting regions at both the subnational and supranational levels.

As pivotal actors in the development community, NGOs are engaged in a dialogue of competing and contradictory discourses of social change, progress, and equity. This is manifest in the complexities and inconsistencies of the everyday practices of grassroots NGOs. In the following pages I outline two popular strategies in the Community Development Programs of grassroots NGOs in New Delhi in order to illustrate the complex and at times contradictory nature of NGO identity, discourse, and practice. The strategies I look at are the promotion of mahila mandals or 'women's circles,' and the creation of income generation programs (also primarily for women). While neither of these strategies is new to development initiatives in India, over the last ten years they have been redefined to achieve different ends from those of their earlier counterparts.

For example, in their current incarnation, income generation programs (IGP) go beyond trying to empower women by giving them an income. Today, these programs seek to re-educate women in the principles of entrepreneurship. The discourse of entrepreneurship (and more broadly, privatization) in NGOs is a powerful articulation of how these groups reconcile an earlier tradition of Gandhian, Marxist, and/or feminist activism while facing a landscape increasingly shaped by economic liberalization, multinational

8. Appadurai 1996: 3.

corporations, an even more powerful Indian industrialist class, a besieged (often desperate) bureaucratic class, and tremendous environmental degradation and crises.

What we learn when we understand these two development strategies in relation to discourses like feminism, and more recently, privatization, is that there is a struggle over ideas, practice, and politics in grassroots development. By focusing on the practices of NGOs (versus looking at them as unified organizations/ subjects) we can better appreciate how a single organization can pursue programs that seem to be logically and ideologically at odds. This is significant for understanding the role of NGOs in changing the course of planned development because it repudiates such reductive characterizations of NGOs as being either 'social enterprises' or social crusaders. Finally, by highlighting the tensions that are generated in NGO practices, particularly as they respond to discourses of development generated by international movements, we begin to interrogate the romanticization of the local and better understand the role NGOs play in constituting regional modernities.

INCOME GENERATION STRATEGIES IN NEW DELHI NGOS: FROM SELF-EMPLOYED TO MICROENTREPRENEUR

A standard rationalization for income generation programs for women since the 1970s has been based in the liberal feminist assertion that women who work outside of the domestic sphere and have an income gain some degree of economic independence. However, the extent to which working outside of the domestic sphere has actually meant economic independence has been the subject of debate.[9] Women who earn an income do not automatically see an improvement in their status within their families and/ or communities.[10] Despite the debate, income generation programs continue to be a central strategy in the community development schemes of grassroots NGOs in New Delhi.

9. See Diane Elson's (1994) discussion of the World Bank's understanding of women's economic participation.

10. Young 1993: 83.

The influence of feminism on development and specifically on NGOs needs to be understood in terms of two different perspectives in feminism. Liberal feminist groups, which have generally defined political struggle as the protection of women's individual rights,[11] have focused on inserting women into the development process and have not really questioned the fundamental assumptions of that process.[12] Kate Young points out that, 'the focuses and strategies of institutional WID [Women in Development] derived from the concerns of the mainstream, so that WID proponents moved from concern with welfare to poverty to efficiency as did mainstream development practitioners.'[13] In other words, within the development establishment there has occurred a marriage of convenience between the advocates of liberal feminism and the proponents of neo-liberal development economics.

Furthermore, as Young herself notes, liberal feminism has not been the only response by women to the development establishment. At the UN World Conference on Women in Mexico City in 1975, there were demands for 'equity strategies' as well as trenchant critiques of patriarchal institutions.[14] This other more radical feminist perspective is what Leslie Calman calls the 'empowerment' perspective.[15] Groups that embrace the empowerment perspective focus on the class and caste differences among women and the structures of exploitation that these differences perpetuate. In the context of the Indian women's movement the empowerment perspective has become more prominent since the 1970s[16] and has increasingly become associated with organizations that work with urban and rural poor women, which are focused on 'economic and social rights...from below, not the conferring of rights or economic development from above.'[17] These more radical feminist organizations are a significant part of the contemporary Indian NGO sector.

But the growing emphasis on entrepreneurism in women's income generation programs cannot be explained solely in terms of

11. Jagger 1983; Young 1993.
12. Escobar 1995: 177–80; Young 1993: 129.
13. Young 1993: 131.
14. Ibid.
15. Calman 1992.
16. See Calman 1992: 15–17; Mazumdar 1985: 5–6.
17. Calman 1992: 15.

feminism. We need to look at the growing dominance of privatization ideology in the development community.[18] By 'privatization' I mean political and economic discourses that advocate the transfer of various public services like welfare programs, public education, waste management, and other public works from government agencies to private contractors. Income generation programs are viewed by many in the development world as part of a broader movement towards privatization, and NGOs themselves are often represented as private development enterprises or 'microenterprises.'

The growing support for the 'microenterprise' or informal sectors of Third World economies by organizations like the World Bank is part of the incorporation of privatization perspectives in the development programs of many NGOs.[19] For example, the Bank's 'Consultative Group to Assist the Poorest' (CGAP) established in 1995, has defined its poverty alleviation agenda almost entirely in terms of microenterprise promotion.[20] Through its Economic Development Institute (EDI), the Bank runs a program in India called the Women's Enterprise Management Training Outreach Program that 'works through some 30 NGOs to design and deliver management training to enhance the income generating capability and self-reliance of women microentrepreneurs.'[21] The Bank's emphasis on microenterprise as the solution to poverty alleviation is clear in the objectives of these two groups—the CGAP and EDI. This characterization of the informal sector as a 'microenterprise' sector is problematic in that it understates the harsh conditions of work and lack of self-determination many of those working in the informal sector experience. The Indian organization Public Interest Research Group (PIRG) makes the following comments on this re-definition of the informal sector:

The focus of research in the informal sector shifted from describing the prevalence of poverty and social insecurity to looking for policy initiatives, which would make this sector dynamic and significant for the growth of modern industry.[22]

18. See Kothari 1995; Zaidi 1999.
19. Webster 1996: 18; World Bank 1996: 12.
20. World Bank 1996: 11–12.
21. Ibid.
22. PIRG 1995: 20.

Ironically the story of entrepreneurism in NGOs does not begin at the World Bank.[23] The success of South Asian NGOs like the Self-Employed Women's Association (SEWA) and the Grameen Bank in Bangladesh, in creating credit unions for women played an important role in popularizing the discourse of poor women as entrepreneurs.[24] Although in World Bank documents[25] there is no acknowledgment of whether the Bank was directly influenced by the successes of these (and other) NGOs, the microenterprise programs seem to be at least partially inspired by the successes of NGOs in this area.

It is, of course, important to distinguish the discourse of entrepreneurship that NGOs like SEWA have employed from that of the World Bank. These NGOs defined their clients as 'self-employed' persons, whereas the Bank's interest in 'micro-entrepreneurs' is in the context of 'private sector development (including micro, small, and medium enterprises),'[26] and seems invested in a more orthodox conceptualization of the entrepreneur as growth and profit-motivated. While these are not entirely contradictory or even mutually exclusive connotations, they do represent two different visions of economic well being, and my contention in the next section is that the latter discourse is becoming a dominant one. In other words, although some in the NGO sector view their programs in entrepreneurial educa-tion as an extension of social and economic empowerment, in fact it has a tendency to become a means for incorporating work-ers from the informal sector into more disciplined capitalist relations.

Finally, this relatively new incarnation of income generation programs must be understood in the context of the privatization

23. Obviously, the World Bank is not the only organization to promote IGPs through NGOs. Other organizations, for example, that provided funding to NGOs in my fieldwork are the ILO, the Ford Foundation, and CRY (an Indian funding agency). These funds were applied to IGPs as well as other programs.

24. First Lady Hillary Rodham-Clinton spoke at length about the efforts of the Grameen Bank in furthering the cause of women and girls in the subcontinent and globally (Mrs Rodham-Clinton's address on 29 March 1995, Rajiv Gandhi Center, New Delhi).

25. E.g. World Bank 1996; Webster 1996.

26. World Bank 1996: 12.

and structural adjustment program of the Indian government.[27] Since the late 1980s, the Indian government has pursued a structural adjustment program in which it has privatized and deregulated many sectors of the economy.[28] Concurrently, there has been tremendous growth in the overall economy.[29] Although the growth is concentrated in the upper and middle classes and has not translated into more or better jobs for working Indians,[30] there is a general sentiment that opportunities exist for those ready and willing to seize them. In other words, the new wealth experienced by some Indians has contributed to the false notion that the prosperity of this period is equally available to all.[31] It is not surprising, then, that in such a climate income generation programs espousing entrepreneurial principles would seem the best, even the only, solution to poverty alleviation in the nation. Furthermore, because they look like private development enterprises, NGOs are doing well (judging by the growth in numbers of organizations in the last ten years) in this period of privatization.

Even organizations like OXFAM and UNICEF, which have critiqued the structural adjustment and privatization agenda of the World Bank and the IMF,[32] fund NGOs working with this discourse of entrepreneurship. The support from these organizations may be explained because the donors interpret entrepreneurist discourse as one prioritizing 'self-employment' and not a logic of profit;[33] and because privatization has gained so much discursive

27. There is even a brief discussion of the need to provide entrepreneurship training in the *National Policy on Education* (GoI 1986: 13, 17), and in regard to women's education in the *Programme of Action: National Policy on Education* (GoI 1986: 110).

28. Government cutbacks have generally not affected development programs—what are referred to in the Five-Year Plans as the 'social' or 'welfare' sectors of the economy (see Sen 1993: 161).

29. Parikh 1999.

30. PIRG 1995: 1, 17–22.

31. Rajni Kothari (1995) describes this false sense of well being as an 'amnesia' towards poverty in his most recent book.

32. Bird 1996.

33. Diane Elson's (1994) analysis of 'people-centered development' versus 'money-centered development' is useful in understanding how development programs can become money or profit-centered even when they are trying not to be.

currency that even groups that opposed it at the macro level accept it at the micro level. The current climate, favoring private micro-entrepreneurial forms of development, is described in the following discussion of the 1995 World Summit on Social Development in Copenhagen:

Adherence to the principles and policies advocated in Copenhagen leads to the conclusion that the new World Social Order is based on *'market fundamentalism'* which will create its own social values and beliefs. Its basic ideology is to emphasize individual rather than collective welfare expressed in these words in the Declaration: 'We affirm that in both economic and social terms the most productive policies and investments are those which empower people to maximize their capacities, resources and opportunities.' In this way, 'human resources' are linked to the dynamism of the market and open competition is linked to inefficiencies in expenditure on social services.[34]

In the next section I will explore how the discourses of entrepreneurship, 'market fundamentalism,' and privatization echo in the everyday practice of income generation programs. Through some examples from my fieldwork, I will outline dilemmas that NGO staff face as they try to reconcile the goal of income generation for self-employment and empowerment with the relatively newer incarnation of income generation as microenterprise.

'LEARNING TO ENTERPRISE':[35]
NGOs AS MICROENTERPRISES

Soma: *In today's climate the market rules.*
Gauri: *In today's climate everyone wants to know what the benefit to themselves is.*[36]

It was a warm November afternoon when I walked into the Jangpura office of the NGO Action India. Gauri, one of the founders of Action India (AI hereafter), and Soma, a visiting consultant, were leading a brainstorming session with members of a grain coopera-tive project that AI was sponsoring. As I joined the group sitting in a circle on the cool floor of the main room, I was able to hear

34. PIRG 1995: 32, emphasis mine.
35. I am paraphrasing the title of Paul Willis' (1977) excellent ethnography on working class children and schooling in England.
36. Action India, November 1995.

the tail end of a discussion of one of AI's loan and credit schemes for a small typing school. There was a pause and Gauri asked Sumitra, a middle-aged woman who had worked as a weaver until 1984, when she joined AI as a healthworker, to describe the Grain Bank project. Sumitra and another woman, Virmati, are coordinators of the Grain Bank scheme. Sumitra spoke confidently in front of the group. All of her discussion was in Hindi with a few choice English words thrown in—like 'quality' and 'risk' or 'joking.' She explained that they have collected Rs 60,000—20,000 from 20 women and a matching loan from AI of 2000 per head—and found a place to store grain. They have also researched where and when to buy the grain by going to nearby farms and talking to farmers about when it is harvested and how to get the grain at cheaper rates. They visited wholesale markets to compare costs and to learn about how the grain is bought and distributed to ration stores. What they found was that the best point to get grain was to buy it from transporters en route from farm to market. If you could buy a whole load, the transporters were more than happy to get rid of it for a cheaper rate than the market. The problem for Sumitra and the cooperative was that one truckload amounted to about three months' worth of grain they could sell in their stores, and they were afraid of the risk of investing so much of their money. They were also still not confident about their ability to safely store the surplus grain.

Till date they have not bought or sold any grain because they are afraid of the risk involved. Once Sumitra had made this point, Soma spent a lot of time talking about the nature of their fear. This part of the discussion was awkward because Soma, Gauri, and myself, to an extent, discussed this in English and switched back to Hindi to address Sumitra, Virmati and a few other women who did not speak English. Soma was trying to get them to understand that it was their fear of risk that was stopping them from moving forward in the project because they had clearly done enough research into running the business. This seemed to be accurate and Sumitra nodded her head in agreement. Then Soma turned to Gauri (and to me sitting behind Gauri) and started talking about the nature of this fear because most women are not socialized to taking risks with money—rather they are in the habit of trying to minimize risk. To this Gauri responded that for Sumitra and the other women in the coooperative it was more the fear of losing the money matched by Action India than their own that stopped them. The session ended on this note and most of the participants broke up into small groups for lunch or left the office. I hung on for a little longer in order to talk to Gauri about AI and her views on the NGO scene in general.

Despite an almost flippant attitude to the class differences on the part of the development consultant—she seemed to view the class-based nature of the fear of risk as inconsequential—Action India encouraged such sessions for the women participating in their programs. In addition, the Grain Bank is an unusual IGP in that the idea for it was inspired by the rampant corruption that occurs in government ration shops. By contrast, the IGPs of other organizations I observed seemed to be based on a fairly conservative stereotypical blueprint of what women's work is or can be. Most IGPs offer training in sewing, cooking, embroidery etc., and in doing so reproduce gender stereotypes.[37] Finally, the cooperative model of this IGP highlights a desire to encourage collective action. But it is important to see two forces or perspectives being struggled with in this case. Even with its innovative methods and progressive goals (promoting collective action and providing economic opportunities that do not reproduce tired gender stereotypes), the question of the bottom line looms large. The discussion basically ended on the note that the IGP will only be successful if the women can be transformed into savvy, risk-taking entrepreneurs. [38]

Devi, who has been active in Action India for some years and who is participating in another IGP within the same organization, most succinctly described this dilemma. Devi is involved in an AI

37. See Anand 1985. Also Patricia Kaplan's (1985) work on women's organizations in South India outlines how middle-class values about gender are imposed on working class women. The IGPs I discuss here do not adequately represent the extent to which gender stereotypes are reinforced. But in the course of fieldwork I came across numerous other IGPs which did: for example, one which offered beautician training to adolescent girls and numerous others which offered sewing and clothing design courses.

38. Throughout the discussion of the grain bank and the other IGPs the following were some words/phrases that were commonly used: the market, *jokin* or risk, *karz* or debt, quality or *sahi cheez*, profit, *vyapari* or businessmen, shareholders, *sanyog* or fate, costs or *khharcha*, salary or *tankha*, entrepreneurship, feminism, sharing, self-help, cooperative, and cooperation.

program to develop a business around the production and sale of ayurvedic and herbal medicines, which are commonly used as substitutes for Western medicine or as supplements to it. When Devi was explaining the project to me she said that she worried that the project would become just another *dhundha* or business. She worried that for the sake of *kamai* or earnings, they would take shortcuts in the production process, which would result in the medicines losing their original potency or 'shakti' and value. For her the project represented something greater than simply the manufacture and sale of some commodity—it was a craft that needed to be respected otherwise whatever unique 'shakti' those medicines might have would be lost in an increasingly impersonalized production process. As I began to reflect more on the choices NGOs must make—some of them paradoxical—I began to realize the astuteness of Devi's observations.

In other organizations, I observed, when problems or obstacles arose in an income generation project the middle-class NGO staff would usually just go ahead and make a decision without any discussion with the participating women. The extent to which an NGO allows the participants of its IGPs to deal with problems that arise is critical, because it is at that point that many IGPs face an ideological or pedagogical dilemma. That is, they must choose between slowing down the progress of the IGP for the sake of educational discussion with all of those participating, or foregoing discussion and allowing management decisions to be made by an elite few for the sake of expediency and ultimately success in generating income.

The model of entrepreneurship is not only applied to the 'clients' of NGOs, but often it is also imposed on the lower echelons of NGO staff who are often from the communities they serve. In reference to NGO staff, the entrepreneurial model is often referred to as 'social entrepreneurship' or the 'social entrepreneurs program.' For example, in Deepalaya Education Society, teachers working in non-formal education centers for children and adults were being transferred from purely salaried work to a commission-based or 'fee-for-service' model. The 'social entrepreneurs program' entailed that the salary of teachers working in NGO centers would be determined by the number of students they were able to enroll and keep in their respective programs. The teachers would charge their students a nominal fee that would be matched or doubled by the NGO, and from this would be generated their salaries. The rationalization for the social entrepreneurs program is that it provides greater incentive for the staff to go out and push the programs of the organization to the community. Implicit to the social entrepreneurs program is the idea that competition for students amongst teachers will encourage a better system.

When I spoke to teachers about the social entrepreneurs program, they were very much against it because it created financial insecurity for them.[39] More importantly, they felt that the program generated hostility towards them within the communities in which they worked. The hostility they described was because parents of children who attended the non-formal education schools saw teachers who approached them as doing so only for their own self-interest. The program, in the eyes of teachers, generated an atmosphere of distrust and cynicism between the teachers and the community residents. Finally, it is important to point out that those staff members who were working in higher administrative or coordinating positions, and who were mostly from middle-class backgrounds, were not asked to submit to any kind of social entrepreneurs program.

In the NGO Khazana, a similar program was being instituted in another income generation program in which women were making lunches for a take-out lunch service for local businesses and for children in the NGO's non-formal school. The women who had been working for a fixed salary were told that they would now be getting less salary, but would each get a share of profits they generated from the take-out lunch program. When I spoke to some of the women about the change they were quite upset. They felt the cut was unfair—their salaries were already quite low to begin with—and they had not been given an opportunity to discuss the change before it happened.

In this case the director of the income generation program was sympathetic with the concerns of the women, but rationalized

---

39. I think it is important to note that the average salary of these teachers, approximately Rs 800 to 1200 per month, was quite minimal given the cost of living in Delhi today. For comparison in 1996 the average salary of a teacher in a private English-medium school was approximately Rs 4000 to 5000 per month.

the new policy in pedagogical terms. She felt that the new policy would encourage the women to think of ways to expand their business and thus learn more management, marketing, and accounting skills. One has to wonder, however, if the same effect could not have been generated in a more positive manner by simply adding the incentive of commissions on top of the original salary level. In addition, the policy change seemed to imply that the participating women were complacent and would not actively try to improve a situation without being prodded by negative measures. This case illustrates how management and labor get differentiated within NGOs.

Thus, within many NGOs there are the same class-based divisions of labor and prejudices that are prevalent in Indian society at large. The attitude that 'the poor' are complacent at best (and at worst, lazy) persists. Although most IGPs claim to be teaching working-class women all aspects of running a business including the managerial aspects, they are often relegated to the labor roles. The middle-class staff monopolize managerial and marketing roles. When I questioned NGO staff about this reproduction of class relations, they responded that the women are not yet ready or willing to take on managerial roles or to face the public in marketing their product or service. That the women are not ready or willing begs the question: what is the purpose of the program other than to prepare the women for these roles?

One must then ask why IGP coordinators do not see the contradiction between the maintenance of such a division of labor and the goals of their organizations? And, if they do, why do they not act to correct the situation? Although within the NGO community at large this problem is often explained away as being the result of 'insincerity' on the part of the staff, the rhetoric of 'insincerity' or 'fraud' was a black box used to explain many forms of failure and/or abuse in the system. One reason many IGP coordinators are reluctant to deal with this issue is because they feel it can jeopardize an organization's reputation and thus its viability. In other words, because they are accountable to funding agencies, risking the failure of a project like an IGP is like risking the viability of the organization as a whole. Thus, in order to keep things running smoothly and to some extent for their own convenience, coordinators take on the management responsibilities themselves or delegate these to others whom they know already have the knowledge or skills to get the work done.[40] When IGP coordinators make such a choice, they are really reacting to the pressures of the market, in particular to the need to make their projects look like efficient microenterprises. Herein lies a great paradox for NGOs in the age of privatization: in order to present the IGP as a successful microenterprise, the staff often sacrifice pedagogical goals of passing on skills that would enable their clients to succeed in the private sector beyond the NGO. Funding agencies must take some responsibility for this contradiction. The scrutiny of funding agents who want to see quick and easily measurable progress can only lead to staff cutting corners in the educational process.

I have to qualify my critique, however, by pointing out that although most NGOs have not been able to successfully transfer real decision-making power to working-class women, they do not engage in the really corrupt employment practices that are rampant in Indian society at large. For example, NGOs almost always provide on-site day-care for their workers' children. They try to pay moderately competitive wages. They do not fire women who have just had a child or just been married, and women working in NGO programs do not face the kinds of sexual harassment so prevalent outside.

Some observers have faulted the whole concept of income generation as rooted in the liberal bias of middle-class development workers who continue to assume that the poor and in particular poor women are not already laboring. Anita Anand makes the following observation of income generation programs in contemporary development schemes: 'As women make up 60 to 90 percent of the agriculture labor force and produce 44 percent of all food, why is it crucial to talk of income generating projects? Rather, would it not be better to recognize *women's current productivity.*'[41] Anand's comments get to the heart of why many income generation programs seem jejune in the face of the living and working conditions that poor rural and urban women face daily.

The organization SEWA, Self-Employed Women's Association, has contributed to the recognition and growing legitimation of women working in the informal sector.[42] SEWA began as the

40. In fact, IGP coordinators in two different organizations even asked me to help them with the marketing of their particular product or service.
41. Anand 1985: 9, emphasis mine.
42. Rose 1992.

women's wing of the Textile Labor Association in the city of Ahmedabad, but soon broke off to become an independent organization of 'self-employed' women.[43] SEWA's name not only describes its constituency, but also was chosen as part of its program to generate awareness of and economic and legal legitimacy for workers in the non-formal sector.[44]

The basic principle that shapes the work of SEWA is that women need more control over the work they are *already* doing. In addition, from its inception SEWA has advocated that working-class women already own an impressive body of knowledge about the conditions of their work and lives as well as about the people and processes that exploit them. Accordingly, the middle-class professionals who work in SEWA are expected to build upon that body of knowledge; not attempt to replace it.

Through the voice of its leading spokesperson, Ela Bhatt, SEWA has been able to influence both national and international policy on the rights of workers in the 'self-employed' or informal sectors throughout the world. In 1989, Ela Bhatt was the first woman to be appointed to the National Planning Commission that drafts the nation's Five-Year Plans.[45] During this time, Bhatt authored, *Shramshakti: Report of the National Commission on Self-Employed Women and Women in the Informal Sector*.[46] In 1990, as a result of the efforts of activists like Bhatt, the International Labor Organization began to officially recognize self-employed workers worldwide and to work to identify and remedy their unique labor problems.[47] Ultimately, SEWA works towards creating a more equitable working environment for women. In this sense, SEWA's approach to economic independence for women is less market-driven than the income generation programs I observed in my fieldwork in New Delhi.[48]

My intent here is not to showcase SEWA as a 'model' NGO, because like every organization it has had its problems and

43. Ibid.: 19.
44. Ibid.: 17.
45. Ibid.: 31.
46. Ibid.: 99–100.
47. Ibid.: 30.
48. This is not to suggest that the work that women in the informal sector do is not market-driven, because it is. But because SEWA functions more along the lines of a labor union, it is less focused on the bottom line.

failures.[49] Rather, I want to compare two different approaches to the question of enhancing the economic status of working-class women. I have argued that IGPs today are dominated by the principles of privatization, which stress efficiency over education and profitability over improving the conditions of labor. IGPs today claim to be educating women in entrepreneurial skills that will enable them to succeed in the private sector but in fact many of them ignore the work skills and experience that so many Indian women already have.

The tendency of many contemporary NGOs to short-change the education of their participants for the sake of greater efficiency and profitability in the income generation program, and thus to compromise their original objective, is greater when the NGO is trying to start a microenterprise in-house. That is when the program does not take into account what the women they are serving do to earn a living outside of the context of the NGO. In these cases there is greater risk of the IGP becoming a kind of NGO-based sweatshop (albeit with child-care facilities and relatively milder working conditions) with the working-class women providing labor and the middle-class administrators making management decisions. Conversely the tendency to compromise pedagogical concerns and to reproduce class relations and gender caricatures is less in those IGPs that focus on enhancing the ongoing economic activities of the women that join them through credit unions and cooperatives, for example.

Although in the discussion above I have argued for the growing discursive prominence of entrepreneurism—punctuated by liberal feminism—in the practices of NGOs, there are other discourses of development and progress competing for the hearts of NGO workers. For example, there are a number of discourses of collective action for empowerment, which manifest themselves in IGPs organized as economic cooperatives, and in the creation of programs focused on activism and advocacy, like the mahila mandals or women's circles I discuss in the next section. The co-existence of different, often competing discourses illustrates the heterodoxy of contemporary discourse and practice within and between NGOs, community groups, governmental development agencies, and international development organizations. All of these participate in the bricolage of a regional modernity.

49. Rose 1992.

EMPOWERMENT THROUGH MAHILA MANDALS

We are not an NGO, We are Activists![50]

The strategy examined in this section is about the empowerment of women through the creation of community-based women's groups or mahila mandals. Unlike the mahila mandals of the 1950s and 1960s,[51] primarily feminist perspectives on development define the mahila mandals described in this paper.[52] The NGOs in my fieldwork, for example, focused overwhelmingly on women in their adult programs and routinely employed some variety of feminist rhetoric in articulating their goals.

Over the course of twelve months of fieldwork I was struck by the use of the English word 'empowerment' by primarily Hindi-speaking NGO workers to describe their programs in slum communities, and particularly in reference to programs for women. The practice of organizing women's groups, or mahila mandals, is grounded in the belief that communities of the poor, and in particular women, need to be better organized to actively confront the institutions and groups that exploit them. When we consider the notion of empowerment as it is used by NGOs, we find a number of senses associated with it and a variety of practices or programs organized around it. The concept can be traced to at least three discourses: feminism (i.e. 'giving women a voice'), leftist or Marxist notions of empowerment (i.e. 'generating a class conscious-ness'), and in particular the notion of empowerment through 'consciencization' authored by the Brazilian activist, writer, and pedagogue Paolo Freire.[53] Freire actually combines the concerns and methods of the first two discourses in his term, consciencization. That is, he argues that 'the oppressed' can achieve a class conscious-ness, a concern of Marxists, through the process of dialogue or finding their own voice—a central concern of feminists both Western and Indian.

50. Asha, Janawadi Mahila Samiti, November 1995.

51. Kim Berry (this volume) presents an excellent discussion of mahila mandals in government sponsored community development programs in the 1950s and 1960s.

52 See Diane Elson's (1997) discussion of feminist economics and critiques of development for a more general analysis of the feminist intervention on development discourse.

53. Freire 1989.

In the past decade on the Indian development scene, Freire and feminism have become cornerstones of NGO development methodology and are particularly relevant to the strategy of creating mandals for women in slum communities. Most NGOs, upon entering a community, will try to initiate a dialogue by extending an open invitation to the entire community to meet with some of the NGO staff. In the first meetings, the staff introduce themselves and the organization to the community, and they encourage the community's members to talk about what kinds of programs they would like to see implemented. The first programs introduced are related to children's education, health programs for children, and health programs for women. Once the NGO has a sense that the community is open to its presence, a few members of the staff are assigned to organize local women into mahila mandals or *samitis*, literally 'committees.' Enlisting the participation of men and women in the community who have some social standing facilitates the creation of mandals. Men with influence are often called *pradhans*, literally 'ministers,' they are relatively wealthier and have connections to political parties. Women with influence are often politically active or are midwives who provide traditional health services.

A central goal for mahila mandals is to encourage women to talk about and eventually confront problems that they may all face: for example, harassment by police, domestic violence, harassment for dowry for their daughters, sexual harassment, extortion from petty bureaucrats from whom they must seek certain services like getting rations cards, and being ignored by the teachers and administrators of their children's schools. Proponents of this methodology believe that through the process of 'narration' and autobiography women can attain a 'critical consciousness' which will enable them to collectively confront their problems.[54] The collective nature of the process is the key for its success.

It is important to note that the majority of NGOs working directly in slum-based centers in New Delhi tend to pursue *both* strategies I have discussed above: that is, they run income generation programs and facilitate women's groups. In fact there is a great deal of overlap between those women participating in the IGPs and those women active in the mandals or circles. During the course

54. Bapat and Patel 1993: 466; Rose 1992.

of fieldwork I found that the mandals, if they met on a regular basis, were more popular than the income generation programs. In part this is because the women who were able to attend mandal meetings were those who either did not need to work (because their husbands or fathers or brothers had regular employment) or were not allowed to work by husbands, fathers, or brothers regardless of the family's economic situation. More significantly, the mandals fill an important social void that many of these women who have migrated from rural areas experience. When these women arrive in cities they live away from kin and community networks for the first time in their lives and therefore experience a great sense of isolation.[55] The mandals can provide at least a partial remedy for this.

From the perspective of NGOs mandals are an important part of their response to the turbulent political economy of contemporary India. In other words, NGOs are trying to help communities that face economic and social exploitation become better agents of social change while helping them to adjust to growing pressures of market forces as the nation undergoes privatization. Income generation or 'microenterprise' programs are development's answer to privatization for (and, to some extent, of) the poor and as such are not usually a challenge to the prevailing system. Rather, they are about helping the poor find a niche in it. The mandals, on the other hand, represent a development strategy invested in confronting the status quo. While most IGPs are ultimately based on the principle of individual competition and success, the mandals are about collective action.

Although I have argued for a specific correspondence between these strategies and the discourses of feminism and privatization, I am not suggesting a teleological relationship between specific practices and discourses. There are elements of feminism that emphasize the well being of the individual over that of the group— for example, the quest of the women's movement to secure the rights of women as individuals. The same is true of privatization and entrepreneurism. There can be forms of entrepreneurism that value collective action, as in, for example, the cooperative model some IGPs encourage. However, the particular constellation I have described above is accurate in describing the nature of NGO

55. Fernandes 1990.

practices at this time. More importantly, I have tried to recount the difficult, often paradoxical choices NGOs face as they try to make their mark on, and are made by, a dynamic Indian modernity.

References

Anand, Anita, 1985. 'Women in development: a critique of mainstream models.' *Alternatives* 12(3/4): 8–12.

Appadurai, Arjun, 1990. 'Disjuncture and difference in the global cultural economy.' *Public Culture* 2(2).

———, 1991. 'Global ethnoscapes: Notes and queries for a transnational anthropology.' In Richard G. Fox (ed.), *Recapturing Anthropology: Working in the Present.* Santa Fe: School of American Research Press.

———, 1996. *Modernity at Large: Cultural Dimensions of Globalisation.* Minnesota: Minneapolis University Press.

Bapat, Meera and Sheela Patel, 1993. 'Shelter, women and development: Beating a path towards women's participation.' *Economic and Political Weekly* 28(11): 465–72.

Bhasin, Kamla (ed.), 1985. *Towards Empowerment: Report of an FAO-FFHC/AD South Asia Training for Women Development Workers.* New Delhi.

Bhatt, Anil, 1989. *Development and Social Justice: Micro Action by Weaker Sections.* New Delhi: Sage publications.

Bhattacharjee, Abhijit, 1989. *A Decade of Deepalaya: Deepalaya Education Society.* New Delhi: Foster Parents Plan International Inc.

Bird, Graham, 1996. 'The International Monetary Fund and developing countries: A review of the evidence and policy options.' *International Organization* 50(3): 477–511.

Calman, Leslie J., 1992. *Toward Empowerment: Women and Movement Politics in India.* San Francisco: Westview Press.

Carroll, Thomas F., 1992. *Intermediary NGOs: The Supporting Link in Grassroots Development.* West Hartford: Kumarian Press.

Chatterjee, Jyotsna, 1985. *The Women's Decade 1975–1985: An Assessment.* New Delhi: ISPCK.

Dhanagare, D. N., 1991. 'Developing human resources: India.' *Indian Council of Social Science Research Newsletter* 22(2).

Dirlik, Arif, 1996. 'The global in the local.' In Rob Wilson and Wimal Dissanayake (eds.), *Global/Local: Cultural Production and Transnational Imaginary.* Durham: Duke University Press.

Elson, Diane, 1994. 'People, development and international financial institutions: An interpretation of the Bretton Woods System.' *Review of African Political Economy* (62): 511–24.

————, 1997. 'Economic paradigms old and new: The case of human development.' In Roy Culpeper, Albert Berry, and Frances Stewart (eds.), *Global Development Fifty Years after Bretton Woods: Essays in Honour of Gerald K. Helleiner*. New York: St. Martin's Press.

Emmerji, Louis, 1987. 'Preface.' In Louis Emmerji (ed.), *Development Policies and the Crisis of the 1980s*. Paris: Organization for Economic Co-operation and Development.

Escobar, Arturo, 1995. *Encountering Development: The Making and Un-making of the Third World*. Princeton: Princeton University Press.

Farrington, John, 1993. 'Introduction.' In John Farrington, David J. Lewis, S. Satish and Aurea Miclat-Teves (eds.), *Non-Governmental Organizations and the State in Asia*. London: Routledge.

Farrington, John, David J. Lewis, S. Satish and Aurea Miclat-Teves (eds.), 1993. *Non-Governmental Organizations and the State in Asia*. London: Routledge.

Fernandes, Walter, 1990. *Women's Status in the Delhi Bastis: Urbanisation, Economic Forces and Voluntary Organisations*. New Delhi: Indian Social Institute.

Finnemore, Martha, 1997. 'Redefining Development at the World Bank.' In Frederick Cooper and Randall Packard (eds.), *International Development and the Social Sciences: Essays on the History and Politics of Knowledge*. Berkeley: University of California Press.

Freire, Paolo, 1989. *The Pedagogy of the Oppressed*. New York: Continuum.

Government of India, Planning Commission, 1992. *Eighth Five-Year Plan 1992–1997: Volume I Objectives, Perspective, Macro-Dimensions, Policy Framework and Resources*. New Delhi: GoI.

————, 1992. *Eighth Five-Year Plan 1992–1997: Volume II, Sectoral Programmes of Development*. New Delhi: GoI.

Gulhati, Ravi, Kaval Gulhati, Ajay Mehra, and Janaki Rajan, 1995. *Strengthening Voluntary Action in India: Health–Family Planning, the Environment, and Women's Development*. New Delhi: Konark.

Jagger, Allison, 1983. *Feminist Politics and Human Nature*. Brighton: The Harvester Press.

Jain, Nabhi Kumar (ed.), 1995. *Nabhi's New Industrial Policy & Procedures*, 5th edition. New Delhi: Nabhi Publications.

Johnson-Odim, Cheryl, 1991. 'Common themes, different contexts: Third World women and feminism.' In Chandra T. Mohanty, Ann Russo, and Lourdes Torres (eds.), *Third World Women and the Politics of Feminism*. Bloomington: Indiana University Press.

Joshi, Charu Lata, 1995. 'Chasing the greenbucks: Voluntary organisations.' *India Today* 15: 164–9.

Kaplan, Patricia, 1985. *Class and Gender in India: Women and their Organizations in a South Indian City*. New York: Tavistock.

Karat, Prakash, 1984. 'Action groups/voluntary organisations: A factor in imperialist strategy.' *The Marxist: Theoretical Quarterly of the Communist Party of India (Marxist)* 2: 19–53.

Kothari, Rajni, 1984. 'The non-party political process.' *Economic and Political Weekly* 19(5): 216–24.

———, 1995. *Poverty: Human Consciousness and the Amnesia of Development.* New Jersey: Zed Books.

Lokayan, 1985. 'Mission statement.' *Lokayan Bulletin* 3(2).

Mazumdar, Vina, 1979. 'Editor's note.' In Vina Mazumdar (ed.), *Symbols of Power: Studies on the Political Status of Women in India.* Bombay: Allied Publishers.

———, 1985. *Emergence of Women's Question and Role of Women's Studies.* New Delhi: Centre for Women's Development and Studies.

Ministry of Education and Social Welfare, Govt. of India, 1974. *Towards Equality—Report of the Committee on the Status of Women in India.* New Delhi: GoI.

Mishra, S. N., 1984. *Participation and Development.* New Delhi: NBO Publishers' Distributors.

Mohanty, Chandra T., 1991. 'Introduction: Cartographies of struggle, Third World women and the politics of feminism.' In Chandra T. Mohanty, Ann Russo, and Lourdes Torres (eds.), *Third World Women and the Politics of Feminism.* Bloomington: Indiana University Press.

Pandey, Shashi R., 1991. *Community Action for Social Justice: Grassroots Organizations in India.* New Delhi: Sage Publications.

Parikh, Kirit S., 1999. *India Development Report, 1999–2000.* New Delhi: Oxford University Press.

Pietila, Hilkka and Jeanne Vickers, 1990. *Making Women Matter: The Role of the United Nations.* London: Zed Books.

Pigg, Stacy L., 1992. 'Constructing social categories through place: Social representations and development in Nepal.' *Comparative Studies in Society and History* 34(3): 491–513.

PIRG (Public Interest Research Group), 1995. The State of India's Economy: 1994-1995. New Delhi: Unpublished manuscript.

PRIA (Society for Participatory Research in Asia), 1991. Voluntary Development Organizations in India: A Study of History, Roles, and Future Challenges. New Delhi: PRIA, November.

Rose, Kalima, 1992. *Where Women are Leaders: The SEWA Movement in India.* New Delhi: Vistaar Publications.

Scott, James, 1985. *Weapons of the Weak: Everyday Forms of Peasant Resistance.* New Haven: Yale University Press.

Sen, Ilina, 1990. 'Introduction.' In Ilina Sen (ed.), *A Space within the Struggle: Women's Participation in People's Movements.* New Delhi: Kali for Women.

Sen, Jai, 1986. 'On anti-voluntarism.' *Lokayan Bulletin* 4(3/4): 9–37.

Sen, Tapas Kumar, 1993. 'Public expenditure on human development in India: Trends and issues.' In Kirit S. Parikh and R. Sudharshan (eds.), *Human Development and Structural Adjustment.* Madras: Macmillan.

Sethi, Harsh, 1984. 'Groups in a new politics of transformation.' *Economic and Political Weekly* 19(7): 305–16.

————, 1985. 'The immoral 'other': Debate between party and non-party groups.' *Economic and Political Weekly* 20(9): 378–80.

Sethi, Harsh and Smitu Kothari, 1985. 'On threats to the non-party political process.' *Lokayan Bulletin* 3(2): 37–49.

————, 1986. 'Editorial.' *Lokayan Bulletin* 4(3/4): 1–8.

Sheth, D. L., 1984. 'Grassroots initiatives in India.' *Economic and Political Weekly* 19(6): 259–64.

————, 1987. 'Alternative development as political practice.' *Alternatives* 12: 155–71.

Smith, Brian H., 1990. *More than Altruism: The Politics of Private Foreign Aid.* Princeton: Princeton University Press.

Society for Participatory Research in Asia (PRIA), 1991. *Non-Governmental Organisations in India—A Critical Study.* New Delhi: PRIA (January).

————, 1991. *Voluntary Development Organisations in India: A Study of History, Roles, and Future Challenges.* New Delhi: PRIA (November).

Tandon, Rajesh, 1986. 'Regulating NGOs.' *Lokayan Bulletin* 4(3/4): 38–48.

Toye, John, 1987. 'Development theory and the experience of development: Issues for the future.' In Louis Emmerji (ed.), *Development Policies and the Crisis of the 1980s.* Paris: Organisation for Economic Co-operation and Development.

United Nations, 1992. 'Chapter 27, 27.1.' In *Agenda 21: Report of the United Nations Conference on Environment and Development.* Rio de Janeiro: UN.

————, 1985. *World Survey on the Role of Women in Development.* New York: UN.

Volken, Henry, 1984. 'Action groups: Beginning or end of a dream?' *Social Text: A Quarterly Review of Social Trends* 34(2): 115–31.

Webster, Leila M, 1996. *World Bank Lending for Small Enterprises 1989–1993.* Washington, DC: The World Bank.

Willis, Paul, 1977. *Learning to Labor: How Working Class Kids Get Working Class Jobs.* New York: Columbia University Press.

World Bank, 1979. *Recognizing the 'Invisible' Woman in Development: The World Bank's Experience.* Washington, DC: World Bank.

————, 1996. *The World Bank's Partnership with Nongovernmental Organizations.* Washington, DC: World Bank.

Young, Kate, 1993. *Planning Development with Women.* New York: St. Martin's Press.

Zachariah, Mathew and R. Sooryamoorthy, 1994. *Science for Social Revolution: Achievements and Dilemmas of a Development Movement—The Kerala Sastra Sahitya Parishad.* New Delhi: Vistaar Publications.

Zaidi, S. Akbar, 1999. *The New Development Paradigm: Papers on Institutions, NGOs, Gender and Local Government.* Karachi: Oxford University Press.

10

Mukkuvar Modernity: Development as a Cultural Identity

AJANTHA SUBRAMANIAN

In the general elections of 1996, a village of Catholic fishers from the south Indian district of Kanyakumari voted overwhelmingly for the Hindu nationalist Bharatiya Janata Party. In this essay, I explore the cultural politics of development that led to this curious alliance between a group of low caste (Mukkuvar) Catholics and a majoritarian politics that has consistently defined India's Christians and Muslims as alien threats to the 'Hindu nation.' My essay begins in the 1950s with the uneven development of Kanyakumari's fishery that benefited a section of the district's Mukkuvar Catholic population. I narrate the gradual crystallization within this group of local beneficiaries of a middle-class Mukkuvar identity defined in opposition, first to the wider artisanal fishing population, and then to a Catholic clergy mobilized to 'opt for the poor' through the embrace of liberation theology. I end in the 1990s, when Indian economic liberalization permitted foreign capital access to national waters. This most recent shift in the political economy of development, I show, finally ruptured the relationship between these 'modern' Mukkuvars and the developmentalist state, and delivered them into the hands of Hindu nationalism.

This story, then, is about class and cultural identity. But it is also a story about place. Kanyakumari is an arena where communities have been crafted through a politics of place-making, a process of carving out 'geographies of difference'[1] from within more encompassing spaces of power and mapping identities onto these imagined geographies. As I narrate below, Kanyakumari's middle-class Mukkuvars were situated at the confluence of several currents of place-making including Dravidian regionalism, Hindu nationalism, Catholic liberation theology, and global environmentalism. They appropriated the geographical imaginaries generated by these currents to creatively rework development imperatives and craft what I call a 'Mukkuvar modernity.'

How does this local story engage with current debates on development? What does it offer to an understanding of regional modernities and storytelling? First, Tamil Nadu is in many ways an ideal context for documenting regional particularity. State development intervention and social movements in Tamil Nadu have been characterized by a cultural idiom that commonly references the particularities of regional language, caste, and ethnicity. As a consequence, state policy and local practice have generated notions of community and place that constitute a regional, or vernacular, formation of modernity. Second, the cultural history of community and place-making in Kanyakumari speaks to the question of development hegemony. I argue that the open-endedness of community and place-making in the district points to the impossibility of a neat correspondence between a global discourse of development and its uses and meanings in specific locales. While development does restructure both communities and places, it does not operate in a deterministic or monolithic way. In Kanyakumari, development traveled unstable terrain where the contested meanings ascribed to community and place conditioned its outcomes. Third, this 'development situation' highlights the necessity of attending to the stories told by particular subjects in particular locales. The story that middle-class Mukkuvars in Kanyakumari tell of themselves reveals the importance of development as a material and symbolic system, its mutual implication with other discursive formations, and the impossibility of predicting its cultural and political outcomes.

1. Harvey 1996.

COMMUNITY, PLACE, AND TECHNOLOGICAL CHANGE

Decolonization ushered in the structural transformation of the Indian fishery. On the eve of Independence, India's development planners formulated a national fisheries policy that anticipated the rapid introduction of capitalist technologies into the domestic fishery. The National Planning Commission (NPC)'s recommendation of rapid technological change for alleviating coastal poverty, raising the Indian fisher's standard of living, and increasing levels of production was justified by perceptions of the coastal population as socially backward. The Commission characterized the existing fishery sector as 'largely of a primitive character, carried on by ignorant, unorganized, and ill-equipped fishermen. Their techniques are rudimentary, their tackle elementary, their capital equipment slight and inefficient.'[2] There was also a cultural component to this evaluation. The Commission determined that the poor productivity of indigenous fishing technologies was largely attributable to coastal culture, characterized by indolence, lack of thrift, resistance to change, and violence, and itself a product of social isolation. The incorporation of the coast into a national framework of development would help undermine those aspects of coastal culture that were inimical to social progress.

The incorporation of the coast into the developing nation was to be facilitated through the incorporation of the nation in turn into what Arturo Escobar calls 'the post-War global development regime.'[3] Foreign experts from First World nation-states with developed fishing industries would be the conduits for introducing modern technologies into the Indian fishery. Post-Independence India's fisheries policy thus reflected the complex relationship between India and the global developmentalism. At the core of the Nehru government's vision of a self-sufficient, sovereign, postcolonial nation lay a continued dependence on Western technology and knowhow as necessary for modern nationhood.

As Daniel Klingensmith[4] notes, however, it would be too simple to conclude from this instance of what he calls 'development borrowing' that Indian fisheries development was simply derivative of the West's. While the NPC encouraged coastal state

2. Shah 1948 quoted in Kurien 1985.
3. Escobar 1985.
4. Klingensmith, this volume.

governments to follow the developmental path hewn by Western nation-states, it also recognized the disparities of wealth that could result from rapid capitalist development. In order to promote social equality alongside economic growth, NPC advocates sought a more 'culturally sensitive' approach to developing coastal India. They finally determined that the Community Development Program would be the ideal approach for ensuring the smooth transformation of the coast. This emphasis on a communitarian approach to rural development reflected a preoccupation with carving out a geography of difference from within global modernity. India's modernity would adhere to certain 'universal' principles of social transformation while maintaining its 'cultural core.'

Community development represented the NPC's application of the Gandhian prescription for national reconstruction to rural India. It envisioned the uplift of rural Indians in their own localities, a process that would tap the organic solidarity of the village with its self-governing institutions and principles of 'moral economy.' Through community development, subsistence production was to give way to production for profit, but without exacerbating existing inequalities.[5] In accordance with Gandhian notions of the decentralized, self-governing village republic, fisheries community development identified the need to sustain the organic solidarity of the fishing village as a foundation for development. Within this framework, the fishing village would be the basic unit of the development process. By making 'community' the basic social unit of development, the Commission hoped to mitigate the turbulence of change. In keeping with Gandhi's vision, it placed the village at the heart of the community development agenda and promoted nation-building as a process extending from India's rural communities.

In its final incarnation, community development was a peculiar blend of goals: it invoked the 'village community' as an organic place of 'moral economy' that would provide a moral foundation for the nation *and* it sought to restructure the village to suit the needs of nation-building. The program thus had conflicting aims: it sought to dissolve the boundaries of 'traditional,' place-based economies and communities by integrating them into a national developmental framework, and in an articulation of what Ajay

5. Frankel 1978.

Skaria calls 'the primitivism of development,'[6] it reified its target populations as traditional collectives characterized by a timeless unity of will and practice.

THE POLICY AND POLITICS OF TAMIL NADU'S FISHERIES DEVELOPMENT PROGRAM

While Tamil Nadu Fisheries Department documents reflect faithful adherence to the national project of development, they are less clear on whether and how fisheries development *practice* responded to the political culture of the state. How was development promoted in Tamil Nadu? And, in what ways did its chosen channels mold fisheries development as a regionally specific process?

In Tamil Nadu, the state fisheries department took up the task of fisheries development with some amount of caution. Instead of the wholesale introduction of a new technology, the department collaborated with the United Nation's Food and Agricultural Organization (FAO) to introduce 'new but traditional designs' that would motorize indigenous crafts without significantly changing the structure of the fishery.[7] Under the expanded technical assistance program of the FAO, two naval architects, one Danish and the other Norwegian, were assigned the task of motorizing the *kattumaram* and *vallam*—the indigenous crafts of the Tamil Nadu coast.

But by 1955, the department had also begun tests to introduce mechanized crafts used in the temperate waters of Europe. Fisheries officials conducted exploratory surveys in various methods of mechanized fishing using foreign crafts, after which they embarked on the construction of mechanized gill-netters and trawlers. In order to distribute these crafts to important fishing centers, the department revitalized the village fisheries cooperative societies that were started during the colonial period but had become dormant for lack of purpose. These institutions effectively localized the presence of the state, channeling technologies and subsidies to fishing villages. Importantly, the cooperatives also provided

6. Skaria, this volume.
7. Administrative Report of the Tamil Nadu Fisheries Department, 1955–6. Madras: Government Press.

loans with a view to 'eliminat[ing] middlemen.'[8] As Ludden remarks in the case of colonial agriculture, the 'removal of intermediaries' meant 'an increase in centralized state power and rationality.... Putting the peasant and state face to face, with no mediating institutions between them [implied] that the state would become part of every farm's operation.'[9] Similarly, postcolonial fisheries development inserted the state into the everyday life of the fisher.

In addition to cooperatives, the fisheries department also started training schools at important fishing centers to instruct fishermen in:

(a) elements of navigation, including the compass and its uses;

(b) the upkeep and maintenance of marine diesel engines;

(c) fishing gear utility in different types of fishing and modes of operation;

(d) theoretical knowledge of fish habits, oceanography, fishing craft, and boat building.

These centers shifted the locus of knowledge from the experience of the fisher to the scientific expertise of the state. Now, those who spent their daily lives at sea came to these centers to learn how to fish.

The new mechanization program was widely advertised by the department. It began publishing and distributing a monthly newsletter in Tamil to educate fishermen on department activities and give them technical advice. It also deputed an audio-visual unit to tour the state and exhibit films on fisheries development. This unit toured all the coastal districts and exhibited films in 157 centers. A special post, propaganda assistant, was created for the sole purpose of advertising the department's endeavors, and the man occupying this post in 1962 was sent to New Delhi to attend the International Industries Fair where he could study the latest techniques used by foreign governments, other state governments, and private industrialists in the construction, decoration, and display of exhibits.[10]

8. Administrative Report of the Tamil Nadu Fisheries Department, 1961–2. Madras: Government Press.

9. Ludden 1992: 275.

10. Administrative Report of the Tamil Nadu Fisheries Department, 1961–2. Madras: Government Press.

In an interesting twist on the process by which colonized peoples were made objects of a colonial gaze,[11] these publicity stunts put modernization itself on display as a spectacle to be consumed and desired. The goal to achieve national modernity was to become the personal desire of every Indian citizen.

From department documents, one gets the sense that fisheries policy was an entirely rational exercise insulated from the volatility of politics. But there was no line dividing policy from politics. As Subir Sinha[12] points out in reference to Indian forestry policy, the need to balance capital accumulation with political legitimation made planned development an arena, not of domination but of contestation.

So how did the policies of fisheries development intersect with the politics of modernization in Tamil Nadu? During the period of the Second Five-Year Plan, Tamil Nadu under Congress Chief Minister K. Kamaraj got a significant share of the Indian government's industrial projects, becoming the second most industrialized state by the late 1950s. Kamaraj was an avid modernizer. He distributed contracts and industrial licenses associated with Second Plan projects to habitual supporters and to win over other industrialists.[13] The other side of modernization was the community development scheme for the Tamil poor. This was also used to expand the Congress patronage network, but with a difference in approach. In true paternalist style, Kamaraj appealed to these marginal social groups through their 'traditional' leaders.

Fisheries development in Tamil Nadu reflected the patern-alism inherent to Congress community development strategy. The general elections had been held just the previous year and Kamaraj had chosen Lourdammal Simon, a Catholic woman from Kanyakumari's Mukkuvar fishing caste, as fisheries minister.[14] The Congress presented this choice of a low-caste, Catholic woman as its commitment to religious minority and low-caste represen-tation in the party, and to gender equality.[15] Kamaraj's efforts won

11. Said 1978; Mitchell 1991.
12. Sinha, this volume.
13. Subramanian 1999.
14. Interviews with N. Dennis, Congress Member of Parliament, Nagercoil; M. C. Balan, ex-DMK Member of Legislative Assembly.
15. Interview with Lourdammal Simon, Minister of Fisheries, Tamil Nadu Government, 1958–62.

him the support of the local Catholic Church. Even prior to his selection of a Catholic candidate, the groundswell of support for the Communist Party of India in the neighboring state of Kerala had set off warning bells in Kanyakumari's churches and consolidated clerical support for the Congress. Lourdammal Simon's selection only strengthened the Kanyakumari clergy's political allegiance to the Congress. On the eve of the 1957 elections, the Bishop of Kanyakumari's Kottar diocese sent out a circular requesting the faithful to exercise their franchise by electing candidates who would fight for freedom of religion, for educational rights of private institutions, and against birth control, all of which the Congress guaranteed under the rubric of religious minority rights.[16] In response, Catholics in Kanyakumari voted overwhelmingly for the Congress.

Lourdammal Simon initiated fisheries development in 1958. In tune with the community development agenda, membership in the fisheries cooperative societies was limited to 'active fishermen' for whom fishing was a subsistence occupation to help them increase their levels of productivity. In Tamil Nadu, this category of 'active fishermen' was translated to mean those belonging to castes traditionally engaged in the occupation of fishing. Fishers across the state, therefore, experienced modernization not through the erosion of caste but *as* members of castes.

In Kanyakumari, the mechanization program was fully backed by the local Catholic clergy. For many of them who were themselves from elite coastal families, modern technology meant escape from coastal penury and a new means to compete with the upwardly mobile castes of the 'interior.' These priests had themselves left fishing for the clerical life, and their theological training in centers far from the Kanyakumari coast had given them a new perspective on their home, one that starkly contrasted Mukkuvar cultural life with those of upwardly mobile groups. Returning to the coast as religious leaders, they were a local elite who were *from* but no longer simply *of* the coast. When the state introduced the development program, these priests were quick to identify it as a much-needed catalyst for Mukkuvar integration into the national economic and cultural mainstream. Through them, mechanization was given religious sanction as a means to minority advance.

16. Narchison *et al.* 1983.

Lourdammal Simon set about implementing the mechanization program across Tamil Nadu, with particular attention to her home district of Kanyakumari. Although the program's stated intention was to ensure an even spread of subsidized crafts, they were channeled mainly to the village of Colachel, a natural harbor in an otherwise turbulent coastline that made it a good test-case for the technology. Coincidentally, it was also the minister's marital village where her husband Simon was president of the cooperative society. Simon was succeeded by a series of three presidents, all Congress loyalists like him, which firmly secured Colachel's place within the Congress party's patronage system.[17] In the first five years of the distribution scheme, over 70 percent of crafts went to Colachel.[18]

The concentration of crafts in one village called into question the meaning of community development. It now appeared to be more a process of class differentiation than one of community uplift. However, early challenges to the development program were stifled by the continued promise of social progress through technological change. It was not until the prawn rush of the 1960s that the polarization of the coast was sealed and more effective challenges to the development project emerged.

The direction and pace of fisheries development shifted dramatically in the mid-1960s due to the rise in demand for prawn in the international fisheries market. In Tamil Nadu, the 'pink gold rush' signaled the subordination of cooperative development for domestic consumption to the export trade in prawn. The earlier goals of crafting 'new but traditional designs' and building cooperative institutions were rapidly superseded by a new focus on trawlerization by a government hungry for foreign exchange. Accordingly, the Tamil Nadu fisheries department shifted emphasis to the rapid distribution of subsidized trawling boats for prawn harvests. The pink gold rush restructured domestic fishing for monocrop, export-oriented production.

Apart from increasing levels of fish harvest, the pink gold rush radically altered social dynamics across the Indian coastal belt.

17. Interview with Peter, current president of Colachel Fisheries Cooperative Society.

18. Mechanization scheme records from the District Fisheries Department office, Nagercoil.

Since prawn are most abundant in shallow waters, trawler owners equipped with the capital-intensive technology to take them to offshore fishing grounds now preferred to remain in the area closest to shore to avail of this valuable commodity. The crowding of the inshore sea has led to violent confrontations between trawler and artisanal fishers over access and use of the coastal waters. These conflicts have increased in intensity from the mid-1970s, after which the overcapitalization of the fishery and overfishing of the resource began to result in a decline in total landings. Artisanal fishers now found themselves competing on unequal technical terms for a depleting resource.

The elevation of Colachel as the local success of Tamil Nadu fisheries marked the Kanyakumari coast as a space of uneven development. The concentration of trawlers in a single village disrupted the system of resource and conflict management built on the mutual cooperation of villages. Suddenly, there was a clear advantage of one village over the others that threatened the system of inter-village cooperation. With the new technology came an alternative, state-endorsed system privileging scientific technologies over traditional ones, a formalized, legal code of individual property rights over the existing set of customary rights, and national economic priorities over local ones. Backed by this new framework of rights, Colachel's beneficiaries defied community-based regulative measures and claimed unlimited access to the resource. Alarmed by the impressive catch volumes of the new crafts, artisanal fishers bypassed by the development program finally attacked Colachel and destroyed several trawlers.

The reaction of Congress party leaders and Catholic clergy to the attack reflected the regional character of development. On the one hand, they condemned the action as the 'natural impulse' of a backward caste threatened by change. At the same time, they held up Colachel's embrace of mechanization as evidence of the transformation of consciousness made possible through technological change. What this amounted to was a hierarchical divide between the modern and traditional groups of a single caste, with technology serving as the yardstick.[19] Coastal modernity had emerged as a particular regional variant of national modernity, and the modern

19. Interviews with Minister Lourdammal Simon and Fr Jacob Lopez, parish priest of Colachel from 1957–62.

Mukkuvar as a fisher who understood technological progress, not in an abstract sense, but as a means to caste and religious minority empowerment. Significantly, the landscape of uneven development spatially anchored this difference. Colachel village was marked as a place of development more nationally oriented than the rest of the coast, which, by contrast, came to symbolize reactive isolationism and resistance to progress.

NATIONAL VERSUS REGIONAL MODERNITY

In the previous section, I illustrated the process by which fisheries development policy was subject to a regional political idiom. I pointed to the cultural embedding of development, the process by which developmental constructions of community and place took on locally specific meanings. This was the case in spite of the fact that Tamil Nadu's Congress government faithfully echoed the national agenda of modernization. By the 1960s, however, the mutual constitution of development and regional culture was transformed from an implicit cultural process to an explicit political agenda by the Dravidian movement.

E. V. Ramaswami Naicker (popularly known as *Periar* or Great Leader) had launched the movement in the 1930s in response to the dominance of the Brahmin caste in the public spheres created during colonial rule—namely English educational institutions, the bureaucracy, and the Congress party itself.[20] With the emergence of its offshoot, the Dravida Munnetra Kazhagam (Party of Dravidian Uplift, or DMK), the movement shifted focus from a critique of the Brahmin to a critique of both state and central governments. In 1967, the DMK finally supplanted the Congress and became the first regional party to secure state power.

The crafting of a Tamil modern was central to the Dravidianist platform. The DMK charged the Congress with promoting a development agenda that was culturally alien, and therefore imperialist, in nature. Party ideologues argued that the Congress party's economic and social policies were irrelevant to the needs of Tamils and contrary to the property regime rooted in Tamil tradition.[21] Instead, they associated themselves with the small propertied low castes, and recast Tamil modernity in terms of the economic and

20. Subramanian 1999.
21. Washbrook 1989.

political interests of this social group. When the DMK came to power, it was with the support of middle-class Tamils who were socially powerful but nevertheless marginal to national politics. But there were also poorer Congress supporters who were won over to the DMK by actor-turned-politician, M. G. Ramachandran, popularly known as MGR. MGR's use of carefully crafted screen personalities as agricultural laborer, urban worker, and fisherman had a tremendous impact on the Tamil poor who for the first time were seeing their identities and social reality represented in the mainstream media.[22]

With the spread of the Dravidian movement, fishing communities across Tamil Nadu moved away from the Congress. The spread of coastal support for the DMK is attributable to MGR's rise to prominence within the party. From the late 1950s, MGR fan clubs had sprouted in fisher villages. His roles as a boatman in 'Padakotti' (Boatman) and as a poor fisherman in 'Meenavar Nanban' (Friend of Fishermen) consolidated the bulk of the fisher vote behind the DMK. Even in Kanyakumari, which for the most part remained a Congress bastion resistant to the Dravidianist wave, the coastal population defied church authority and voted overwhelmingly for the DMK in the 1967 elections.[23] The sole exception to this coastal shift away from national party support was Colachel, which continued to vote for the Congress. Colachel's villagers remained loyal to the party of Kamaraj and the Simons, the party that had provided them with the means to social mobility.

The tension between the two different kinds of class appeals— DMK Chief Minister M. Karunanidhi's to the middle classes and MGR's to the poor—finally led to MGR's expulsion from the party in 1972. MGR formed his own party, the Anna-DMK and the poor across Tamil Nadu, including the majority of fishers, switched loyalties. In a five-year vilification campaign that finally won him the regional government, MGR used populist imagery to brand the DMK a middle-class party with no sympathies for the poor. In the fisheries arena, MGR highlighted the fact that many DMK leaders had bought trawlers with the generous loans granted to

22. Baskaran 1981; Dickey 1993; Pandian 1992; Subramanian 1999.
23. Interviews with N. Dennis, Congress Member of Parliament (Nagercoil), M. C. Balan, ex-Member of Legislative Assembly (Padmanabhapuram).

entrepreneurs during DMK rule, and aligned himself with the artisanal sector.[24] By the time the ADMK came to power in 1977, Dravidian rule, and by extension regional development, had come to take on distinct meanings in the two-party frameworks: the DMK represented middle-class self-assertion and a Tamil modernity rooted in middle-class success; the ADMK transformed Dravidianism into a politics of the poor centered on the figure of a charismatic leader and a future Tamil prosperity ensured by MGR's benevolence. As a result of this difference in rhetorical emphasis, class rivalries in many parts of Tamil Nadu were played out in terms of support for one or the other party,[25] and for one or the other image of Tamil modernity.

MGR's electoral triumph in 1977 is most often seen as a masterstroke by a canny politician adept at crafting his image for mass appeal.[26] However, image-makers rarely have complete control over their masterpieces. Four months after the ADMK formed the government in Tamil Nadu, the simmering tensions between artisanal and mechanized fishers exploded into large-scale riots that shook Madras city and thrust artisanal fishers into the spotlight. The intensity of the inter-sectoral clashes, the active role played by MGR's fan clubs in the violence against trawlers, and their invocation of MGR as an inspiration in their fight for economic justice forced the ADMK government to formulate an official policy to regulate trawling. In 1983, the Tamil Nadu government implemented the Marine Fisheries Regulation Act. The Act created geographical zones to separate the antagonists: artisanal fishermen would work the sea up to three nautical miles from shore while trawlers would carry out operations only beyond this limit. This territorial approach to management was primarily compelled by 'law and order' concerns: its primary purpose was to separate fisher antagonists into distinct zones to stave off conflict while continuing to promote development through mechanization. In effect, however, the Act exacerbated tensions between warring fishers and territorially grounded the claims of fisher artisans.

In Kanyakumari, artisanal fishers took full advantage of the new Act. The line in the sea substituted a horizontal boundary for the

24. Interviews with F. M. Rajaratnam, ADMK ex-Member of Legislative Aseembly, and with members of the MGR fan association.

25. Subramanian 1999.

26. Pandian 1992.

vertical ones separating villages and became a territorial marker for the divisive hostility between Colachel and its surrounding villages. This redrawing of territory in sectoral rather than village terms crystallized the oppositional dynamic between the warring groups of fishers and the three-mile zone quickly became a potent symbol of artisanal identity. It came to symbolize the convergence between the community of artisans and a particular place, giving artisanal fishers territorial sovereignty over the inshore sea.

Through this period of transition from DMK to ADMK rule, the DMK's identification with Tamil Nadu's propertied classes slowly began to appeal to Colachel's mechanized fishers. That a number of DMK leaders had themselves invested in trawlers only made this link stronger. Over the 1970s, Colachel's fishers began to identify with the DMK's rhetoric of self-empowerment and reject MGR's version of Dravidianism as 'a politics of the illiterate and the poor.'[27] They began to see the DMK as the party of choice for an upwardly mobile low caste and the Dravidianist agenda as compatible with middle-class modernity. As 'being developed' became more central to their self-image and more threatened by the artisanal fishers' appropriation of ADMK politics, Colachel's fishers began to 'regionalize' their own understanding of middle-class identity and look to the DMK for support. The 1983 Act further underscored the importance of alignment with a regional party that would address their needs in Tamil Nadu's political arena.

PLAYING HINDUS AGAINST CHRISTIANS: THE REASSERTION OF A NATIONAL MODERN

By the 1980s, the two groups of Kanyakumari's fishers had come to understand community, place, and development, not in terms of global or national prescriptions, but more through opposing interpretations of a regional idiom given political legitimacy by the Dravidian movement. However, the ascendance of Dravidianist cultural politics did not mean a complete overshadowing of national politics. The continued resonance of a national idiom and agenda was especially witnessed in Kanyakumari, with its nearly 50 percent Christian population. Over two decades of increasing

27. Subramanian 1999.

coastal polarization and the spread of Dravidianist politics along the Kanyakumari coast, another political movement was growing. Just as had the early Dravidianists, Hindu nationalists gained ground in the district by highlighting disparities in community representation in the bureaucracy and in educational institutions. The primary difference was that the Rashtriya Swayamsevak Sangh (RSS), the parent Hindu nationalist organization, identified the *Christian* and not the Brahmin as the primary beneficiary of Congress and Dravidian rule in Kanyakumari. Hindu nationalists crafted a politics of territory that transformed fisher claims to shore and sea into acts of 'Catholic' aggression against the 'Hindu' nation.

In opposition to perceived 'Christian domination,' the RSS and its offshoot, the Bharatiya Janata Party (BJP), appealed to Hindus to consolidate their power against church control of educational institutions and the dominance of Christians in the professions and in electoral politics. RSS and BJP ideologues pointed out that only 'Christian' sectors of the district economy, such as education and fishing, were provided development incentives by the state, while the 'Hindu' sectors of agriculture, coir manufacturing, and oil production were totally ignored. Charging the Congress and Dravidian parties with 'pandering to minority sentiment,' they claimed that Hindus were fast becoming an endangered group in their 'own' country. In place of these 'pseudo-secular' parties that played undemocratic 'vote bank politics,' the RSS offered the 'truly secular' BJP. The BJP's 'real' secularism would involve a recognition of the cultural and territorial integrity of the nation and of the *Hindu* heritage shared by all citizens. Furthermore, in Kanyakumari, it would ensure the 'recovery' of the Catholic coast for the Hindu nation.

Even at the outset, the Catholic fishing community became representative of the 'Christian problem' identified by the RSS. The RSS had gained a foothold in the district in the early 1960s through its role in the construction of the Rock Memorial, a monument built to honor Swami Vivekananda. This project was marked by hostility between the RSS and the fishing community because building the monument required the dredging of the resource-rich inshore waters, a move that the fishing community opposed on the grounds that it was disruptive to their livelihood.[28]

28. *The Hindu*, September 1965.

As the RSS started to highlight the importance of Kanyakumari in the sacred geography of the Hindu nation, this original conflict with the fishing community too was integrated into the mytho-history of the resurgence of Hindu identity in the face of the alien faiths of Christianity and Islam. Kanyakumari's Catholic fishers became the residues of European colonialism and their opposition to a Hindu monument an instance of Christian aggression against Indian spirituality. The RSS's systematic campaign to polarize Hindus and Christians finally erupted in riots in 1982 in which the coastal fishing villages were the worst affected. Geographically isolated and socially marginal, the fishing population, as the largest group of Christians in a confined territory, was an easy target of attack.

Following the riots in which six fishermen were killed, one fishing village razed to the ground, a number of coastal churches looted and desecrated, and coastal wells poisoned, the MGR government instituted the P. Venugopal Commission of Inquiry to investigate the causes of violence. Most remarkable about the Commission's report was the evidence it provided of the cross-caste consolidation of Hindus against a perceived Christian threat, including those Hindus within the district's administrative and law enforcement machinery. By way of explaining the firings on groups of fishers, police officials and district administrators spoke of the defiance of the fishing community, which only recognized the rule of religion. In statements echoing RSS rhetoric about a monolithic minority impervious to national law and order, they depicted the coast as a theocracy within a secular nation-state and attributed fisher 'intransigence' to the consolidation of Christian clerical power on the coast and the increase in money power through fisheries development.

At the same time, then, Kanyakumari's coast was shaped by a Dravidian politics that interpellated fishers and their coast as part of a Tamil region, and a Hindu nationalism that identified the coast and its Catholics as an alien presence within the Hindu nation. How did these parallel currents of community and place-making intersect?

In response to Hindu nationalist attacks on 'alien' Christianity, fishers and clergy deployed the cultural rhetoric of Dravidianism to declare Hindu nationalism an alien presence within the Tamil region. It was the RSS, they claimed, that had introduced the

'Aryan disease' of communalism into a region characterized by the absence of inter-religious violence. During the inter-religious clashes of 1981 and 1982, there was a noticeable absence of hostility between mechanized and artisanal fishers as the need of the hour was caste and religious community solidarity in the face of a growing majoritarian threat. There are even instances of Colachel's boats providing food supplies to artisanal villages cut off from interior markets by the RSS.[29] The Catholic church too stood solidly behind its fisher congregation and played a major role in recording and presenting evidence of the coastal tragedy to the investigative body set up by MGR.

However, changes in church ideology and practice that accompanied its entry into the development arena once again escalated the hostility between mechanized and artisanal fishers. As I show in the following sections, RSS representations of the coast and its fisher population eventually began to circulate among Colachel's upwardly mobile Catholics who, by the 1990s, began to adopt Hindu nationalist rhetoric to critique their church and fellow fishers as barriers to development and to craft a new definition of community and place that 'fit' their middle-class status.

'LIBERATION TECHNOLOGY' AND MUKKUVAR MODERNITY

The truce between the mechanized and artisanal sectors of Kanyakumari's fishery during the Hindu-Christian clashes of the early 1980s was broken by a shift in the political economy of development. As Sangeeta Luthra notes (this volume, section II), the post-Emergency period in India witnessed a shift in national development strategy to accommodate the greater involvement of non-governmental organizations that variously linked the local to the global. In Kanyakumari, this shift ushered the Catholic church, arguably the largest global NGO, into the development arena.

Two decades after the onset of uneven development and frequent clashes between an increasingly prosperous minority and the wider artisanal population, a section of the Kanyakumari clergy began to question the liberatory potential of the state's development agenda

29. From newspaper reports and court testimonies of victims, police, and clergy.

and rethink their own role as moral custodians of the coast. Drawing inspiration from Latin American liberation theology, they started talking about the cultural rights of the poor and the loss of community allegiance on the part of mechanized fishers. When a Belgian Catholic priest of the local church proposed a second development experiment to motorize artisanal crafts, the church's social service society took up the task of filling what, in its view, were the development gaps left by the state. With official approval of this non-governmental initiative, the Indo-Belgian project was initiated and the motorization of indigenous crafts began. Once this scheme came within the state's subsidy program, the use of motors proliferated among Kanyakumari's artisanal fishers.[30]

These events had a dramatic impact on the polarization of the two sectors. Motorization increased the speed and range of artisanal crafts, making possible head-on confrontation with the mechanized trawlers at sea. In the absence of a government coast guard, artisanal fishers themselves took on vigilance activity to ensure trawler compliance of the 1983 Marine Regulation Act. They began to attack trawlers that crossed the boundary into the inshore three-mile zone. In addition, artisanal village councils whose legislative authority had been undermined by their inability to restrict trawling were now revitalized through the deployment of vigilante canoes. With every attack, the three-mile zone became an even more powerful territorial marker of artisanal identity and rights.

This new, more militant artisanal politics pushed Colachel's mechanized fishers into a new, more assertive form of cultural politics at the end of the 1980s. Through the decade, they had gradually differentiated themselves from their wider community in a variety of ways. Many of Colachel's trawler owners diversified their investments, buying land as well as more trawling boats. The ownership of property away from the coast brought them into

30. A comprehensive account of the Kottar social service society's project in intermediate technology is provided by Pierre Gillet, one of the Belgian priests, who was also an engineer with the project, in his 1985 manuscript, *Small is Difficult: The Pangs and Successes of Small Boat Technology Transfer in South India*. Maarten Bavinck also discusses the impact of motorized craft on the power dynamic between the trawlers and artisanal sector in 'Changing Balance of Power at Sea: Motorization of Artisanal Fishing Craft,' in *Economic and Political Weekly*, 1 February 1997.

greater contact with agrarian and urban caste groups and enhanced their new middle-class affiliation. Interestingly, they began to describe their own set of changing values by using the primitivizing language used by state officials to distinguish coastal from national culture. A disposition to save money, to foster an ethic of cleanliness, to resolve conflict through dialogue not force, and to accept change were some of the ways in which they characterized their cultural transformation from 'primitive' to 'modern' fishers. Their consumption practices also changed dramatically. Big concrete homes, motorcycles, and cars became a more common sight in Colachel, as did increasing rates of dowry. These markers of 'civilization' further insulated Colachel from other artisanal villages.

Most significantly, Colachel's mechanized fishers responded to artisanal opposition by invoking their greater contribution to the nation. In the early 1990s, Colachel's trawl boat association began an information campaign by distributing pamphlets defending their position against the artisanal sector. Some pamphlets highlighted their contribution to India's foreign exchange earnings and used 'scientific' reasoning to invalidate the artisanal sector's opposition to trawling. Other pamphlets defended their position on the basis of more 'traditional' identities. These denounced the un-Christian values of the artisanal fishers who 'only practice violence while the trawlers multiply the fish just as Jesus did.' In contrast to these 'bad' fishers are the trawler owners who 'contribute financially to Catholic festivals and to the upkeep of parish churches' and have 'given Kanyakumari's Catholics a national name.' Through these publications, Colachel's mechanized fishers underscored the greater contribution of trawler over artisanal fishing to the building of both church and nation. By rhetorically fusing sector, community, and nation, they constructed Colachel as a place of nation-building, their own interest as the national interest, and their success as the success of the Catholic community.

Their experience of social mobility and exposure to social dynamics outside the coast also generated middle-class Mukkuvar resentment towards church authority. The Catholic Church's role at the center of coastal social organization set the fishing villages apart from both agrarian and urban communities in the district, where competing institutional forces circumscribed the power of religious institutions. Colachel's mechanized minority began speaking of the illegitimacy of church activity in secular arenas and the clergy's investment in keeping their congregation poor and dependent. Interestingly, their demands for greater fisher self-determination echoed the language of the RSS. Colachel's fishers began to echo Hindu nationalist critiques of Christian social organization and turn them against their own religious leaders. Their attempt to redefine Catholic Mukkuvar identity in 'modern' terms signaled a growing intolerance towards church authority even as it normalized the RSS's demand for religious minority assimilation into the national (read Hindu) mainstream.

NEOLIBERALISM AND NEW ANTI-IMPERIALISMS

In 1991, at the height of ongoing struggles within the domestic fishery, the Indian government responded to World Bank and IMF demands for structural adjustment by deregulating its 200-mile Exclusive Economic Zone to permit the operations of foreign industrial fishing vessels. According to the new logic of modernization, India could only achieve full modernity by freeing itself from the shackles of state control and opening up to global capitalism. This most recent vision of national development effectively marginalized both sectors of the Indian fishery by pronouncing them equally inadequate for building a truly modern nation.

National opposition to the deep sea fishing policy arose primarily from two quarters: the National Fishworkers Forum (NFF) and the Swadeshi Jagaran Manch (SJM). The NFF, an umbrella body of artisanal fisher unions, began a campaign that inverted the Indian government's development paradigm by identifying localized artisanal economies as the best foundation for development. Furthermore, it equated trawling with destruction, not production, and pronounced artisanal fishing the only means to a sustainable future. At the same time that it forged a national collective of small fishers, the Forum started working to build a global movement uniting small fishers opposed to the detrimental impact of capital-intensive fishing on marine resources. The NFF link with global environmental groups strengthened its critique of the Indian government's developmental choices and offered an alternative to both state and global capitalism.

Another group that opposed the deep sea fishing policy was the Swadeshi Jagaran Manch, the economic wing of the Hindu nationalist front. But instead of opposing capital-intensive fishing like the

NFF, the Manch advocated upscaling the mechanization of the domestic fishery. Sustainability in the era of globalization, Manch leaders argued, is sustainable national resistance to Western domination which can be ensured only by industrialization under the auspices of a strong Hindu state. According to the SJM, real sustainability could not be based on alien concepts such as socialism or environmentalism, but on a Hinduism which would modernize local economies towards strengthening the nation globally.

In Kanyakumari, artisanal fishers participated en masse in the NFF's campaign. Linking up with small fishers globally further strengthened their critique of mechanization and sense of being the rightful heirs to the local resource. They began to speak of trawling, not simply as an expression of greed and unequal distribution, but as destructive and unsustainable. The link between artisanal fishing and the sustainable future of the resource reinforced a collective consciousness as custodians of the sea and the moral arbiters of local conflict.

For Colachel's mechanized fishers, globalization was a twist in the logic of development that turned the tables against them. Suddenly, they found themselves sandwiched between two new global threats: the environmentalism of the NFF and the embrace of foreign capital by a liberalizing Indian state. At the same time, local tensions were building. In 1995, they finally exploded in a devastating clash in which artisanal fishers burned fourteen trawlers and mechanized fishers destroyed one artisanal village. During this three-day conflict, both church and state were paralyzed and Colachel's villagers had to flee to interior areas where they were offered shelter by Hindu families.

Immediately after, Colachel's trawler owners approached the SJM for protection in exchange for which they offered to support the BJP during the general elections of March 1996. This move ensured the backing of a national party that supported the middle classes nationally. The choice of a Hindu nationalist party that had grown locally through opposition to Christianity and to Dravidianism also expressed their feeling of betrayal by the Catholic Church and regional parties. Vincent, one of Colachel's boat owners elaborated the logic of community and place that lay behind this decision. He began with a cultural map of the district strikingly similar to the RSS's own chauvinistic cartography. 'The Catholic coast,' he explained, 'is hemmed in by the Hindu interior.

On the coast, the church is the real authority; in the interior, it's the state.' He then laid out two kinds of community dynamics, one local and the other national. Speaking of the local situation, Vincent defined Colachel's villagers as a 'community' besieged by the combined force of artisanal aggression and religious orthodoxy. To defend *their* rights on the coast, he explained, Colachel's villagers had to turn to the national community to which they belonged. The force of the national, as represented by the RSS and BJP, would curb the local power of the Catholic church and its artisanal fishers. 'Now, if the artisanal fishers attack Colachel,' he exclaimed triumphantly, 'we can escape to the interior Hindu villages which are controlled by the BJP and the RSS. Our Bishop is scared because he knows that if they attack us, we have the RSS on our side. The church can't tell us what to do anymore. We're with the BJP now.'

In Vincent's story of Colachel's fight for justice, the concerns of Colachel's boat owners were seamlessly integrated with national interests, even as he identified local tensions with their church and artisanal brethren as the primary cause of their turn to the BJP. This identification with a middle-class nation marked a radical departure from the wider politics of the coast. While the artisanal sector's critique of globalization established a link between local crises across the globe, in the process erasing the boundary between the local and global, Colachel's mechanized fishers fell back on territorial nationhood and middle-class privilege within the nation to show the violence of both liberalization and environmentalism.

On their part, BJP leaders exhibited their new secular image by insisting that Colachel's fishers did not convert to Hinduism. After all, they argued, the BJP is not about religion at all but about national Hindu culture to which all Indians regardless of faith belonged. This definition of Hinduism as culture, not faith, finally sealed the alliance with Colachel's mechanized fishers. 'If our own Christian brethren and priests are against us,' they reasoned, 'why not place our trust in a Hindu party which is willing to help us without even asking us to convert?'

CONCLUSION

In this essay, I have analysed the cultural specificity of Indian developmentalism by looking at one strand of the development process. State intervention in a local fishery, I have argued, generated forms of community and place that, rather than playing out a predetermined course of modernization, were products of a specific cultural environment. While the teleologies associated with modernization theory would dictate the erosion of 'Other' imaginings by development, I submit that it intersected with Dravidian, theological, Hindu nationalist, and environmental discourses in the self-representations and political practices of the Catholic Mukkuvars.

Finally, I have argued that just as India's developmentalism should not be seen as derivative of a global formation, local phenomena too should be seen as influenced by but not reduced to the logic of the national. The Catholic Mukkuvars' alignment with the BJP must not be understood simply in terms of a national pattern of middle-class support for Hindu nationalism, but as the dynamic outcome of community and place-making at the local level.

References

Appadurai, Arjun, 1996. *Modernity at Large: Cultural Dimensions of Globalization*. Minneapolis: University of Minnesota Press.

Baskaran, Theodore, 1981. *The Message Bearers: Nationalist Politics and the Entertainment Media in South India, 1880–1945*. Madras: Cre-A.

Bavinck, Maarten, 1997. 'Changing balance of power at sea: Motorization of artisanal fishing craft.' *Economic and Political Weekly* 32(5).

Chatterjee, Partha, 1993. *The Nation and Its Fragments: Colonial and Postcolonial Histories*. Princeton: Princeton University Press.

Dickey, Sara, 1993. *Cinema and the Urban Poor in South India*. Cambridge: Cambridge University Press.

Dirlik, Arif, 1994. *After the Revolution: Waking to Global Capitalism*. Hanover: Wesleyan University Press.

Escobar, Arturo, 1995. *Encountering Development: The Making and Unmaking of the Third World*. Princeton: Princeton University Press.

Ferguson, James, [1990] 1994. *The Anti-Politics Machine: 'Development,' Depoliticization and Bureaucratic Power in Lesotho*. Minneapolis: University of Minnesota Press.

Fox, Richard, 1989. *Gandhian Utopia: Experiments with Culture*. Boston: Beacon Press.

———, 1984. 'Urban class and communal consciousness in colonial Punjab: The genesis of India's intermediate regime.' *Modern Asian Studies* 18: 459–89.

Frankel, Francine, 1978. *India's Political Economy, 1947–77: The Gradual Revolution.* Princeton: Princeton University Press.

Gillet, Pierre, 1985. *Small is Difficult: The Pangs and Successes of Small Boat Technology Transfer in South India.* Nagercoil: Centre for Appropriate Technology.

Harvey, David, 1996. *Justice, Nature, and the Geography of Difference.* Oxford: Blackwell.

Kurien, John, 1978. 'Entry of big business into fishing: Its impact on fish economy.' *Economic and Political Weekly* 13(36): 1557–64.

———, 1985. 'Technical assistance projects and socio-economic change: Norwegian intervention in Kerala's fisheries development.' *Economic and Political Weekly,* Review of Agriculture 20(25–6): A70–A88.

Ludden, David (ed.), 1992. 'India's development regime,' In Nicholas B. Dirks (ed.), *Colonialism and Culture.* Ann Arbor: University of Michigan Press.

———, 1996. *Making India Hindu: Religion, Community, and the Politics of Democracy in India.* Bombay: Oxford University Press.

Mintz, Sidney, 1977. 'The so-called world system: Local initiative and local response.' *Dialectical Anthropology* 2: 253–70.

Mitchell, Timothy, 1991. *Colonising Egypt.* Berkeley: University of California Press.

Narchison, J. R., V. Paul Leon, E. Francis, and F. Wilfred, 1983. *Called to Serve: A Profile of the Diocese of Kottar.* Nagercoil: Assisi Press.

Pandian, M. S. S., 1992. *The Image Trap: M. G. Ramachandran in Film and Politics.* Delhi: Sage Publications.

Ram, Kalpana, 1990. *Mukkuvar Women: Gender, Hegemony and Capitalist Transformation in a South Indian Fishing Village.* New Delhi: Kali for Women.

Sachs, Wolfgang (ed.), 1992. *The Development Dictionary.* London: Zed Books.

Said, Edward, 1978. *Orientalism.* New York: Pantheon.

Smith, Neil, 1985. *Uneven Development: Nature, Capital, and the Production of Space.* Oxford: Blackwell.

Subramanian, Narendra, 1999. *Ethnicity and Populist Mobilization: Political Parties, Citizens and Democracy in South India.* New Delhi: Oxford University Press.

Washbrook, David, 1989. 'Caste, class and dominance in modern Tamil Nadu: Non-Brahminism, Dravidianism, and Tamil Nationalism.' In F. Frankel and M. S. A. Rao (eds.), Dominance and State Power in Modern India, vol. 1. New Delhi: Oxford University Press.

———, 1997. 'The rhetoric of democracy and development in late colonial India.' In Bose, S. and A. Jalal (eds.), *Nationalism, Democracy and Development: State and Politics in India.* New Delhi: Oxford University Press.

11

Development Counter-Narratives: Taking Social Movements Seriously

SUBIR SINHA

DEVELOPMENT: CHRONICLES OF A DEATH PREMATURELY?

Rumor has had it for some time that 'the development project' is dying, that it is dead already, and indeed that it is now putrefying.[1] These intimations have come from those who believe that as a global project development should die, and whose political preferences are alternatives emerging from the popular politics of 'grassroots,' 'local,' 'indigenous,' located in 'community' or 'civil society,' etc. Esteva indicts development as a failed attempt to impose a 'single cultural model on the whole world.' Escobar argues that planning, the engine of state-led development, was at core a process of domination and social control, a concept alien to the Third World, imposed upon it by the West. Illich argues that the notion of basic needs, while well meaning, had created networks of domination and dependency. Shiva rues the desacralizing of nature into resources and commodities through the instruments

---

1. Illich (1993) observes that 'development is dying'; Escobar (1995) that 'development is dead' already; and Esteva (1987) that 'development stinks'.

of science and markets underpinning development projects, which, for all their claims to emancipation, enabled the oppressive insertion of the state in ever-newer arenas of everyday life.[2] Confronting and moving beyond this oppressive imperium of development, these commentators whom I shall identify here as the 'new radical critics' see far-reaching changes being brought by social movements. Shiva, for instance, sees in the collective action of 'little people' challenges to reductionist Baconian and Cartesian science.[3] It is by way of a reconsideration of the relation between domination and resistance in their formulations that the paper approaches the question of 'regional modernities.'

I see the new radical critique as encompassing two distinct components. The first is the importation of Foucault into the study of development, the chief effect of which has been to show development as domination. Ferguson shows that the unintended but structurally systematic effect of development was to expand bureaucratic power in Lesotho. The ability of development as discourse to produce material effects is common also to the arguments of Escobar and of Mitchell in different country contexts. The totality of domination produced by development projects seems to constitute an imperium, within which lie no possibilities of liberation. Ferguson's 'anti-politics machine' implies the production by the power of development of a contained political field. Where resistance is theorized, it is in autonomous, primarily 'cultural,' spaces. This identification of resistance and alternatives in new forms of conviviality and sociality is the point of intersection between this approach to domination and writings on resistance by academics, intellectuals, and activists associated with specific social movements. Despite the different temporal frames in which they locate the moment of origin of the development project, these two components agree on the alien-ness of development to those in whose name it is justified, its domination over them, and the autonomy of new cultural initiatives. It is in their view of development as domination and coercion, and resistance as pure, that the new radical critique intersects with what we have elsewhere

2. See essays in Sachs 1992.

3. 'Protest against reductionist science is emerging in all spheres. In India, for instance, the famous 'Chipko' movement is a movement against reductionist forestry.' (Shiva in Nandy 1988: 255)

identified as the 'new traditionalist' discourses.[4] Ferguson's preference for civil-society type initiatives, Esteva's for absolutely local
actions, Escobar's for agents that are located outside of sites colonized by development merge seamlessly with the idealized protagonists of new traditionalist accounts of movements such as Chipko.
This maintains the formulation the state and community as strictly
separate domains, one the center of a network of domination, the
other the domain from which other ways of seeing, doing, and
being may emerge. It is in this way that certain local stories become
part of the global counter-narrative of development offered by the
new radical critics.

Essays in this volume have challenged the new radical view of
domination. As Subramanian shows, differentially positioned
fishers incorporated dominant discourses (of development, but also
of caste, region, nation-building, etc.) into their overall strategies
to claim power over each other, over marine resources and production inputs, and over the state. Klingensmith documents
the multiple individual and collective claims made around the
Damodar Valley dam project. Skaria notes that the spectacle
through which the colonial state wished to institutionalize its
domination over Bhils was used by them for a host of other
purposes. At the very least, these examples indicate a level of
engagement between a range of social groups and the modernizing
or developmentalist state, rather than a rejection of the modernizing or developmentalist agendas *in toto*. Similarly, interested
in the ways in which development discourses do not close but
make possible new forms of agency and subjectivity, here I review
the ways in which the Sarvodaya and Chipko movements in the
1960s and 1970s engaged with development in the western
Himalayas, and to what effect.

The claim that development freezes the field of politics and is
the prime mode for the proliferation of an abstract, placeless, and
agentless mentality of rule, 'governmentality,' sits uneasily with
the implication in new radical accounts of agency that there is an
'outside' to development, which is the site from which new agents
will dismantle it. As the Introduction has argued, the local is not
a space of splendid isolation, but a product of specific articulations.
Along these lines, this paper is interested in the ways in which

4. Sinha *et al*. 1997.

actors supposedly located outside development's imperium engaged with the programmatic agenda of development embodied in the state.

The paper is organized in the following way. In the first section, by way of a brief review of the history of the Indian development project, and of Indian forestry particularly, I develop the idea that development was the product of a politics of legitimization and contestation between the colonial state and nationalist challengers. In the second section, I show the relation of the Gandhian—socialist Sarvodaya movement to the Nehruvian project of 'community development' in post-Independence India. Following this, I consider in detail some programmatic documents of the Chipko movement, analysing them in relation to the supposedly dominant agenda of planned development. I close with a consideration of the ways in which contestations over development produced regional collective identities, and the effect this had in reshaping development.

THE TIME AND PLACE OF DEVELOPMENT

It is not merely a quibble over chronology to dispute the position that the development project is a post-war phenomenon. As Ludden, Bose, and others have shown, the late colonial state in India, already challenged by nationalists for managing the economy against the interests of a putative national community (to which colonialists by definition could not belong), as well as by vigorous armed responses aimed at overthrowing its rule, initiated development as a justification for its continued presence, as part of its overall unsuccessful attempts to convert its power into authority, coercion to domination and hegemony. Well before its emergence as an international agenda at the end of the Second World War, development was produced in the regional context by this politics of legitimization.[5]

5. It could be convincingly argued that elements of the development project were emerging as arenas of 'international concern' from the late nineteenth century. See essays in Boli and Thomas (1999). Here I am interested only in arguing that before development became the agenda of international agencies and of superpowers, it arose in the context of anti-colonial struggles and colonial responses to them.

In India, since its inception in the late nineteenth century the development project has constantly been challenged and reshaped by struggles over the nature and control of the state between nationalists and colonialists.[6] In 1901, calling the attention of the colonial state to agriculture, the Indian National Congress urged that it 'adopt all those measures for its improvement and development which have been made in America, Russia, Holland, Belgium and several other countries.'[7] This foreshadowed the later role of the state as teacher, guide, financier, buyer and seller to agriculturists. As Mishra points out, early nationalist political-economic critiques of colonialism, such as those formulated by Dadabhoy Naoroji, bore the conviction that 'without an active intervention of the state, [the] Indian economy could not develop.' By the early twentieth century, the state's primary mission, both sides agreed, 'was to apply European scientific methods to Indian agriculture.'[8] This articulation of development as a domain of state action, meant as an indictment of the colonial state, had two effects. It simultaneously pushed the colonial state to adopt a more explicitly developmentalist agenda, and prepared the ground for it to become a raison d'être of the post-colonial state.

By the early 1940s, the main current of nationalist economic thinking was that national development was necessary, but that the colonial state was an obstacle to it. National development was possible only under a nation-state, not under colonial rule: 'Self-government was...necessary because it represented the historically necessary form of national development...[T]he new state represented the only legitimate form of exercise of power because it was a necessary condition for the development of the

6. See Partha Chatterjee 1995, esp. chapter 10. Little and Painter (1995) make the argument for colonial contexts in general: 'What did emerge following World War II was a consensus among the wealthy nations that, if the emerging nationalist, anti-colonialist and anti-imperialist struggles were to be confronted successfully, military occupation and direct colonial rule could not be the only contexts for promoting modernization in poor areas of the world. They thus created an institutional structure charged with promoting the expansion of capitalist production relations and linking that expansion with aspirations for better living conditions.'

7. Zaidi 1988: 34.

8. Mishra 1988: 12; Manak 1979: 73, quoted in Ludden 1993.

nation.'[9] Progress and development thus became critical components of the logic of the nationalist movement and later of the postcolonial state.[10] My point here is that development was a product of a process marked by asymmetrical power relations through which the colonial state claimed hegemony, and nationalists challenged it. Insofar as each conjured up a 'public' or a 'nation,' and claimed to represent the public good or national interest, they also entered into a relation of legitimization in relation to the 'public' and the 'nation.' This articulation was to have effects on colonial and post-1947 development projects.

The development project in Indian forestry took shape over a long nineteenth century. Guha provides evidence of the wide variety of temporary arrangements into which the early colonial state entered with forest dwellers. Initially, agents of the colonial state saw forests as abundant and inexhaustible.[11] The lack of coherent state policy or interest toward forests in the early years of colonial rule can be attributed to this view.[12] This verdant abundance was sometimes seen as a hindrance to other state objectives, such as revenue.[13]

The introduction of forest contracts in the 1840s in the Uttar Pradesh (UP) hills initiated a set of far reaching changes, and something like 'forest policy' began to take shape. The colonial state reapportioned property rights and rights of access to forests, asserting its ownership of them, with the aim to make them productive. This involved the creation of a new forest bureaucracy, the introduction of forest legislation, outlawing a range of activities key to the reproduction of rural society, and the use of scientific forestry, based in the Forest Research Institute, to find more lucrative uses for forests. Forestry thus became a sector of the colonial economy, organized to provide revenue through auctions of forest contracts, timber to provide railway sleepers, housing

9. Chatterjee in Byres 1994.

10. Ludden 1992.

11. Harwicke (1809), visiting the Himalayan kingdom of Garhwal in 1793, noted that 'the forests of oak, fir and *boorans* are here more extensive and the trees of greater magnitude than I have ever seen.' See also views attributed to J. H. Batten in Guha (1989: 35).

12. See Chaturvedi 1961: 45. Of course, it can also be argued that in this period, 'the colonial state' did not yet exist as a coherent entity.

13. Richards and McAlpin in Tucker and Richards 1983: 87.

furniture, pulp and paper, rayon fiber, packaging material, particle boards, plywood, carved wooden articles, wooden utensils, and safety matches.

Forestry legislation, reflecting the colonial will to expand its control over new domains, was also meant to reshape the relation between Himalayan forests and hill peasants. Their pasture rights had already been curtailed by the Cattle Trespass Act of 1871, under which forest officers and police officers were empowered to seize or impound any cattle grazing in forests deemed legally closed. The Act of 1927 prohibited making fresh clearings; setting fires; grazing cattle without permission; felling or otherwise damaging trees; and the removal of stones or 'forest produce.' Infringements of any of these rules were punishable by fines, as was clearing land for cultivation or other purposes. Section 72 of the Act endowed the forest bureaucracy with additional coercive capacity to enter, survey, demarcate, and map absolutely any land. The Act also empowered the state to grant portions of reserved, protected, or other forests to villages to be managed as village forests, and to withdraw such grants. Local autonomy over village forests was greatly curtailed under the Act. The state retained the right to make rules for regulating the management of village forests, prescribing the conditions under which the communities were granted rights to timber, fodder, and other forest produce, and their duties for the protection and improvement of such forest.[14] By the last few decades of colonial rule, apart from revenue imperatives, the state justified its claims over forests on principles of stewardship. Section 35 of the Act of 1927 claimed that these efforts at control, restrictions, and prohibitions were aimed at protecting the hills from extremes of weather, soil preservation, hydrological concerns, protecting lines of communication between the frontier and the city, and public health.[15]

While this scenario of increasing state control over forests and forest dwellers would seem to confirm the formulations of the new radical critics, it is to be noted that key aspects of colonial forestry were shared by the nationalist opponents of the colonial state. G. B. Pant's advocacy of 'modernizing' the hills included 'educated young men' encouraged to settle in the hills to 'develop agriculture along improved lines.' He lamented that the hills were 'deprived

14. Malik 1981: 18, 25.
15. Ibid.: 46–8.

of state activities for agricultural development, whether research, investigation, demonstration, propaganda or teaching,' and suggested that a more extensive network of roads to facilitate the movement of agricultural and dairy products from the hills to the markets in the plains. He urged the colonial state to get more directly involved in the hill economy, promoting the vine and raisin industry as in Switzerland, importing and popularizing Australian sheep, and writing off the considerable loans the hill peasants had contracted over the years.[16] By this time, both the colonial state and its nationalist challengers had become committed to the idea of state led modern forestry.

The harsh restrictions and penalties over forest users also met with organized and militant response from the latter half of the nineteenth century.[17] Protesting against the colonial-influenced policies of the Tehri state in 1906, villagers attacked forest officials who had put curbs on forest use, claiming 'full and extensive rights' over all forests.[18] Recognizing peasant demand for more access to forests, Pant supported the lifting of some major restrictions on local rights to hunt and to collect forest produce.[19] It was perhaps by framing the forest question in these terms, of the rights of the peasantry to have increased access to forests, that Pant hoped to integrate them within nationalist politics. Rawat notes that these demands found their way into colonial forest policy. In 1931, the colonial state granted the right to village communities to constitute common forests. Likewise, in 1941, as nationalist conflicts with the colonial state intensified, the forestry department relaxed grazing in Kumaon, giving every person who had resided there for at least 12 years the right to graze 'horses, ponies, mules, cows, bulls, bullocks, buffaloes, sheep and goat.'[20] Domination and resistance were working out in at least three ways. First, nationalist resistance to colonial rule actually legitimated some key elements of that rule, notably the role of the state, an agenda of guarded capitalist development, and of scientific and bureaucratic rationality. Second, nationalism legitimated its claim to represent

16. Pant 1927.
17. Guha (1999) provides evidence that the question of control over forests remained a contentious issue throughout colonial rule in the Sahyadri region.
18. Guha 1989; Rawat 1990: 20.
19. Pant 1927.
20. Rawat 1990: 24–5.

a 'national community in the making' by incorporating, at the regional level, demands made by subaltern movements. And third, the colonial state also incorporated some nationalist and subaltern demands, reflected in policy changes. This politics of legitimization, which formed the context for the formation of the development agendas, underwent transformation in the post-1947 period of planned development for the national economy.

PLANNED DEVELOPMENT AND THE RECONSTITUTION OF LEGITIMACY

The chief role assigned to the state in post-1947 development planning was to oversee rapid capital accumulation. In keeping with the populist notion of 'social transformation without social conflict,' planning aimed to mitigate the social upheavals that accumulation might cause, and to legitimate it through the wide diffusion of its benefits.[21] Perceptions of the agricultural sector, including forestry, were rooted in the 'theory of agricultural constraints to growth,' which argued that in a poor and primarily agricultural country, slow growth of the agricultural sector places a limit on the maximum non-inflationary rate of GDP growth.[22] Over the first two Five-Year Plans, relatively lower levels of state interventions prevailed in the 'traditional sector,' which became more open to modernization from the Third Plan onwards, following the fiscal and foreign exchange crises of the early 1960s.[23] Seth points out that it was this intertwining of nationalism, productivism, and development that marked the 'socialism' of Nehruvian development.[24] Similarly, Chatterjee argues that balancing regimes of accumulation with those of legitimization, planned development constituted a Gramscian 'passive revolution' to bring about capitalism with gradual, incremental changes with minimum social conflict and the redistribution of national wealth.[25] The domination of the development project and the state was contingent on the extent to which accumulation and modernization gained popular legitimacy.

21. Chakravarty 1987: 14.
22. Sen 1991: PE–63.
23. Chatterjee 1995: 210–11.
24. Seth 1993.
25. Chatterjee 1994.

As Bose points out, the legitimization imperative prevented planned development from achieving its purely apolitical ideal.[26] The necessity of development as a project of accumulation was premised on its ability to eradicate poverty, provide employment, deliver community development, and meet basic needs. In an upward spiral, these goals were at the same time desirable, as well as necessary to create new productive citizens who would aspire to and achieve ever higher levels of affluence, employment, development and needs provision. As the First Five-Year Plan document puts it:

There has to be a dominant purpose around which the enthusiasm of the people can be aroused and sustained, a purpose which can draw forth in the people and those who assist them on behalf of the Government the will to work as well as a sense of urgency. The aim should be to create in the rural population a burning desire for a higher standard of living— a will to live better.[27]

The relation between 'the people' and the state in these formulations of 'community development' was complex. While 'the principal responsibility for improving their own condition… rest [ed.] with the people,' at the same time the central agency in community development was vested in 'network of extension workers' who would 'initiate a process of transformation of the social and economic life of the villages.'[28] 'The people' were important actors but ultimately inadequate to change their collective lot; this made it necessary for the state to intervene in social life, and at the same time for it to seek the 'cooperation' of the people. Improved standards of living as a legitimating principle thus placed the state and the people in a dynamic relationship, though it did not resolve the tension between the agency of the state and of 'the people' in achieving it. One attempt was to mobilize Gandhian self-help groups in order to supplement the state's extension efforts with those from the 'voluntary sector.' By the early 1960s, the Planning Commission's Program Evaluation Agency was reporting that community development had failed both to increase agricultural production and to decrease rural poverty and inequality. Fiscal and foreign exchange crises of the early 1960s provided the immediate context for the shift in official priorities

26. Bose in Cooper and Packard 1997.
27. GoI 1952: 223.
28. Ibid.: 222.

from gradualism to accelerated productivity increases through the Green Revolution. Mira Behn was among the more prominent Gandhians to have felt the increasing gap between them and the developmentalist state.[29]

Early post-1947 planned forestry development aimed to balance productivity enhancement and stock management. The National Forest Resolution of 1952 reiterated the objectives of state forestry: 'the value of forests was recognized not only in the physical field, such as conservation of moisture and prevention of erosion, but also in the economic field such as development of agriculture, industry and communication.'[30] The plywood industry was established countrywide, adding new demands on the forests.[31] The Second Plan at the same time recognized the need to increase forested area from 22 percent to 33 percent, and to do so in a way that would increase the industrial availability of timber, for which transport, scientific, and statistical research were promoted.[32] With this in view, the powers of the forest bureaucracy were further expanded in 1966. From the Third Plan, productivity enhancement became the primary objective of state intervention. There was rapid expansion of forest-based industries in the plains, such as paper mills and turpentine. By 1980, India's 3788 wood-based industries and 4091 paper and paper product units together consumed 150,000 tons of timber annually.[33] In 1980-1, forests accounted for 3.2 percent of the national revenue, in several states accounting for up to 10 percent of the revenue. From the late 1970s, India entered the world market as an exporter of timber, mainly to the lucrative Japanese market.[34]

While planning achieved accelerated rates of capital accumulation in forestry, it failed to meet the countervailing objectives of legitimization and conservation. The expansion of state power over forests, and the increasing primacy given to capitalist and industrial use of forests, sought legitimization on two grounds, namely the welfare of local forest dwellers through Community Development Programs, and the practice of sustainable forestry

29. Behn 1964.
30. D'Abreo 1985: 4.
31. PUDR 1983: 8.
32. GoI 1956: 98.
33. GoI 1981: 66-7.
34. Ibid.: 9-12.

(i.e. avoiding deforestation, soil erosion, and threats to local water sources.) However, the persistence of forest contracts and poverty in the hills both contributed to accelerated environmental degradation. By the 1960s, there was evidence of extensive deforestation in the districts of the UP Himalayas, which remained among the poorest in the country, and now faced increased incidence of landslides and floods.

Across the UP hills, Sarvodaya groups, who had long-term presence, had organized and registered block-level cooperative societies to participate in and take advantage of the official community development.[35] Their activism went beyond the official agenda, including schools,[36] and involvement in the anti-alcohol and anti-caste movements. In the next section, I will review the Sarvodaya and later Chipko movements to understand the ways in which they drew upon community development to constitute new local and regional political practices and identities.

AGENDAS OF RESISTANCE: A LONG VIEW

As colonial forest policy of increased state control was taking shape, alternative agendas were proposed that stressed the need for the autonomy of the 'village community' in its use of the forest. The Poona Sarvajanik Sabha reacting to the Forest Act of 1878, demanded the participation of villagers in maintaining forest cover, and autonomy in managing their forests.[37] Likewise, Gandhi made extensive arguments in favor of village autonomy, including in the management of all forms of common property.[38] New radicals such as Shiva have argued that Chipko, with its supposed emphasis on locality and community, is the latest in this long line of indigenous thinking. It can, of course, be argued that notions of community were present and influential within colonial development thinking.[39] More importantly, Gandhian thinking itself was not static, frozen in time from the 1930s. The Sarvodaya movement consciously attempted to reconcile Gandhian political philosophy

35. See Sinha 1999.
36. See Klenk's account, this volume.
37. Quoted in Guha 1994: 2192.
38. See, in particular, Gandhi 1959.
39. Hunt 1938, chapter 3; Mosse 1999; Gilmartin, in Madsen 1999. Gandhi's own understanding of village communities owes something to Maine.

with socialism. In addition, as noted above, Sarvodaya groups had participated, with diminishing hope for success, in the state's community development programs. In this section, I will analyse development counter-narratives emerging from the Sarvodaya movement and a selection of essays by Sundarlal Bahuguna and Chandi Prasad Bhatt, Chipko activists who earlier were activists of the Sarvodaya movement, to understand how issues of state, community, and the relation between the two were articulated.

Sarvodaya was based on the idea of *sampoorna kranti* (total revolution) in social relations. Activists interpreted 'national independence' to mean village self-sufficiency, achieved through a total reconstruction of village life. Inspired by Gandhi's 'constructive programme,' sarvodayis called for a transition from *rajniti* (politics of state power) to *lokniti* (people's power), aimed at making state power irrelevant in meeting the needs of rural people.[40] Sarvodaya's goal, like that of early Indian planning, was social transformation without social conflict. To prevent class conflict on the land question, activists hoped to persuade to give land to the landless (*bhoodan*), and then to persuade all owners to gift land to the village community (*gramdan*). Activists such as Vinoba Bhave had undertaken foot marches to popularize bhoodan and gramdan. Several of the Chipko activists had participated in these programs in the hill areas and elsewhere in India.

'Lokniti,' however, could be made real only if people were capable of taking full charge of their own lives. Bhave argued that the Gandhian idea of *swaraj* (self-rule) required that people should refuse to be governed by the state, practice self-government, and refrain from exercising power over others. The refusal to be governed by the state came from the belief that even if the government had genuinely good intentions, 'the seat of power' limited its ability to do constructive work. People organized in village communities must work for the decentralization of state power, constituting, in effect, mini-republics, linked in concentric circles: '[T]he politics of Sarvodaya can have no party and no concern with power. Rather, its aim will be to see that all centers of power are abolished. The more this new politics grows the more the old politics shrinks. A real withering away of the state!'[41] Such

40. Gandhi 1941; see also Narayan 1964.
41. Narayan 1964: 51.

a decentralization of power implied also decentralizing technology and the economy: thus, the stress within Sarvodaya on humanizing technology, and the organization of local cooperatives and small-scale industries. Sarvodayis claimed to draw strength from their faith in God and in the power of the people (*bhagwan ki bhakti aur janata ki shakti*).[42] It was these activists who constituted the core organizations of the movement, such as the Dasholi Gram Swaraj Sangh (DGSS, later the DGSM, associated with Bhatt), and the Parvatiya Navjeevan Mandal (Mountain New-Life Society, later the Navjivan Ashram, NJA, associated with Bahuguna).

Autonomous village communities were the cornerstones of the Sarvodaya alternative. Autonomy required enabling people to reduce their dependence on the state, and to create new interdependence between and within communities. It was with the aim to increase the capacity of village communities that hill Sarvodayis supported and participated in community development.[43] They established village self-rule societies that included labor collectives, *khadi* spinning groups, and small-scale 'cottage' industries. Bhatt argued that the main reason for their limited success was that the government did not make adequate amounts of wood available to them, and urged the forest department to open more timber depots and help set up cooperatively owned small-scale forest industries to manufacture pencils, mathematical instruments, etc.[44] The Sarvodayi demands for village industries or for common property were thus not only about bringing benefits locally, they were also political acts aimed at creating a new kind of social power in which the state would not be the central actor. But one problem was that considerable assistance from the state was required in order to ultimately become autonomous from it.

Still, some hill cooperatives were able to provide higher incomes to their members, though temporarily. The Malla Nagpur Cooperative Labor Society was started in 1962, bid competitively for road building contracts, and later, with support from the Village Industries Commission, established small iron- and wood-based industry. The 700 members of this cooperative were able to double the wages from those under previous labor arrangements. Labor

42. C. P. Bhatt, 'Sundarlalji Bahuguna ke naam sandesh.' Letter dated 29 December 1973.
43. Narayan 1964: 249–52.
44. See Bhatt 1972.

contractors who saw the threat posed by increased wages bribed local bureaucrats to award non-profitable construction contracts to the cooperatives. Forced to choose between entering into competitive bribery or falling wages for members, the cooperative left construction contracts altogether, deciding to focus on forest-based small-scale industries. The DGSS, which was to play a central role in the Chipko movement, was formed for this purpose in the late 1960s.[45]

With accelerating deforestation and persistent poverty, and with their own space to maneuver within official policy squeezed by productivism in its formulation and corruption in its implementation, Sarvodaya activists became increasingly critical of the post-independence state. They argued that, while seeking legitimization on the Gandhian socialist ideal of 'total revolution,' the state had failed to change the direction of forest policy.[46] Centralization invested the state with enormous power; at the same time, it made it difficult for the state to acquire the knowledge on which a responsible exercise of power must be based. In Bhatt's analysis, planning from above promised to 'remove our backwardness,' but instead it degraded the local environment and further impoverished hill villagers, many of whom fled to the cities for employment. He pointed to the distance between planners and those on whose behalf they drew their projects: 'planners are unable to grasp the problems of the villagers, and the villagers are not asked to participate in the planning process.... [I]t is for this reason that the pace of rural development is slow.' While Sarvodayis had initially hoped to complement state policy, they now opposed it.

Sarvodayis now developed a critique of the relation between hill villages and the planning state. Condemning the urban domination of the planning process, Bhatt wrote: 'Planning is done through book knowledge. Village planning is done in air-conditioned rooms in far away cities and thus lacks a sensitivity to village problems.'[47] For Bahuguna, planned development made the hills dependent upon the state capital of Lucknow, which in turn was dependent

45. Weber 1988: 35–6.
46. Pathak 1978.
47. C. P. Bhatt, 'Path of Rural Development.' Typescript dated 5 August 1981.

upon New Delhi.[48] He was critical of the logic of aggregate planning, since in the middle Himalayas there was wide variation in conditions and problems between villages at different altitudes. Further, he argued that planning was based on an inadequate understanding of demographic specificities. On the basis of the 1971 Census, the urban population of Uttarakhand was 15 percent compared to the national average of 20 percent. However, Uttarakhand included a few large urban centers such as Dehra Dun, with an urban population of 46 percent, as well as districts such as Tehri Garhwal with a 3 percent urban population. Moreover, since development funds were allocated on the basis of population, the hill districts, because of relatively low figures, never became high priority. Likewise, while the per capita incomes of Nainital and Dehra Dun were among the highest in the country, those of Tehri Garhwal were among the very lowest.[49] Aggregate planning done in state and national capitals was unable to understand regional specificity.

Faced with deforestation and its effects, Sarvodayis collaborated with a range of other political formations in the UP hills collectively known as the Chipko movement.[50] I shall continue to read essays by Bhatt and Bahuguna as representing Sarvodayi contributions to Chipko.[51] By 1974, Sarvodaya organizations such as the DGSM had established a clear theory of agency regarding the degradation of the hill environment: massive illegal cutting of trees, carried out mostly with state support though also involving local peasants, led to landslides and floods.[52] Activists blamed the policies of the forest department, its negligence, and the venality of its lower officials.[53] In Mandal village, they saw the nexus between forest contractors and forest administration as leading to excessive felling. In Dungri-Paintoli, in spite of the government's

48. Bahuguna 1973.

49. Ibid.

50. See Linkenbach 1994.

51. Sarvodaya itself can be said to encompass not one but a range of positions, from Vinoba Bhave's Gandhian purism to Jayaprakash Narayan's search for Indian 'socialism.'

52. 'Simant kshetra me chipko andolan bhadka.' *Uttarakhand Observer* (UO), 8 April 1974.

53. Citizens of Joshimath, 'Van Bachao, Joshimath Bachao.' Letter to the editor, UO, 28 October 1974.

directive against indiscriminate felling of oak forests, the forest department was presiding over large-scale felling, ironically, for the purposes of setting up a government nursery. In Malai, Banauli and Dewal villages in Chamoli district, the department planned to plant commercial pines in oak forests, despite the fact that hill peasants had little use for pine and a clearly expressed preference for oaks. This contravened the department's own directive that pines be planted only in elevations over 1500 meters.[54] With little to show for the state's aims of poverty reduction and environmental stability, the movement challenged its legitimacy.

Emphasizing the need for an alternative forest policy, Bhatt invoked the recommendations of the Kumaon Forest Facts Finding Committee of 1959. The committee had proposed a new forest policy in which the protection, development, and extension of forests would be core, but in a way that would recognize the needs and rights of local, particularly rural people. It recommended the participation of local people organized in village councils and zonal committees in afforestation and reforestation programs. To broaden the income base, it suggested state support for the cultivation of medicinal herbs, and setting up a cooperatively operated pharmaceutical industry. To increase collective rights over forests, it recommended that forests close to villages be declared their common property managed by newly constituted village forest councils, and an extension of the rights of local people to collect forest products. It suggested the appointment of a special officer in Almora, Nainital, and Garhwal for the specific purpose of nurturing village councils. In keeping with the emphasis of the late 1950s, the Committee recommended that local cooperatives be given sole rights for resin tapping, and the involvement of the forest department in helping the establishment of these bodies. Bhatt also agreed with the suggestion that nomadic populations should be settled in Saharanpur and Bijnaur districts, and limits should be placed on their cattle holdings.[55] The recommendations of this Committee were never implemented. Likewise, the recommendations of the Virendra Kumar Commission of Inquiry,

54. Pahari 1987. Pinewood was useless for the purposes of making agricultural implements because, being resinous, it stuck to the skins of animals and caused abrasions. Interview with Murarilal, village Papriana, 7 June 1992.

55. Bhatt 1975.

similar to those listed above, did not elicit any response from the state government. At the same time, these commissions of inquiry informed the agenda of alternative development championed by Sarvodayis within Chipko.

Bahuguna argued that current development could not meet even its own stated objectives of providing basic needs and community development to hill dwellers, and indeed could not meet them while persisting with the contract system. He recalled that at the start of community development in 1952, Mira Behn, his mentor and a noted Gandhian active in the UP hills, had suggested a locally oriented forest policy, which was turned down by the UP government. The government's own Dhebhar Commission had recommended similar changes in forest policy, specifically that the forest department should generate jobs in forest areas through farming, animal husbandry, and small-scale industry. The contract system created few local jobs, as contractors preferred migrant laborers willing to work for less pay and in worse conditions. Likewise, jobs in afforestation and cutting forest paths were not priorities of the forest department. Most effectively, employment could be created in small-scale forest-based industries, but so far they were located in the plains. Bahuguna pointed out that the government's own experts had opined that the closer the industries were to the forests, the more the forests will be protected, as local people would have more of a stake in them. Sarvodayis argued that cooperatives would eliminate middlemen, and local volunteer 'self-help' (*swayam sewak*) societies would be involved in the marketing of these goods.[56]

Bahuguna proposed that development planning should not only promise direct benefits to local people, but also include them in deciding what 'development' should mean and how it should be carried out. This 'localism' was tied to national interests, but in a way different from those visualized by planners. Local interest and participation in preserving hill forests were necessary for the prosperity and welfare of the entire country. Deforestation in the middle Himalayas was against the national interest, since all major north Indian rivers emerged from these hills. It would accelerate soil erosion, undermining the viability of the many multipurpose dams in the hills. From this standpoint, Bahuguna

56. Bahuguna 1973.

recommended a minimum of 60 percent forest cover. Since local control and self-government of forests were the best ways to combat and reverse deforestation, for Bahuguna these expressions of people's power were consistent with the national interest. Part of the critique was presented in terms of a cost/benefit calculation. Sarvodayis wanted to force the government to consider: was it wise to sell forests worth Rs 50 million to get floods that cause damages of over Rs 500 million?[57]

Bhatt, too, linked local rights and regional stability with 'national security,' that power-laden idea which has been one of the key constituents of the modern and developmentalist state.[58] In the Himalayas, national security had become a particularly sensitive issue since India lost a war with China in 1962. The inclusion of hill dwellers in planning was a national security issue, since the best line of national defense was a satisfied populace. Indian borders would be more secure if hill dwellers were made full participants and beneficiaries of the process through which state policies were formulated and implemented.[59] At the same time the paramount role of the state in defining and defending national security was not questioned. Indeed, some struggles were suspended during periods of perceived threats to national security.[60]

The Sarvodaya alternative to state forestry was not aimed against the market per se. Bahuguna argued that local populations must have rights over forest products, with the Hill Development Council facilitating their entry into the market and guaranteeing a fair price for them. This Council would encourage people to participate in afforestation and reforestation schemes that would plant mostly broad-leaved trees to provide fodder for stall-fed animals and manure, rather than commercial species. For optimum forest use in which local communities made judicious use of

57. Pathak 1978.
58. Abraham, this volume.
59. Key activists such as Bhatt (1968) described the 'gramdan' projects as necessary for the security of the borders. (*Graamdaan hamaare liye seema suraksha ka karyakram hai.*)
60. 'Keeping in mind the war-like situation that had developed between India and Pakistan, squatting and picketing was suspended, since the state would have had to send additional police forces. Those involved in the movement wanted that during this moment of external crisis, the state should be free from internal problems.' (Mishra 1973: 29, translations mine)

forests, Bahuguna recommended village ownership and responsibility over them, but at the same time, state coordination and market incentives were key parts of the Sarvodaya plans.

The Sarvodaya development alternative was not against the kind of technology favored by the state. Bahuguna supported the generation of electricity from the dam on the Bhagirathi in Maneri and plans for the construction of the Tehri dam. He hoped that with the survey of the Alaknanda river, plans would be made for several smaller dams as well. Electricity would help first in lift irrigation in high altitude villages. Domestic electric supply would minimize the use of wood for lighting purposes and for fuel. It would make possible ropeways for the easy and less ecological damaging transportation of goods. Given the potentially important role electricity could play in alleviating pressures on forests, Bahuguna demanded state subsidies for its provision.[61]

Community authority was supplemented in the Sarvodaya project with extensive state intervention in the rural economy. Since agriculture remained the primary occupation in the hill villages, its alternative development policy emphasized irrigation, with traditional guhls supplemented by new facilities, such as small dams to check soil erosion during the monsoons, and to contribute to the longevity of the larger dams such as Tehri downstream. Bahuguna urged a further role of the state in redefining the rural economy, through the introduction of horticulture, mainly apple cultivation, and animal husbandry.[62]

There was a close resemblance, then, between Sarvodayi demands and the recommendations of government commissions of inquiry, as well as the overall goals of community development. Pervasive in Sarvodaya counter-narratives is the strong support for the kind of 'socialism' that had been pitched as the objective of state planning, tinged with regret that state policies had failed to achieve it. Sarvodaya counter-narratives also show a concern with rural employment, and with incentives for peasants to use forests and land judiciously. It was with this in mind that Bahuguna favored labor cooperatives to provide labor to contractors for cutting roads and forests, and transportation: projects condemned later for causing deforestation. It is for the same reason that

61. Bahuguna 1973: pt 5.
62. Bahuguna 1973: pt 6.

Sarvodayis supported industrial use of forests. Bahuguna recommended local wood-based industry to manufacture the same products that were currently being made by industrial units in the plains. The argument was not that forests should not be used as resources, but only that the scale should be reduced, value added retained in the hills, and terms of trade between the hills and the plains equalized. The role of the state was to create local employment, to catalyze local industrialization, to offer support prices for local products and to facilitate new market linkages. Autonomy from the state, in other words, could only be brought about by considerable state intervention.

The state/community opposition of the new radicals is complicated also by the Sarvodayi understanding of deforestation. Bahuguna emphasized the responsibility of local people in causing deforestation, primarily through their extension of agriculture, and the consequent need to curb their forest use practices. The rights of local communities favored by Sarvodayis were justifiable only when they took the responsibility for sustainable land and forest use. The difference here between planners and Sarvodayis is that even though they shared views about local contribution to deforestation, while the state saw this as justification for disempowering the peasantry, Bahuguna saw in local control the set of incentives that would lead local users to adopt sustainable practices. The Sarvodayi support for electricity provision, and thus for dam construction, was for precisely the same reasons cited by planners: namely, the provision of electricity that would reduce the burden on forests for fuel, and provide electrified ropeways which would make villages more connected with each other. The incorporation of technology into the popular perception of state obligations and people's needs reflects another blurring of distinctions between official and oppositional agendas.

There are more fundamental areas of agreement between statist development and its Sarvodayi opponents, especially on community development and basic needs. The very measures of official development were articulated by Bhatt as the *janmasiddha adhikar* (birthright) of forest dwellers. They had the right to irrigation, health care, education, transportation and so forth. Far from repudiating the development agenda, Sarvodayis incorporated precisely those elements of it which were supposed to legitimate resource use for capital accumulation in the official formulation. What to make of these slippages between official and oppositional agendas? First, planners relied on Gandhian and Nehruvian socialist ideas to formulate the parameters for legitimating development. Second, Sarvodayis saw these legitimating principles (e.g., employment, basic needs, participation, community development) as the basis for the state's relation with village communities. Within Chipko, Sarvodayis expanded the notion of legitimization to include environmental concerns, without which socially just development was not possible. That good development planning was a necessary pre-condition for achieving social justice, even 'socialism,' was not questioned. In this way Sarvodya and later Chipko operated within the accumulation–legitimization dialectic of development planning rather than outside it.

CONCLUSION

I do not dispute that development is a powerful project, and that developmentalist states, international agencies and foundations seek legitimacy on its basis, nor that it has overall created new systems of coercion, domination, and dependence. My engagement instead has been with the claim made by the new radical critics that social movements are 'unmaking development' and 'bringing about a post-development era.' My arguments have been that (a) the development project in Indian forestry arose out of conflict and negotiation between the colonial state, nationalists, and autonomous peasant movements; and (b) new movements such as Sarvodaya, including as part of Chipko, operate within the parameters of the development project. From their perspective, the movement was the mechanism through which local centers of lokniti would be formed, which would then seize and shape development as a people's agenda. I have shown above the extent to which Sarvodayi activists used the components of the development project to challenge state power. The non-fulfillment of state objectives was the object of critique and opposition, not the objectives themselves.[63]

63. As Gupta (1997) has recently argued on the basis of quite a different movement, populist claims made by developmentalist states make them vulnerable to populist opposition.

Sarvodaya and Chipko constructed a notion of a regional political collectivity in articulating a localist, communitarian critique of the nation-state. The UP hills had been planning and administrative units in colonial and post-1947 forest policies, separated as the Kumaon and the Garhwal divisions. While a significant sense of cultural distinctiveness between these two entities persists, the Sarvodayis were part of a wider political current that reconstituted them as 'hill districts' (and later as Uttarakhand), in similar relation to forests, to external markets and the state, and thus requiring a similar re-articulation. Their critique of planning signaled that already existing regional entities, such as the state of Uttar Pradesh, were inadequate to deal with the problems of the hills. A new regional entity was the necessary precondition for local rights and proper planning. In this way, they contributed to the political processes that articulated the demand for the creation of the state of Uttarakhand, leading ultimately to the formation of Uttaranchal. Their demands for integrating environmental sustainability with employment and poverty alleviation, drawing from earlier planning and Gandhian concepts, informed the changes in forestry legislation from 1980, as well as the more recent agenda of 'watershed development' and 'rural livelihoods' in the UP hills.[64]

Social movements, by contesting and appropriating it, give new shape and form to the development project, deploying it for new political programs, and for creating new bases for social and political life. That development is an increasingly global project is undeniable, but regionally and locally it is constituted and used in ways different from those outlined in the new radical perspective. I have shown that domination and resistance have always been, to some extent, hybrids of one another. The colonial state's incorporation of 'community' was a key moment in the formation of 'rural development' agendas. Nationalists posited relations between the village community in relation to the larger, national community, articulated through the state. The post-1947 community development agenda itself was a hybrid one, drawing not only on Gandhian and Nehruvian ideas, but also on colonial development thinking, experiments carried by American missionaries from the

---

64. The World Bank sought the DGSM's advice on its Himalayan watershed programmes in the mid-1980s.

1910s, and so on. Sarvodayi involvement in it transmitted not only Gandhian ideas to the hills but also those of community development. Given the strong support for the Communists in the hills until the 1980s, regional collective agendas had other external influences as well. Resistance as much as domination was part of the mode through which modernity was generalized across this regional political space. Forms of resistance adopted development discourses productively, that is, to produce critiques of development comprehensible on its own terms. This had two effects. New collective actors, such as hill dwellers and forest dwellers, ceased being mere 'population' categories, incorporating calls for state formation, demands for collective village rights on forests, justified on the state's own stated objectives. In other words, forms of resistance were part of the forces dissolving 'subaltern consciousness' of some pure, local type, in effect producing political subjects demanding rights in the language of the state. Second, these forms of resistance became channels through which the demand for joining environmental concerns with employment generation, poverty alleviation, gender empowerment and participation came into the consciousness of policy makers, though often with formulaic results. Insofar as official agendas informed oppositional ones and were affected by them in the medium term, forms of resistance blurred the boundaries between not only policy and politics but also between state and society.

The process I have described above is situated at the moment of the unraveling of the balance between accumulation and legitimization that underpinned the passive revolution of planned development in India until the mid-1960s. It is tempting to see this crisis as a local symptom of the dying of a global project, but as I have argued, both the crisis and the popular–political responses to it are better understood in terms of their regional specificities: of specific environmental factors within which petty commodity production in the hills was located, and of specific politics of legitimation between hill peasants and the planning state, for example. While drawing on a range of influences, Sarvodaya and Chipko were regionally specific political formations, collaborating with other entities to draw up an agenda of regionally and sectorally specific demands. As such, they are mechanisms through which modernity gets generalized as well as regionally reproduced and transformed.

References

Anon, 1927. *Report of the Royal Commission on Agriculture.* London: His Majesty's Stationary.

Anon, 1974. 'Simant kshetra me chipko andolan bhadka.' (Chipko movement flares up in border areas), *Uttarakhand Observer*, 8 April.

Bahuguna, S. L., 1973. 'Uttarakhand ka niyojan: Samasyayen aur prathmiktayen.' (The re-organization of Uttarakhand: Problems and Priorities), *Uttarakhand Observer*, 4 December 1972–22 January 1973 (UNSP parts 4, 5, 6).

Behn, Mira, 1964. *The Spirit's Pilgrimage.* London: Allen and Unwin.

Bhatt, C. P., 1968. '31 October ko Shri Jayaprakash Narayan ke sammaan me aayojit saarvajanik sabha me Uttarakhand Observer ke karyakari sampaadak Shri Chandi Prasad Bhatt ka swaagat bhaashan.' *Uttarakhand Observer* (Welcome address of Chandi Prasad Bhatt, Acting Editor of *Uttarakhand Observer*, made to the Public Meeting organized to honor Shri Jayaprakash on 31 October), 4 November.

———, 1972. 'Parvatiya zilon me van sampada par adharit udyog.' (Industry based on forest resources in hill districts), *Uttarakhand Observer*, 3 July.

———, 1975. 'Uttarakhand ki van samasyayen aur samadhan.' *Uttarakhand Observer* (Uttarakhand's forest problems and their solutions), 2 October.

Boli, J. and G. Thomas (eds.), 1999. *Constructing World Culture: International Non-governmental Organizations from 1875.* Palo Alto: Stanford University Press.

Bose, Sugata, 1997. 'Instruments and idioms of colonial and national development: India's historical experience in comparative perspective.' In Frederick Cooper and Randall Packard (eds.), *International Development and the Social Sciences.* Berkeley: University of California Press.

Byres, T. J. (ed.), 1994. *The State and Development Planning in India.* New Delhi: Oxford University Press.

Chakravarty, Sukhamoy, 1987. *Development Planning: The Indian Experience.* Oxford: Clarendon Press.

Chatterjee, Partha, 1994. 'Development planning and the Indian state.' In Terence Byres (ed.), *The State and Development Planning in India.* New Delhi: Oxford University Press.

———, 1995. *The Nation and Its Fragments.* Princeton: Princeton University Press.

Chaturvedi, M. D., 1961. 'Abstract from recollections and reflections.' In *100 Years of Indian Forestry, 1861–1961*, vol. 1. Dehradun: Forest Research Institute.

Citizens of Joshimath, 1974. 'Van bachao, joshimath bachao.' Letter to the editor, *Uttarakhand Observer*, 28 October.

D'Abreo, Desmond, 1985. *People and Forests: The Forest Bill and a New Forest Policy.* New Delhi: Indian Social Institute.

Escobar, Arturo, 1995. *Encountering Development.* Princeton: Princeton University Press.

Esteva, Gustavo, 1987. 'Regenerating peoples' spaces,' *Alternatives* 12(1).

Gandhi, Mohandas K., 1941. *The Constructive Programme: Its Meaning and Place.* Ahmedabad: Navjivan Publishing House.

———, 1959. *Panchayat Raj.* Ahmedabad: Navjivan Publishing House.

Gilmartin, David, 1999. 'The irrigating public: The state and local management in colonial irrigation'. In S. Toft Madsen (ed.), *State, Society and Environment in South Asia.* Richmond: Curzon.

Government of India, 1952. *The First Five-Year Plan.* New Delhi: Planning Commission.

———, 1956. *Second Five-Year Plan: A Draft Outline.* New Delhi: Planning Commission.

———, 1981. *Statistical Pocket Book.* New Delhi: Ministry of Planning.

Guha, Ramachandra, 1989. *The Unquiet Woods.* New Delhi: Oxford University Press.

———, 1994. 'Forestry Debate and Draft Forest Act.' *Economic and Political Weekly* 29(34).

Guha, Sumit, 1999. *Environment and Ethnicity in Western India, 1201–1981.* Cambridge: Cambridge University Press.

Gupta, Akhil, 1997. 'Agrarian populism in the development of a modern nation (India).' In Frederick Cooper and Randall Packard (eds.), *International Development and the Social Sciences: Essays on the History and Politics of Knowledge.* Berkeley: University of California Press.

Harwicke, Thomas, 1809. 'Narrative of a journey to Srinagar.' *Asiatic Researches* 6.

Hunt, Sir Edward, 1938. *Social Service in India.* London: His Majesty's Stationary Office.

Illich, Ivan, 1993. 'Basic needs.' In Wolfgang Sachs (ed.), *The Development Dictionary.* London: Zed.

Linkenbach, A., 1994. 'Environmental movements and the critique of development: Agents and interpreters.' *Thesis Eleven* (39).

Little, Peter and Michael Painter, 1995. 'Discourse, politics and the development process: Reflections on Escobar's "Anthropology and the development encounter."' *American Ethnologist* 22(3).

Ludden, David, 1992. 'India's development regime.' In Nicholas Dirks (ed.), *Colonialism and Culture.* Ann Arbor: University of Michigan Press.

Malik, P. L., 1981. *The Law Relating to Forests in Uttar Pradesh.* Lucknow: Eastern Books.

Manak, Elizabeth, 1979. 'Formulation of agricultural policy in imperial India, 1872–1929.' Ph.D. Thesis, University of Hawaii.

Mishra, Anupam, 1973. 'Daru ko dait aige, dait bhagola, Hita didi, hita muli chala Tehri jaula.' (If the demon of alcohol comes, we'll chase it away, come older sister, come little girl, we are going Tehri way.) *Dinman* 15 April.

Mishra, Girish, 1988. *Nehru and the Congress Economic Policies.* New Delhi: Sterling.

Mosse, David, 1999. 'Colonial and contemporary ideologies of "community management": The case of tank irrigation in South India' *Modern Asian Studies* 32(1).

Narayan, Jayaprakash, 1964. *Socialism, Sarvodaya, and Democracy.* Bombay: Asia Publishing House.

Pahari, Ramesh, 1987. 'Chipko andolan ke pandrah saal.' *Pahar* 1.

Pant, G. B., Deposition, Written and Oral Evidence, *Report of the Royal Commission on Agriculture,* London: His Majesty's Stationary Office, 1927: 345–67.

Pathak, Shekhar, 1978. 'Nainital se Reni tak.' In S. Pant (ed.), *Uttariya.* New Delhi: Kurmanchal Press.

PUDR (People's Union for Democratic Rights), 1983. *The Undeclared War.* New Delhi: PUDR.

Rawat, Ajay S., 1990. 'Commentary on G. B. Pant.' In *Forest Problem in Kumaon.* Naini Tal: Gyanodaya.

Richards, John F. and M. McAlpin, 1983. 'Cotton cultivation and land clearing in the Bombay Deccan and Karnatak: 1818–1920.' In Richard Tucker and John Richards (eds.), *Global Deforestation and the Nineteenth Century World Economy.* Durham: Duke University Press.

Sachs, W., 1992. *The Development Dictionary.* London: Zed Books.

Sen, Pronab, 1991. 'Growth theories and development strategies: Lessons from the Indian experience.' *Economic and Political Weekly* 26(30): PE 63.

Seth, Sanjay, 1993. 'Nehruvian socialism, 1927–37: Nationalism, marxism and the pursuit of modernity.' *Alternatives* 18(4).

Shiva, Vandana, 1988. 'Reductionist science as epistemological violence.' In Ashis Nandy (ed.), *Science, Hegemony and Violence: A Requiem for Modernity.* New Delhi: Oxford University Press.

———, 1999. 'Is community internal to the logic of the developmentalist state?' Paper presented to the South Asia Anthropology Group Annual Conference, 18–19 September. SOAS, University of London.

Sinha, Subir; Shubhra Gururani, and Brian Greenberg, 1997. 'The "new traditionalist" discourse of Indian environmentalism.' *Journal of Peasant Studies* 24(3).

Weber, Thomas, 1988. *Hugging the Trees.* New Delhi: Penguin.

Zaidi, A. Moin (ed.), 1988. *A Tryst with Destiny: A Study of Economic Policy Resolutions of the INC Passed during the Last One Hundred Years.* New Delhi: Indian Institute of Applied Political Research.

Part III

Transgressing Boundaries

12

Rethinking Boundaries

ANGELIQUE HAUGERUD

INTRODUCTION

Gone are yesterday's notions of boundaries as fixed, natural, or inevitable. How boundaries—between the local and the global, the indigenous and the Western, the traditional and the modern—are made and unmade is this section's focus. The four authors illustrate the analytical potency of the ethnographic, micro-political, micro-historical turn in development studies advocated in the editors' introduction. That shift necessarily de-emphasizes familiar modes of analysis of wider political–economic contexts in which identities are formed and contested, knowledges (re-)constituted, or state projects of modernization envisioned and accomplished. Analysis of those wider contexts has often invited precisely the kinds of elisions, linear trajectories, and structural logics the editors wish to escape. It is the 'incoherence that lurks at the heart of all development efforts,' as they put it, that demands attention. Hence, their emphasis on stories that capture historical contingency, multiple sites of production, multiple vocalities, and boundary contestation.

Does the editors' analytical framework mean that we must celebrate disorder, chaos, and uncertainty in ways that preclude the discovery of new forms of order, pattern, and predictability? The focus on 'regional modernities'[1] is intended precisely to avoid a descent into postmodern narratives of fragmentation. Indeed, the editors' theoretical redirections signal a wish to avoid two extremes: on the one hand, emphasizing indeterminacy and contingency to an extent that obliterates wider patterns and connections, and on the other, reading development as a monolithic script or discourse that expunges the multiple subjectivities of actors and the variable ways development and regional modernities are produced. Mediating this opposition, of course, is not easy.

FOREIGNERS, FICTION, FISH AND FORESTS

The chapters by Abraham, Brodt, Kumar, and Robbins uncover subtle processes that are obscured by the global/local dyad and by portrayals of development as an imposed discourse without agents. Abraham and Kumar adopt textual approaches, while Brodt and Robbins write of their ethnographic field research. All call attention to boundaries as sites of key social struggles and remind us that to reproduce or maintain boundaries, as well as to challenge, transgress, or alter them entails a struggle and a process. Their analyses reveal individuals' capacities to maneuver within development institutions and in networks and struggles at the sites where development occurs or where modernity is defined.

Itty Abraham tells two stories about how states struggle to impose identities on subjects and how they 'resolve the difference between nationality and citizenship' when the post-colonial nation is 'not contained within the territorial limits of the state.' First, he examines the 1955 Asian-African Conference in Bandung, Indonesia (from which the Non-Aligned Movement originated) as a site of struggles over postures toward Communism and the Cold War, a zone of agreement on opposing global militarization and colonialism, and a means of expanding inter-Asian communication rather than simply following European precepts. At the same time, the so-called Colombo powers denied their own histories, Abraham argues, by ignoring the effect of Japanese imperialism on the way

1. Here, we are to discard the idea of region as a fixed or bounded geographic space, and think of it instead as a nonspatial site for the production of varied modernities. The editors invite attention to how the 'local,' the 'regional,' and the 'global' are produced or socially constructed, rather than assuming they are natural units to be discovered.

Asia was defined, and especially by ignoring Asia's profound multi-ethnicity—its long histories of inter-Asian movement of people. Immigrant populations and their ambiguous loyalties threatened standard post-war notions of national sovereignty and racial citizenship. Asian states consigned such populations to the category of 'minority' rather than viewing their neighboring states as 'ethnic mirrors of themselves, with intertwined and intermingled histories.'

Abraham's second story illustrates processes obscured by the boundary in political science between international relations and comparative politics.[2] He takes the Indian media tale of a supposed spy ring, the collapse of that narrative into a familiar and sordid tale of domestic corruption, and the absence of an espionage genre in regional literature as signs of the effort required to produce national difference in South Asia, or to establish a boundary between the national and the international, the citizen and the foreigner. That is, these are not natural or static boundaries (rather they are socially and historically produced), though the divide has been institutionalized and naturalized in political science. The latter point suggests that studies such as Abraham's may constitute useful boundary skirmishes within academia itself.

He also argues that the state's inability to define unambiguous political boundaries without undermining its own legitimacy 'redirects the technologies of state power onto people' and recreates within the nation the otherwise missing inside/outside opposition. Minorities thus emerge as unspoken threats to the global script of sovereignty and state-ness, and the state's quest for hegemony over nation and territory remains incomplete. State struggles to mask this weakness sometimes entail violence against their own populations, such as state-sponsored ethnic riots.

In Amitava Kumar's chapter, we enter the world of the literary text, with analysis of works by London-based immigrant authors such as Hanif Kureishi and Salman Rushdie. Kumar's study is a contribution to what Appadurai[3] terms 'ethnography of the imagination,' or work that suggests how expressive forms such as novels and films contribute to the 'conceptual repertoire of

2. He mentioned this theme in the version of this chapter presented at the conference from which this volume originates.
3. Appadurai 1996: 55–8.

contemporary societies,' inspire ordinary lives, or help to constitute modern subjectivities. Kumar discusses one of the most powerful examples of the blurred boundary between fiction and ethnography, or fiction and life—namely, the work of Salman Rushdie. The reaction to Rushdie's *Satanic Verses*, Ortner observes, 'shows in particularly dramatic form that the novelist can no longer pretend that, in contrast to ethnography or history, there is nobody on the other side of his or her text nor that fiction can escape resistance.'[4] That is, consumers of such texts can be moved to passionate action, and the producers or authors of these texts do indeed help to constitute their readers' social and moral maps.[5]

Literary fantasies, such as magical realism, 'tell us something about displacement, disorientation, and agency in the contemporary world.'[6] Magical realism, Kumar suggests, has especially become a tool of the expatriate writer and 'has given the writer illusory short-cuts to the heart of history. Not only because it is easier to write a poem than organizing a march... but also because the real as a difficulty or challenge becomes merely a textual affair and not a social one.' That is, literary texts signal both escape from and engagement with the social world.

Kumar's chapter is not ethnographic in the sense of focusing on the lives of individuals studied through participant observation. Rather, his interest is how India is narrativized from outside the subcontinent, specifically how in stories about South Asian immigrants 'modernity emerges as a contested project.' Immigrant modernities, Kumar suggests, invoke the processes by which interstitial cultures are produced, and 'the writings that emerge from these contexts will, quite inevitably, be impure, unstable, indeterminate.' In Kumar's figure of speech, South Asian immigrants bring various brands, various burdens of divided modernity, in their suitcases. These transportable modernities become part of those global processes in which boundaries between center and periphery are blurred, as the peripheries penetrate the centers in ways that transform both. Scattered throughout Kumar's chapter are tantalizing questions about the status of the author, the significance of the act of writing, consciousness of its status as artifice, and in the final two paragraphs, the reflexive persona of

4. Ortner 1995: 189.
5. Appadurai 1996: 58.
6. Ibid.

the chapter's author himself. Kumar leaves the reader to devise answers to questions Kureishi raised about '"writing" as the site where contradictions would be addressed and seemingly resolved.'

Kumar offers a textual landscape that celebrates immigrant experiences as domains of hybridity, interstitiality, and ambivalence. Cultural forms of globalization, such as flows of images across mediascapes, take center stage here. But the chapter offers us fleeting glimpses of more. Kumar asks, for example, what others in Kureishi's and Rushdie's novels are doing while the immigrant authors/protagonists wrestle with modernist doubts. The 'others' include Asian friends who display different subjectivities, politics, and class positions from those of the usually male protagonists. These differences suggest how various brands or interpretations of modernity may clash, how modernity's uses are open to contestation. Thus, in one of Kureishi's novels (*The Black Album*), a female tutor explains to the male protagonist (a successful student) how the bleak employment prospects afforded youths under Thatcherism shape his fellow-students' more negative attitudes toward education. Kumar also alludes to a connection between religion's shifting role and particular forms or logics of capitalism. When difference or identity is reproduced as exoticism, Kumar implies, political–economic contextualization can help to explain why. He also remarks, in discussing a passage from Rushdie's *Satanic Verses*, upon the absence of political–economic explanations such as the economic dynamics of labor migration from India and Pakistan to the Persian Gulf. Such allusions point to important connections between aesthetic and political–economic domains. In what ways, for example, are accelerated global cultural flows across Appadurai's mediascapes linked to growing disruptions, economic dislocation, and social conflicts in everyday life in particular places?

Kumar's discussion of diasporic imaginations, of how South Asian immigrants negotiate individual and community identities and conflictual modernities, could be used to explore identity categories as both vehicles of oppression and means of challenging that oppression.[7] What forms of social action are inspired or what kinds of individual subjectivities are shaped by images flowing across mediascapes? One might explore how identity categories or

7. Cf. Dirks *et al.* 1994: 24.

cultural understandings are re-examined and reworked through literary texts and through devices such as the images of reversal with which the paper concludes—when Kumar invokes images of people jubilantly flinging crowns in the air and toppling thrones to the ground as a dictatorship collapses.

In Sonja Brodt's chapter we leave the world of the literary text for that of tree farmers in central India making decisions such as whether to apply fish, or ashes and buttermilk, or cowdung to their trees. Brodt problematizes the concept of indigenous knowledge by illustrating how individuals create their own knowledge hybrids out of multiple sources and scales of knowledge. She places these hybrids along a continuum—rather than a dichotomy—of types containing varied proportions of localized versions of folk knowledge on the one hand, and formal or global scientific knowledge on the other. These knowledge hybrids are characterized as well by varied levels of abstraction (the latter not being coterminous with the local/global distinction). Brodt emphasizes the importance of local learning opportunities, direct observation, and experimentation, so that 'what may have originated as global knowledge may take on different forms in different places.' She offers clear examples of how farmers in different structural positions possess different types of knowledge about tree farming.

One question raised by this analysis (and others) concerns the implications of reinvoking some of the very dichotomies one wishes to overcome. Thus, Brodt uses contrasts such as local/global and folk/scientific to construct a typology of individuals, noting that if one wishes to explore the 'mechanics of knowledge recombination,' it is necessary to define clear categories of which things are to be combined. Such categories then can allow us to understand 'how different knowledge systems can be seen as broadly complementary, overlapping, and/or interpenetrating.' Brodt recognizes, however, that it is not necessarily possible to ascertain 'exact pedigrees of particular elements of knowledge.' Indeed, the difficulty with the definition of knowledge categories, as Agrawal discusses in a different context, is that 'what is today known and classified as indigenous knowledge has been in intimate interaction with Western knowledge since at least the fifteenth century.'[8] Furthermore, a binary categorization of knowledge

8. Agrawal 1995: 422.

types relies on the false 'possibility that a finite and small number of characteristics can define the elements contained within the categories.'[9] Instead, the principal dimensions along which indigenous and western knowledges are presumed to differ (the substantive, the methodological and epistemological, and the contextual) are all problematic, as he shows.

At least as important as the mix of supposedly folk and scientific knowledge in particular individuals is the variation within these categories; that is, variation within what are today classified as indigenous and scientific knowledges.[10] Brodt's chapter offers intriguing glimpses of such differences. She notes, for example, the contrasting types of local knowledge about tree husbandry held by farmers who occupy different parts of the local landscape and different structural positions (with a contrast drawn, for instance, between poor and recently landless arrivals versus longer-term residents). That is, Brodt describes how folk knowledge of tree husbandry is unevenly distributed among two communities of marginalized minorities. In addition, she observes that within her study village, access to particular knowledge sources varies according to gender, class, caste, and sometimes age, though even individuals within similar socio-economic categories display 'widely varying sets of tree management knowledge.' Thus, experiential learning is important—in this case, the ways individuals learn through their own direct personal experience with and observation of tree management. Brodt suggests that those individuals in the middle of her posited continuum of local–global knowledge—the farmers who possess significant knowledge of folk and formal Indian science as well as 'access to technological ideas from global science'—may be best positioned to acquire and adapt rich knowledge bases. That is, they have the widest 'potential repertoire of ideas from which to draw in any given management situation.' Here, as in many other small farmer settings, diversification (of knowledge types, economic activities, land types, crop cultivars, personal networks, and so on) appears to be advantageous.

The variable distribution of knowledge and of learning opportunities among individuals signals the importance of the politics of

9. Ibid.: 421.
10. See Agrawal 1995.

knowledge. At least as important as an outside analyst's classification of types of tree management knowledge as folk or scientific is the strategic labeling and deployment of such knowledge by local and other actors, as well as the processes by which some bodies of knowledge come to carry more weight or to be more influential than others in a community, and the environmental and economic consequences of such processes. There is a politics to the fate of particular types of local and nonlocal knowledge—if one wishes to use those binary categories—and to the labeling of knowledge as local. And, there is an ecology of consequences, as illustrated in Robbins' chapter.

Robbins explicitly addresses how agrarian practices informed by particular types of environmental knowledge alter the landscape or affect the trajectory of biotic change. Combining attention to discourse and material outcomes, he understands the terms global and local not as scales of activity or discrete physical locations or isolated processes, but rather as 'discrete discursive locations where knowledges, categories, and languages about the world are produced and naturalized.' He notes that how professionals (environmental specialists, bureaucrats, and managers) interpret narratives about both the global environment and local ecology shapes 'real-world actions: tree-planting, fence-building, irrigation, and well-digging.' In such ways, the local and global environmental narratives that meet in the minds of forestry professionals are 'written into the landscape.' Robbins contrasts local narratives of 'access and control' with global stories of 'decline and rescue,' while recognizing the permeability of such categories. To explore how such narratives encounter one another and with what effect, he focuses on the experiences of state forestry officers in an arid region of India.

One particular forestry official (Chaudri), who operates as a development broker, embodies the 'struggle between global and local definitions of the environment.' This mid-level bureaucrat mediates opposing discourses and becomes an active agent rather than simply an instrument of state power. Thus, we see how the forestry department 'recreates the ecological imagination of the forester,' as he assimilates new categories of environmental knowledge offered by the state, and how the state uses him as a vehicle to enact global constructs of development, so that he 'fit(s) the modeled forest of state planning.' At the same time, however,

Robbins shows how the forester can appropriate, refashion, and occasionally challenge such constructs. Studies of such professionals and their 'situated knowledges and actions' are rare[11] for reasons Robbins discusses.

One question raised by this analysis is just how much room for maneuver do individuals such as Chaudri have; how confined are they by what Robbins characterizes as static knowledge categories of bureaucracies such as the Indian forestry department? Robbins notes that some local environmental information does flow upward in the bureaucracy, and that Chaudri observes some small shifts in the forestry department's priorities (in choice of tree species, for example). Explanations of such shifts are likely to vary among individuals who occupy different positions in the bureaucracy.

As such a forester advances in the administrative hierarchy, however, his own ecological and social knowledge and the lessons of his own field experience recede and gradually are replaced by priorities and knowledge categories from the central office. For example, local vernacular identifications of species as hot or cold, edible or toxic, auspicious or inauspicious are replaced by the new binaries slow- or fast-growing and high- or low-value, which 'better fit the notion of a forest offered by the state.' The power to define the environment, to name landscapes ('pristine wilderness,' 'degraded forest') and record their elements is also the power to control the environment, as Robbins notes. The act of naming or categorizing is always political. The institutional sites where such categorizing occurs, he writes, are sites where local and global are mutually constituted and where 'regional modernities' are produced.

The case of Chaudri the forester affords a view of an important site of political struggle about which we need much more research. Additional studies might show us how development brokers such as Chaudri negotiate environmental understandings with both their superiors and their subordinates; and how small changes, innovations, and subversions are accomplished in sites such as forest nurseries, agricultural experiment stations, extension offices, and national agricultural research institutes. (All of these are locations of struggles over the value of particular types of knowledge,

11. See Dove 1994.

practice, and policy; and they are sites of struggles over how to classify and understand the environment.) These are certainly, as Robbins suggests, loci of collision between more globally and more locally produced narratives, but most important they are the points where these narratives are reworked and where alternatives to dominant categorical systems can emerge. Though the rate of change may be glacial and may have to occur within officially recognized environmental categories, even small shifts in such conceptual systems may prove significant. Robbins' study offers a glimpse of how local and nonlocal knowledges move both up and down administrative hierarchies, and illustrates the value of examining how both local and nonlocal actors in various structural positions find room for maneuver and effect small changes that may have large consequences.

CONCLUSION

It is tempting to seek a larger framing story in these stories[12] about the (re-)production of state power, identities, landscapes, and the knowledge and practices of farmers and foresters. Scholars[13] emphasize the need to understand the larger histories that have produced and connected in particular ways the apparently disjointed or fragmented elements of contemporary life. Are structural or historical connections discernible among particular practices, customs, institutions, social groups, or states?[14] Must pursuit of such connections entail adoption of models, or totalizing theories of functionalist integration, holism, or mechanical evolutionism? As we address new imaginings of space and locality, some would urge us to locate diasporic imaginations[15] in changing 'global'

12. See the editors' introduction for explanation of their use of 'stories' as opposed to 'narratives' of development. They emphasize that stories better capture the incoherence of development efforts, the variable power of actors in creating development discourse, and the 'historical contingency, multiple sites of production, and contention within presumed areas of consent.' Narratives, on the other hand, stress linearity and discourses emphasize a structural logic.

13. Such as Watts 1992; Polier and Roseberry 1989; and Coronil 1992.

14. See Polier and Roseberry's (1989) discussion of this theme and of the question raised in the sentence that follows.

15. Cf. Kumar, this volume.

political and economic conditions.[16] Once characterized as global, the political and economic processes in some paradigms are easily essentialized, homogenized, naturalized, and reduced to an inevitable structural logic. Can we avoid such traps while nonetheless envisioning, for example, clearer connections between migrants' dreams and imaginings[17] on the one hand, and varieties of capitalism that help to propel vast numbers of South Asians to the Persian Gulf and United Kingdom on the other?

In short, how to theorize such connections or to describe the mechanisms by which they occur without resorting to economic determinism or totalizing models such as a 'world system' or a homogeneous modernity remains a challenge.[18] Some scholars have suggested we think in terms of a 'totality of fragments'[19] or of differentiated totalities.[20] In any case, to comprehend these wider contexts, which are conceived today as discontinuous rather than systematic, must we posit a logic (or logics) of connection among various ethnographic or discursive sites?[21]

If so, we need better ways than globalization metaphors to understand how spatial linkages and boundaries change over time.[22] In this respect, the notion of regional modernities helps to fill a gap Cooper identifies,[23] namely the urgent need for social science 'concepts that...emphasize both the nature of spatial linkages and their limits, which seek to analyse change with historical specificity rather than in terms of a vaguely defined and unattainable end-point.' It is possible, Cooper suggests, to analyse

16. Gupta and Ferguson 1997: 39.

17. See Kumar's chapter.

18. In focusing on stories rather than narratives of development, this volume's editors caution that 'a "narrative" comes into focus only when the tensions and indeterminacies of its construction have been relegated to the background if not completely expunged.' Larger-scale political–economic processes enter their analytic framework as these supralocal formations 'selectively empower or undermine particular local processes and phenomena.'

19. Watts 1992.

20. Polier and Roseberry 1989.

21. Cf. Marcus (1995: 99): 'The global is an emergent dimension of arguing about the connection among sites in a multi-sited ethnography.'

22. Cooper 2001: 195, 213.

23. Ibid.: 192.

large-scale, long-term processes without neglecting specificity, contingency, and contestation.[24]

That analytical balancing act reflects profound oppositions in the social sciences—indeed a great divide in today's academic culture that historian Thomas Bender[25] believes is more difficult to bridge now than at any time in the past half-century.[26] On one side of the gulf are scholars in disciplines such as economics, political science, and sociology who wish to emulate the natural sciences rather than humanities, who constitute tight subfields, and who favor 'objective' methods and eschew particularism. On the other side are disciplines such as anthropology and history whose boundaries are porous, whose members are more likely to avow value commitments, and whose analyses tend toward particularism. Associated tensions concern essentialism versus contingency, the precision of simplifying models versus complexity, epistemological certainty versus uncertainty, deduction versus induction, and social causation versus subjective meaning. These polarities are as pronounced within as they are between disciplines, with particular fields tilting in different directions. In political science and sociology, for example, but not in socio-cultural anthropology, the discipline's scientistic, quantitative wing dominates. Such leanings, of course, are subject to historical pendulum shifts.

Contemporary anthropologists' and historians' disenchantment with reductionistic or causal models and structuralist logics is not shared by many political scientists or economists. Yet, the notion of regional modernities—this volume's conceptual innovation—defies certain academic hierarchies of authority. As Mosse suggests, the 'regional modernities' concept averts the presumed marginality of regionalism (parochial, particular) by 'critically re-appropriating universal concepts' circulating in development studies.[27]

Regional modernities are not variations on a global theme; rather, they contradict the misplaced teleology and coherence of globalization theory. Thus, Brodt (this volume) suggests that '"stories of development" are often more meaningful than grand

24. Ibid.: 200.
25. Bender 1997.
26. Material in this paragraph draws on Haugerud and Cadge (2000).
27. Mosse, this volume.

generalizations.' Such stories highlight the historical contingency and particularity of connections and networks. As such, they are a crucial corrective to the overemphasis in much globalization talk (and in earlier modernization theory) on order, structural logic, coherence, directionality, and determinacy. This volume also challenges, as noted earlier, naturalized distinctions such as the national vs. the international (see Abraham's chapter), which political science institutionalizes as the boundary between international relations and comparative politics. In short, redirecting attention to networks and connections and refusing to take boundaries for granted—whether disciplinary, subdisciplinary, or geographic—are inspiriting moves toward better understanding development and modernity.

References

Agrawal, Arun, 1995. 'Dismantling the divide between indigenous and scientific knowledge.' *Development and Change* 26: 413–39.

Appadurai, Arjun, 1996. *Modernity at Large: Cultural Dimensions of Globalization*. Minneapolis: Univeristy of Minnesota Press.

Bender, Thomas, 1997. 'Politics, intellect, and the American University,' In Thomas Bender and Carl Schorske (eds.), *American Academic Culture in Transformation: Fifty Years, Four Disciplines.* Princeton: Princeton University Press.

Cooper, Frederick, 2001. 'What is the concept of globalization good for? An African historian's perspective.' *African Affairs* 100: 189–213.

Coronil, Fernando, 1992. 'Can postcoloniality be decolonized? Imperial banality and postcolonial power.' *Public Culture* 5(1): 89–108.

Dirks, Nicholas B., Geoff Eley, and Sherry B. Ortner, 1994. 'Introduction.' In Nicholas B. Dirks, Geoff Eley, and Sherry B. Ortner (eds.), *Culture/Power/History: A Reader in Contemporary Social Theory.* Princeton: Princeton University Press.

Dove, Michael, 1994. 'The existential status of the Pakistani farmer: Studying official constructions of social reality.' *Ethnology* 33(4): 331–51.

Gupta, Akhil and James Ferguson, 1997. 'Culture, power, place: Ethnography at the end of an era.' In Akhil Gupta and James Ferguson (eds.), *Culture, Power, Place: Explorations in Critical Anthropology.* Durham: Duke University Press.

Haugerud, Angelique and Wendy Cadge, 2000. 'The social sciences and area studies: The SSRC's international predissertation fellowship program, 1991–2000.' Report to the Ford Foundation.

————, 2001. 'Forging links between disciplines and area studies. *Items and Issues* 2(1–2), Social Science Research Council.

Marcus, George, 1995. 'Ethnography in/of the world system: The emergence of multi-sited ethnography.' *Annual Review of Anthropology* 24: 95–117.

Ortner, Sherry, 1995. 'Resistance and the problem of ethnographic refusal.' *Comparative Studies in Society and History* 37(1): 173–93.

Polier, Nicole and William Roseberry, 1989. 'Tristes tropes: Post-modern anthropologists encounter the other and discover themselves.' *Economy and Society* 18(2): 245–62.

Watts, Michael J., 1992. 'Capitalisms, crises, and cultures I: Notes toward a totality of fragments.' In Allan Pred and Michael J. Watts (eds.), *Reworking Modernity: Capitalisms and Symbolic Discontent.* New Brunswick: Rutgers University Press.

13

On Binaries and Boundaries

DAVID MOSSE

In part three of this volume the authors are concerned in different ways with the making and transgressing of boundaries between 'the local' and 'the global.' These, it should be understood from the outset, are not defined as spaces, or even as the product of economic processes (e.g., globalization driven by the movement of global capital) but as forms of knowing, 'discrete discursive locations of knowledge and institutions.'[1]

The authors concur that the binaries of local and global, tradition and modernity, non-Western and Western, parochial and cosmopolitan (among others) have outlived their usefulness as analytical frameworks for comprehending social processes of development. Indeed, the burden of these chapters is to advance a challenge to such oppositional thinking, firstly by situating research precisely in boundary zones where local–global polarities become meaningless as framing metaphors, and secondly by taking the perspective of 'doing' and engagement, identifying the distinctive and creative ways in which people make themselves 'modern.'

The chapters present four rather different instances of boundary zones or meeting points as subjects for discussion. The first is a set of 'hybridized' tree management practices in rural Madhya Pradesh (Brodt); the second, the practices of state forestry officers

1. As Robbins puts it in this volume.

in Rajasthan that straddle the 'global environmental narrative' of (forest) loss and recovery, on the one hand, and the local politics of resources access and control, on the other (Robbins). The third setting is the self-critical imaginative world of immigrant Asian writers in Britain and the contested modernities of their characters (Kumar); and the fourth is the fragile frontier between the modern and the immodern, established and maintained through secrecy in an Indian space installation (Abraham). Individually and together these cases make it harder for 'bloated images of single modernity [to] suppress envisionings of [the] several and chequered and contradictory modernities.'[2]

The difficulties of forging a genuinely new departure from existing (modern?) patterns of thought on development and modernity are not, however, to be underestimated. To speak of frontier zones or boundaries (even their transgression) is already to imply the very distinctions, and opposed states of mind, which new analyses seeks to eliminate, but which prove almost impossible to un-think. Indeed, these chapters do in various ways end up reinvoking the binary categories that the boundaries mark, even while treating them in new ways. Whether in the vocabulary of hybridizing, rearticulating, folding, straddling, layering or colliding differences, boundaries are simultaneously dismissed and re-created by the same overarching oppositional categories (e.g., as literate/oral, formal/folk, conceptual/pragmatic).

Brodt's piece is illustrative of a certain resilience in the oppositional logic of our analyses. For instance, having usefully established that learning of all types is a 'local' process, she suggests that what are produced are hybrids, formed from contrasting knowledge types: 'global science' and 'local knowledge.' But, does not the metaphor of hybridizing itself encourage us to invoke and juxtapose distinct knowledge types where they may not exist;[3] or involve tracing genealogies of knowledge where they do not matter? Robbins, too, reinvokes a contrast between the local and global through the metaphor of the borderland between the two. Reading his paper, one can hardly doubt the heuristic value of conceiving of a contrast between a unified 'degradation–restoration' narrative of environmental change, on the one hand, and a local

2. Dube 1998: xii.
3. See Agrawal 1995.

narrative of conflict over access to and control over resources, on the other. But it would be easy to read too much into this contrast, both about the unified and 'global' nature of environmental narratives of degradation, and the local nature of conflicts over access and control.

After all, 'global' narratives are themselves also forged in the context of a politics of resource allocation. Representations of environmental change are part of a struggle over state (or international) resources and institutional legitimacy. Work on the dominating discourses of environmental degradation, scarcity, or deforestation illustrates this.[4] A recent study of the Kutch region in western India, for example, suggests that state and popular discourses of scarcity are 'manufactured' as part of a regional politics of access to water and validation of the Narmada valley Sardar Sarovar large dam project.[5] In other words, 'global' development policies and their rationalizing scientific discourses are rendered altogether more contingent, 'local,' vernacular, multi-stranded, and tied to institutional interests in recent writing.[6] The observation that 'global' narratives of environmental degradation justify and consolidate state power both colonial and postcolonial, has become commonplace—although it would be a mistake to identify discourses of degradation too strongly with assertions of state power and to ignore the way in which tragic landscapes of neglect[7] have underpinned challenges to the legitimacy of rulers and overlords as part of a popular (or 'local') moral critique of the state. But Robbins is demonstrating something further, namely how these narratives (and their technical choices) create professional identities and sustain bureaucratic hierarchies; how they are part of a micropolitics of careers, promotions, and the reproduction of rank and position within organizations like the Rajasthan state forestry department, and between them and the village beneficiaries; and finally how they are deployed by individuals negotiating their own multiple identities (as Rajput, farmer, forest officer).

4. E.g., Fairhead and Leach 1998.
5. Mehta 1998.
6. See also Ferguson [1990] 1994, and Sivaramakrishnan and Agrawal's introduction to this volume.
7. E.g., of south Indian irrigated landscapes, see Mosse 2003.

If the 'global' (or universal)—as a category of thought and action—is de-legitimized as partisan, incoherent, or socially embedded, its opposite the 'local' (indigenous, or traditional) has also lost its distinctive moorings. Local knowledges and indigenous traditions again and again turn out to be non-locally produced; the product of layered histories of governance, built out of the reified categories of colonial census makers, or revenue settlement officers and their official glossaries. Indian village 'traditions' have been unmasked as the product of the exigencies of colonial government, its discourses of 'localization' or their effects.[8] And, there is good reason to suppose that the exigencies of contemporary state policies (e.g., of decentralization, whether joint forest management, participatory irrigation, or *panchayati raj*) will create new community 'traditions' and new forms of 'local knowledge' through new rules and regulations as 'people acquire stakes in the new dispensation.'[9] So, just as 'global' discourses of degradation are found also to be idioms of 'local' resistance, so too the 'local' language of access, rights and control, turns out to be central to a 'global' policy discourse.

As empirically meaningful categories of knowledge and practice, 'global science' and 'local knowledge' (or state/community and the like) constantly dissolve, but as a mode of thought created by modernity the power of such distinctions is undiminished. They are deployed in the rhetorics of metropolitan arguments today, which are as often counter-modernist (counter/alternative development) as modernist: the celebration of 'indigenous knowledge' in contrast to the ignorance of 'global science;' the reversal (rather than dismissal) of orientalist accounts of other peoples (i.e. the wisdom of people and the ignorance of science); or the challenging of scientific discourses of degradation from the perspective of local knowledge-practices. It is not necessary to take these binaries seriously as sociological description to appreciate the significance of the ideological and political work they do. These are strategic representations deployed in policy debates aimed at advocating rights and mobilizing opinion (public and official) in favor of policy change—part of the politics of resource use they describe.[10] But this way of thinking and the analytical problems it appears to

8. Fuller 1989; Ludden 1993.
9. Sundar 2000: 260.
10. Li 1996.

generate remain, some argue, part of one (Euro-American) distinct regional modernity. As Leach and Fairhead[11] point out, contrasts or confrontations between 'local practices' and 'global' policy science turn out to be abstractions that imply 'argumentative interactions' where none exists. Models of the engagement of 'citizen science' and expert institutions derived from the European experience of science and public policy are not readily transferable to African or Asian contexts.[12]

Clearly, then, talk of hybrids, boundary-crossings and the like risks imposing external analytical problems onto local practices, or hypothesizing processes such as hybridizing or straddling, which may be abstract analytical shortcuts avoiding deference to the multiple categorizations of experience and knowing and the diverse modernities they produce. In this respect, the chapters of this section of the book struggle for freedom from the problems they have set themselves, choosing to follow the editors of the volume by turning away from the mediation of global/local narratives, to '"stories" [which] return us relentlessly to the moments of production [its micropolitics]'[13]—moments as disparate as the fertilizing of saplings, the work of state forestry professionals, the practices of national security surveillance, and the writing of immigrants.

But no sooner have we dispensed with the local/global, underdeveloped/developed, traditional/modern, Indian/Western, etc., as universal ordering categories of knowledge, and redirected our energies to the stories of villagers or policy makers, than the same binaries reappear, now filling our notebooks as idioms through which social experiences are interpreted, social differences marked or aspirations expressed, whether in south Rajasthan or south London. As Pigg[14] shows from ethnography in Nepal, people need to contend with the way others see them. 'Development' and some views of the modern and its opposite have become a powerful idiom of social differentiation. Modernization is no longer only a theory providing legitimizing or delegitimizing charters for nationalists, environmentalists, NGOs or others, but is part of the everyday contest of identity and social position. Here, it is not the death of the grand narrative which is prominent, but its reworking

11. Leach and Fairhead 2000.
12. Ibid.: 38.
13. Introduction, this volume.
14. Pigg 1992, 1995.

as a vehicle for the negotiation of identity as 'villagers...come, increasingly, to define themselves in and through the terms that objectify them.'[15] So, like the distinction between Sanskritic and non-Sanskritic religion, that of 'global science' and 'local knowledge' (and related distinctions), while empirically meaningless, has nonetheless, become a basis for judgments on the practices of others, for claiming status and producing distinctive 'regional modernities.' Brodt and Robbins both demonstrate this social location of knowing, describing the social relations and networks, caste/class configurations, or bureaucratic hierarchies that determine what counts as knowledge, or skill or 'science,' showing how knowledge and ignorance are socially produced,[16] and have social effects. Styles of agriculture or tree growing (practical and linguistic) convey social meanings as well as produce successful harvests.

'Regional modernities' are contested spaces in which distinctions of local/global, underdeveloped/developed are rearticulated through divisions of class–caste, ethnicity, and gender. Ultimately, these binaries are relations of power reproduced at many different levels. Knowledge/practices will always be differentiated in terms of who possesses and uses them. The knowledge of those with the greatest discursive and non-discursive resources will count as 'global' and be established as hegemonic; the knowledge of those with fewer resources will be 'local.' 'Global' thinking will be used to define, co-opt, or exclude, even while its rules for what counts as developed, modern, scientific, or intellectually respectable are challenged by 'local' or oppositional groups.[17] As Sivaramakrishnan and Agrawal suggest,[18] the alternative to grand analytical oppositions is not an infinite 'proliferation of difference,' but rather an ethnographic and historical focus on the social processes which make and remake the polarities of 'locality,' 'globality,' or 'modernity.' And, these are processes shaped by inequalities of power such that some (transnational institutions, nation states, etc.) will define the dreams and aspirations of others.

If one way out of the analytics of local–global type binaries is to conflate the distinctions (through hybridizations, straddling, collisions, etc.) and to allow them to be refashioned in an ethnog-

15. Pigg 1995: 267.
16. See Pottier 1989.
17. See Berry, this volume.
18. Sivaramakrishnan and Agrawal, this volume.

raphy of development practices, another is to refuse local–global, tradition–modernity a coherence in the first place. This is the sense, it seems to me, in which the chapters of Kumar and Abraham occupy 'boundary zones.' In his account of expatriate cosmopolitan fiction, Kumar gives binary categories of modernity/tradition an altogether less secure foundation, showing how in the imaginative inventions of immigrant writers, modernity is never allowed to cohere. The West is but a dream-becoming-nightmare in which doubt and the hand of the inventor-writer is only partially veiled. The 'interstitial cultures' of the immigrant are imagined not as hybrids or bridges but unstable and indeterminate—modernity is divided, is 'up for grabs,' for negotiation or refusal (i.e. in various fundamentalisms); distance is both created and erased, and all this in the practices and products of writing. These are writers—Rushdie, Kureishi—struggling with their own agency and with the politics of representation, and doing so by amplifying uncertainty, displacing history into magical fantasy, writing into dreaming. This is writing which both challenges and reinscribes orientalist imaginings, blends difference, exoticism and betrayal.

If Kumar provided glimpses into a literary world in which distinctions and boundaries are never permitted to cohere, then Abraham, through another kind of storytelling, draws us into a quite different landscape of state and national security where there is an imperative to mark boundaries that signify the nation and its modernity. As with other authors in this volume, for Abraham, modernity is not a condition but a becoming, a 'time-in-waiting' ('a predicament of incompleteness').[19] Modernity is not a 'present' set in contrast to past tradition, but is a future that has constantly to be forged. The task is the making of modernity out of the present/past, that is to say the *creation* of difference not the mediation of it. In this context, 'postcolonial' means naturalizing the modern as an Indian state of being. Abraham's cases are Asian regional cooperation and India's space program, both in their own way showing how, precisely, because of the weak cultural definition of the modern Indian state, there is an obsession with boundaries to 'establish beyond doubt where national space begins and ends.' The question is not then the crossing or bridging of boundaries, or even their literary confusion or dissolution, but rather their making and protection, in this case through the

19. Ibid.

mechanism of secrecy and the idiom of national security that radically distinguish the inside from the outside.

The chapters in this section, then, are clearly written against the idea of an inevitable tension between globalization and the protection of locality, and find instead multiple and regional modernities, which are historically specific endeavors and processes. I close with the suggestion that we have here a metaphor for the dilemmas of our own (as regionalists/anthropologists) scholarly practice that involves its own hierarchies of authority.[20] The appeal to historical and ethnographic 'localization' has itself to contend, in disciplinary terms, with a hierarchization of 'the universal' (global), 'the regional,' and 'the local' in the social sciences. The local–global polarity translates into the dichotomies of universal/particular, abstract/concrete, and pure/applied that order our scholarly worlds. We appear to work in a 'globalizing' environment that reinforces the hierarchy between 'superior' universalist disciplines producing abstract explanatory theory (e.g. economics) and regional (i.e. historical, ethnographic) studies considered increasingly parochial and subordinate in a postcolonial, post-Cold War, postmodern world: '*We* are universalists, *you* are regionalists, *they* are locals.'[21] In this context, the notion of 'regional modernities' helps set a scholarly agenda in which, as Christopher Davis put it, regions are resources (not impediments) for the interrogation of disciplines 'such that we see the analytic tools we use in our disciplines...as bearing the stamp of the particular historical moment and social space from where they are derived.' The marginality of regionalism (of all kinds) is averted by critically reappropriating universal concepts, especially those produced in the seemingly 'reunified discursive world' of development pragmatics and its framing concepts such as community or 'social capital.' In short, we may be encouraged to generate our own analytical 'regional modernities' in interrogating development policy.

References

Agrawal, Arun, 1995. 'Dismantling the divide between indigenous and scientific knowledge.' *Development and Change* 26: 413–39.

20. I quote, in what follows, from the contribution of Christopher Davis (1998) to the debates on academic priorities at SOAS, University of London.
21. Turton 1998.

Davis, Christopher, 1998. 'Area studies and cross-regional studies.' Debates on academic priorities. November–December. London: SOAS.

Dube, Saurabh, 1998. *Untouchable Pasts: Religion, Identity, and Power among a Central Indian Community, 1780–1950.* Albany: State University of New York Press.

Fairhead, James and Melissa Leach, 1998. *Reframing Deforestation: Global Analysis and Local Realities: Studies in West Africa.* London: Routledge.

Ferguson, James, [1990] 1994. *The Anti-politics Machine: Development, Depoliticisation and Bureaucratic Power in Lesotho.* Cambridge: Cambridge University Press.

Fuller, C. J., 1989. 'Misconceiving the grain heap: A critique of the concept of the Indian Jajmani system.' In J. Parry and M. Bloch (eds.), *Money and the Morality of Exchange.* Cambridge: Cambridge University Press.

Leach, Melissa and James Fairhead, 2000. 'Fashioned forest pasts, occluded histories? International environmental analysis in West African locales.' *Development and Change* 31(1): 35–59.

Li, T. M., 1996. 'Images of community: Discourse and strategy in property relations.' *Development and Change* 27: 501–27.

Ludden, David, 1993. 'Orientalist empiricism: Transformations of colonial knowledge.' In Carol A. Breckenridge and Peter van der Veer (eds.), *Orientalism and the Postcolonial Predicament: Perspectives on South Asia.* Philadelphia: University of Pennsylvania Press, pp. 250–78.

Mehta, Lyla, 1998. 'Contexts of scarcity: The political ecology of water in Kutch, India.' D. Phil dissertation, University of Sussex.

Mosse, David, 1995. 'Found in most traditional societies: Traditional medical practitioners between Culture and Development.' In J. Crush (ed.), *The Power of Development.* London: Routledge.

———, 1998. 'Colonial and contemporary ideologies of "community management": The case of tank irrigation development in south India.' *Modern Asian Studies* 33(2): 303–39.

———, 2003. *The Rule of Water: Statecraft, Ecology and Collective Action in South India.* Delhi: Oxford University Press.

Pigg, Stacy Leigh, 1992. 'Inventing social categories through place: Social representations and development in Nepal.' *Comparative Studies in Society and History* 34: 491–513.

Pottier, J., 1989. '"Three is a crowd": Knowledge, ignorance and power in the context of urban agriculture in Rwanda.' *Africa* 54(4): 461–77.

Sundar, N., 2000. 'Unpacking the "joint" in joint forest management.' *Development and Change* 31: 255–79.

Turton, Andrew, 1998. Discussion paper on 'Area studies and cross-regional studies in the academic priorities at SOAS Review.' October–December. London: SOAS.

14

Beyond the Local/Global Divide: Knowledge for Tree Management in Madhya Pradesh*

SONJA BRODT

INTRODUCTION

Traditional environmental knowledge has often been portrayed in the development literature as something held by exclusive 'indigenous' groups and confined to distinct localities separate from global knowledge formations. Drawing from a study of rural tree management in Madhya Pradesh, India, this chapter will question this dichotomous pigeon-holing of knowledge into either local or global, 'indigenous' or 'scientific' forms. Rather, I will use the life stories of individuals and groups of people encountered in a particular locality to show how they cross these conventionally described boundaries between knowledge types to construct their own modern knowledge systems of tree management. Moreover, I will show how people's access to various tangible as well as intangible resources, including knowledge resources, are in part determined by 'historically sedimented social, economic, and

* This chapter is published with permission from the Society for Applied Anthropology. An earlier version of this article first appeared in *Human Organization* 61: 1.

spatial structures'[1] and that these differences in access result in substantial differences in knowledge from one person to the next. Despite being situated in potentially limiting structures, however, we will also see that most individuals can exercise at least a small degree of personal agency in pursuing opportunities for learning. This agency is the important message behind the concept of 'stories' as elucidated by Sivaramakrishnan and Agrawal in the introduction to this volume, as it reminds us that development and the knowledge associated with it are not just abstract processes, but that they exist as a whole host of lived situations experienced and created by real people in real localities.[2]

DEFINITION AND PROBLEMATIZATION OF TERMS

In this paper, the term 'global science' is used to designate that science that is taught and practised by professional scientists in universities and research centers throughout the world. I prefer this term to the more popular term 'Western science' because it more aptly portrays how this type of science is globally constructed through the aid of modern-day communication technologies and internationally published journals that allow interaction of practising scientists around the world, not just in the West. The use and meaning of this term itself could be problematized, especially in terms of questioning the universality of thought of scientists located in different cultures around the world. However, the definition as stated here will be operative for the duration of this paper, with the assumption that some basic 'culture of science' is held in common by all or most practitioners.

The term 'local knowledge' in this study is opposed to 'global knowledge' only in the sense that it signifies any particular body of knowledge held and used by an individual or group of individuals situated in a particular geographical, cultural, and political economic context. In this sense, not only do villagers possess local knowledge, but any particular scientist at a research institute would also use his own brand of local knowledge in, for example, carrying out research trials on a particular plot of land that he knows well. Therefore, local knowledge can be seen as 'situated practice' and

1. Sivaramakrishnan and Agrawal, this volume.
2. See also Klenk, this volume.

is not necessarily synonymous with 'traditional knowledge,' 'folk knowledge,' or 'indigenous knowledge.'[3]

ANALYTICAL APPROACH TO KNOWLEDGE SYSTEMS

As will be shown in this paper, knowledge of different geographical and socio-political origins can be blended or combined into hybrid knowledge systems at the local level. This hybridization does not, however, occur in a random, unorganized way. The detailed mechanics of knowledge recombination can best be understood by viewing knowledge as composed of different levels of abstraction, ranging from concrete practices to abstract concepts. Horton, Kalland, and Ingold distinguish two or more different levels in any knowledge system.[4] Practices, which compose the 'primary level,' consist of pieces of information resulting from simple cognition of objects in the environment, and their cause-and-effect, spatial, and temporal relationships. Concepts, at the 'secondary level' consist of those overlying constructs that are abstracted from the information level and that explain and unify the information pieces into a meaningful whole, the knowledge system. Therefore, whereas the primary level is closely tied to physical reality and concrete actions, the conceptual level is one step removed from the physical.

This perception of knowledge as composed of multiple levels offers several possibilities for combining knowledge from diverse origins. Primary-level practices, perceptions, or 'facts' derived or learned from an outside source may be subsumed under secondary-level interpretive concepts from the pre-existing system. Conversely, newly-acquired secondary-level concepts may be adopted or expanded to explain the practices of the existing system. Knowledge pieces may also be compartmentalized, with information from one origin being used for one subject area, and from another origin for another subject area.

THE STUDY SITE

This study was conducted in a small group of villages located approximately 40 kilometers southwest of Bhopal, the state capital

---

3. See also Kloppenburg 1991; Sivaramakrishnan 1999.
4. Horton 1982; Kalland 1994; and Ingold 1992.

of Madhya Pradesh, and connected with this large city and other smaller towns by regular bus service. These villages, consisting of from 550 to 2000 inhabitants, are home to mixed populations of numerous Hindu castes, Muslims, and Gond and Bhil tribal people. While proportions vary considerably from village to village, the overall proportions for the three study villages, roughly calculated from national census data, are just under 75 percent caste Hindus, somewhat over 15 percent mixed tribal, and less than 5 percent Muslim, giving this area a much larger Hindu representation than the more tribal-dominated eastern portion of the state.[5]

Medium to good quality teak and mixed forest on state-owned land is accessible to all villages for firewood collection, grazing of livestock, and collection of various non-timber forest products such as the edible *mahua* flowers, fruits, fibers, and medicinal plants. With these forest resources close by, people do not grow any trees expressly for fodder or fuelwood on their own farmland or in their home gardens. Instead, they concentrate mostly on fruiting and flowering trees such as mango, guava, papaya, custard apple, ber (*Zizyphus jujuba*), oleander, plumeria and certain specialty trees such as eucalyptus, bamboo, and sacred tree species like peepal, or bodhi (*Ficus religiosa*) and tulsi, or holy basil (*Ocimum sanctum*).

HISTORICAL AND PRESENT-DAY CONTACT
WITH EXTERNAL KNOWLEDGE

The specific nature of regional modernity in this area was foreshadowed almost a century ago in the modernization efforts of the nawab, ruler of the erstwhile state of Bhopal, which encompassed the study area prior to Independence. Although Bhopal was never entirely annexed by British India, the last few nawabs nevertheless, understood the expediency of currying favor with the British, and they were keen to show off their modernity by bringing European styles and technologies into the everyday workings of their realm. Situated on the outskirts of the central study village, for example, was a country estate of the nawab, which boasted an elaborate mansion built and decorated in a

---

5. For more details see Brodt 1998.

distinctly European art deco style, still visible in the now uninhabited and deteriorating buildings. And, as in his personal tastes, so in his official duties did the nawab try through various means to inculcate his subjects' farming practices with a modernity adopted from outside. Older village residents can still remember, for example, the agricultural fairs sponsored by the nawab's government in the early decades of the twentieth century, in which demonstrations were made of new implements and farm management techniques. On his own farmland, the nawab used state-of-the-art tractors imported from England, the United States, and Germany. In addition, his own estate employed local residents to care for prized ornamental and fruit trees, many of which had been brought from distant parts of India and elsewhere and were otherwise unknown in the area.

How these external influences actually played out in farmers' fields and gardens at that time can only be surmised from few available sources, a task which is beyond the scope of this essay. However, some of the legacy of 'modernization from outside', left not only by the nawab's government but also by postcolonial national and state government policies, is still present in knowledge exchanges within this region today. Externally-derived information continues to enter local communities through the agricultural extension system, the forest department, formal schooling, mass media such as radio and television programs, and commercial vendors of agricultural inputs. Certain well-traveled and influential farmers also act as conduits of information about the latest technology available in the national and global market systems.

The extent of contact with these sources, however, differs markedly across the village population due to constraints of class, caste, gender, and sometimes age. Members of poorer and socially more isolated classes, scheduled and backward castes, and women of various classes, especially the very poor and the very rich, are the least likely to have any direct contact with extra-village information sources. Numerous communication obstacles account for this discrepancy, including the impropriety of communicating directly across status and gender gaps, illiteracy, and lack of mobility. In addition, the poor, lacking large farms and orchards, are unable to attract the attention of professional knowledge agents from outside. Significantly, however, the data collected did not yield a very neat pattern with a clear, positive, linear relationship between socio-economic status and knowledge. Rather, individuals even in similar socio-economic classifications evinced widely varying sets of tree management knowledge. These results suggest that knowledge is also acquired through other means, especially experiential learning.

LOCAL EXPERIENTIAL LEARNING OF TREE-RELATED KNOWLEDGE

Villagers themselves often asserted that they had learned everything they needed to know about tree management through their own experience, without being taught by anyone, and therefore a lack of knowledge is due to a lack of experience. Indeed, when asked whether she thought that cowdung or commercial urea fertilizer is better for trees, one poor tribal woman responded that she could not say, since she has never had a chance to see for herself the effects of applying urea to her trees due to its prohibitive cost. Villagers' own emphasis on personal experience as well as their wide variation in knowledge suggest that it is actually this experiential knowledge combined with observation of other local people that forms the central matrix into which outside information is incorporated.

Interviews and exercises conducted with children support this hypothesis. Groups of even quite young children, from about the age of eight and older, could give step-by-step instructions for planting trees that matched that of adults, but rarely could they match this simple factual information with as much explanatory knowledge. Their good familiarity with practices and their lesser ability to articulate the secondary-level concepts behind the practices points to the significance of observation in learning. Practices can most easily be observed and absorbed, whereas concepts have to be taught or developed through experience and reflection. Young children are typically involved in regular household chores which often include tasks such as watering trees, and they are also very likely to acquire information just from watching their elders engaging in activities such as tree planting. Having older relatives or other close associates who have an interest in tree cultivation and are knowledgable is thus likely to be an important factor in children's learning. Indeed, many young people explicitly cited parents and grandparents as their most significant teachers, after personal experience.

People assigned significantly less importance to verbal communication with others in the local setting. Many people reported that they do not talk at all to other people about tree cultivation. One teenage girl, for example, noted that, although she had learned about trees from her father, much of this learning was through simple observation, and only occasionally did her father give any direct verbal instruction. To some extent, people's assertions that they talk with no one about tree growing may have been overstated as a generalized answer to a very general question. On the other hand, an overall paucity of verbal communication is not implausible. Trees occupy only a small economic or subsistence niche and in most cases are considered as luxuries or even hobbies. Thus, it is understandable that they are not the most common topic of conversation.

The emphasis on personal experience and observation implies that learning is an inherently local process, contingent upon which trees fill which parts of the local landscape and who has access to those parts of the landscape. Evidence from the study suggests, for example, that people who grow up around rich, carefully managed home gardens are somewhat more likely to have a richer knowledge base for tree management.[6] While this point may seem obvious for populations with little formal education, it also holds for those wealthier farmers with high school or even university educations. Given the now widely acknowledged experimental nature of most farmers' work,[7] even those with substantial 'abstracted' knowledge learned in a classroom bring that knowledge to fruition via their own experience forged in their own particularistic gardens and fields. Therefore, even knowledge that might be globally disseminated is ultimately encountered and integrated in the minds of real people in very local contexts. This integration, then, is the essence of the concept of regional modernity presented in the introduction to this volume, where localities are the 'places,' both real and figurative (village landscapes and people's minds) where modern knowledges are continually produced using

6. Brodt 1998.
7. See Chambers 1983; Biggelaar 1996; Rhoades and Bebbington 1995; Richards 1985.

information gleaned from local conditions, drawn through the lens of a larger, regionally-based culture and historically-determined circumstances, and broadened with information gained from globally circulated sources.

EXAMPLES OF
KNOWLEDGE PRODUCTION

Just how such local knowledge integration takes place can best be understood by observing some examples of local tree management. Villagers spoke of a variety of practices as well as concepts used to deal with soil fertility and tree growth. At the level of practices, most farmers in this region, except the very poorest, make some use of commercial, inorganic fertilizer, especially urea, on their crop fields, and many have experimented with it on the fruit trees in their home gardens. Most, however, continue to use the more traditional cowdung as a manure, often in combination with urea for crops, or by itself for trees. Some people use fish as a nutritive soil amendment for trees, and some also apply buttermilk and ashes.

On a conceptual level, many farmers explain several of these practices using the humoral concept of a hot/cold balance. According to villagers, 'heat' and 'cold' must be balanced in trees and plants, as in human beings. Heat is often associated with potency or fertility and is responsible for the good green color and growth of plants, but too much heat can damage them, just like very powerful drugs can have undesirable side effects in people. The concept of hot and cold is found in distinctly Indian theories of medicine, as evidenced, for example, by the science of ayurveda.[8] It is also widely used by lay people throughout India to understand the effects of food on the body, and can likewise be found in medicinal traditions around the world. The exact origins of the concept are difficult to surmise; however, it is certainly a concept foreign to the now predominant scientific establishment.

Another prominent concept is the idea that plants require certain types of 'food,' or fertilizer. This concept may have arisen separately within local knowledges of many areas, and it is

8. See Dash and Junius 1983.

certainly also a part of the global scientific agricultural paradigm that guides the production of commercial inorganic fertilizers such as urea.

These diverse practices and concepts, stemming perhaps from equally diverse cultural geographic origins, are mixed and matched by villagers in characteristic ways. For example, the application of ashes and buttermilk, two traditional practices in this locality, is explained entirely by the hot/cold concept, because these substances are said to cool trees during the hot season. Amending the soil with fish, also an apparently traditional practice in this area, is explained by the nutrition concept, which is shared with global scientific endeavors. Cowdung manuring, also long practised in an area which traditionally raised many cattle, is explained by both concepts, cowdung being said to be a cooling agent as well as a nutritive fertilizer. Urea application, a practice developed by the international scientific establishment, is also dually covered by these diverse concepts, but urea is considered hot in addition to being nutritive.

The above is just a brief example of how pieces of knowledge that seem to be coming from different loci, from local, to regional, to global, are gathered together and woven into a workable local model of tree management, sometimes integrated to such an extent that the actual origins of any part are difficult to differentiate. In the next section I will illustrate more precisely how real people in actual localities carry out such processes of hybridization and how local and regional particularities pertaining to questions of power relations and access influence opportunities for knowledge acquisition.

INDIVIDUAL CASE HISTORIES OF LEARNING AND KNOWLEDGE HYBRIDIZATION

The following mini-case studies span a continuum of connectedness with social, cultural, and natural resources. I will begin with individuals having poor access to both local and global resources and move on to those with high local but poor global connectivity, and finally to those with strong global but lesser local connections. In each case I will demonstrate how a person's or a group's socioeconomic and natural milieu influences the particular composition of that person's or group's knowledge of tree management.

BHIL TRIBAL GROUP:
ISOLATED NEW ARRIVALS

I will begin with a small, relatively isolated community consisting of Bhil tribal people who recently settled on a small area of marginal, hilly land somewhat apart from other villages. The 15 households that constitute the village are the offshoots of four original families that had migrated 25 years previously in search of work and land from another district. They had been landless or nearly landless and had been displaced from their homes by a large-scale irrigation project. Most of the families of this small, cohesive group now hold titles to small parcels of land. Owing to their previous near landlessness, however, they have a general lack of experience in farming and growing trees. One informant even indicated that no trees grew around his childhood home in his parental district. Informants described the first years in this new location as difficult, because they had to learn farming by their own trial and error. Their newness to the locality entails a lack of knowledge of local conditions, such as distinctions between black and yellow soil, which are otherwise widely known in this area. In addition, the small parcels of land that they do own, amounting to 1.6 hectares or less for each of the surveyed households (about 10 hectares total for all households), is very hilly, creating more challenges for farming. The nearest forest area from which they gather firewood and a few other products is also quite sparse and open.

Although they have received government subsidies for traditional style wells and gasoline-run irrigation pumps, they otherwise seem to have less access to outside informational and educational resources than other farmers in the area. They have very little or no contact with the forest department and their children mostly do not attend school, since they would have to walk quite far to reach the nearest school in the neighboring village, which, moreover, consists of different, non-Bhil people.

Currently, thus, they are neither very locally nor very globally connected, a state which has left a mark on their tree-related knowledge. Several trips to their settlement revealed no one among even the more willing informants who was very articulate about the specialized, technical practices of tree care described by people elsewhere in the study area. If anything, as a group they seemed the least knowledgable of all. Although aware of the most basic practices such as the use of cowdung for soil fertility and the building of small bunds around trees for water retention, none expressed familiarity with the more specialized practices such as pruning or the application of different substances to the soil besides cowdung that were often mentioned by other people. Only one Bhil interviewed expressed an awareness of different effects on plants of different types of soils, while others expressed unfamiliarity with such a difference.

Nevertheless, given these limitations, several households did have mature mango and other fruit trees. In addition, they used some expressive metaphors and similes when talking about trees, such as trees requiring care and attention just like children do. At least one informant was also able to articulate a pertinent criterion for choosing between cowdung and urea for crop fields. Such reflective observations show evidence of some hands-on learning, and the higher-level metaphorical comments could be interpreted as evidence of a real interest in tree growing. Overall, however, a few secondary-level metaphorical concepts preside over a seemingly sparse primary level of observations and practices. This top-heavy nature of the knowledge system suggests a relative lack of significant experiential learning opportunities.

This more insular and environmentally disadvantaged group of people thus aptly demonstrates the role of the local landscape in affecting knowledge acquisition. Neither in their original home district nor in their current new home were many physical resources, such as extensive home gardens, initially available for learning about trees. Their knowledge subsequently seems overall sparser, as a group, than that of other groups of people in this area. (It should be noted, however, that while they seemed less knowledgable overall as a group, as individuals they did not seem strikingly less knowledgable than some individuals interviewed in other communities.) Having some land, now, however, makes it possible to learn by doing, and many households are already engaged in tree growing. Because they are physically and socially isolated from other communities and therefore more exclusively dependent on local resources (both physical and social), it may take some time for the Bhils to build up the sort of specialized expertise at all levels of knowledge as exemplified by some members of the surrounding communities. On the other hand, with their high within-group cohesion and physical proximity to each other, they can quickly gain from each other's experiences and lessons in tree growing.

GOND TRIBAL COMMUNITY: LONG-TERM LOCAL RESIDENTS

The small Bhil community just described can be contrasted with the community of approximately 40 households of Gond tribals living in a nearby village. The Gonds are also a very cohesive and somewhat insular group, and are very reserved with outsiders. Overall, however, they create an impression of greater expertise in tree care, with several people among those interviewed being able to speak at some length about commonly mentioned practices, especially those originating more clearly from local or regional folk knowledge. Secondary concepts such as the hot/cold dichotomy, nutritional ideas, and pest control also seemed to be fairly well-represented here. In addition, one notable community leader was particularly knowledgable about some specialized practices that were not mentioned by anyone else in the entire study, such as incising the bark of mango trees to facilitate fruit development.

One factor that distinguishes these Gond people from the Bhils is their longer residence of three to four generations in this same area. This longer time period has allowed for the development of a significantly altered tree cover within and around the village, with many cultivated fruit and flowering trees distinct from the natural forest vegetation. Learning opportunities therefore abound from early childhood onward, with many residents having inherited trees and gardens from their elders. In addition, their significantly larger but still cohesive group of approximately 40 households provides a larger set of people who are potentially creating and sharing new information.

This group also has notably more contact with external information sources. The forest department had very recently initiated the formation of a forest protection committee in their village to help protect the moderate to good forest cover located immediately adjacent to the village. Forest officers now have greater contact with villagers and also impart tree planting advice at meetings. In addition, committee members now have access to free seedlings from the forest department's nursery, and several men mentioned planting exotics such as eucalyptus and acacia, which they may not have been able to afford to purchase previously. The official attention seems to be working a change within the village, as noted by the knowledgable Committee president, who observed that people are becoming increasingly interested in growing trees in the village and on their fields, and that a few opinion leaders such as himself are trying to set an example to encourage people in this regard. Besides the exotics mentioned above, farmers are also extensively involved in transplanting seedlings of the more traditional fruit trees from each other's gardens and fields where they have germinated spontaneously. Some of these mango trees, however, also originated from seeds obtained from the nawab's orchard, the fruit of which is highly prized among all local people.

Both the Gond and Bhil communities are considered equally marginalized minorities within the larger society of this region, but a comparison of the two reveals how a blend of some contact with external factors combined with a strong base in a local landscape and community can diversify and enrich learning opportunities. The Gond community, on the one hand, enjoys the benefits of long-term access and control over a richly diverse treed landscape, consisting of many cultivated as well as forest species which provide a space in which children can learn from elders. The Bhil community, on the other hand, is still working through its first, displaced generation just learning from scratch how to come to terms with its new environment. Moreover, it has a poorer environment to begin with, having arrived later than surrounding communities and therefore having had to settle for hilly, vegetation-poor land which had probably already been picked over by earlier forest felling operations. And, while the more favorable forest resources available to the Gond community garner it more attention from the incipient global-scale program of joint forest management, the Bhil community is left to itself, as of yet on the outskirts of the official limelight. Moreover, although only two to three kilometers separate the two communities, contact between them seems quite limited, as not only do they fall under the jurisdiction of different villages, but members of both groups tend to associate primarily with those of their own ethnicity.

YADAV MAN: LOCAL KNOWLEDGE
WITH GLOBAL INFLUENCES

One of the knowledge 'stars' of the study was Mahesh (name changed), an elderly man of the Yadav caste, officially classified as a backward caste. Mahesh could not only speak articulately about unique practices and insights about trees, but he also had an impressive home garden to vouch for his expertise. Mahesh seemed to be an avid observer and experimenter and, like other villagers, had gained much of his knowledge through trial and error. In addition, he had also been able to make the most of some formative experiences, including employment as a laborer at the nawab's nearby estate during his youth. There, he had observed some of the fertilization practices being implemented for the fruit trees, such as the use of fish, which he currently uses on some of his own trees. He also subsequently worked on other large, commercial farms, where he was able to obtain good seedlings of fruit trees for his own garden. In addition, he reported being intrigued when, on one of his travels to a distant district to visit relatives, he observed the practice of growing two kinds of fruit trees next to each other in order to improve the flavor of the fruit. He expressed an interest in applying this new idea from someone else's personal knowledge in his own garden.

Thus, although he is of a disadvantaged group, with little or no formal education, and with only a small plot of land near his current home, Mahesh nevertheless has been able to tap into larger-scale enterprises that themselves are much more integrated into global-scale knowledge structures. From these he has gleaned selected practices, such as fertilization techniques. At the same time, from other grassroots practitioners he gathers ideas that can serve as fodder for his own very individualistic and localized experimentation. His overall knowledge framework, especially at the higher conceptual levels, is therefore dominated by elements of his own experiential 'craft' knowledge, melded with regionally prevalent traditional concepts, with particular bits and pieces gleaned from globally circulated sources embedded predominantly at the lower, primary level of practices.

WELL-TO-DO HINDU FARMER

A second example from the middle of the spectrum is Sita Ram (name changed), a middle-aged male member of one of the more prosperous Hindu households in the large central village of the study. Sita Ram exemplifies someone whose knowledge comes from having one foot firmly planted in local lore while the other treads the global ground of agricultural extension services. Approximately 13 to 14 years ago he and his two brothers established a mango orchard on part of their farmland with 30-5 grafted mango seedlings. These had been specially ordered from a nursery in another district through the local block office (the government office charged with agricultural extension and other development activities), located in a nearby town. The family maintains close relations with this office, and the block officer even makes periodic visits to their house, especially since the family plays an important role in the village panchayat, or council. They, thus, obtain information on chemical pesticides for the trees, when necessary, and have applied commercial fertilizers when the trees were smaller. In addition, Sita Ram's son and nephews are getting or have already acquired university education in nearby Bhopal, and other branches of the family are involved in various commercial enterprises at a regional level. Besides these family connections, he is also friendly with the manager of the large commercial farm that belongs to the erstwhile nawab's estate. This manager has a Master of Science degree in agriculture and occasionally lends advice to the family on crop-related matters. Sita Ram's contact with global-scale processes, including agricultural and horticultural science, is therefore quite high.

His understanding of other types of informal knowledge not generated at research institutions, however, is also somewhat exceptional, and he is able to articulate detailed ideas about many of the practices and concepts used by other, less 'worldly' farmers in the area. For example, although cognizant of the nutritional and pest control roles of chemical fertilizers and pesticides, respectively, he can also explain how these substances as well as trees themselves have humoral qualities of hot and cold, and what proportions of different local soils should be used when planting trees. Significantly, one of his close friends is an elderly neighbor, a respected Brahmin with little formal education but a large store of experiential knowledge, whose family has long roots in this locality.

Overall, then, Sita Ram is another of the knowledge 'stars' of this study, possessing a rich knowledge base stemming from diverse sources and traditions. His manner of acquiring this knowledge, moreover, clearly stems from a combination of both local and global-level factors and processes. While the economic power of his family ensures access to prime land for growing trees locally, it also allows for globally-oriented aspirations such as commercialization of their farm enterprise, acquisition of special tree varieties not available locally, and higher education. It is these types of aspirations that bring him into contact with global knowledge structures. At the same time, local friendships and relations with family and neighbors help to reinforce informal, regionally distinct types of knowledge, so that his vocabulary is a mixture of both practices and concepts which, while stemming from many realms of knowledge, mingle relatively boundary-free within his mind.

ELITE GENTLEMAN FARMER

Finally, at the extreme global end of the spectrum stands a wealthy Muslim farmer, Ahmed (name changed), with a substantial landholding near the study villages and a large residence in Bhopal. A descendant of a family with close ties to the erstwhile nawab, Ahmed inherited many of his present assets from his privileged forebears and acquired a worldly education from university training and frequent overseas travel. He also provides farm employment to local people such as Mahesh and thereby continues the tradition, of sorts, of informal knowledge transfer to local villagers started by the nawab. And like the nawab, he is a progressive thinker highly conversant in global agricultural trends and environmentalist thinking, at all levels of knowledge, and he applies these with great interest to his own land. He has experimented with organic fertilizers (with which even the local extension agent is unfamiliar) and the latest machinery, and also contracts with a Bhopal seed company to grow out new varieties of crop seeds on his land. Like the farmer above, he has started a substantial mango orchard with special varieties imported from a breeding center in another state. At the secondary, paradigmatic level, he expressed an unusual, environmentalist interest in preserving patches of native forest species on his land. He also espouses the global environmental discourse of ecological crisis and remediation described by Robbins,[9] holding his poorer neighbors responsible for the decline of forest cover in the local area.

9. See Robbins, this volume.

This farmer's connection to the national and international scientific knowledge establishment is thus quite strong, and he himself is even directly involved in its production and continuation at multiple levels, from the primary level of seed varieties to the more abstract levels of soil chemistry ideas and discourses of environmental decline. On the other hand, although he talks to local farmers and maintains particularly close relations with the locally powerful family of Sita Ram, above, he is less conversant with some of the more purely 'folk' conceptions circulated locally and regionally, such as the humoral hot/cold classification. Although he is generally aware that some farmers may use this idea to talk about trees and crops, he himself only vaguely understands the conceptual mechanism. Moreover, he did not evince any significant interest in it, having an already substantial toolbox of scientific ideas coming from an entirely different frame of reference with which to make sense of his farm. He does, however, utilize a few traditional local practices, such as the application of cowdung as fertilizer. Ahmed therefore presents almost a mirror image of Mahesh, with just a few primary level practices from regional culture, such as the use of cowdung, embedded in a knowledge framework otherwise heavily dominated by globally-generated science, especially at the higher levels.

CONCLUSION

The above series of examples suggests that most people have incorporated some elements of knowledge from diverse sources, ranging from international scientific institutions to parents' inherited wisdom to their own experience, into their personal understandings of growing trees. What the exact proportions of different types of knowledge are for any individual, however, is contingent upon a number of factors present in each person's own story of development. Access to extra-village sources, in particular, is related to factors such as economic power, education, landholding, and social status (whether high or low caste or tribal). It is also contingent on idiosyncratic opportunities and individual choices of employment and personal associations and friendships. Acquisition of knowledge with local or family origins is similarly contingent on contact with appropriate, knowledgable people.

The efficacy of accessing any of these knowledge types and sources, however, is ultimately mediated by availability of spaces for tree growing, as personal experience seems to be one of the most important factors in developing knowledge. Access to the necessary land is in turn roughly correlated with factors such as economic power, gender, and social status, and, true to our understanding of regional modernity, history plays an important role in determining each of these factors. We should also remember that personality traits such as inventiveness and curiosity ultimately intersect with learning opportunities to affect knowledge acquisition; in other words, individual agency can significantly influence the course of each personal story of learning.

These observations raise some important points about globalization and regional modernities. First, they illustrate that conventionally described boundaries between 'global' and 'local,' or 'modern science' and 'traditional knowledge' are not necessarily as strictly defined as earlier literature would have one believe; moreover, any such boundaries that may be constructed are often transgressed by people actually using knowledge in their everyday lives. In addition, we have seen that personal, local knowledge is not only under continual production, but that it also exists in relation to, indeed draws from, externally-derived knowledge, such as that which is produced in international research centers.

Finally, globalization is not necessarily just a one-way street. Local villagers do not simply receive knowledge from outside and use it to displace whatever 'traditional' knowledge may have existed previously. Rather, they create knowledge systems using a whole host of resources, of which elements of external knowledge are but one type. Moreover, communication can also occur in the other direction. Careful research into the historical development of modern European botanical science, for instance, suggests that it owes much to scientific explorations of 'indigenous knowledge' throughout Asia during the eighteenth and nineteenth century and earlier.[10]

Modernity of knowledge systems, therefore, can be seen as a condition in which knowledge in multiple 'places' (international institutions as well as village farmers' fields) exists in relation to, and is continually being constructed from, other knowledge

10. See Ellen and Harris 1997.

systems. Moreover, such modernity is distinctly regional because all knowledge formations pertaining to natural resource management are ultimately dependent on regionally-specific, historically-determined circumstances for articulation, and the intersections of access to information with access to local land and tree resources will play out differently in each specific locality.

These perspectives on local and global aspects of environmental management hold two implications for development. The first is that access to land where farming and gardening can be practised is important for creating and maintaining viable knowledge, perhaps even more so than simple verbal communication between people. For the poor who do not have an adequate land base of their own, thus, access to common land or employment on landscapes richer than their own can constitute important opportunities for learning.

The second implication stems from the unique perspective that the concept of regional modernity brings to the project of development. This perspective promotes a view of knowledge that emphasizes diversity, flexibility, and continual, locally-relevant innovation. This view differs substantially from the commonly expressed crisis attitude which predicts the catastrophic loss of uniquely local and traditional knowledge due to the violent penetration of global influences via insensitively conducted development projects and market forces.[11] This perspective is not intended to imply that the two-way street along the global–local spectrum is necessarily evenly divided and that we should not be concerned about the effects of globally-circulated knowledge entering local vocabularies faster than locally-generated concepts travel in the other direction. For, as Robbins warns us, the power to define the landscape is often the power to control it, and whose definition and knowledge dominates, therefore, remains a crucial issue for the poor and disenfranchized who depend on that landscape for their livelihoods.[12] However, this perspective is intended as a recognition of the continual evolution of all knowledge, and the idea that those systems and cultures that can adapt to changing circumstances, rather than just trying to resist them, are the most likely to persist over time.[13] It is also a suggestion

11. See Shiva 1997.
12. Robbins, this volume.
13. See Bebbington 1996; Brodt 2001.

that those in the middle of the knowledge spectrum, with the largest potential repertoire of ideas to draw from, may indeed be better off in the long run that those at either end. Only time can tell if even the elite farmer, despite his ability to draw upon far-reaching information sources, lacks the diversity of knowledge types and perspectives of some of his less elite neighbors that may provide answers in times of crisis. Therefore, it may be most expedient for development workers to examine whether and how rural communities might manage to maintain elements of multiple perspectives in their local settings so that they could benefit from the increased knowledge richness, while at the same time addressing knowledge and resource poverty among their most underprivileged members.

ACKNOWLEDGMENTS

I wish foremost to thank all the residents of the study villages whose cooperation and patient assistance made this research possible. Several staff members of the Obedullaganj Forest Division were also particularly helpful in facilitating my field work, especially Mr B. P. Singh and Mr P. K. Tripathi and their assistants. Dr Achal Singh Pawar provided much valuable assistance in the field, and the Indian Institute of Forest Management in Bhopal sponsored this project.

Financial support for this study was provided by the National Science Foundation under Grant Number SBR–9508550 and the East–West Center. In addition, the University of Hawai'i, Manoa, and the Agricultural and Resource Economics Department, University of California, Davis, provided computer resources. Any opinions, findings, and conclusions or recommendations expressed in this material are those of the author and do not necessarily reflect the views of the National Science Foundation, the East–West Center, the University of Hawai'i, the University of California, or any individuals named above.

References

Bebbington, Anthony, 1996. 'Movements, modernizations, and markets: Indigenous organizations and agrarian strategies in Ecuador.' In R. Peet and M. Watts (eds.), *Liberation Ecologies: Environment, Development, Social Movements*. London: Routledge.

Biggelaar, Christoffel den, 1996. *Farmer Experimentation and Innovation: A Case Study of Knowledge Generation Processes in Agroforestry Systems in Rwanda.* Rome: Food and Agriculture Organization of the United Nations.

Brodt, Sonja B., 1998. 'Learning from the land: Local knowledge systems of tree management in central India.' Ph.D. thesis. University of Hawai'i, Manoa.

———, 2001. 'A systems perspective on the conservation and erosion of indigenous agricultural knowledge in central India.' *Human Ecology* 29(1): 99–120.

Chambers, Robert, 1983. *Rural Development: Putting the Last First.* Essex: Longman Scientific and Technical.

Dash, Bhagwan and Manfred M. Junius, 1983. *A Hand Book of Ayurveda.* New Delhi: Concept Publishing.

Ellen, Roy and Holly Harris, 1997. *Concepts of Indigenous Environmental Knowledge in Scientific and Development Studies Literature. A Critical Assessment.* APFT Working Paper No. 2. Avenir des Peuples des Forêts Tropicales project. Canterbury: University of Kent.

Horton, Robin, 1982. 'Tradition and modernity revisited.' In M. Hollis and S. Lukes (eds.), *Rationality and Relativism.* Cambridge: MIT Press.

Ingold, Timothy, 1992. 'Culture and the perception of the environment.' In E. Croll and D. Parkin (eds.), *Bush Base: Forest Farm: Culture, Environment and Development.* London: Routledge.

Kalland, Arne, 1994. 'Indigenous knowledge—local knowledge: Prospects and limitations.' Paper presented at the AEPS Seminar on Integration of Indigenous Peoples' Knowledge, Reykjavík, September 20–3.

Kloppenburg, Jack, 1991. 'Social theory and the de/reconstruction of agricultural science: Local knowledge for an alternative agriculture.' *Rural Sociology* 56(4): 519–48.

Rhoades, Robert and Anthony Bebbington, 1995. 'Farmers who experiment: An untapped resource for agricultural research and development.' In D. Michael Warren, L. Jan Slikkerveer, and David Brokensha (eds.), *The Cultural Dimension of Development: Indigenous Knowledge Systems.* London: Intermediate Technology Publications.

Richards, Paul, 1985. *Indigenous Agricultural Revolution: Ecology and Food Production in West Africa.* London: Hutchinson.

Shiva, Vandana, 1997. *The Plunder of Nature and Knowledge.* Boston: South End Press.

Sivaramakrishnan, K. 1999. *Modern Forests: Statemaking and Environmental Change in Colonial Eastern India.* Stanford: Stanford University.

15

Modernity in a Suitcase:
An Essay on Immigrant Indian Writing

AMITAVA KUMAR

As the editors of this volume point out, there have been several critics who have been interested in questioning the presumed homogeneity of the developmentalist imagination; in the brief paper that follows, I am more interested in discerning, in some detail, how it is precisely in the domain described as the imagination that the presumed homogeneity of the world is shattered. In commenting on the work of Indian writers based in the West, I want to elaborate what we might call 'immigrant modernities'; by dealing with fiction, I am taking rather literally the editors' call for thinking of storytelling as a particularly viable way of understanding the 'disjunctive experiences' under modernity. I want to ask how it is that in the stories that are written by immigrant writers from India modernity emerges as a contested project.

The appeal to the immigrant, and, more specifically, to the immigrant writer, provides a visa of entry into the zones of representation. Who is the one talking about modernity, and where is this conversation taking place? Where does it find its echo? It is with these basic questions that this paper wrestles. The displacements that the editors seek to bring about in the conversation on modernity vis-à-vis India must engage that crucial, quite literal, displacement to which we give the name 'immigration.' It seems to me that the editors' preference for not giving a fixed spatial anchoring to the idea of 'regional modernity' partakes, in some mesasure, of the mobility that this split between the nation and the diaspora produces.

In the special issue of the *New Yorker*, published to commemorate India's 50th anniversary of Independence and devoted entirely to Indian fiction, there was a photograph of the contributing writers. The editor informed the reader in his introductory note that this photograph had been taken in London, and only one of the writers in the photograph had journeyed from India—'and that was because he had been visiting his family; he lives in Washington, DC.'[1] The rest were living or traveling outside India's borders. This, of course, raises the question of, among other things, the class-profile of these writers working in English; however, that does not entirely exhaust the issue of how India does get narrativized in many significant ways from outside its own geographical space. It is this point that serves as a point of departure for this paper.

I

First, the West as a dream. And, its discovery as a dream—or as a nightmare—in the writing of those who have bitten into the fruit of the history of colonialism.

What is the entanglement of this writing with the contradictions of modernity? How does this narrative unravel in the lives—rather, in the lines—of writers of South Asian origin living in the West, writers like Hanif Kureishi and Salman Rushdie?

'Then a disturbing incident occurred which seemed to encapsulate the going-away fever.'[2] The incident that the London-based Kureishi is describing is of an 18-year-old girl in a Pakistani village called Chakwal. In the pages of a journalistic travelog, Kureishi tells us of the girl's dream one night—the villagers walking across the Arabian Sea to Karbala, where they found work and money.

I still say the West as a dream, even though these villagers were going only as far West as Saudi Arabia. That's where the more working class South Asians go, as the wealthy fly further west to the cities of Great Britain and North America.

1. Buford 1997: 6–8.
2. Kureishi 1987.

Following this dream, people from my village set off one night for the beach, which happened to be near my uncle's house in fashionable Clifton. Here lived politicians and diplomats in L.A.-style white bungalows with sprinklers on the lawns, Mercedes in the drives, and dogs and watchmen at the gates. On the beach, the site of barbecues and late-night parties, the men of Chakwal packed their women and children into trunks and pushed them into the sea. Then they followed them into the water in the direction of Karbala. Soon all but twenty of the potential *emigrés* were drowned. The survivors were charged with illegal immigration.

When Kureishi writes of what he calls the 'Gulf Syndrome'— 'a dangerous psychological cocktail consisting of ambition, suppressed excitement, bitterness and sexual longing'—his readers are treading a landscape that one could, in a kind of shorthand, call a place mined by the conflicts of development and desire. There is much to be examined and understood there, but let me insist on getting there by limiting our interest, as it were, to the operations of writing itself. How, then, does the dream of the 18-year-old girl, in a Pakistani village called Chakwal, reappear as another dream?

Part four of Salman Rushdie's novel, *The Satanic Verses*, is entitled 'Ayesha.' The first page of this section offers the words: 'Who is he? An exile. Which must not be confused with, allowed to run into, all the other words that people throw around: emigre, expatriate, refugee, immigrant, silence, cunning. Exile is a dream of glorious return. Exile is a vision of revolution. Elba, not St Helena.'[3] The revolution that is announced in the pages that follow—ending almost where the book ends, with a section called 'The parting of the Arabian sea'—is that of a woman, naked except for the butterflies that surround her bodies, leading her followers, a few of them rich but mostly poor, to their deaths in the rushing waters of the Arabian Sea. She has had a dream in which the Archangel Gibreel told her that they were all destined to go to Mecca by walking over water.

What is lost in this retelling? The modern appeal of the Gulf and its contradictory articulation through traditional underpinnings is turned by Rushdie into a tale of adequate flatness that is nothing more than a mystical narrative about the search for a mysterious God. In this retelling, the tantalizing lure, even the legitimating insignia of divinity, is provided only by the butterflies. There is no mention of the attraction of the Gulf which draws

3. Rushdie 1988.

millions of laborers from countries like India and Pakistan; those who as drivers, carpenters, servants, or nannies, provide service in the sheikdoms of the Middle East and other states in the area. Rushdie clearly could not have foreseen the spectacle of millions of displaced migrant workers stranded or wandering in the desert when the combined assault of Western Allied forces played havoc with the lives of those who are simply called 'contract labor' in the zones of shifting, global capital. But, nevertheless, the dream of the Gulf, suddenly reachable, giving faith to the poor in the village of Chakwal in Pakistan—and leading to that immense tragedy—is turned into a magical fable.

Jobs, development, and change are figures in the dream of a village girl. Why does this dream not appear in Rushdie's fiction as a narrative about immigration? The would-be immigrants suddenly begin to appear to us also as shadowy figures who populate the dreams that can be collectively identified as cosmopolitan fictions. In the case of Indian writers, most prominently Rushdie, magical realism has of course been 'positively' linked to the realities of the Indian subcontinent.[4] My own understanding of its use in Rushdie is closer to Gayatri Chakravorty Spivak's when she writes:

Whereas the topical caricature of the Bombay urban worlds of the popular film industry, of rhapsodic 'left' politics, of Muslim high society, of the general atmosphere of communalism, carries an idiomatic conviction, it is at least this reader's sense that so-called 'magical realism' becomes an alibi in the fabrication of Titlipur Chatnapatna, the village and the country town.[5]

In other words, magical realism is adopted by writers based in the West as a way of approaching and representing rural life, while things more familiar, like the details of life in the Indian cities, are rendered in a manner more familiar. In this mapping, modernity is located in the cities, while tradition reigns in the villages. Of course, from a different location, in opposition to such magical realist writings it is possible to see even in the dreams of village girls the displaced visions of development, of miraculous acts of flight and levitation, of roads to heaven, of bridges that fly over water.

4. Sangari 1987.
5. Spivak 1993.

In cosmopolitan fictions, it is often that one encounters what the editors of this volume decry, the symmetrical oppositions that create a binaristic universe divided between the rational urban folk and the benighted rural masses. This could be a result of the distance of an expatriate existence or, more plainly, the urban elite's distrust and distaste of the peasantry. Or something else entirely. In any case, Rushdie's representation in *The Moor's Last Sigh* of a rural populace thirsty for blood is nothing if not touched by fantasy in its apocalyptic vision that is at once manichean and homogenizing:

In the city we are for secular India but the village is for Ram. And, they say Ishwar and Allah is your name but they don't mean it, they mean only Ram himself, king of Raghu clan, purifier of sinnners along with Sita. In the end I am afraid the villagers will march on the cities and people like us will have to lock our doors and there will come a Battering Ram.[6]

And yet, is that all that can be said about the agency of such writing? In approaching the West as a dream, and its discovery as a dream or a nightmare in the works of authors of immigrant origins, I want to privilege the writing that carries a sharp consciousness of its own status as an artifice. In the new historiography that has been written about South Asia in recent years, a lot of attention has been given to the status of writing itself. Witness, for example, Gyan Prakash's declaration that 'the term postcolonial...refers to a position of reinscription, and its conditions of possibility imply the displacement of colonial discourses in the process of their dissemination.'[7] This idea of reinscription, the one that Rushdie characterized as the empire writing back, appears with a further twist in a short story entitled 'With your tongue down my throat' by Kureishi.[8]

6. This statement by Rushdie (1995)—even with its place as prophecy in the novel, with the narrative touching upon the demolition of the Babri Masjid by Hindu zealots in 1992—is to be challenged by pointing to works like Anand Patwardhan's *Ram ke Naam*, a brilliant documentary effort showing not only the heterogeneity of opinion among the masses but also their resistance.

For a critique of Rushdie's inability 'to conceive of a real possibility of regenerative projects on the part of the people who actually exist within our contemporary social reality,' see Ahmad 1992.

7. Prakash 1996.

8. Kureishi 1998b.

In Kureishi's story, the young, female narrator Nina, with a
Pakistani father and a white British mother, takes us through her
junkie days as a punk on the streets of London and then her visit
to her privileged father's home in Pakistan. In London, at the
Community Centre, the 'communists and worthies' are all over
her: 'I'm oppressed, you see, beaten up, pig-ignorant with an
arranged marriage and a certain suttee ahead.' On the streets, kids
harass her: 'Curry breath, curry breath, curry breath!' On her visit
to Pakistan, Nina accelerates through scenes from a neo-Orientalist's
fantasy: car accidents in which people literally lose their heads,
decadent parties, and streets filled with the requisite quota of
limbless beggars and shit under her shoes. Her authoritarian father
shows his affection by shouting at her: 'No, don't interrupt! A half-
caste wastrel, a belong-nowhere, a problem to everyone, wandering
around the face of the earth with no home like a stupid-mistake-
mongrel dog that no one wants and everyone kicks in the backside.'

The last section of the story begins with the words of Nina's
mother's lover, addressing us from his quarters in London, which
he calls his 'sock': 'Hello, reader. As I'm sure you've noticed by
now, I, Howard, have written this Nina and Nadia stuff in my
sock, without leaving the country, sitting right here on my spreading arse and listening to John Coltrane.... Do you think Nina
could have managed phrases like "an accent as thick as treacle"'.

Nina's voice is actually Howard's: 'So I became her, entered her.
Sorry.' Through this device, the story makes a simple point: the
postcolonial reinscription might, indeed, once again only be a
*re*inscription, a reinforcing of that which had first appeared about
to be displaced. This gesture not only calls attention to the scene of
writing; it seems to undermine the certainty of authoritative representations. The wily indeterminacy at play presents writing as a
performance.[9] In this theater of writing, we cannot get away without asking who is representing whom. I was earlier railing against

9. Consider Spivak 1993: 'Postcolonial women and men, in different ways,
utter metropolitan performatives on the stage of migrancy as they utter
'cultural-origin' performatives in a simultaneous shadow play; thus perhaps
revealing the constitutive theatricality of all performances.'
Spivak's argument, quite rightly, should place both Rushdie and Kureishi
in the realm of the performative. My own attempt, however, to play with
the ambiguities between the two positions is itself a performative gesture—
and its politics are a part of the paper's subject.

the use of writing in Rushdie to erase distance. Here, in Kureishi, what I am supporting is the use of writing to underline distance—distance, not as a given fact, but an unstable, questionable one.

The immigrant as if in a dream...

II

The device of a dream to cast doubt on authoritative certitudes is also a ploy of modernism. As Rushdie never tired of repeating in his defense of his novel *The Satanic Verses*, what readers had found insulting is actually narrated as a dream inside the head of a dying, slightly demented, Hindi film actor. More pointedly, Rushdie responded thus to an interviewer's question:

Everything we know is pervaded by doubt and not by certainty. And, that is the basis of the great artistic movement known as Modernism. Now the fact that the orthodox figures in the Muslim world have declared a jihad against Modernism is not my fault. It doesn't validate an entire way of looking at the world which is, to my mind, the most important new contribution of the 20th century to the way in which the human race discusses itself.[10]

For the purposes of this conversation, I want to posit that modernism—and that strand of it that today goes more commonly by the label of postmodernism—is the name for the rejection of totalizing universals. If we widen our category to include practices outside the aesthetic sphere, and certainly the practices outside the sphere called Europe, then these cultural practices would have as their telos what Dipesh Chakrabarty formulates as the goal of postcolonial historiography: 'The idea is to write into the history of modernity the ambivalences, contradictions, the use of force, and the tragedies and ironies that attend it.'[11] I do want to submit, however, that the aesthetic sphere remains a privileged, ideological space for the expression of doubts. The image of the individual artist, isolated and alone, beset with agonizing doubt, is very much a part of the modernist ethos. This is certainly true of characters in Kureishi's fiction, and even in Rushdie's, where the epic ambitions of his novels cannot always rule out the preoccupation with a single, main male protagonist.

10. Appignanesi and Maitland 1990.
11. Chakrabarty 1992.

In such a scenario, the question that takes shape is this: while the modernist immigrant writer/protagonist battles with doubt, what are the others doing?

In Kureishi's second novel, *The Black Album*, the protagonist and narrator Shahid lacks all conviction, while his fellow Asian Muslim brethren are full of passionate intensity.[12] This novel was written in the wake of the Rushdie affair. While the battle over the book rages around him, Shahid vacillates. He goes back and forth between his cultural studies tutor Deedee Osgood and the hardline preacher, Riaz. The tutor distrusts Shahid's Asian friends because 'they are devoid of doubt'; the preacher, Riaz, does not need anyone to tell him that there is only the truth and 'all fiction is, by its very nature, a form of lying.' Osgood becomes Shahid's lover and he dreams of composing an erotic story for her called 'The prayer-mat of the flesh.' In an act reminiscent of Rushdie's immigrant writer Salman who, in *The Satanic Verses*, rewrites the verses of the Prophet Muhammad, Shahid even rewrites Riaz's poems, inserting between his lines the odor of bodies in sexual heat. At the same time, however, seeing that 'everyone was insisting on their identity...Shahid, too, wanted to belong to his people.' But, when Rushdie's book gets burned by his friends in his college yard, Shahid's feelings begin to change. 'He wanted to crawl back to his room, slam the door and sit down with a pen; that was how he would reclaim himself.... He had been taught much about what he didn't like; now he would embrace uncertainty.'

The crowd that had burned the book, their faces had shown 'such ecstatic rigidity! The stupidity of the demonstration appalled him. How narrow they were, how unintelligent, how...embarrassing it all was!' Shahid asks himself whether he could think he was better only because he lacked the fervor. No, he replies to himself. 'He was not simple enough!' And yet, on the narrative's own evidence, the others are not so simple.

Shahid's fellow Asian Muslims are those who have brought their own brand of modernity in their suitcases. When a liberal Englishman turns up his nose at the condition of the projects, Riaz reminds him of the privileges that the people living there readily enjoy. 'And do you think our brothers in the Third World, as you

12. Kureishi 1995.

like to call most people other than you, have a fraction of this?
Do our villages have electricity? Have you ever seen a village?'
Modernity as an incomplete project, indeed!

Standing near the crowd that has come to get a glimpse of the
aubergine in which 'God had inscribed holy words,' Riaz asks
Shahid: 'Are you not with your people? Look at them, they are
from villages, half-literate, and not wanted here. All day they
suffer poverty and abuse. Don't we, in this land of so-called
free expression, have to give them a voice?' Isn't this portrayal of
the intellectual a part of modernity's political equation of representation and political institutions? In the same way, Shahid's
sister-in-law, the wealthy socialite, Zulma, represents modernity's
own complicitous, instrumental understanding of the ends of
irrationality: 'The peasants and all—they need superstition, otherwise they would be living like animals. You don't understand it,
being in a civilized country, but those simpletons require strict
rules for living, otherwise they would still think the earth sits
on three fishes.'

Hanif Kureishi's immigrants have brought with them their own
particular histories, which means that they carry as a part of their
baggage the burden of divided modernities. These include the
rationalities that, sometimes perversely and at other times not, run
counter to the rationalities of the colonizers. There are no easy,
or even predictable, distinctions to be made. In other works of
Kureishi, too, as in his screenplay for 'Sammy and Rosie Get Laid,'
there are fierce repudiations of one kind of modernity. When
Rafi grandly proclaims that he likes rebels and defiance, Alice pulls
him up short: 'You funny little fraud, you shot your rioters
dead in the street! The things we enjoy—Chopin, Constable,
claret—are a middle-class creation. The proletarian and theocratic
ideas you theoretically admire grind civilization into dust!' Earlier
in the film, Rafi, confronted by Rosie who had learned of the
tortures he sanctioned, reminds her not only of what has been
modernity's underside but also its origins: 'I come from a land
ground into dust by 200 years of imperialism. We are still
dominated by the West and you reproach us for using the methods
you taught us.' Modernity is up for grabs and its uses are open to
contestation. If we seek any further answers in the act of *The Black
Album*'s protaganist taking up a pen, what kind of materalist
framework might we provide those answers?

Early on in the novel, Deedee Osgood tells Shahid that he is a good student while most of the others are not. When he asks her the reason for the others, she gives him a thumbnail sketch of life under Thatcherism: 'Because they know there's no work. They're not being educated, just kept off the dole. I've never known such a lack of inner belief.' In a scenario where to find work is to find inner belief, Shahid's finding his vocation as a writer is also the discovery of an inner faith. In many ways, this comes only through a negotiation of the conflictual modernities: Prince, Madonna, neo-fascism, Thatcherism, drugs, Salman Rushdie and the Prophet, resurgent Islam, postcolonial diaspora.... And, it is impossible not to believe that it is a particular kind of community—human solidarities that are different, if not also opposed, to modernity's valorized mode of social association, citizens of a nation-state—that is being celebrated when the negotiation of such conflicts takes Shahid to the mosque where he finds a new world:

Men of so many types and nationalities—Tunisians, Indians, Algerians, Scots, French—gathered there, chatting in the entrance, where they removed their shoes and then retired to wash, that it would have been difficult, to tell which country the mosque was in.

Here, race and class barriers had been suspended. There were business-men in expensive suits, others in London Underground and Post Office uniforms; bowed old men in *salwar kamiz* fiddled with beads.... There were dozens of languages. Strangers spoke to one another. The atmo-sphere was uncompetitive, peaceful, meditative.[13]

Even if my recuperative reading is found acceptable, the question remains: is this, after all, only a community of men? In Kureishi's writings, although women do not necessarily step into public spaces of empowerment, lesbian as well as straight South

13. In an interview, Kureishi (1996: 34–8) described the kids he met and talked to at college near his house: 'Most of their parents had come here to work hard, to do well in Britain and make money for their families. The immigrant dream. But the dream had kind of run out quite quickly. In the sense that the kids didn't really believe it anymore. They were kind of disillusioned with England. They knew that it was difficult for them to get on—a lot of racism, bad housing, bad education, you know. They were right at the bottom of everything. So, fundamentalism really appealed to them because *it gave them a lot of strength and unity between them*. It was their own.' (emphasis mine).

Asian women often become the locus of resistance. In *The Buddha of Suburbia*, Jamila invites the narrator, Karim's, admiration and sometimes only a boyish misogyny; nonetheless, at the novel's end, Karim offers a fond eulogy:

Her feminism, her sense of self and fight it engendered, the schemes and plans she had, the relationships—which she desired to take this form and not that form—the things she had made herself know, and all the understanding this gave, seemed to illuminate her tonight as she went forward, an Indian woman, to live a useful life in white England.[14]

In the shared space of solidarity between Jamila and her mother, Jeeta, we see the forging of an autonomous sphere of modernity: 'But as the days passed I watched Jeeta's progress. She certainly didn't want to go home. It was as if Jamila had educated her in possibility, the child being an example to the parent.' In matters as mundane as the ambition to acquire a liquor license or to sell newspapers we find the outlines of immigrant dreams.

Even while calling into question the status of writing—or the status of the author in stories like 'With your tongue down my throat'—what Kureishi is also certainly doing elsewhere is calling attention to the act of writing—most prominently in a novel like *The Black Album*—as the site where immigrant experience is given shape. If the former gesture signals, in part, the absence of a community, the latter, I'm arguing, goes in search of one. In that role, it discovers in a whole range of places, the negotiation of mixed cultures of modernity. The new and the old—and the old and the very old or the very new—feed into each other, as in this description of West London that Kureishi offers in a diary he kept while his film was being made:

The music starts. The music is extraordinary. After years of colonialism and immigration and Asian life in Britain; after years of black American and reggae music in Britain comes this weird fusion. A cocktail of blues and R 'n' B shaken with Indian film songs in Hindi, cut with heavy guitar solos and electric violin runs and African drumming, a result of all the music in the world being available in an affluent Asian area, Southall, near Heathrow airport—it is Bhangra music! Detroit and Delhi, in London!

14. Kureishi 1990.

For a few seconds no one moves. The dance floor is a forbidden zone with everyone perched like tense runners around it. Then no one can hold themselves back. Men fly on to the floor.... Women and girls dance with each other; women dance with tiny babies.

And they all know each other, these people.[15]

Immigrant modernities are the processes whereby interstitial cultures take root and spread, in proliferating new forms. The writings that emerge from these contexts will, quite inevitably, be impure, unstable, indeterminate. More than other objects of criticism, the assessment of these writings gets done on the basis of a salient calculation: what are the consequences of this act—in saying this, what has the writer done? It means taking representation seriously.

That, to an extent, is also a pedagogical inquiry. I turn to that issue in the final section of this paper.

III

Stuart Hall has written that under threat from a globalizing postmodernity, ethnic movements can take either progressive or reactionary forms. Commenting on the latter trend, he writes: 'We have seen that happen: the refusal of modernity that takes the form of a return, a rediscovery of identity that constitutes a form of fundamentalism.'[16] Is there a lesson for the classroom here? At one level, Hall's move represents an argument for what we ask so often of our students and our colleagues: contextualization. Here, it means taking seriously the responsibility of examining 'reactive' phenomena as a part of modernity rather than any kind of regression in a vacuum.

At another level, the labor of contextualization—at least based on Hall's reasoning in the essay from which I've quoted above—is also the effort to map capitalism's 'contradictory terrain—precisely how particularity is engaged, how it is woven in, how it presents its resistances, how it is partly overcome, and how these overcomings then appear again.' With this in mind, one cannot remain with the idea that religion, for example, 'ought by now to have been modernized out of existence'; instead, what emerges as

15. Kureishi 1988a.
16. Hall 1997: 173–87.

a challenge is the task of explaining religion's shifting role, the differential logic of capital, and its production and exploitation of particularisms and difference.

Let me take up first, however, the issue of difference being reproduced as exoticism. Young Karim, in *The Buddha of Suburbia*, is trapped in the theater director Shadwell's *fixed* economy of difference. 'You've never had that dust in your nostrils?' he asks. Shadwell is disappointed that Karim has never visited the subcontinent:

What a breed of people two hundred years of imperialism has given birth to. If the pioneers from the East India Company could see you. What puzzlement there'd be. Everyone looks at you, I'm sure, and thinks: an Indian boy, how exotic, how interesting, what stories of aunties and elephants we'll hear now from him. And, you're from Orpington.

In another part of the book, though, Karim's representation of Anwar begets opposition from Tracey, a black performer in the group. Anwar is a shopkeeper from Bombay, raving in the streets of South London against the neo-fascists, and now on a hunger strike to force his daughter, Jamila, to go for an arranged marriage. Tracey's opposition is cogent and her questions directed politically—pedagogically—at what I had earlier called 'contextualization'; her responses to all of Karim's objections are nothing if not edifying:

Your picture is what white people already think of us. That we're funny, with strange habits and weird customs. To the white man we're already people without humanity, and then you go and have Anwar madly waving his stick at the white boys. I can't believe that anything like this could happen. You show us as unorganized aggressors. Why do you hate yourself and all black people so much, Karim?

This forces Karim, under pressure from the director Matthew Pyke, to change his choice of character. He decides to portray another friend, Changez. Changez is called Tariq in Karim's rewritten narrative; he has a crippled hand and an accent that 'would sound, to white ears, bizarre, funny and characteristic of India.' This performance of a character—'eagerly arriving at Heathrow with his gnat-ridden suitcase, having been informed in Bombay by a race-track acquaintance that you merely had to whisper the word "undress" in England and white women would start slipping out of their underwear'—is no less open to the criticisms that Tracey had provided regarding Anwar. But this time, Pyke does not allow Tracey to speak. He recommends a story line involving the immigrant in England: 'Girls fall for him all over the place because of his weakness and need to be mothered. So. We have class, race, fucking and farce. What more could you want as an evening's entertainment?' More than the exoticization, the feeling that stays with Karim—a feeling that must have been compounded by Pyke's absolute power of judgment—is the one of having betrayed, if not one's community, then one's friend. (Changez had threatened Karim: 'And if you try and steal me I can't see how we can be friends to talk to each other again!')[17]

The entry into the process of negotiating identities—one's own as an immigrant, and its relation to one's community, rather, communities—constitutes an attempt at contextualization. In Kureishi's case, this effort was being made in *The Black Album*. In that book, as I have mentioned before in this paper, Kureishi had presented the idea of 'writing' as the site where contradictions would be addressed and also seemingly resolved. In a short story, 'My Son The Fanatic,' first published in early 1994 in *The New*

17. In an interview conducted four years after the publication of the book, and soon after the release of its film version, Kureishi, who was being interviewed along with filmmaker Gurinder Chadha, had this to say about representating his community (Kureishi and Chadha 1994: 50-4):

HK: There isn't such a thing as an essential Asian experience any more than there is any other essential experience. Nobody's life can be reduced in that way.

GC: What's interesting now are the responses from the Asian community to our work. I didn't see Asians jumping up and down about *Buddha*, whereas ten years ago they did when *Laundrette* came out.

HK: They're getting used to it now. (laughter)

GC: They're getting used to it, used to...

HK: Used to being represented as gay drug dealers. (laughter)

GC: Of course, I am a good Indian girl so I'd never put sex or drugs in any of my work. But, you've smashed those definitions, so people can't jump up and down and say, he's being pejorative about the community. Well, who's the community? Is it Gin and Tonic from *Buddha*? Who is it?

HK: Well they exhausted themselves with *The Satanic Verses* as well.

GC: Exactly, that's the other thing.

HK: Which was the crisis and also the end of the crisis, really.

Yorker (but probably written around the same time as *The Black Album* which came out the following year), Kureishi explores the appeal of fundamentalism among the South Asian youth in Britain. Here, writing as artifice gives way in a more explicit sense to writing as a staging of politics and identity. Distance cannot be the primary fact in this story; its place has been taken by the demands of the surrounding society. The story is narrated from the position of the cab driver, Parvez. He is a nonplused father who, even though he is a Muslim, enjoys eating pork pies and drinking alcohol, and has as his principal confidante and friend a prostitute with a golden heart. The reader discovers—sharing the father's shock—the transformation of the son, Ali. Ali presents his reasons with confidence. And, his resolve is unyielding. Parvez, on the other hand, is fearful and distressed at the loss of his son. He becomes powerless, and, as we discover at the story's end, fanatical in his opposition to his son.

If the story performs the pedagogical task of contextualization, it is one that helps us understand in some measure the reactions to the publication of *The Satanic Verses*. It also calls into question any quick attribution of the charges of fanaticism. However, the central mode through which this point gets made is a fairly conventional one: the familiar device of the ironic and surprising twist at the end of the short story. Whether Kureishi wanted this or not, it is once again writing itself that functions as the response to contradictions. The form of the narrative allows the overturning, if not the resolution, of the crisis of ideology that the content of the narrative had opened up. Where would an insistence on an alternative pedagogy lead us? What form would such a strategy take?

A few days after Khomeini's *fatwa*, a letter written by one Inayatyllah Zaigham and published in the London newspaper, *Independent*, explained to the readers that Rushdie's was 'a serious crime against the Muslim Ummah (universal brotherhood of Muslims), much more serious than high treason is against a state of which one is a citizen.'[18] The analogy of the nation-state is being provided by the letter-writer as a universal category; the pedagogical truth, of course, lies in pointing out the limits of both. What is being excluded from the calculations of the nation-state and

18. Appignanesi and Maitland 1990.

from this brotherhood? Spivak's exhortation seems appropriate here: 'whenever they bring out the Ayatollah, remember the face that does not come together on the screen, remember Shahbano. She is quite discontinuous with Salman Rushdie's fate as it is being organized on many levels.'[19] When one sees only the well-known face, what also needs to be organized are more difficult truths.[20]

And, at the end of this paper, which began by talking about the immigrant as a dream...I must confess that I am haunted by what I remembered like a dream. I have this memory of a music-cassette playing on a friend's tape player. The time is that of the tyrannical regime of Zia-ul-Haq and Iqbal Bano is singing Faiz; although when I'm listening to the music, that time has passed and the time now is ordinary. I could have been drinking tea. *Hum dekhenge, laazim hai ke hum bhi dekhenge...* The words I can translate very roughly as 'We shall see/it is certain that we shall see/the day that has been promised/the one that has been written in destiny/when the mountains of tyranny and oppression/will be swept away like cotton...' The audience applauds, someone has removed their chains it seems. Everyone claps in unison. *Sab taj ucchaale jayenge, sab takht giraye jayenge...* 'All the crowns will be flung in the air, all thrones will be toppled to the ground...' Shouts and slogans punctuate the singing. The singer is singing that there will only be one name and that name will be Allah, but I am hearing her sing Zia is dead, long live democracy. There is no doubt about that at all. *Aur raj karegi khalq-e-khuda/ Jo main bhi hoon aur tum bhi ho....* 'And, the masses will be the rulers, the one that I am too and you are too.'

In this dreamscape—which is also what Arjun Appadurai would call a 'mediascape,' the subcontinent reterritorialized in a cassette

19. Spivak 1993.

20. 'Recently some NGOs had organized a big 150,000-strong meeting of poor people in Dhaka city where they criticized the macroeconomic policies, structural adjustments, World Bank policies, and also reminded the developmental community and the Bangladeshi government that the whole issue of poverty must not be forgotten. In the process they also criticized the rise of fundamentalism encouraged by this external funding. But when this same news was reported in some Canadian newspaper, the *Globe & Mail*, they said that it was a rally of 100,000 women protesting in Dhaka against fundamentalism, which is far from the complex truth.' (Mazhar 1997: 28–33)

playing in an immigrant's apartment in New York City—it is difficult for me to list all that I desire.[21] I am disturbed by the fact that the pressure that is there in the air in Pakistan when Iqbal Bano is singing—I imagine this to be happening in the night—is imagined by me to be here too, around me, in this city. And, I am not sure whether it is indeed because I have thought about the need to produce secular readings about South Asian lives in the diaspora. But, what it undeniable is the feeling of liberation when I imagine something as irrational as a crown tossed in the air, hanging there above the shouts and slogans for democracy.

References

Ahmad, Aijaz, 1992. 'Salman Rushdie's *Shame*'. In Aijaz Ahmad, *In Theory*. New York: Verso.

Appadurai, Arjun, 1996. *Modernity at Large*. Minneapolis: University of Minnesota Press.

Appignanesi, Lisa and Sara Maitland (eds.), 1990. *The Rushdie File*. Syracuse: Syracuse University Press.

Buford, Bill, 1997. 'Declarations of Independence.' *The New Yorker* 73 (23 and 30 June): 6–8.

Chakrabarty, Dipesh, 1992. 'Postcoloniality and the artifice of history: Who speaks for "Indian Pasts?"' *Representations* 37: 1–26.

Hall, Stuart, 1997. 'The local and the global: Globalization and ethnicity.' In Anne McClintock, Aamir Mufti and Ella Shohat (eds.), *Dangerous Liaisons: Gender, Nation and Postcolonial Perspectives*. Minneapolis: University of Minnesota Press.

Kureishi, Hanif, 1987. 'Erotic politicians and mullahs.' *Granta* (17): 140–51.

———, 1988a. *Sammy and Rosie Get Laid. The Screenplay and the Screenwriter's Diary*. New York: Penguin.

———, 1988b. 'With your tongue down my throat.' *Granta* (22). Reprinted in Hanif Kureishi, 1997. *Love in a Blue Time*. New York: Scribner.

———, 1990. *The Buddha of Suburbia*. London: Faber and Faber.

———, 1995. *The Black Album*. New York: Scribner.

———, 1996. Interview with Jessica Hagedorn. *SAMAR* (Summer): 34–8.

Kureishi, Hanif and Gurinder Chadha, 1994. Interview with Lawrence Chua. *BOMB* (Summer): 50–4.

21. Appadurai 1996.

Mazhar, Farhad, 1997. Interview with Gayatri Chakravorty Spivak. *SAMAR* (Winter): 28–33.

Prakash, Gyan, 1996. 'Who's afraid of postcoloniality?' *Social Text* 49: 187–203.

Rushdie, Salman, 1988. *The Satanic Verses*. New York: Viking.

———, 1990. Interview by Bandung File on 27 January 1989. Reprinted in Lisa Appignanesi and Sara Maitland (ed.), *The Rushdie File*. Syracuse: Syracuse University Press.

———, 1995. *The Moor's Last Sigh*. New York: Vintage Books.

Sangari, Kumkum, 1987. 'The politics of the possible'. *Cultural Critique* (7): 157–86.

Spivak, Gayatri Chakravorty, 1993. 'Reading *The Satanic Verses.*' In Gayatri Spivak, *Outside in the Teaching Machine*. New York: Routledge.

16

Policing and Erasing the Global/Local Border: Rajasthani Foresters and the Narrative Ecology of Modernization

PAUL ROBBINS

In an era when germplasm from Indian vegetables finds its way into cucumbers shelved in the produce sections of North American supermarkets[1] and North American mesquite trees are a favored plantation species across India,[2] it would seem to make little sense to distinguish global and local environments or environmental knowledges. And yet, genes and species, like globally mobile advertisements, currencies, and ideas, are all forced to a temporary halt in real-world locations where they are appropriated, contested, strained, and rearticulated before being set loose again into the circuitry of hypermodern culture and economics. At these places, species are selected, capital is fixed, and television programs are interpreted, all in ways that defy a 'globalization' of knowledge, society, and culture; the global is folded into local reality and specific and distinctive forms emerge. These regional sites are not simply the locations where universal driving forces of modernization act on local particularities. Rather, they become the locations where modernity is itself produced and transnational and local discourses, resources, and power relations are concretized into

1. USDA 1971.
2. Hocking 1993.

practices.[3] At these sites, global and local ecologies are highlighted in their collision.

Nowhere is this more apparent than in the encounter of development-focused global narratives of environmental change with local accounts of ecological transformation. On the one hand, stories of development allied with global institutions of development reflect emergent concerns with 'eco-friendly' and 'sustainable' development where a 'global agenda' directs and solves 'global' environmental 'problems.' In that context, inchoate notions of nature and resources that previously dominated the planners' imagination are increasingly turned into the concrete technocratic category of 'environment.'[4] In this global development story, the vocabulary is one of loss and recovery and of ongoing struggle against an abstract tide of degradation. In narratives common to more local development scenes, on the other hand, awareness and articulation of the politics of ecology and resources are in increasing evidence, but its language takes a different form. Whether in struggles over logging,[5] dam-building[6] or community pasture,[7] local narratives of environment are often geared around the politics and control of domesticated ecology and 'rights to nature.'[8] These narratives of 'access and control' contrast starkly with more global stories of 'decline and rescue.'

In the daily business of development, these distinctions between global and local make no sense. Most people live in a reality lodged within both the story of loss, preservation, and recovery as well as that of access, use, and control. This is especially true of environmental specialists, bureaucrats, and managers who live at the intersection of these interpretations. At the location between the two, where professionals interpret local and global stories, 'global environment' is seeded with elements of 'local ecology' and vice versa. The resulting interpretations, moreover, take the form of real-world hybrid forms: tree-planting, fence-building, irrigation, and well-digging. The encounter of competing development stories in the minds of the professional is, in this way, written into the landscape.

3. Sivaramakrishnan and Agrawal, this volume.
4. Yapa 1996; Sachs 1992.
5. Shiva 1988; Guha 1989.
6. Baviskar 1995.
7. Brara 1987.
8. Hanna et al. 1996.

This paper explores the encounter of these competing stories of environment and development in the arid state of Rajasthan, India. The encounter of global and local discourses of the environment is here shown to produce a unique and regional form of modernity. Here, the terms global and local do not refer to spatial scales of activity or process, as in 'the global market.' Rather, they are understood as discrete discursive locations where knowledges, categories, and languages about the world are produced and naturalized. The encounter of 'global' and 'local' is shown to dissolve here, through the experience of state forestry officers who produce a regional ecology of decline, rescue, access, and control. In negotiating this terrain, foresters act as interpreters and brokers who change the material character of regional landscapes and the trajectory of biotic change. In this way, the process that links discourse to experience, behavior, and material environmental transformation is shown to be one not only of development, but of a specific and regional form of modernization.

The paper is divided into three parts. It begins with a survey of the global story of ecological decline and intervention that characterizes contemporary environmental discourse. This is followed by an exploration of the politics of control that dominates local discourses of environmental change. Using the case study of a local forester, the third section examines the position of the environmental manager between these stories of environmental change, investigating the material outcomes of this tension, in terms of expanding and contracting species on the ground in western Rajasthan. So, even while the agenda of modern state action is predicated on adjudicating and separating global environmental concerns from local subsistence ones, the reality of the landscape is a blurring of any such distinction.

Finally then, if the fictive partition between the global and the local is undermined by the actual practice of those who are supposed to enact it, what are the politics of mapping the emergence of such regional modernities? The essay concludes by suggesting that efforts to map the regional forms of modernity subvert the partitioned patterns of capitalized and institutionalized power by raising the possibility that, following Bruno Latour,[9] we might never have been modern at all.

9. Latour 1993.

THE LANGUAGE OF 'GLOBAL'
ENVIRONMENTAL CHANGE

In the period since the United Nations Conference on Environment and Development (UNCED) at Rio in 1992, the sources and solutions of environmental problems has been thrust onto the center of the world stage. At the same time, however, the character of nature and of the ecological problems facing people throughout the world has been significantly transformed. Where before politicians had spoken of local and regional problems ranging from the loss of forest cover to the decline in water quality, now they spoke of a global environment in crisis. As Sachs observed, 'Nature, when she becomes the object of policy and planning, turns into environment.'[10] Now defined as a global problem, a host of solutions attended, ranging from global agreements to technocratic interventions. What had previously been regionally defined problems came into the purview of a 'Global Ecocracy' to manage 'sustainable development.'[11]

GLOBAL ENVIRONMENTAL DISCOURSE

Beyond the political questions of state sovereignty and local control of resources that this change entailed,[12] one of the central features of this change was the imposition of a unified narrative of environmental change, based on an assumption of degradation and a definition of restoration and rescue. The environment was described as under siege and in need of management. Global environmental problems were to be identified and prioritized and responses were to be engineered. From 'Losing Ground' to 'Our Common Future'[13] a story of decline and salvation was established by academics, politicians, and international development agencies.

This discourse of loss and recovery was in no way novel at Rio, and reflects many of the historical narratives based in a colonial science of control. Historically, these exercises in conservation often focused on the perceived extensive degradation of nature at

10. Sachs 1992: 34.
11. Sachs 1992; Escobar 1996.
12. Surveyed elsewhere in Gadgil and Guha 1992.
13. Eckholm 1976; World Commission on Environment and Development 1987.

the hands of locals and 'the belief that science was capable of unlocking redemptive and regenerative forces on a vast scale.'[14] By offering a degraded and recoverable view of nature, colonial authorities consolidated their power. In South Asia, the East India Company established a brand of colonial science as an arm of empire building that rationalized resources, assured a boom in monoculture and mining, and cemented the idea of managed nature.[15] By articulating the environment as a problem, the state, through its science, justifies its existence and extends its control.[16]

This perspective on nature and conservation carried over from colonial activities to those of the Independence-era state in India. Most prominently, Indian foresters extend their 'discretionary power' through the identification of environmental problems (fuelwood crises, shifting sand dunes, etc.), and their scientific resolution.[17] In the post-Independence era of development, the state would target the crisis of deforestation as a central project.[18] Significantly, issues of resource control and management authority are not articulated in the explanation of the project. Instead, the normative degradation of the resource and its protection in the public trust is emphasized throughout. In this way both colonial conservation science and postcolonial global environmental management share a common narrative thread. In both cases, the environment is understood to be degraded and in need of rescue. The imperatives of such a task justify interventions, secure funding, and extend control. In the case of arid India, where environmental crises like drought and desertification are common tropes in governance, these themes are especially clear.

These forms of knowledge have traditionally been defined as 'global,' largely because of the power and momentum of global-scale institutions in forming and reinforcing them. The global funding and global reach of its advocates include the International Monetary Fund and the World Bank.[19] Even so, such knowledges, as will become apparent later, are in no way 'global' in the sense of their being universal, hegemonic, or inevitable.

14. MacKenzie 1990: 6.
15. Kumar 1990.
16. Nandy 1990.
17. Gadgil and Guha 1995: 153.
18. Haeuber 1993.
19. Lele *et al.* 2000.

Defining the Landscapes of 'Global' Environmental Planning

In the planning documents that characterize the 'global environment' perspective of nature in India, the environment is repeatedly invoked as a landscape of 'tragedy,' succumbing to drought, overpopulation, and degradation. In Rajasthan, a consensus on the character and causes of this environmental change is emerging from the expert community. Desertification and deforestation are described throughout the region and remediation efforts are central concerns of the manager-state.[20] The definitions of environmental change used in these efforts, however, draw on exogenous understandings of the landscape which drive and direct planning to specific ends.

Such understandings have long been a part of environmental development of the region, dating from forestry interventions made during the pre-Independence period. Conservation in the post-Independence era therefore grows indirectly from long-standing traditions in the princely states.[21] The states of Marwar, Jaisalmer, and Bikaner in western Rajasthan, though governed by independent rulers during the colonial period, fell under residency administration; colonial experts and officials typically set the terms of environmental management and were employed to assess and operate forest resources. With the first survey of Marwar's forest in 1887, for example, the British assistant conservator of forests in Ajmer loaned his services to the state to outline a conservation scheme to counter the perceived 'reckless destruction by man' in the region.[22] This required the enclosure of forests, the setting of fines, and the implementation of fire control throughout the region. Thus, for more than a century, there has been a sustained call for action against the disappearing forest and the spreading desert, implemented as a regime of landscape management.

There is certainly evidence to support the claim of environmental degradation. Surveys of villages throughout the western part of Rajasthan reveal a wide range of important local tree species as vanishing or declining.[23] This supports the results of previous

20. Chouhan 1995; Mabbut and Floret 1980.
21. Gold 1997.
22. State of Marwar 1887: 26.
23. Robbins 1998a.

resource surveys and detailed ethnographic work throughout the state that suggest a precipitous decline in important tree and grass species, including khejri (*Prosopis cineraria*) and bordi (*Ziziphus nummularia*) trees and the important sevan (*Lasiuris sindicus*) and dhaman (*Cenchrus spp.*) grasses.[24] All of these species are crucial to local production systems by providing fuel, fodder, medicine, famine-foods, and building materials. These species also serve significant functions in the scrub forest ecosystem. Many of these trees create microclimatic conditions important for the development of undergrowth[25] and most play an important role in the preservation of local animal species. Some form of environmental change is in evidence. The definition of this change, however, varies in the telling.

For the official estimations of environmental change that follow the global environmental model, categories for forest land reflect definitions of forest imported to the region; categories including 'good' forest cover and 'dense forest canopy' are typical.[26] Under such a definition, it is hardly surprising that forestry officials conclude that 'the region has hardly any natural forests.'[27] The employment of these categories in Rajasthan is highly problematic, however, and features of the region's arid ecology make this definition of forest difficult. The tree cover of the area is an open scrub, with fluctuating productivity between years of good and bad rainfall.[28] The annual monsoon, given to failure every four or five years, produces grass cover that lies dormant in root or seedstock and tree cover that may be leafless for long periods. This growth may occur even after long periods where the landscape appears bare or denuded. Additionally, traditional land use practices involve the mixing of wild grasses and trees with domesticated cultivars so that pastures and fields are scattered with trees and herbaceous coverage.[29] These uneven periods of biotic production, coupled with complex land use patterns, make the identification and management of forest resources in Rajasthan difficult. Nevertheless, by defining forest cover in the narrow terms of 'closed canopy,' a

24. Kumar and Bhandari 1992, 1993.
25. Ahuja 1980; Gupta and Saxena 1978.
26. Chakraborty 1994.
27. Mathur 1988: 278.
28. Kumar and Bhandari 1992; Dhir 1987; Sen 1990; Bhandari 1990.
29. Robbins 1988b.

discourse of degradation necessarily emerges. Clearly, under increasing pressure, if such closed cover forest ever existed, it is certainly in decline. Understood in global terms and with the imagined eye of the satellite, deforestation is a regional problem.

By defining the problem in these terms, certain solutions become paramount. First, where forest is best represented by 'closed canopy' cover, a disturbance-free environment is necessary for forestry in this densely populated desert region. Seen in the global language of decline, 'India's best forests are represented by reserved forests.'[30] It is therefore essential to create and institute closed 'reserved forests' by cordoning and enclosing resources. Second, defined as a heavily managed ecological space, this forest is given to expert control. Thus, 'the forest department is the key actor in the care of and management of the forest land.'[31] Third, the central task of this state instrument is to rescue the land. Afforestation is the natural tool to face the crisis. Defined as 'the establishment of a forest...on an area not previously forested...or where other land-use patterns have dominated the landscape for many generations,'[32] afforestation means the transformation of non-forest lands into forested ones, despite any existing systems of communal use and tenure.

In sum, defined in the terms of global crisis, the environmental problem of the region is the decline of closed canopy tree communities. The solution is the implementation of expertise, the seizure of land to be rescued, and the promulgation of vast plantations on lands that may or may not have ever been under such cover. The effects of such a policy are hard to measure, but Rajasthani landscapes are clearly changing.

The Case of Afforestation in Rajasthan

The efforts of the state in this regard appear to have produced significant and tangible results. Census data from the region reveals trends in forest cover, as defined by forest department statisticians (Table 16.1). In the westernmost districts of the state in the period following Independence, forest cover has increased dramatically, outpacing the national average by several times.

30. Chakraborty 1994.
31. Ibid.
32. Dunster and Dunster 1996.

TABLE 16.1
Land use change (in hectares) in western
Rajasthan (Barmer, Bikaner, Jaisalmer,
Jodhpur, and Pali districts), 1976–98

	Forest	Waste
1976	155,812	25,260,929
1980	177,020	20,327,976
1985	180,050	15,548,246
1992	196,350	10,952,906
1998	214,568	6,775,021
1976–8	+37.7%	–73.2%

In fact, much of this change reflects only a transformation on paper. These statistics reflect the expansion of land under the authority of the forest department less than a net increase in actual closed forest cover. The simultaneous decrease in 'wasteland' in the region reflects a loss of local tree cover and pasturage species to expanding cultivation. The species planted in emerging forests, on the other hand, are largely foreign, are integrated poorly into the regional ecology, and meet far fewer of the production demands than indigenous species.[33] Nevertheless, by invoking the language of crisis, defining the land in a way that demands remediation, and organizing a vast bureaucracy for rescue, the forest department has undertaken the 'Promethean' role of 'eco-cratic' experts. The statistical expansion of forests, therefore, more accurately reflects the expansion of forest department authority and power than forest cover per se. The global definition of environmental change, in this way, takes form in the landscape. In the process, the control and remediation of ecological crisis is fitted to the framework of international development, embodied in the 'managed' future forged in manifestos like that of the 1989 report of the World Commission on Environment and Development or The Brundtland Report.[34] The expansion of forest department control throughout Rajasthan is not simply a state exercise in the definition and control of resources; it embodies a vision of development articulated in a global context.

It would be romantic, however, to assume that global narratives of the environment were somehow inherently less 'accurate' and

33. Robbins 1998a.
34. Sachs 1992.

'truthful' than local ones. Just as colonial and postcolonial narratives of ecological change are lodged in the national and international politics of development, so too are local accounts of nature and its transformation situated in struggles over resources and the daily political economy of village life.

THE LANGUAGE OF 'LOCAL' LANDSCAPE STRUGGLE

Accounts of environmental change exchanged locally, like those of currency in global institutions, take narrative form. Unlike the global stories of decline and amelioration, however, local accounts of environmental change are focused on the shifting control of resources and the crises of access. In discussions of the landscape that occur in kitchens, tea shops, and fields, stories usually dwell upon local actors participating in a struggle for resources that results in landscape change or degradation. In many cases, this local story begins in a past that is stable and productive, where the key players, usually prominent families or caste communities, live in tense harmony. These communities are then described as violating norms in resource use, destabilizing institutional systems and, in the process, acting to change the landscape, destroy ground cover, or deny access. Local narratives, in this way, often follow a pattern of blame and end with calls to justice or equity. Significantly, the players who receive attention and the causes of change vary greatly with the narrator. Indeed, the position of the narrator, in terms of gender, occupation, or caste, affects the story greatly. In most all cases, however, the politics of blame are common. The case of a degraded grove in western Rajasthan is demonstrative.

Stories of Conflict and Control: The Case of a Jajwara's Oran

The village of Jajwara (name substituted) is located in the southwestern part of Rajasthan, in the center of Barmer district, formerly the princely state of Marwar. Phyto-geographically it is typical of the region, dominated by khejri (*Prosopis cineraria*) and ker (*Capparis decidua*) trees, and shrubs including phog (*Calligonum polygonoides*), and aak (*Calatropis procera*), and the valuable graze, sevan grass (*Lasiuris sindicus*). It is a large village with a relatively small and sparse population. The dominant *jatis* in the village include Rajputs, the traditional landlord families of the area, Meghwals, an economically marginal leather-working community, and Jats, powerful farming families.

Despite the relatively low population per unit of community land, Jajwara has experienced heavy degradation of its commons, especially its *oran*, a semi-sacred village forest. According to reports by a variety of members from different communities, the large oran was, only a decade before, rich in ker and khejri trees with an understory of fodder grasses and shrubs. A survey of the 'oran' area reveals an open plain, some two or three square kilometers in size, with few trees standing and little in the way of grass or shrub cover. The area is dense with stumps, predominantly of mature ker trees, though including some khejri and bordi trees; 88 percent (176 out of 200 sampled) trees are stumped or have been cut heavily. Many of the stumps appear fresh. The damage inflicted on the scrub forest here was swift, extensive, and recent.

Accounts concerning what happened to the oran differ from community to community. Conversations with tehsil officials, local rajputs, and village meghwals, reveal three distinct histories of the oran's demise. Significantly, none of the groups explained the destruction as a result of population growth. Most vocally recognize that their community lands are considerably larger than most villages in the region.

Rajputs in the village represent the inherited legacy of *jagir* authority. Jajwara was the administrative center for a feudal holding (jagir) including several nearby villages. The family of the local lord (*takor*) who governed here, still lives in the village and holds large areas of land. Interviewed rajputs generally report that it is the disintegration of the jagir system, coming with Independence, that has created the problem. Meghwals and other poorer families, according to interviewed rajputs, started cutting ker trees for fuelwood from the oran as soon as they realized there would be no sanction from traditional authorities. According to members of this group, the local governing body, the *gram panchayat*, is not respected and known the way the takor was. For rajputs, the transition from jagir authority has created an institution that lacks community respect. Control of the resource has shifted and new production demands have depleted the resource.

The meghwal community lives mostly in clustered households (*dhanis*), fairly distant from the oran and village center. They generally collect fuel and construction wood from surrounding fields. In interviews, several meghwal men admit to cutting in the oran in the last few years. They explain however, that they did so only after the land had been 'enclosed' by the gram panchayat, dominated by a *rajput sarpanch*. They report that rajputs began cutting bordi and ker trees for household use and sale outside the village soon after the gram panchayat declared that the land was protected by the government. There was concern that rajput families would lay claim to the resources quickly if other families did not get their share immediately. Unable to gain redress in the official forum, they joined the rajputs in cutting. The results, they say, are unfortunate but part of a general trend in corruption and loss of accountability.

Meghwal women interviewed describe the cutting as largely conducted by men of varying caste communities, mainly harvesting the ker trees for construction materials. The loss of browse and fruits from these trees puts extra burdens on their daily work. Men's control over the resource, they insist, has increased in recent years and they lament the declining beliefs in religious sanctions that traditionally held cutting in check. They insist that they would never cut in the oran, since the act would be an affront to Nagnichi, the local manifestation of the goddess whose shrine sits on the edge of the oran.

It is impossible to assess any truth of these claims in great detail as the oran is effectively destroyed and many of the events described by the people of Jajwara happened several years before. Elements of these stories reflect changes throughout the region. Secularization has reduced some of the power of culturally legitimate authority and the coercive power of the goddess. The transition from jagir authority has reduced the socially legitimate and hegemonic power of the elite rulers. Caste-based divisiveness of gram panchayat institutions has paralyzed the political power of that governing body. These have all played a part in many of the failed institutions in the region. More significant than the verification of one or another explanation of change, however, the stories all share key elements of a local language of production. The losses are articulated in terms of important local species, and the problem for all claimants is not a question of forest cover loss so much as it is a crisis of access and control and problem of production and resources. This pattern reflects what Agrawal describes as 'I don't want it but you can't have it,'[35] the local resource politics in evidence elsewhere in the region.

All these stories might be considered local insofar as they represent a form of account that dominates, with relative stability (in its tropes and morals), over 'local' time and space. While not monolithic, these narratives of environmental change wield influence on a local scale, but they also enforce their own categories and priorities. Like the 'global' narrative, the local one is connected through the power-laden process of narrative politics. Again, however, the global and local are not physical places or isolated processes; they are spaces where discrete discourses are produced and naturalized. Their apparent isolation from one another is enforced through modern modes of explanation, where differing forces are thought to be arrayed at discrete scales.

When traced in the real world, however, these discourses do not operate in isolation. Instead, they encounter one another and interact, giving rise to the material interactions and landscapes experienced on the ground. The case of the Rajasthani forester shows the tensions and outcomes of this struggle between competing definitions of the environment, and subverts the notion of isolated and discrete forms of knowledge.

RAJASTHANI FORESTERS IN REGIONAL MODERNITY

Foresters in Rajasthan occupy a position where the environmental story of decline and rescue competes with the language of production and control. By articulating and acting upon these category systems, these professionals have a significant impact on the political and ecological conditions of the area. The selection of species and implementation of programs, modified by what foresters perceive as local needs or conditions, recreates the region's biota through large-scale plantation.

Placing Foresters

Despite the prominence of these foresters in interpreting environmental meaning and altering the landscape, they are largely

35. Agrawal 1994.

understudied. This follows a more general pattern in analysis of environment and development. Despite the importance of development officers, foresters, and extension agents in contemporary political ecology, little work is done on understanding their role.[36] For environmental studies, this is partly because the processes of degradation are understood to be the products of interaction between local producers and structural forces. In the dominant models of political ecology, explanations of change are focused on the way producers exploit or overexploit natural resources in responses to pressures in the economic and institutional setting. Investigations into questions of landscape change in the dominant paradigm of development research, therefore, seek overgrazing herders and soil depleting farmers.[37] In such a theorization, the development official is seen simply as an instrument of state power, with little agency or efficacy.[38]

Additionally, this silence also reflects more fundamental biases in geography, anthropology, and development studies that focus analysis on the 'periphery' in the domain of an exotic 'Other.' The official is often considered too culturally, economically, and politically proximate to the researcher to be a valuable subject of study. By eliding the developmental or environmental professional, troubling neo-colonial hierarchies are reproduced through orientalist ethnography in this way.[39]

Recent work has provided some exceptions to this trend. Dove's analysis of local foresters in Pakistan demonstrates the power of the official in interpreting and focusing development priorities.[40] Springer's analysis of agricultural extension in southern India demonstrates the way institutional forms and priorities effect the ideas and actions of development officers.[41] Gururani's examination of the Indian forest guard, shows him to be enmeshed in local networks and relationships.[42] So too, Brodt's analysis of the encounter of global and local science demonstrates the specific regional hybrids formed in expert environmental practice during

36. Dove 1994.
37. Blaikie and Brookfield 1987.
38. Dove 1994; Fairfax and Fortmann 1990.
39. Said 1978; Marcus 1986.
40. Dove 1994.
41. Springer 2000.
42. Gururani 2000.

the process of development.[43] These studies reveal the situated knowledges and actions of professionals and explain many of the successes and failures of environmental amelioration programs through a better understanding of professional cultures and knowledges. They show that officials can independently effect the outcome of development but also that these professionals are constrained by larger institutional and political structures.

The Position of the Rajasthani Forester

The application of such approaches to officials in western Rajasthan is made imperative by the unique position occupied by the local state forester. Here, the state forest department represents the only prominent environmental development organization of any type. Foresters act as important vehicles of environmental change, serving both as independent agents as well as constrained representatives of institutional culture and the political bureaucracy. This is reflected in the recruitment and advancement policies of the forest department. Rajasthani state forestry is notable for its recruitment of local talent from within the region and, at the entry level, many of the foresters come from the areas where they manage afforestation projects. At the same time, as foresters continue to advance through the bureaucracy, their advancement is pinned to following expectations from extra-local agencies. Their own notions of appropriate tree cover, significant species, and ecological process are all reformed to fit the modeled forest of state planning. Thus, while recruiting regional expertise amongst its foresters, the bureaucratic structure of the forest department creates a language-world and priority system that devalues local concepts and approaches to arid ecology on the part of its agents. Imposing the knowledge system of state forestry through exogenous categories of 'forest,' the forest department recreates the ecological imagination of the forester. As local people located in larger institutional structures, foresters are thus the targets as well as the agents of global environmental discourse in Rajasthan. The previously described models of fast-growing, 'closed canopy' forest, designed to rescue the land from degradation, are not only

43. Brodt, this volume.

implemented by these officers, they are internalized and natural-ized by them.

The case of one such officer is illustrative of the dilemma of the local forester and shows, at the level of the individual, 'systems of knowledge as systems of domination.'[44] Dayal Lal Chaudri (name substituted) is the forest department range officer for the Shiv Tehsil (sub-district) of Barmer district in southwest Rajasthan. He is a local man who has worked his way up through the forest department hierarchy over the last decade. He had previously worked in the position of forester and hopes to be promoted to the district forest office in the next few years. At that time, he may be moved out of the region and transferred to another part of the state where a position becomes available. Unlike national officials, the training of state foresters like Chaudri is limited and involves considerably less extensive indoctrination than is typical in the Indian state bureaucracy.

Generally the structure of the department's bureaucracy limits the ecological decisions made by Chaudri and other foresters and range officers. The Central District Forest Office uses models drafted in Dehra Dun or at the Central Arid Zone Research Institute (CAZRI) and drafts plans from these. These models lay out the 'targets' for quantity and coverage, determine the choice of species used in plantations, and identify the areas for develop-ment. The central office oversees the success of projects and organizes the promotion of 'successful' foresters and range officers. Range officers choose the distribution of projects, oversee planting and transport, and choose the mix of species from those allowed by the central office. As Chaudri puts it, range officers 'just get the trees where they are going' but it is clear that key decisions effecting land cover are made here in the middle-strata of the bureaucracy. Working under the officers are the local foresters, who oversee plantation labor and distribute work to planters, *chowkidars*, and waterers. These are almost always local men, who know the ecology and social situation in the area.

Figure 16.1 shows the configuration of decision-making and responsibility in the Rajasthan state forest department. The bureau-cracy is more than simply a 'top-down' configuration of decision-making. The structure is also an information system that limits

44. Cashman 1991.

and controls the flow of knowledge into the decision framework and so determines the priorities and choices throughout. Social information and local ecological categories and priorities are sometimes incorporated into the implementation of plantations by the forester, who might hire preferentially, or change slightly the species mix in a plantation based on local conditions. At the same time, priorities from the central office descend the bureaucracy and set the larger agenda for local plantations. The two knowledge systems collide at the level of the local forester and the range officer.

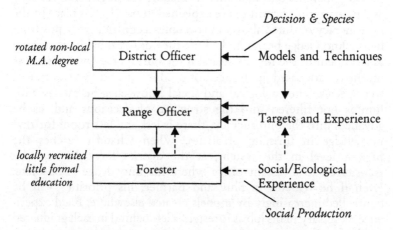

FIGURE 16.1: Flow of decisions and information in state forest bureaucracy (following Robbins 1998a).

This collision is directly reflected in the way Chaudri thinks about and describes regional ecology. In a series of interviews about plantation, landscape change, and the value of fodder grasses and indigenous tree species in the region, Chaudri reveals the contradictory perspectives mandated through his social and institutional position. When discussing sevan (*Lasiuris sindicus*) and khejri, he extols the virtues of local species: 'sevan grass [is] a gift from god for the desert.' A few moments later, he describes sevan as a 'weed' that has to be removed in order to maximize production and growth rate of plantation trees. A few minutes after describing khejri as 'the most useful tree in the desert,' he explains that if it were up to him, he would only plant *Prosopis juliflora, Acacia nimbica*, and *Acacia tortilis*, all exogenous species. He points out that several local grass and tree species are useful for pastoral producers, providing fodder and serving a range of important uses. Planting species that have little fodder value and that are poorly compatible with understory development, he explains, serves the interests of non-pastoral households better than those of regional pastoral castes like Sindhi and Raika. Nevertheless, he insists, *juliflora* and *tortilis* trees, even with leaves that are unpalatable to animal species and germination inhibitors that stunt grass growth, are 'benefiting the people' through plantation.

The apparent contradictions in Chaudri's ecological impressions and intervention priorities are explained in part by his place in the bureaucracy outlined above. He occupies a contradictory position; he is a knowledge bearer and a long-time desert inhabitant, as well as a resident of the middle strata of the bureaucracy where success incentives are based upon speed of production and survival rate of tree species. The ecological and social knowledge he carries with him is not filtered into the structure of decisions and, as he advances into the bureaucracy, there is less and less room for that knowledge in forming priorities. When Chaudri reaches the highest level in the system, at the district level, he may be transferred to a distant office where his knowledge is obsolete. Even if he remains in Shiv and Barmer, his priorities will be controlled increasingly by models created elsewhere. Field experience, necessary in his job as forester, is left behind in each graduated level of authority and a new set of underlying logics come to colonize his concept of the landscape. Plants previously considered appropriate become nuisances, areas with indigenous species cover become degraded. Chaudri's professional development results in the recreation of his fundamental categories of environmental perception.

The experience of the forester reflects Douglas' assertion that 'the entrenching of an idea is a social process' wherein, 'the simple acts of classifying and remembering are institutionalized.'[45] Fundamental analogies underlying his understanding of the environment are transformed in this way. Species in the local vernacular, for example, traditionally are identified as either hot or cold, edible or toxic, and auspicious or inauspicious. In occupying his

45. Douglas 1986.

institutional position, Chaudri has come to identify and value species based on a new set of binaries: slow or fast growing and high or low value. These analogies undergird new categories that better fit the notion of a forest offered by the state. Such a forest has a closed canopy, produces quickly, serves specific uses, and is in need of constant management. The change from one ecology to the other requires an alteration of fundamental cultural analogies, flowing downwards through the priority systems of the bureaucracy.

At the same time, local information moves, to a limited degree, in the opposite direction. In the conclusion of the last of several interviews with Chaudri, he explains that things are changing in the department's priorities. There has been a slight shift away from the planting of *Prosopis juliflora* and towards *Acacia tortilis*. The forest department district director says this is a response to local pressure against *angrezi babul*, but Chaudri confides that the change was, in part, a result of termite vulnerability tests conducted at CAZRI. Similarly, there has been an increase in the plantation of *Prosopis cineraria* in village fuelwood projects (up to 10 percent in every plantation). This has been the result of some pressure brought by local foresters in the bureaucracy. Finally, there was a limited experiment in fodder development projects in which sevan grass was planted, harvested and marketed in surrounding districts and states. This project was discontinued in 1990 because of difficulties in organization, storage, and transport.

These small changes in ecological priorities that have occurred in recent years have come primarily from pressure and information at lower levels of the bureaucracy. The structure of the department, however, disallows fundamental change by institutionalizing the thinking of its lower and middle-level staff. As Douglas observes, the institution not only sets the categories through which we comprehend the world, but further, causes a forgetting of those ideas and priorities that are not so categorized.[46] While the range officer is an agent of environmental change, he is also a subject of institutional structure and can only initiate reform within the static categories defined by the department.

The case of Dayal Lal Chaudri demonstrates that the imposition of exogenous forest is not only a process of foreign species selection,

46. Ibid.

or of the introduction of foreign land cover categories in the region; afforestation is also the layering of a new set of environmental meanings and priorities over an existing ecological imagination. By intervening at the level of information and identity, the centralization of ecological institutions, therefore, represents one of the most far-reaching and dramatic forms of environmental change. These 'monocultures of the mind'[47] are material and discursive colonizations of both landscapes and psyches.

CONCLUSION: FROM NARRATIVE STRUGGLE TO LANDSCAPE POLITICS IN REGIONAL MODERNIZATION

One of the strongest lessons from environmental history is that the power to define the environment is often the power to control it. The simple acts of naming a landscape, recording its elements, and describing the characteristics of its transformation are often contentious and always political.[48] Such acts of naming are not simply rhetorical; they are, rather, the invocation of metaphor and the creation of meaning.[49] When environmental organizations invoke 'pristine wilderness' in an effort to alter resource policy, they render invisible the presence, action, and traditional rights of native peoples on the land.[50] When agricultural engineers describe 'high-yielding' versus 'low-yielding' fields of grain, they turn complex agro-ecological processes into mounds of grain and so justify the logic of capital and chemical intervention.[51] And, when the Indian state, the state forest department, and the village herder deploy and naturalize ideas of 'forest' in Rajasthan, they all give categorical identity to the land and, in so doing, give shape to the actions and debates that are enabled thereby.

The struggle to control resources, landscapes, and environments in India is, therefore, a struggle to define them. Political conflict, therefore, occurs not only in the acts of resistance, evidenced in the Chipko movement or Narmada Dam protest, but in the places where landscapes are defined: census offices and forest nurseries.

47. Following Shiva 1993.
48. Barnes and Duncan 1992.
49. Johnson 1981.
50. Willems-Braun 1997.
51. Shiva 1992; Carson 1962.

These places are not simply static arms of global development policy which merely reflect larger political and economic structures. Nor, are they the professional embodiment of some idealized 'indigenous' or 'local' knowledge. Rather, they are dynamic locations, where categorical contests occur both in the heads of officials and in the knowledges they produce. These institutional locations are sites of 'regional modernity' where global and local are mutually constituted. The emergent research concern with these professional localities, seen in studies of the relationship of knowledge to policy[52] and categories to control[53] in South Asia, might be understood, therefore, as a technique for explaining and participating in ecological politics. By exploring the textual geography of these 'regional modernities,' this work is prerequisite to understanding how the landscape 'serves to mystify particular socio-political systems'[54] and to tracing the effects of powerful institutions on the daily lives of people.

In this sense, the case holds implications for the possibility of reform in environmental management. Though totally absent from the region at the time of research, the Indian state's implementation of a policy of joint forest management (JFM), where control of forestry practice occurs in consultation with local communities,[55] has gained momentum in recent years and will likely enter the region in the future. The case of western Rajasthan suggests that the prospects of success of such a policy, however, depend entirely on the categorical knowledge system and narrative structure that governs the process. If JFM is truly consultative, for example, it must be porous not only to 'participation' in planning but in the very definition of key concepts, tropes, and ideas. How will a forest be defined? What species will be appropriate for plantation? This means not only that forestry officials (especially higher level ones) must surrender enforcement and planning authority, as stated in JFM documents, they will also have to surrender authority as *experts*. The latter may prove far more difficult than the former. In this way, the case shows the barriers and potentialities of modern development and democratization.

52. Saberwal 2000.
53. Rangan 1997; Baker 2000.
54. Duncan 1990: 251.
55. See Khare *et al.* 2000.

More generally, the case sheds light on the locations where the daily realities of modernity are produced. The Rajasthani forester behaves as a broker for modernity. In this role, he is very much like the farmers of Madhya Pradesh described by Brodt,[56] who sort out the specific properties and characteristics of the ecology, drawing across a range of knowledges. So too, he resembles Kumar's expatriate and diasporic Asian writers[57] whose accounts challenge the homogeneity of modernity and the developmentalist imagination. Similarly, Abraham's space scientists, narrating their place between immodern India and hypermodernity[58] are swept up in a constant endeavor of transformation—producing the modern as they go. None of these people act as passive local nodes whose experience of modernization is one of being 'globalized.' Instead, they act to produce the modern themselves, within the restrictive conditions of capitalized and institutionalized power, in altogether new ways, defying universalization of lived experience, and the homogenization of daily life expounded by many observers.[59]

But if the binary partitions of global and local are imaginary, they are themselves the product of modernist partitioning. The urge to divide the traditional from the non-traditional, the cultural from the natural, and the wild from the domesticated is very much a project of modernist state planning and global development policy.[60] The Indian state, through its forestry arm, has consistently tried to isolate the ecological concerns of ecological rescue from the political concerns of local control, the forest ruled by the forest department from the farm and pasture ruled by agricultural extension, the environment from development. Yet, these efforts have failed precisely because of the efforts to enact them. By attempting to enact the modernity imagined by the state, foresters act to undermine that very thing.

What, therefore, does the propagation of 'regional modernities,' like those brokered by the players described above, portend for the modernist project itself? If the global and the local have never

56. Brodt, this volume.
57. Kumar, this volume.
58. Abraham, this volume.
59. Barnet and Cavanagh 1996.
60. Scott 1976.

truly been divided—despite the attempts of modernists to make them so—then, following Latour[61] have we ever really been modern at all? If not, what are the politics of mapping the locations of regional modernities like those of the Rajasthani forester? Arguably, such cartographies expose the struggle over modernization, between those who would exert control through partitioning and those who would re-knit the amputated pieces of economy and ecology, production and reproduction, culture and nature.

This case study is a tentative contribution to writing that geography of modernization. The analysis has attempted to follow the Rajasthani forester in his journey through a modernity in whose creation and destruction he participates, tracing the porousness of narratives traditionally partitioned as 'global' and 'local.' Moreover, it has tried to attend to the material effects and linkages of these narratives; definitions of environmental change and amelioration are far from academic, as they determine the kinds of species that prosper and disappear in a context where biotic resources are central to daily life. Future research must begin from here, exploring the material effects of categorical systems created, imported, or transformed in the process of modernist development. Because these landscapes must be used and inhabited by real people, research must further trace the patterns of control that result from such emergent forms. In the absence of such an attention to modernity's politics, a survey of its regional forms will remain a largely academic exercise.

References

Agrawal, A., 1994. 'I don't want it but you can't have it: Politics on the commons.' Pastoral Development Network Paper 36a. London: Overseas Development Institute.

Ahuja, L. D. 1980. 'Grass production under Khejri (Prosopis cineraria) in the Indian desert: Its role in agroforestry.' In H. S. Mann and S. K. Saxena (eds.), *CAZRI Monograph 11*. Jodhpur, India: Central Arid Zone Research Institute.

Baker, M., 2000. 'Colonial influences on property, community, and land use in Kangra.' In K. Sivaramakrishnan and A. Agrawal (eds.), *Agrarian Transformations: Resources, Representations, and Rule in India*. Durham: Duke University Press.

61. Latour 1993.

Barnes, T. and J. Duncan, 1992. *Writing Worlds: Discourse, Text, and Metaphor in the Representation of Landscape.* London: Routledge.

Barnet, R. and J. Cavanagh, 1996. 'Homogenization of global culture.' In J. Mander and E. Goldsmith (eds.), *The Case Against the Global Economy.* San Francisco: Sierra Club Books.

Baviskar, A., 1995. *In the Belly of the River: Tribal Conflicts over Development in the Narmada Valley.* New Delhi: Oxford University Press.

Bhandari, M. M., 1990. *The Flora of the Indian Desert.* Jodhpur: MPS Reros.

Blaikie, P. and H. Brookfield, 1987. *Land Degradation and Society.* London: Routledge.

Brara, R., 1987. *Shifting Sands: A Study of Rights in Common Pastures.* Jaipur: Institute for Development Studies.

Carson, R., 1962. *Silent Spring.* New York: Houghton Mifflin.

Cashman, K., 1991. 'Systems of knowledge as systems of domination: The limitations of established meaning.' *Agriculture and Human Values* 8(1/2): 49–58.

Chakraborty, M., 1994. 'An analysis of the causes of deforestation in India.' In K. Brown and D. W. Pearce (eds.), *The Causes of Tropical Deforestation.* London: University College Press.

Chouhan, T. S., 1995. *Indian Desert: Resources and Perspectives of Development.* Jaipur: Printwell.

Dhir, R. P., 1987. 'The Indian arid zone in retrospect and prospect.' In M. Shafi and M. Raza (eds.), *Dryland Agriculture in India.* Jaipur: Rawat.

Douglas, M., 1986. *How Institutions Think.* Syracuse: Syracuse University Press.

Dove, M., 1994. 'The existential status of the Pakistani farmer: Studying official constructions of social reality.' *Ethnology* 33(4): 331–51.

Duncan, J., 1990. 'Review of "The iconography of landscape: Essays on the symbolic representation, design, and use of past environments" by D. Cosgrove and S. Daniels.' *The Professional Geographer* 42(2): 251–2.

Dunster, J. and K. Dunster., 1996. *Dictionary of Natural Resource Management.* Vancouver: University of British Columbia Press.

Eckholm, E. P., 1976. *Losing Ground: Environmental Stress and World Food Prospects.* Norton: New York.

Escobar, A., 1996. 'Constructing nature: Elements for a poststructural political ecology.' In R. Peet and M. Watts (eds.), *Liberation Ecologies.* London: Routledge.

Fairfax, S. K. and L. Fortmann, 1990. 'American forestry professionalism in the Third World: Some preliminary observations.' *Population and Environment* 11: 259–72.

Gadgil, M. and R. Guha, 1992. *This Fissured Land: An Ecological History of India.* Berkeley: University of California Press.

————, 1995. *Ecology and Equity: The Use and Abuse of Nature in Contemporary India*. London: Routledge.

Gold, A., 1997. 'Wild pigs and kings: Remembered landscapes in Rajasthan.' *American Anthropologist* 99(1): 70–84.

Government of India, 1973. *Indian Agricultural Statistics*, vol. 1. New Delhi: Government of India.

————, 1975. *Indian Agricultural Statistics*, vol. 11. New Delhi: Government of India.

————, 1977. *Statistical Abstracts of Rajasthan*. Jaipur: Directorate of Economics and Statistics.

————, 1989. *Statistical Abstracts of Rajasthan*. Jaipur: Directorate of Economics and Statistics.

————, 1992. *Agricultural Statistics: Rajasthan*. Jaipur: Directorate of Economics and Statistics.

Guha, R., 1989. *The Unquiet Woods: Ecological Change and Peasant Resistance in the Himalayas*. New Delhi: Oxford University Press.

Gupta, J. P. and S. K. Saxena, 1978. 'Studies of the monitoring of the dynamics of moisture in the soil and the performance of ground flora under desertic communities of trees.' *Indian Journal of Ecology* 5: 30–6.

Gururani, S., 2000. 'Regimes of control, strategies of access: Politics of forest use in the Uttarkhand Himalaya, India.' In K. Sivaramakrishnan and A. Agrawal (eds.), *Agrarian Transformations: Resources, Representations, and Rule in India*. Durham: Duke University Press.

Haeuber, R., 1993. 'Development and deforestation: Indian forestry in perspective.' *The Journal of Developing Areas* 27: 485–514.

Hanna, S. S., C. Folke, *et al.* (eds.), 1996. *Rights to Nature: Ecological, Economic, Cultural, and Political Principles of Institutions for the Environment*. Washington, DC: Island Press.

Hocking, D., 1993. *Trees for Drylands*. New Delhi: Oxford University Press.

Johnson, M., 1981. 'Introduction: Metaphor in the philosophical tradition.' In M. Johnson (ed.), *Philosophical Perspectives on Metaphor*. Minneapolis: University of Minnesota Press.

Khare, A., M. Sarin, N.C. Saxena, S. Palit, S. Bathia, F. Vania and M. Satyanarayana, 2000. *Joint Forest Management: Policy, Practice and Prospects. Policy that Works for Forest and People Series No. 3*. New Delhi: World Wide Fund for Nature—India and London: International Institute for Environment and Development.

Kumar, D., 1990. 'The evolution of colonial science in India.' In J. M. MacKenzie (ed.), *Imperialism and the Natural World*. Manchester: Manchester University Press.

Kumar, M. and M. M. Bhandari, 1992. 'Impact of protection and free grazing on sand dune vegetation in the Rajasthan desert, India.' *Land Degradation and Rehabilitation* 3: 215–27.

————, 1993. 'Impact of human activities on the pattern and process of sand dune vegetation in the Rajasthan desert.' *Desertification Bulletin* 22: 45–54.

Latour, B., 1993. *We Have Never Been Modern.* Cambridge: Harvard University Press.

Lele, U., N. Kumar *et al.*, 2000. *The World Bank Forest Strategy: Striking the Right Balance.* Washington, DC: The World Bank.

Mabbut, J. A. and C. Floret (eds.), 1980. *Case Studies on Desertification.* Paris: UNESCO.

MacKenzie, J. M., 1990. 'Introduction.' In J. M. MacKenzie (ed.), *Imperialism and the Natural World.* Manchester: Manchester University Press.

Marcus, G. E., 1986. 'Contemporary problems of ethnography in the modern world system.' In J. Clifford and G. E. Marcus (eds.), *Writing Culture: The Poetics and Politics of Ethnography.* Berkeley: University of California Press.

Mathur, K. B. L., 1988. 'Afforestation and pasture development on wastelands in the desert region of Rajasthan.' In *Wasteland Development for Fuelwood and Fodder Production.* New Delhi: Government of India.

Nandy, A., 1990. 'Introduction: Science as a reason of state.' In A. Nandy (ed.), *Science, Hegemony, and Violence: A Requiem for Modernity.* New Delhi: Oxford University Press.

Rangan, H., 1997. 'Property versus control: The state and forest management in the Indian Himalaya.' *Development and Change* 28(1): 71–94.

Robbins, P., 1998a. 'Paper forests: Imagining and deploying exogenous ecologies in arid India.' *Geoforum* 29(1): 69–86.

————, 1998b. 'Authority and environment: Institutional landscapes in Rajasthan, India.' *Annals of the Association of American Geographers* 88(3): 410–35.

Saberwal, V. K., 2000. 'Environmental alarm and institutionalized conservation in Himachal Pradesh, 1865–1994.' In K. Sivaramakrishnan and A. Agrawal (eds.), *Agrarian Transformations: Resources, Representations, and Rule in India.* Durham: Duke University Press.

Sachs, W., 1992. 'Environment.' In Wolfgang Sachs (ed.), *The Development Dictionary: A Guide to Knowledge as Power.* London: Zed Books.

Said, E., 1978. *Orientalism.* New York: Random House.

Scott, J. C., 1976. *The Moral Economy of the Peasant: Rebellion and Subsistence in Southeast Asia.* New Haven: Yale University Press.

Sen, D. (ed.), 1990. *Ecology and Vegetation of the Indian Desert.* Bikaner: AgroBotanical Publishers.

Shiva, V., 1988. *Staying Alive: Women, Ecology, and Development.* London: Zed Books.

————, 1992. *The Violence of the Green Revolution.* Goa: The Other India Press.

————, 1993. *Monocultures of the Mind.* Penang: Third World Network.

Springer, J., 2000. 'State power and agricultural transformation in Tamil Nadu.' In K. Sivaramakrishnan and A. Agrawal (eds.), *Agrarian Transformations: Resources, Representations, and Rule in India.* Durham: Duke University Press.

State of Marwar, 1887. *Report of the Administration of the Jodhpur State for the Year 1886–87.* Jodhpur: Marwar State Press.

Willems-Braun, B., 1997. 'Buried epistemologies: The politics of nature in (post)colonial British Columbia.' *Annals of the Association of American Geographers* 87(1): 3–31.

World Commission on Environment and Development, 1987. *Our Common Future.* New York: Oxford University Press.

USDA (United States Department of Agriculture), 1971. *The National Program for the Conservation of Crop Germplasm.* Washington, DC: USDA.

Yapa, L., 1996. 'Improved seeds and constructed scarcity.' In R. Peet and M. Watts (eds.), *Liberation Ecologies.* London: Routledge.

17

State, Place, Identity: Two Stories in the Making of Region

ITTY ABRAHAM

Every state is born of violence...state power endures only by virtue of violence directed toward a space. Each new form of state, each new form of political power, introduces its own particular way of partitioning space, its own particular administrative classification of discourses about space and about things and people in space.

—*Henri Lefebvre*[1]

INTRODUCTION

A discussion of regional modernities requires some reflection on the notion of 'region.' At the outset, it is worth going back to the roots of this and similar words which come from metaphors of power. Region is from *regere* (to command), and province is from *vincere* (to conquer). Foucault in his 'Questions of geography' notes that spatial metaphors help locate the relations between power and knowledge.[2] Region, a 'politico-strategic term is an indication of how the military and the administration actually come to inscribe themselves both on a material soil and within

1. Lefebvre [1974] 1993: 280–1.
2. Foucault 1980.

forms of discourse....The use of spatial metaphors helps one to grasp precisely the points at which discourses are transformed in, through and on the basis of relations of power.'[3] This reminder is important, for it tells us that region is a product of the actions of political agents. In the sense permitted in this volume, 'region' could imply any space marked by systematic patterns of behavior and relatively fixed institutional parameters or where we can locate a cultural identity related to distinct norms of economic and political change. These regional spaces might be subnational, transnational, or international (a categorization that shows in turn my dependence on the frame of nation to orient myself). Yet, if the notion of the regional modern is to become useful, we cannot sidestep the awareness that the unity or coherence given to the region is prior to or at best simultaneous with its identification. In any event, the political agent that institutes a region, or seeks to, cannot be separated from the stories we tell.

As the editors of this volume demonstrate in their introduction, it would be folly to ignore the historical efforts made by the national state in some parts of the world to regionalize—to define its own space of control, to organize, monitor, and develop 'its' territory. While the editors' objective is to establish that a meaningful set of social forms and institutions exist 'between the global and local,' an argument made quite convincingly, in the process we must consider other questions thrown up by these categories. What I am particularly concerned with is the trap of naturalization which modern political power seeks to engender in us. In this case, it would be that which allows us to say without much effort: 'this is a region.' As Lefebvre points out, the ease with which we can identify a region is directly related to the extent of the effort made by organized political power to naturalize its control over that area.[4]

Organized political power takes many shapes of course, but the pre-eminent global institutional form of this power for the last half century is the modern state. The region created by the modern state is not identical to the region created by other modes and institutions of power but is characterized by 'particular way[s] of partitioning space.' To count politically, modern statecraft informs

3. Foucault 1980: 69–70.
4. Lefebvre [1974] 1993.

us, one begins by having a piece of land. The relationship of modern states to territory is specific, defined as sovereign control. This zero-sum relationship is usefully contrasted against the substantially different relationship that, for example, pastoral peoples, fishing communities and common property regimes have to land. And, as the contemporary example of the 'hostilities' between India and Pakistan over the 17,000 feet high Siachen glacier shows, territory is fetishized well beyond the intrinsic value of a piece of land in economic or even symbolic terms. For the political entity seeking to become a state, sole control over a 'national territory' is a prerequisite. Loss of territory, by the same token, marks the secular failure of a state, leads to the fall of governments, the decline of legitimacy, and the reduction of 'state-ness'—the sentiment that all powerful states seek to inculcate and internalize in its human subjects.

For the postcolonial state, born into a world where the rules of political modernity were already in place, the script of state-ness and sovereignty defined a global narrative to aspire to.[5] Corresponding to these state imperatives were the linked but distinct categories that describe the relation of the state to the people— nationality and citizenship. Given the complex movements of people in South Asia and the histories of imperial cartography, however, neither blood nor land was sufficient to resolve the difference between nationality and citizenship. As state managers soon found out, the postcolonial nation was not contained within the territorial limits of the state. Under these conditions, the first step was always trying to establish beyond doubt where national space began and ended. Anxieties over territory have been at the heart of state-making in this region. Indian state security forces have been fighting social forces from Kashmir to Nagaland who have contested their political authority from practically the founding of the country as an independent entity. Hence, the obsession with establishing boundaries.

From the state's point of view the link between territory and political identity is linear, direct, and beyond question. But if we suspend the assumption of political control over territory as a fundamental source of modern identity, we may be able to develop new insights into the making of region. In what follows, I treat

5. Abraham 1998.

the state as a region-making political actor, seeking to describe its actions in local terms. The stories I will recount allow us to reflect upon the stakes in the state's struggle to impose a singular identity on its subjects and help us see its core contradiction. The first story is quite literally regional and is drawn from recent inter-state history: namely, the Asian–African Conference of 1955 held in Bandung, Indonesia, which led to the creation of the Non-Aligned Movement. This was an effort to create a grouping of newly independent states based on a putative anti-colonial sentiment, but was in fact tied to a physical affiliation with the region called Asia. While the state would have identity following naturally from place, it is my argument here that the postcolonial state's effort to mandate, politically, culturally, legally, a singular national identity is necessary precisely because of its inability to establish complete hegemony over nation and territory. The second story is drawn from Indian newspaper accounts of a 'spy story' involving, like all good spy stories, rockets, male scientists, female allure, and international intrigue. The difficulty of sustaining international espionage at the heart of this story and its eventual narrative degeneration point to the problems created by trying to impose a strict distinction between national identities, a prerequisite for the narration of a good spy story. This story helps us see that the inability to define the boundaries of the state unambiguously redirects the technologies of state power onto people, seeking to reproduce within the body of the nation the missing opposition of 'inside' and 'outside.'[6] In both cases, the state seeks to define its boundaries in accordance with the global script of sovereignty and state-ness; as a result the presence of the minority emerges as an unspoken but ineffable threat to the state as conceived through that script. The regional project remains incomplete.

THE MAKING OF AN ASIAN REGION

When I was growing up in 1960s, I lived in Southeast Asia. Two decades later, I found myself in South Asia, without any noticeable change in my surroundings. I never discovered who had changed my location, or why, but this region's present distance from Southeast Asia is palpable. As a result, traveling to Indonesia

6. Walker 1993.

marked a double displacement. My first reaction on seeing the building where the plenary sessions of the Asian–African conference—as the Bandung Conference was referred to at the time—was how small it is. Gedung Merdeka, or Freedom Building as President Sukarno renamed it, is an Art Deco building which dates from the late nineteenth century, located in the heart of Bandung. Bandung itself is akin to a hill station—in South Asian terms—located in the West Java hills three hours from Jakarta. There is even a small train that plies between Jakarta and Bandung that travelers who have been to Ooty and Simla will recognize in terms of spirit, if not vintage. The actual building has a checkered past of its own—it was first a club for well-to-do Dutch planters and colonial officers, and in all likelihood the only natives allowed in at the time entered through the service entrance. After the Japanese invasion of Indonesia, the building was commandeered by the occupying forces, though still to be used as a club and cultural center. After the proclamation of Indonesian independence on 17 August 1945, it was occupied by liberation forces and used as a headquarters in the struggle against the Dutch who were then trying to reclaim their colony. And, to take this story past the Conference momentarily, this building had a future, more sordid, role to play in a key transitional moment in that country's history when, during the military coup of 1966, numbers of Indonesian Chinese and alleged members of the PKI (Communist Party of Indonesia) were held prisoners in Gedung Merdeka. Something about this building clearly caught the popular imagination, for the official reference guide of the Conference museum also records that in the late 1960s, the building was used as a 'place for art shows by unauthorized [persons].'[7]

If you look through the bars that guard the main entrance to the building on Jalan Afrika–Asia, you can see a large shadowy room with the figures of some men at its far end. Entering the main hall from the adjoining library, one realizes that these are wax works, assembled to simulate the opening moment of the Conference. Seated behind the standing figure of President Sukarno, who is seen delivering a speech, are the figures of Jawaharlal Nehru of India, Mohammed Ali of Pakistan, Sir John Kotelawala of Ceylon, Prime Minister of Indonesia Ali Sastroamidjojo, and U Nu of

7. Department of Foreign Affairs, (Indonesia) 1992: 8.

Burma. These individuals were known, collectively, as the Colombo Powers. According to Sir John Kotelawala's memoir, *An Asian Prime Minister's Story*, the idea of an Asian conference was his, something he had been thinking about for some years and which he had first mentioned in a radio broadcast in Rangoon.[8] C. C. Desai, India's High Commissioner to Ceylon, is given the credit for helping Kotelawala find the right time to launch the initiative.[9] Certainly, Kotelawala was responsible for inviting the leaders of India, Pakistan, Burma, and Indonesia to Ceylon to have discussions about common problems facing the independent countries of what was then called South East Asia, which led to the discussion of such a conference. But Indonesia's premier, Ali Sastromidjojo has to be recognized as the one who explicitly called for it in his opening remarks at the Colombo meeting. Not everyone was in favor of a meeting of this kind initially. George Kahin suggests that India and Burma first greeted the proposal with some caution, in contrast to Pakistan and Ceylon.[10] Sastromidjojo took the initiative in making the event happen, offering his country as the host, and taking the lead in sounding out international opinion.

The idea of something called the 'Colombo Powers' sounds anachronistic today but that should not blind us to the surprising importance of the group at the time. Although the countries involved had very different foreign policies and indeed views of the prevailing world system,[11] what did bind them was what might be called a pan-Asian sentiment, borne especially of the sense of having all gone through the trauma of European colonialism. Where the voice of the Colombo Powers might have had their

8. Two important precursors to the Bandung conference were the Asian Relations Conference, held in Delhi in March–April 1947, some months before India's independence, and the 19-member Asian Conference on Indonesia, also held in Delhi in January 1949. In both, India was the instigator and key participant.

9. Kotelawala 1956: 117, 174.

10. Kahin 1956: 2.

11. Kotelawala (1956: 124) writes: 'At another stage (in the discussion in Kandy), one of the Premiers lost control of himself, banged the table, and shouted at another, "You are nothing but an American stooge!" To which the other retorted with equal heat, "And you are nothing but a Russian stooge!" Notwithstanding its playground quality, this is clearly a reference to Nehru of India and Mohammed Ali of Pakistan, respectively.

greatest impact, apart from sponsoring the Asia–Africa Conference itself, was in their influence on the Geneva 'Far East' peace negotiations then underway.[12] What is often forgotten today is simply how novel was the idea of four militarily weak and newly independent countries of Asia feeling confident enough to make their collective voice heard, speaking from a point of view that was beholden neither to the USA nor the USSR, and that in fact sought to bridge the gap between them. Recall how nascent was the present international system at the time—much of Africa was still under colonial rule, in fact the only official invitees to the Conference from Africa were Ghana (then called the Gold Coast), Liberia, Egypt, Ethiopia, Libya, and Sudan. The Central African Republic was invited but didn't come. The following countries had not yet even been admitted into the United Nations: Cambodia, Ceylon, Jordan, Libya, Nepal and—Japan! Formosa, or Taiwan, occupied the Chinese seat at the United Nations. And, that brings us to a major subtext of the Conference—the People's Republic of China.

China was at this point in time a source of great uncertainty in the international system. While the Communists controlled the Chinese mainland, remnants of the Chinese Nationalists, the Guomindang, were ensconced in Taiwan having looted the national treasury before their departure, while fragments of its army were holed up in Burma and Thailand. There had been a near-war with the US over the islands of Quemoy and Matsu, off the Chinese mainland, one the earliest flashpoints of the Cold War. The PRC had aligned with its fraternal ally, the Soviet Union, it had fought the US and the UN to a standstill in Korea, and it had ongoing border disputes with a number of countries. A number of Southeast Asian countries saw the Chinese as inherently expansionist, thanks in the first instance to Communism, but made more dangerous by a potential fifth column of overseas Chinese all over the region, especially in Indonesia, Thailand, and the Philippines. Though few knew it at the time, the disastrous Great Leap Forward policy had been started a few years earlier which would lead to major famines and devastation of the rural population. China was deeply isolated and outside of the world community, such as it was.

12. Rajan 1964: 128–31.

An invitation to China to attend the meeting seems incongru-
ous, given the ideological and political compulsions of a majority
of the Colombo Powers. Pakistan was then aligned with Turkey
and Iraq as part of an American policy of global containment of
communism, Ceylon was led by a rabidly anti-Communist premier, and Indonesia was deeply concerned about the loyalties of
its large Chinese population who held dual citizenship. Burma had
a Guomindang rump army sitting on its border. Only India, it
seemed, was unconcerned about the real intentions of the Chinese.
India was in the forefront of efforts, internationally and bilaterally,
to bring China out of isolation and into the world community
because it was too important to be ignored. With hindsight we
know that Nehru would be deeply humiliated and publicly
castigated when this policy seemed to backfire on him some years
later. At the time he seemed to be sure that if leaders could get
to meet the Chinese and hear from them about their intentions,
and if the Chinese in turn were exposed to the variety and range
of opinion in the region, this situation would change for the better.
This seems to have been what happened in the Conference, thanks
to the diplomacy and abilities of Chou En-lai, the Chinese foreign
minister.[13]

But Nehru's support still does not fully explain why the Chinese
were invited in the first place. Short of any evidence that Nehru
made China's attendance a condition of going ahead with the
Conference, what made China's presence necessary and acceptable
to the event's other sponsors? Some clues can be provided by events
of the time, and by the issues on which there was disagreement
between the Colombo Powers. The 1954 Geneva Conference on
the Far East seeking to end the war in Korea and the military and
political standoff in Vietnam, Cambodia, and Laos, had no Asian
members other than the belligerents. Nehru in particular made a
series of pungent remarks about the absence of Asian participants,
given how important the issue was to that region, and promptly
sent Krishna Menon off to Geneva to play what is generally accepted as a positive role behind the scenes. So, in the first instance,
there was anger at the arrogance of the Western powers, including

13. As U Nu is reported to have said, 'there would have been no conference
without Nehru and no success without Chou En-Lai.' Reported in M. S. Rajan
1964: 212.

the Soviet Union, who presumed that they could make decisions about the world without consulting those who were living in the region and were directly affected by their decisions.

This anger fed into the common sense of all the newly independent Colombo Powers that the practice of colonial rule was far from banished, even if its form was less visible. This event only confirmed the sense that the end of the Second World War had not changed the behavior of the European colonial powers, promises made to the contrary notwithstanding. But there were some successes to turn to which bolstered the sense that it was worth acting and that change was possible. After all, it was only following the extraordinary Delhi conference on Indonesia in 1949, convened by India and attended by delegates from 19 countries, that the Dutch came to realize that they had lost their major colonial possession forever.

The Colombo Powers also agreed that the major problems facing the world were the manufacture and testing of weapons of mass destruction, especially the hydrogen bomb, the need for positive steps toward disarmament, that France should release its colonial possessions in North Africa, and the need for a just solution to the Palestine problem and the rehabilitation of Arab refugees in their original homes. On these international issues, one can see the consistency in their views that remnants of the colonial system had to be abolished, and that global militarization was antithetical to economic development, the most important issue for them all.

But there was substantial disagreement in some major issues as well, as is evidenced by the delicately phrased statement in their final communiqué that 'the subject of Communism in its national and international aspects were generally discussed and the prime ministers made known to each other their respective views on and attitudes towards Communist ideologies.' This was followed by a statement reaffirming their commitment to democracy and its institutions, and their 'unshakable determination to resist interference in the affairs of their countries by external Communist, anti-Communist or other agencies.'[14] The simultaneous attention to Communism and on respecting national sovereignty points to the ongoing pressures by both the USA and the USSR to make the

14. Department of Foreign Affairs (Indonesia) 1983: 193–4.

newly independent countries of Asia and Africa commit themselves to one side or the other. Affirmations of neutrality in this context were seen as suspicious, with both sides trapped in a mutually reinforcing dualism which had no room for a middle ground.

The disagreements between the Colombo Powers are to my mind more revealing about what united them than their stated points of agreement. The statement above, which makes clear that the parties had a substantial difference of views on a major international issue also reminds us that it was not significant enough to derail the meeting altogether. The parties would, as the phase today has it, 'agree to disagree,' and would continue to work together on other issues of common interest. This kind of bracketing of disagreement is a typical example of what Nehru appears to have had in mind when he raised the term 'peaceful co-existence' to the level of foreign policy doctrine in the 1954 Panchsheel agreement with China.

'Peaceful co-existence' was one of those code words of the time that was closely associated with Communist leanings, being usually used to describe the character of interaction between fraternal states sharing a common socialist ideology. But Nehru wanted to elevate the term to mean something else altogether. For him, peaceful co-existence meant the recognition of difference, and the ability to live with it. It was a deeply humanist idea and one that he felt would be particularly valuable in determining the nature of interaction between the states of Asia, given their enormous differences. President Sukarno placed the sentiment behind the term squarely on the table in his eloquent opening speech, when he said '[This Conference] is a body of enlightened, tolerant opinion which seeks to impress on the world that all men and all countries have their place under the sun—to impress upon the world that it is possible to live together, meet together, speak to each other, without losing one's individual identity; and yet contribute to the general understanding of matters of common concern, and to develop a true consciousness of the interdependence of men and nations for their well being and survival on earth.'[15]

This viewpoint sounds a lot more reasonable today, in the era of avowed multi-culturalism, but in the deeply divided and power politics world of the 1950s this came across as a naive and

15. Ibid.: 10.

unorthodox view. Ironically, given the contemporary state of knowledge among Asian countries, it was quite realistic. Most Asian intellectuals and policy makers knew much more about the countries of Europe than their Asian neighbors. There had to be space given for inter-Asian communication to be developed, if countries of this region were not going to simply follow precepts laid down in Paris, London, or the Hague. And thus we come back to China. The Chinese inclusion in the Bandung conference was on the one hand a recognition of the size and importance of the country in Asia. More important, however, it was a rigorous test of the presumption that Asian countries had something in common, that they could sit down with each other, notwithstanding differences, and learn from the interaction, and by the end of it, they might be a step closer in understanding what was Asian about Asia. Peaceful co-existence was, from the Indian point of view, a generalized recognition that there was very little in common among the countries of Asia, beyond a general aversion to colonialism and a desire to speak to the world as equals, which they were not. Including the Chinese into the Conference was a way of showing that Asians were not bound by the ideological limits of the West, of testing the idea that Asians had something in common, but most important, given that China was the sign of their greatest disagreement and anxiety, its inclusion was a sign that the possibility that they had proposed—peaceful co-existence—was more than a fancy phrase.

However, in this minimalist strategy of defining Asia in pragmatic terms—the ability to sit down and talk and to respect the differences one saw in the other—the Colombo Powers were succumbing to a greater problem. Idealism built on geography—in the sense of what Asia meant—was being set up to confront History, and the Colombo Powers were in effect denying their own histories. First, they had chosen not to confront the importance of appreciating that one of the ways in which Asia was defined, post-Second World War, was via the effect of Japanese imperialism, the first political formation that united diverse colonies that had been under the influence of the British, French, Portuguese, and Dutch powers. The very term Southeast Asia, as Vicente Rafael points out, was first used by the Allies to describe a theater of war. Second, and even more importantly, they were denying the histories of inter-Asian movement, where thanks to long-standing flows of people from every country, but especially India and China, Asia was a profoundly multi-ethnic world. More than once during the discussions, the issue of Irian Jaya, the western half of Papua, came up in the discussions. The Dutch had not left this half of the island and the Indonesians were using all the pressure at their disposal to get them out, with the full support of the Asian–African conference members. Also mentioned in this regard were Goa and East Timor, still held by the Portuguese, and Indochina. By seeing the presence of Europeans in Asia as the only issue worth agreeing about, the Conference members assumed that the correct response to that was to elevate national sovereignty to the highest level, and to insist on being sole masters in their own domain.

By the same token, what they had done in this process was to consign the fates of 'their' people—people who had migrated, moved, traveled—to the decisions of another state. This is less a problem, I would argue, for the 'sending' countries than the 'receiving' ones. Indeed, both China and India were quite happy to ignore the overseas Chinese and Indians until they began to be, in more recent years, a potential source of capital. But for the countries in which these overseas populations were sojourning, their presence was more threatening. By the logic of national sovereignty and racial citizenship, foundational pillars of post-war sovereignty, the loyalties of these populations could never be known unambiguously, notwithstanding their often long-standing residence there, because of their race and their foreign origins. The most primitive sign of this anxiety was ethnic riots, in more than one case state-sponsored.

So, taking the Colombo Powers alone, we see essentially multi-ethnic states beginning the process of national integration without fully coming to terms with these divided and moving populations within their midst, except to see them as a problem to be dealt with, ultimately with force. Indonesia had East Timor, Irian Jaya, and now Aceh; India has Kashmir and the Northeast; Pakistan had East Pakistan and Sindh, and perhaps also Baluchistan; Ceylon/Sri Lanka has Jaffna and the Northeast, and Burma has never been able to claim that the north of the country, home of the Shan, Wa, and Tai-speaking hill peoples, is truly under its control. Asia, no less than Africa, had suffered the multiple scars of cartographic surgery as a result of the colonial experience.

By taking mutual co-existence as a founding principle of regional relations, the states of Asia were resigning themselves to the perpetual anxiety of fearing the loyalties of their own people, consigning them to the permanent category of 'minority.' Instead of seeing their neighbors as ethnic mirrors of themselves, with intertwined and intermingled histories, the Colombo Powers made the fatal error of reinscribing the lines between them with greater force, now sanctioned with the power of independence. Minorities became a problem for the law-and-order state to deal with, rather than a cause of instituting structures of governance that took protection of minorities as their first principle. At the very moment when they were groping toward a definition of the region of Asia as a mark of identity shaped by normative considerations beyond territory (though not proximity), Asia broke down into national states. The Asian region fell back upon national sovereignty as the only way to resolve their mutual concerns and to cover up their need to address the political anxieties caused by having to face up to the absence of homogenous populations. Instead of elevating the existence of intertwined histories and common ethnicities to the level of a principle that defined their difference from the rest of the world, the states of this region chose to turn their backs on this question by reaffirming the boundaries between them. Interstate relations would now be conducted according to Geneva Rules: formal, official, and between recognized parties. All relations, that is, except espionage.

A Modern Spy Story

I began thinking about spy stories in contemporary India through my observation of a relative absence. The absence can be framed as a question: why has a full-fledged espionage genre not emerged in South Asian literature and popular culture? On the face of it, all the preconditions that allowed for a flourishing literary cottage industry during the West's Cold War are in place on the subcontinent. It could be argued that India and Pakistan are locked into a historic battle of epic proportions; the battle has gone on long enough to have resonance in daily life: each state is identified as the mirror image of the other, especially from the point of view of the extremists on either side; the relationship never seems to rise above a zero-sum calculus; and, importantly, spy scandals involving each state are common enough to be reported frequently.

That both states are engaged heavily in espionage is well known. Every day references to the Indian foreign intelligence service, the Research and Analysis Wing (more commonly known as RAW), and Pakistan's Inter-Service Intelligence (ISI), appear in newspapers. Horrible tragedies and stunning successes are credited to these organizations even as little is known about them or how they operate, who runs them, or what their budgets are. Yet, while there are a few short stories and films that deploy characters identified as spies (usually from the opposite side), it is difficult to identify sufficiently common narrative conditions that would suggest the existence of a full-fledged espionage genre. Indeed, perhaps it is in fact the ever-ready presence of these agencies and their activities in daily news coverage that preempts the rise of a fictional counterpart. Hence, in the absence of a fictional counterpart from which to draw on, we must turn to journalism. What does a 'real-life' spy story look like?

In the first telling of this story, this is what the newspapers reported. Sometime in 1994 a directive went out from the home ministry in New Delhi to all state police headquarters informing them of a drive to crack down on foreigners staying illegally in India.[16] Soon after, on 20 October 1994, Mariam Rasheeda, an 'attractive thirty-year-old' from the Maldives, was arrested by the special branch of the Kerala police for overstaying her three-month visa. In the course of her interrogation, Mariam Rasheeda mentioned that D. Sasikumaran, a scientist at the nearby Vikram Sarabhai Space Center (VSSC), could vouch for her good character and innocence. The Vikram Sarabhai Space Center is an integral part of the Indian Space Research Organization (ISRO), which in turn is a key node in the Indian strategic enclave, or military–scientific complex, the institution responsible for developing the technology used in the present generation of India's

16. This first account of the 'spy scandal' has been summarized from a series of articles published in the popular English press. See 'Mariam's mission,' *The Week*, 11 December 1994; 'Spies in space,' *India Today*, 15 December 1994; 'A spy ring,' *Frontline*, 16 December 1994; 'Space for spies: Looking for the wider network,' *Frontline*, 30 December 1994; 'Too many loose ends,' *India Today*, 31 December 1994; 'The great espionage mess,' *India Today*, 31 January 1995. My thanks to Krishna Gopalan who helped gather this material.

medium range ballistic missiles.[17] Realizing the international rami-
fications of this connection, the Kerala police hurriedly put
together a special team under the aegis of the Kerala police, a
team which included representatives of both India's foreign intelligence service—RAW—and the domestic counter-intelligence
agency, the Intelligence Bureau. The police informed ISRO that
one of their scientists had been associating with an unauthorized
foreigner and was probably in violation of the many regulations
that control the activities of state scientists. At first glance, an
important espionage case seemed to have been cracked open by
some astute police work, also suggesting the source of these initial
reports.

After an internal investigation, Sasikumaran was summoned to
ISRO headquarters in Bangalore and transferred to a new job at the
Space Applications Center in Ahmedabad. In early November
1994, and on the same day that Mariam Rasheeda was remanded
to custody for a further fortnight, Fouzia Hussain, a former Maldivan
TV actress, was arrested by the Intelligence Bureau, allegedly as she
was about to leave the country. Fouzia had stayed with Rasheeda
in Thiruvananthapuram's Samrat Hotel and they were good friends.
In the meanwhile, Rasheeda's ongoing interrogation had revealed
another contact. The new figure was K. Chandrasekharan, a Bangalore businessman who had close ties with both ISRO and the
Russian space agency, Glavkosmos. Chandrasekharan was arrested
after a search of his office and house by RAW and IB personnel.
The circle appeared to be closing when it was revealed that
Chandrasekharan was the one who had introduced Rasheeda to the
disgraced scientist, Sasikumaran. On 21 November 1994,
Sasikumaran was arrested in Ahmedabad by the Kerala police
special team. Soon after, Sasikumaran's boss in the VSSC's Liquid
Propulsion Centre, S. Nambinarayanan, submitted his resignation.
The resignation was not accepted. Later that year, the Kerala Police
special team called in the Central Bureau of Investigation (CBI). On
6 December, Chandrasekharan and Sasikumaran were transferred
to the custody of the CBI. A few days later, the CBI also took into
custody Nambinarayanan and Sudhir Kumar Sharma, another
Bangalore businessman with ISRO connections. In all, there were
now six accused: two Maldivan women, Rasheeda and Fouzia, two

17. For an elaboration of the term see Abraham (1992: 231–52).

scientists, Sasikumaran and Nambinarayanan, and two Bangalore businessmen, Chandrasekharan and Sudhir Kumar Sharma. The national press lapped up these initial reports and soon stories began to circulate of a full-blown spy ring seeking to gather information about India's space program. Stories appeared in the Malayalam press that Rasheeda had been seen driving around town in a Ferrari. Suspicions mounted about the origins of the spy ring, with repeated suggestions that Pakistani ISI agents operating from the (Urdu-speaking) Maldives were behind the whole event.

The six were transferred to Chennai for 'uninterrupted questioning'—a process made both easier and sinister by holding the six in a house on Greenways Road named 'Malligai,' where the special team investigating Rajiv Gandhi's assassination was based. Yet all was not over. Still at large was the mysterious figure of 'Brigadier' Srivastava, who had been mentioned by a number of the accused during their interrogation. The Brigadier was alleged in news reports to be Kerala Inspector General of Police Raman Srivastava. This high ranking police official was said to be living well beyond his means, but complicating the issue was the fact that he was also very close to Kerala's Congress (I) Chief Minister K. Karunakaran. The chief minister defended his man as best he could, but this proved counter-productive as the press and opposition were baying for blood. Srivastava was arrested and Karunakaran resigned as chief minister soon after. At this point the intense media scrutiny of the event died down, and much of the remaining activity took place in the courts. Following their investigation, the CBI dropped its case against all the accused in May 1996 asserting that no espionage had taken place. Most peculiarly, the Kerala government, now under the Left Front, withdrew their invitation to the CBI and re-established the case under its own police force. The six accused challenged this executive decision in the courts, and finally, the Supreme Court weighed in on their side. Castigating the state government for having taken this unusual decision, in April 1996, the Supreme Court awarded the plaintiffs Rs 100,000 compensation for their persecution and ordered them released at once. Rasheeda's trial however was not complete. She had to remain in India to answer charges in a defamation case brought against her by the original arresting officers.

As time went on, a few journalists kept at the story and, based on their reporting, one can put together the pieces of another 'spy story.'[18] This is also what might have happened. Rasheeda first went to the Foreigners Registration Office attached to the Thiruvananthapuram Commissioner of Police's office on 8 October 1994. There, she met Inspector Vijayan of the Special Branch. Maldives nationals do not need visas for India provided their stay is less than 90 days. Due to a plague scare, flights to the Maldives had been cancelled, and Rasheeda was concerned that she would have to stay in India beyond 17 October, the end of a 90-day stay. Inspector Vijayan took her passport and confirmed air ticket. A few days later, he dropped by the Hotel Samrat where she was staying with her friend Fowzia Hassan. According to Rasheeda, Vijayan asked Hassan to leave the room, first asked her if she had any dollars, and then made a sexual pass at her. She refused. Vijayan left the room without returning her passport and tickets. According to her, although she went daily to the police station she wasn't able to meet him or get her tickets and passport back. On 20 October she was asked to come to the police station in the afternoon and was arrested for having overstayed her visa. Her hotel room was raided. The police found a telephone diary and checked the hotel phone logs. One of the numbers that had been repeatedly called was Sasikumaran's, the ISRO scientist. He admits

18. Venu Menon, 'Sinner or sinned against? The tangled tale of Mariam Rasheeda,' *http://www.rediff.com/news/aug/19spy.htm*; Ritu Sarin, 'Petitioners in ISRO spy case to file suits for compensation,'*http://www.expressindia.com/ ie/daily/19980430/12050644.html*; 'For Maldivian Rasheeda, the ISRO espionage case nightmare is finally over,' *http://www.rediff.com/news/1998/apr/ 30isro.htm*; 'SC raps Nayanar Govt. in ISRO case, acquits all,' http:// www.expressindia.com/ie/daily/19980430/12050514.html; T. V. R. Shenoy, 'The trial of Mariam Rasheeda and others was a giant smokescreen,' *http:// www.rediff.com/news/1998/may/07flip.htm*; Prem Panicker, 'What happened to the four years of life they have been robbed of?,' *http://www.rediff.com/ news/1998/may/08isro.htm*; Venu Menon, 'We would not have proceeded with the ISRO case if the high court had prevented us,'*http://www.rediff.com/ news/may/11isro.htm*; The Rediff Interview with D. Sasikumaran, 20 May 1998, http://www.rediff.com/news/1998/may/20keral1.htm; The Rediff Special/Mariam Rasheeda (interview with Venu Menon),*http://www.rediff.com/ news/aug/19spy1.htm*; M. D. Riti, 'Scientist seeks damages to end "loose talk"' *http://www.rediff.com/news/1999/feb/24nambi.htm*; The Rediff interview with S. Nambinarayanan,*http://www.rediff.com/news/2001/mar/17inter1.htm*; Sam George, 'Kerala High Court stays compensation to ISRO scientist,' *http:// www.indiaabroaddaily.com/2001/05/23/23isro.html*.

knowing Rasheeda, saying defiantly in an interview, 'It was a purely social contact. I have no restriction meeting anyone. It is my right and I will continue to do so.'[19] But how would a junior ISRO scientist meet someone like Rasheeda?

The Indian space program, like a number of other strategic civil-military projects, depends on a number of components, designs, and artifacts from foreign countries in order to produce their supposedly indigenous products. A number of middle-men and suppliers have grown up to feed this system, suppliers who operate on a cost-plus basis and who depend on personal contacts in both the Indian space program and foreign countries, in this case the Russian agency Glavkosmos. Continued goodwill—and profits—at home depends on keeping the scientists in charge of purchasing supplies happy. It is said that gifts of cash and kind are common, and, in a surreal mapping of a traditional anthropological narrative, these brokers give key scientists land, women, and cash in exchange for the permission to do business with them. Rasheeda might just have been one such exchange-gift, and Sasikumaran the beneficiary. Police IGP Srivastava was, it seems, also involved in the chain of favors, complicated by his association and defense by the Congress (I) chief minister. Following the beneficiaries of ISRO equipment purchases led to Hyderabad and to associates of then Congress (I) Prime Mininster P. V. Narasimha Rao, all of which caused the CBI to drop the espionage charges rapidly. The Congress connection is what appears to be what brought the Left Front government back into the picture a few years later. Had they pursued a simple corruption case, they might have succeeded, as the espionage charges by that time were clearly unfounded. But they chose otherwise, leading to the rebuke by the Supreme Court. From being a spy story with treasonous scientists selling the nation's secrets for the lust of a beautiful woman, from sinister figures lurking in a nether world populated by techno-gadgets, cryogenic engines, and mysterious foreigners, the story appeared to have become an all too common and sordid tale of greed followed by corruption, and of business as usual in the upper reaches of power.

The chain of links within ISRO appears to have been in the first place the result of physical abuse and torture. We may speculate that Sasikumaran turned in his boss Nambinarayan, in much the

19. The Rediff interview with D. Sasikumaran, 20 May 1998, *http://www.rediff.com/news/1998/may/20keral1.htm.*

same way that Nambinarayan was threatened by the police to implicate his superior, A. E. Muthunayakom. Nambinarayan reports that he was told that the police would then get Muthunayakom to implicate U. R. Rao, the chairman of ISRO.[20]

Also adding fuel to the fire were the anonymous comments made by ISRO scientists to the media and the police, suggesting that the accused scientists, Nambinarayanan and Sasikumaran, might have been involved in something shady. This innuendo, including the suggestion that the two scientists had passed classified information about the rocket engine program to the French, was the closest the Maldives case came to 'really' being a spy story. Apparently, both scientists had spent some years in France in the 1970s, where they had studied the development of the Viking rocket. On their return to India they had used this information to help develop rocket engines in the Indian space program. Not surprisingly, they had continued to have communications with their French counterparts, and, given that ISRO represents itself as a purely civilian scientific organization, had passed information back to the French, keeping them informed about the state of Indian progress in the field. Possibly, the fact of French involvement upset the deployment of familiar narratives. By not being the Pakistanis or the Americans, usually expected to represent the subversive 'foreign hand' in such dealings, this angle remained relatively unexplored, though it came closest to actually being espionage. However, one additional factor needed to be included for this to come off, namely, that it would have to be admitted that ISRO's work was in fact vital to India's strategic enclave. As a result, the business of espionage seems little different from a gentlemanly exchange of favors, and equally, can hardly be distinguished from the exchange of information that apparently takes place between scientists all over the world on a regular basis. Perhaps, now we can understand better the comforting comment by ISRO Chairman K. Kasturi Rangan, after a tour of ISRO facilities in the wake of the non-scandal: 'all working groups and systems [are] in order.'[21]

At a minimum, the ability to tell credible espionage stories depends on the ability to sustain the difference between 'inside' and 'outside.' The undercover spy, for instance, derives her unique

20. The Rediff interview with S. Nambinarayanan, *http://www.rediff.com/news/2001/mar/17inter1.htm.*

21. Quoted in *Frontline* (Madras) 30 December 1994, p. 125.

character from being able to pass for the Other. Being able to 'pass,' as has been pointed out in studies of racial passing especially, means being more original than the original. In the context of espionage, that usually refers to the 'mole' who has burrowed deep into enemy territory and in due course of time becomes indistinguishable from her neighbors. The greatest compliment paid to such individuals is when, following their capture, their neighbors say, 'But, it can't be! She was just like one of us.' However, when one assumes irreconcilable distance as a precondition for the definition of the Other, as Shiv Visvanathan has pointed out, the tension embodied here is the danger of passing too well.[22] To be too much like the other is to raise at once the possibility of betrayal, the central narrative theme of the John le Carre-style Cold War espionage novel.[23] Faced with this possibility, the Western state raises enormously the threshold of national entry, seeking through a barrage of Walls, Borders, Cards, and Permits to prevent the spy from one side crossing over to the other.

In the South Asian context, given the intertwined political, ethnic, cultural and geographic histories of India and Pakistan, the question of passing is moot. Given the enormous movements of population from and through this region, going back hundreds of years, being from somewhere does not tell you definitively which national identity they profess or admit to. The presence of minorities on one side of the border who are the majority on the other side means that for practical purposes the mole is already in place, simultaneous with the creation of the state. By that token, the scale of the potential spy population is staggering. No state could admit to this possibility without breaking apart, but the suspicion of the fifth column within is a constant refrain that can never go away either.

The inability of popular culture to sustain espionage as a genre coupled with its incomplete form as journalism points us to a central anxiety of the postcolonial state. This anxiety is not how to retain their difference in the face of historical porosity— espionage imagined as border crossings—but how to produce difference in the first place. If these texts are anything to go by, the hollowness of espionage as a structuring ploy points to how

---

22. Visvanathan and Sethi 1998.
23. See 'The Glasnost Spy,' *IUMDA Newsletter*, 2-3 (1990): 76-90.

the boundaries of domestic space are contested, not the international. The postcolonial project in this region is the production of national difference, based on the fragile hope that eventually it will be possible to know definitively on which side of the border we are.

CONCLUSION

In this effort to discuss the political imposition of boundaries implied by 'region' we realize how much effort, absence, silence, and coercion goes into producing a naturalized distinction between regions, into demarcating inside and outside. The weight of the internationally sanctioned imperative of sovereignty prevents the postcolonial state from fully acknowledging its multiple histories. In a region which is defined in the first instance by contestations over territory, in an international context where that lack of control can never be admitted, we find an easy slippage from the control of land to the control of people. What the first story tries to show is how the postcolonial state's 'cartographic anxiety,' as Sankaran Krishna elegantly puts it, leads it to disavow the mobile histories of the people who live within and around it thus foreclosing the making of a uniquely new regional identity and definition.[24] The second story—a spy story that wasn't—seeks to uncover some of the silences embedded in the desire to have meaningful boundaries, in the deployment of legally sanctioned but historically problematic distinctions between citizens and foreigners. The narrative reaches a cul-de-sac, leading to a shift in genres from the weak and underdeveloped spy story to the more familiar and sustainable domestic corruption tale.

In both cases, state efforts to make the political boundaries of the region distinct leads to recognition of their disjuncture from social and historical boundaries. A region marked by the mobility of people has ethnicities, languages, and identities spread across many nations, few of which dare acknowledge them. Faced with the inability to distinguish between its own people and others without drawing into question the state's own legitimacy, the state seeks to divide people again. Internal divisions stand in for the preferred division of inside and outside due to the historical contradictions of the relationship between state, place, and identity.

24. For a discussion see Krishna (1996: 193–214).

References

Abraham, Itty, 1992. 'India's "strategic enclave": Civilian scientists and military technologies.' *Armed Forces and Society* 18(2): 231–52.

——, 1998. *The Making of the Indian Atomic Bomb: Science, Secrecy and the Postcolonial State.* London: Zed Books.

Department of Foreign Affairs, Indonesia. Report on the First Afro-Asian Conference, Bandung Jakarta: Dept. of Foreign Affairs, 1992: 8; 1983: 193–4.

Foucault, Michel, 1980. 'Questions of geography'. In Colin Gordon (ed.), *Power/Knowledge: Selected Interviews and Other Writings, 1972–1977/ Michel Foucault.* New York: Pantheon Books.

Kahin, George McTurnan, 1956. *The Asian-African Conference, Bandung, Indonesia, April 1955.* Ithaca: Cornell University Press.

Kotelawala, John Lionel, Sir, 1956. *An Asian Prime Minister's Story.* London: G. G. Harrap.

Krishna, Sankaran, 1996. 'Cartographic anxiety: Mapping the body politic in India.' In Michael J. Shapiro and Hayward R. Alker (eds.), *Challenging Boundaries: Global Flows, Territorial Identities.* Minneapolis: University of Minnesota Press.

Lefebvre, Henri, [1974] 1993. *The Production of Space.* Oxford: Blackwell.

Rajan, M. S., 1964. *India in World Affairs, 1954–1956.* New Delhi: ICWA.

Visvanathan, Shiv and Harsh Sethi (eds.), 1998. *Foul Play: Chronicles of Corruption.* New Delhi: Banyan Books.

Walker, R. B. J., 1993. Inside/Outside: *International Relations as Political Theory.* Cambridge: Cambridge University Press.

Index

WITHDRAWN
FROM STOCK
QMUL LIBRARY

CPSIA information can be obtained
at www.ICGtesting.com
Printed in the USA
BVOW06s1119190118
505752BV00001B/69/P